THE PROMISE OF PATRIARCHY

THE JOHN HOPE FRANKLIN SERIES
IN AFRICAN AMERICAN HISTORY AND CULTURE

Waldo E. Martin Jr. and Patricia Sullivan, editors

THE PROMISE OF PATRIARCHY

[**WOMEN AND THE NATION OF ISLAM**]

Ula Yvette Taylor

THE UNIVERSITY OF NORTH CAROLINA PRESS

CHAPEL HILL

Designed by April Leidig
Set in Electra by Copperline Book Services, Inc.
Manufactured in the United States of America

The University of North Carolina Press has been a
member of the Green Press Initiative since 2003.

Cover illustration: *White Robed Women at Black Muslim Convention*,
Chicago Coliseum, 1965. Courtesy of Sun-Times Media.

Library of Congress Cataloging-in-Publication Data
Names: Taylor, Ula Y., author.
Title: The promise of patriarchy : women and the
Nation of Islam / Ula Yvette Taylor.
Other titles: John Hope Franklin series in
African American history and culture.
Description: Chapel Hill : University of North Carolina Press, [2017] |
Series: The John Hope Franklin series in African American history and culture |
Includes bibliographical references and index.
Identifiers: LCCN 2017021189 | ISBN 9781469633923 (cloth : alk. paper) |
ISBN 9781469633930 (pbk : alk. paper) | ISBN 9781469633947 (ebook)
Subjects: LCSH: Nation of Islam (Chicago, Ill.)—History—20th century. |
Black Muslims—Social conditions. | African American women—Social
conditions—History—20th century. | Muslim women—United States—
Social conditions—History—20th century. | Patriarchy.
Classification: LCC BP221 .T39 2017 | DDC 297.8/7—dc23

LC record available at https://lccn.loc.gov/2017021189

FOR JAVANE STRONG

Who wipes away my tears
and prays away fears

CONTENTS

FIGURES

ACKNOWLEDGMENTS

I wrote this book while grieving the loss of my best friend and last surviving sibling, Willa Nanette Taylor. She was my joy. Sadly, her passing was accompanied by that of other dear ones: my maternal grandmother, Willie Rogers; my paternal aunt Jean Cole; and friends who were also family — VeVe Clark, Lamonte Toney, Sharla Dundy-Millender, Lynnea Stephens, Benita Robinson, Laurie Warren, and Marti Adams. My work has sustained me. Thinking, writing, and teaching about historical subjects who have done so much with so little, who daily reinvent ways to make meaning and share love, have served as an example of how to move forward as you hold in your heart those who have gone before you.

If I were a poet, I would utilize the haiku form, which concisely captures so much emotion and passion, to express my gratitude to all who have supported my efforts to write this book about women and the Nation of Islam between 1930 and 1975. What follows is a modest attempt; I cannot properly thank everyone in a few lines, because I lack exquisite poetic gifts.

I am very thankful to archivists and reference librarians who have replied to my emails, returned my phone calls, copied materials, and located documents. I am extremely grateful to Rebecca Darby, a reference specialist of microfilm and newspaper collections, and to Jesse Silva, a government information archivist, both at the University of California, Berkeley; as well as to Louis Jones and Elizabeth Clemens at Reuther Library at Wayne State University. Equally significant, Best Efforts Inc., a research powerhouse under the direction of one scholar, Paul Lee, has met my numerous requests with patience and generous care for detail and accuracy. I am so grateful that Paul Lee consistently pressed me to write an honest story. You are a brilliant scholar and a blessing to all who know you.

In addition to traditional archivists, scholars who were aware of my work sent me citations and leads that I otherwise would have missed. I especially appreciate Zain Abdullah, Garrett Felber, Harry Edwards, Gerald Horne, and Peter Goldman (who even purchased eBay material on my behalf). Robyn Spencer and Baiyina Muhammad, gifted scholars of Black Women's history, forwarded materials and intellectually motivated me.

I interviewed numerous former members of the Nation of Islam. They trusted me with their personal thoughts, hopes, and joys. I have done my best to honor their experiences. In particular, I am deeply grateful to Khalilah Camacho-Ali, J. Tarika Lewis, Waheedah Muhammad, Baheejah Shakur, Doris Shahrokhi-manesh, Sara Sharif, Sonia Sanchez, and Zoharrah Simmons. Nur and Me-dina Mohammed gave me permission to reprint the lovely 1932 image of their mother, Reformer Burnsteen Mohammad, and I cannot thank them enough for their generosity.

My colleagues and students in the African American Studies Department at the University of California, Berkeley, have been awesome. Lindsey Herbert Villarreal, who has literarily picked me up off my office floor twice, has been there for me when I most needed it. I very much appreciate the ladder faculty who help to maintain the integrity of our department. My colleagues (Brandi Wilkins Catanese, Nikki Jones, Leigh Raiford, Stephen Small, Ugo Nwokeji, Sam Mchombo, Michael Cohen, Darieck Scott, Tianna Paschel, Jovan Lewis, and Chiyuma Elliott) are transforming the fields of African American and Afri-can diaspora studies, and I feel honored to share the sixth floor of Barrows Hall with you.

I am a proud technological dinosaur. At times, however, it's a tremendous bur-den, so I deeply appreciate my graduate students Jarvis Givens, Zachary Manditch-Prottas, Ronald Williams, Christina Bush, Jessyka Finley, Ameer Loggins, Amani Morrison, Kia Middleton, Selina Makana, as well as my undergraduate, Summer Masson, who were all only a scream away.

I received financial support to pay for image permissions from both the UC Consortium for Black Studies and the H. Michael and Jeanne Williams Depart-ment of African American Studies Chair.

At the University of North Carolina Press, Waldo Martin (series editor) and Jad Adkins (assistant to Charles Grench) encouraged me and brought clarity to the project. Tera Hunter and Saidiya Hartman, my brilliant writing partners, who read every chapter closely and weighed in on how to conceptually com-pose a narrative about women who made choices that rubbed against my fem-inist sensibilities, evidence how sister-friends can provide beautiful, generous critiques. Our summer retreats held me accountable and forced me to write during the academic year. I most appreciate that both of you gave me permis-sion to write convoluted drafts! Paul Lee, Peter Goldman, and Imam Malik Mubashshir also read numerous drafted chapters, corrected my mistakes, and provided unparalleled insight on an array of documents and concerns related to the Nation of Islam. My copy editor, Susan Whitlock, helped me present a more polished manuscript. As a result of these colleagues' collective criticism, my book has fewer errors than it would have otherwise contained.

When you lose as many loved ones as I have, sometimes it is hard to simply get out of bed in the morning. Family and friends have kept me lifted up in their prayers. I can always count on receiving check-in phone calls from Marisa Fuentes, Cara Stanley, Rose Robinson, Amy Gardner, Beverly Peterson, Lisa Ze Winters, my cousins Felicia Hughes and Diana Weaver, and my niece Kasia Miller. The Agos family (Arden, Kyelle, and Hoche) cheered me on. My Farmerville, Louisiana, cousins Debra and Donna Cole keep me connected to my father's rural roots. Marisa Fuentes, my intellectual daughter, makes me proud and sent me a monitor because my computer is so ancient. Saidiya Hartman, Tamara Lewis, and Lynnette Wooten, my sisters on earth, have loved me with unwavering compassion. I simply could not have written this book without Saidiya Hartman's encouraging, gracious, fun-loving spirit. My mother, Lillian Taylor, has always believed in and supported my intellectual work. You keep me informed about the world and daily remind me that I am loved. Lastly, my Greenridge Drive family — my lovely Aunt Mary Wooten (thank you so much for cooking five-star meals), Euneisha Crowd, Leenah Saunders, and my awesome husband, Javane Strong — remind me daily about the power of laughter, love, and chocolate.

THE PROMISE OF PATRIARCHY

INTRODUCTION

I became initially drawn to women and the Nation of Islam (NOI) as a scholarly project when Spike Lee's movie *Malcolm X* premiered in 1992. As a young assistant professor, I was asked to participate on a panel after the movie for a question-and-answer session with the audience. Given that I was the only female panelist, I knew I would be expected to answer any woman-related question. It was during my preparation for the event that the glaring void in the literature on women in the original NOI became evident. I published an essay in 1998 based on my initial findings and assumed I was done![1]

But over time, I would occasionally tinker with the materials in my office — truckloads of copies of *Muhammad Speaks* and secondary literature on the NOI — largely because the possibilities of building a black nation in the United States continued to fascinate me. In 2003, I marshaled a chapter on NOI women for an edited collection on the Northern freedom struggle.[2] Again, I thought I was done! Still, I followed with interest as other scholars completed dissertations and book chapters on the topic. These tended to focus on individuals, such as Sister Clara Muhammad, or on later periods, post-1960s. I began to wonder even more about the early years in Detroit. During my winter break in 2006, I ventured to the city for a three-day research trip. When I located a 1934 report commissioned by the Detroit Welfare Department at the main branch of the public library, I finally realized that I was not done! This document, an investigation into families of the "Detroit Moslem Cult" who had pulled their children out of public schools, had not been quoted in any of the materials I had seen, and it fully reinvigorated my interest in the NOI.

At the present time, the NOI is largely thought about in terms of the Million Man March under the leadership of Minister Louis Farrakhan. It is an organization that celebrates black achievement and a willingness to shoulder the burden of blackness in America. Whether "atoning" for not fully executing patriarchal mandates to provide for and protect black women or supplying security for drug-infested public housing projects, Farrakhan's Nation considers itself the leader in the redemption of black America.

It also considers itself a leader in promoting the best interests of African American girls and women. In this, today's NOI is a direct descendant of the original NOI, founded in 1930 by Master Fard Muhammad and led for decades by the Honorable Elijah Muhammad. From the beginning, the NOI held out that to create a massive divide between black women and exploitative labor practices, harmful encounters, and lustful immorality, it must shield them from the depravity of the white world.

Although Islam and the African American experience share a long tradition, the NOI was a "homegrown religion" with strong connections to the Ahmadiyah, the Moorish Science Temple, and the Universal Negro Improvement Association (Marcus Garvey).[3] Largely viewed by naysayers as a cult at best and an un-American religion at worst, the original NOI critiqued whites as "devils" and "uncivilized." Reversing the racial order, it held up the so-called Negro in America as the "cream of the planet earth," superior to the rest of humankind, especially the immoral beast that had profited from the transatlantic slave trade. Taking pride in blackness and elevating NOI culture above white hegemonic society constituted an empowering endeavor in a world that loathed, exploited, and brutalized African Americans principally based on race.

The NOI leadership anchored its mission with a two-pronged strategy: blunting the force of domination with a religious ideology that reduced whites to primitive beings and creating alternative institutions steeped in a self-help catechism to meet the needs of its believers. Schools, grocery stores, dry cleaners, restaurants, a newspaper, a clothing factory, and a host of small entrepreneurial ventures cluttered the landscape near each NOI temple (renamed mosques in 1962). An independent service economy distanced its membership from whites and provided tangible evidence of nation-building.

Racial justice, for NOI members, was linked to separation from whites, and the Nation's leadership blasted any movement to desegregate America as wrong and led by a pitifully duped black leadership. Taking a hard-core position against the civil rights movement, the NOI was deliberately out of step with mainstream black America. Nation believers did not want to participate in a decadent political system; thus, they had no desire to vote. They also did not wish to educate their children in the company of "uncivilized" white children. Proper schooling was fundamental to their mission. In fact, the Honorable Elijah Muhammad proclaimed that all so-called Negroes, regardless of age or learnedness, needed to be reeducated.

Some of this reeducation took place at the Sunday meetings of the NOI, which provided an opportunity for all black people to bear witness to "scientific truth-telling." Registered NOI members and guests listened to male ministers teach on a variety of subjects. The persuasive power of the speakers ran the gamut from the captivating cadences of Malcolm X to the well-intentioned but uncharismatic declamations of a local minister. The men gave their best instruction to convince others to join the NOI movement. Their most popular teachings aimed to transform Christian thinking about the origins of humankind. The white race had come, Master Fard and his followers held, not from Adam and Eve but from a scientist, Yacub, who had grafted them from the "Asiatic black man," the first and model human, who was the direct ancestor of the so-called Negroes. The NOI ministers crafted a history to explain the pressing problems that plagued black America, from describing how animal-like whites crawled in caves to denouncing oppressive institutions that removed black men and women from their "natural" gendered roles.

Black women attracted to these teachings faced a choice. Joining the NOI meant entering a process of remaking; for women, it involved shaping a puritanical feminine identity, in marked contrast to the supposedly masculinized woman who took root during North American slavery. Proscriptions regarding appropriate feminine behavior were linked with self-sacrifice, self-love, and loving others, and, ultimately, with agreeing to build a separate black Islamic nation. But why would one participate in an endeavor that required so much?

At the core of this book is a fascinating group of women who joined the NOI at different historical junctures. A few resonate in the popular imagination, such as Belinda Ali (Khalilah), the former wife of legendary boxer Muhammad Ali. The vast majority who enter this history, however, were hardworking and unlettered black women determined to assist their men in the development of a black Islamic society. It was not a task for the faint of heart: "A nation is built not from the soft, sophisticated, but by those who love life and who are not afraid of getting 'dear old mother earth' on their hands," wrote Sister Ruby Williams, a rank-and-file member who pledged membership in the early 1950s. She continued, "They are adventurous, fearless, and militant. Most of all they have a burning desire to worship God as they understand him to be."[4]

Sister Ruby's own explanation of her NOI membership no doubt resonated with other black women. She became a black Muslim because "it's a known fact that the black woman has had to work away from home from dawn till dusk, with child or without. She has had to submit to the beast-like nature of men of all races regardless of her desires, and in most cases, her own man has been helpless to defend her. Many of them are even instrumental in making her plight worse. She has been unable to get substantial protection from any source and the least from the government under which she serves."[5]

One is hard-pressed to locate an organization or movement outside the NOI that wavered so little in keeping central and fundamental to its success the kind of protection that Sister Ruby sought. Equally significant, throughout its history, the NOI has promised its converts an escape from poverty. "If you have ever been on welfare, collected food stamps, lived in low-income housing, and lacked medical insurance, and someone promises to change your life, how can you not give it a try," said Sister Doris 9X, a rank-and-file member who joined the NOI in 1972.[6]

Sister Clara Mohammed (Poole) had attended the legendary early meetings with Master Fard Mohammed in Detroit in 1930, during a time when her family was destitute. Her alcoholic husband, Elijah, was an irresponsible husband and father. Forced to work as a maid in the homes of white folks, Sister Clara was in desperate need of support and direction on how to persuade her husband to fulfill his responsibilities to their family. Listening to Master Fard Muhammad, and encouraging her husband to attend the lectures as well, ultimately transformed their family into a financially secure, patriarchal unit.

A new government, or nation, that promised black women a source of protection, financial stability, and loving husbands stirred feelings of racial pride. The NOI also vowed to confront the devaluation of black womanhood and its damaging consequences. It inverted the racist belief that black women were immoral and unworthy of praise and safeguarding. Though the slippery slope between loving protection and the control of one's "property" certainly affected the lived realities of NOI women, the life-changing espousal of providing for and protecting the honor of black women fueled their dedication to a paternalistic movement constructed on the religious covenant of a presumed truth.

Jesus said, "The truth will set you free," but the Honorable Elijah Muhammad told his followers that Jesus's truth was on the side of white America. It was not humanity that had been enslaved on southern plantations and later "freed" to have their labor power exploited; that unique form of degradation rested firmly on the backs of black folks. Moreover, white supremacist power was enforced by violence — rape, lynching, castration, murder — and sanctioned by the courts of law and vicious mob rule. Given this history, no wonder many women welcomed the opportunity to escape the white world of haters and exploiters by embracing a black Nation that was separate from and superior to this cruel way of life.

The words and deeds of NOI members drew the attention of supporters and cynics. Admirers attended street rallies, utilized its services, and purchased its baked goods and its newspaper, *Muhammad Speaks*. Detractors, on the other hand, called Elijah Muhammad a "hate teacher," including his converts in the attack. The local police and the Federal Bureau of Investigation (FBI) closely monitored Elijah Muhammad and other notable NOI followers. In fact, not a decade has passed in which we do not find NOI members under surveillance or jailed. Although women do not feature as prominently as men in these records, on occasion women too were accused of unlawful behavior, harassed because of their willingness to stand up for themselves and their religion, and incarcerated to be taught a lesson about ultimate power and authority. Such tumultuous turning points make known subjects who would have otherwise fallen outside of the chronicled past, such as Sister Pauline Bahar, who was charged with sedition during World War II. The intensity of these moments undermined the NOI, and its institutions were often shut down by authorities. Yet each setback proved an opportunity to rebuild, marked by the addition of new female believers who pledged membership into a movement invested in a vision of racial justice and entitlement.

It is at the intersection of women and their well-being that black life bumps directly into American culture and all of its contradictions created by racial, gender, and class oppression. There are few historical opportunities that allow scholars a lens to explore this crossroads from the vantage point of an ideology of liberation through subordination. In essence, the Nation of Islam becomes a vehicle to understand how freedom and prosperity comingle around patriarchy.

The present book explores the lives of black women who joined the NOI between 1930 and 1975. The period under consideration encompasses the Great Depression, World War II, the Cold War, the modern civil rights and Black Power movements, and the feminist movement. How this history figured into black women's choices to remake themselves into "new women" dedicated to a seemingly threatening religion lies at the heart of my exploration.

"Since 9/11 Islam has acquired so many layers and dimensions and textures," said Salim Muwakkil, the former editor of *Muhammad Speaks*. In fact, "When the Nation of Islam was considered as a threatening religion, traditional Islam was seen as a gentle alternative, and now, quite the contrary. The Nation of Islam is seen as a tame domestic version and traditional Islam is seen as the threatening thing."[7] This shift speaks to a changing world, because the NOI never sought the approval of traditional Muslim societies and never swayed from its mission.

Perhaps more so than any other black nation-building movement, the NOI provided a space for women who had been disrespected, abused, and who had struggled to find a "home" in racial America. How each woman sought to make meaning of her NOI membership is of course impossible to capture in full. There exist, nonetheless, uniform declarations by female believers that ring loud in the ears of all who care to listen. Securing husbands under obligation to provide, respect, and protect was intrinsic to their Nationhood choice: the

NOI leadership promised responsible patriarchs for the betterment of the nuclear family and, ultimately, the larger black nation. How women negotiated an investment in patriarchy shaped their experiences and the multiple forms of subordination they experienced. The result is a powerful narrative of resilience and resistance; a story of unapologetic love and the conscious choice to be remade for the larger good of the black race.

[CHAPTER ONE]

MRS. CLARA POOLE

Clara Bell Evans must have been in love, because all Elijah Poole could offer her were his dreams. They married on March 17, 1919, in the small town of Cordele, Georgia, when she was twenty and he was twenty-two. Her parents, Quartus and Mary Lou (Thomas) Evans, were a bit disappointed in their daughter's marital choice.[1] Although both families were Christian, the Poole family was poorer than the Evanses, and no doubt it was hard for Clara's parents to imagine Elijah providing for their beloved daughter. Her seventh-grade education also exceeded Elijah's shoddy fourth-grade schooling.[2] Like many young lovers, they were full of infatuation and devotion.

From Georgia to Detroit

The newlywed couple struggled financially. Georgia was a tough place to live. As the Harlem Renaissance writer Jean Toomer declared in *Cane*, "Things [were] so immediate in Georgia": the majority of black southerners were exploited by the sharecropping system, and other forms of work did not guarantee income either, since racist employers withheld wages.[3] Toomer captured the thoughts and feelings of many black Georgians with a character who shouted out loud, "How did I ever land in such a hole? Ugh. One might just as well be in his grave."[4] Clara and Elijah kept the full weight of the Georgia pit at bay by clinging to each other. Their family quickly multiplied: Emmanuel was born in 1921, and Ethel in 1922. But an expanding family certainly magnified their problems in a former Confederate state known for lynching in the early 1920s. As one Atlanta minister said, "In many of the rural sections of Georgia . . . [a black person leads] a life of constant fear. . . . To him a beat of horses' hooves on the road at night, the rustling sound of a motor car, or the sudden call of a human voice, may be his death summons."[5] It is no wonder the Pooles soon searched for a home elsewhere. Trailing behind the droves of African Americans who migrated from

Southern cities during World War I, they left Georgia in 1923 to settle closer to his parents, who had relocated to Detroit, Michigan, two years earlier.

The population of black Detroit multiplied by a whopping 600 percent between 1910 and 1920.[6] Residentially segregated into the northeast side of downtown, seemingly presciently named the "Black Bottom" in the nineteenth century due to its rich soil, African Americans lived alongside European immigrants where landlords gouged them with excessively high rents.[7] It did not take long for black folks to learn that the haters who steered them away from the west side of town had mastered a northern style of racial boldness. Although new to the city, Elijah was an astute observer. Describing the distinction between Georgia's and Detroit's white violence, he stated, "Now I left the South so as to get out of the territory where such things are going on all the time and now I find it here before me in the police department. The difference is that they do not hang them up to the trees but they kill them right here on the streets."[8] Elijah had not exaggerated the tensions between African Americans and policemen. In a fury of hatred, officers, many of whom were secretly Klansmen, shot fifty-five black people in the first six months of 1925.[9] "Any Negro," John C. Dancy of the Urban League recalled, "even though he might be a doctor, professor, or substantial business man, could expect, if stopped by an officer, to be greeted with a patronizing, 'Well, boy, what are you doing around here?'"[10]

In this industrial metropolis teeming with Jim Crow enforcers, assembly lines, and African Americans determined to earn "big money," Elijah's work life resembled the sporadic underemployment that had spurred his flight from Georgia. His work history was plagued with firings and layoffs at a number of factory jobs: American Nut Company, American Wire and Brass Company, Detroit Copper Company, and Briggs Body and Chevrolet Axle Company.[11] According to one analyst, a man had to be able to "stand on [his] feet all day, to lift heavy things, to withstand the stifling heat of a foundry" to keep a steady job.[12] Having a diminutive 5'6" stature and a limited skill set certainly impeded Elijah's work performance; but his personal habits of drinking and gambling were also implicated in his inability to achieve financial success in Detroit.[13]

Detroit owed its status as a manufacturing mecca largely to Henry Ford, who employed about 50 percent of the African American autoworkers in the entire industry in his Motor City plants. Ford's paternalistic capitalism demanded that workers be "sober, saving, steady, industrious." Each worker had to "satisfy the . . . staff that his money was not wasted on riotous living."[14] Intrusive supervisors kept employees under surveillance. Elijah, who "would get paid and get drunk on Friday nights," lived riotously on the edge of intoxication.[15] Chasing excitement or an escape from his daily circumstances, he ran afoul of Ford's mandated abstinence. While Elijah himself did not work for Ford, it is a safe bet that the same expectations spread to other employers. Binge drinking (usually more than five drinks in a row) had a devastating impact on him and his family.

On one occasion a neighbor warned Clara, "Oh, Mrs. Poole! Your husband is laying out on the railroad track. You better go get him because the train is going to be coming soon."[16] Clara and their eldest son Emmanuel ran out to the tracks, where they bent down and gathered Elijah in their arms. One can imagine that Clara felt the full burden of her sagging husband as they dragged him home. Only in their private quarters would Clara unleash her disappointment. Their daughter Lottie (born 1925) recalled that her "mother would be [so] mad," she would go on a rampage, "hitting on him" because Elijah "was an alcoholic" who "would lose all of his money."[17] Yet despite a rage sometimes channeled into physical blows, there is no record of Clara threatening to leave her husband. Understandably, separating from him would still leave her in need of money to provide for their children. Her coping strategies were practical: she tried to head him off at the pass, looking for him before he started to drink and gamble "all his money away before he got home."[18]

Over time, Clara no doubt came to dread Elijah's return home, but she must also have feared that one of his disappearances would turn out to be permanent. Clara and her son did their best to keep starvation at bay. Emmanuel later remembered how his wisp of a mother supported the family by working "for white folks as a maid. She cooked their food. She sewed clothes for white folks' children. She scrubbed their floors, washed dishes, washed walls."[19] She was lucky to earn one dollar a day, and the work was hard, because white women would traditionally hire help only once a month. "That's why the dust was so heavy under the beds, and that's why the floors were so dirty you didn't know the color of them."[20] If Clara's hue had been a tad lighter, she might have found better employment serving the public, perhaps in a department store or a restaurant that served African Americans on St. Antoine Street.[21] Locked down by her race, color, and gender in Detroit, Clara's work options were slim, but as a mother struggling to support her family, she could not afford to find any form of domestic service beneath her. Emmanuel did his best to help out and worked hard as a "junker." He would go "up and down alleys with [his] little wagon and junk for cardboard, paper, milk bottles, brass, copper, and all these other things" to sell.[22] He also pulled out vegetables from garbage cans behind stores for family meals.[23] Elijah's contributions to the family income seldom expanded "beyond selling firewood" for fifty cents a stack.[24]

The Promised Land had turned into a barren field for the Poole family. Additional children in 1926 (Nathaniel) and 1929 (Herbert) increased the financial strain and impeded Clara's ability to work. As one female Detroiter has noted, most pregnant "women in those days went in after a certain time, after so many months. They stayed home. They didn't want anybody to see them."[25] In all likelihood, Clara followed this common practice, but the pressure to manage the expanding household fell squarely on her slight shoulders. With five children and an unemployed husband, her circumstances spiraled downward with the national economy. During the most difficult days it was tempting for Clara to give up on life. There was a moment, she confessed to a grandson, when she contemplated "call[ing] all of the children to take a nap and just put [her] head in the oven and then turn on the gas."[26]

During the Great Depression the Pooles were able to keep a roof over the family's heads only by sharing a home with Marie Thomas and her two sons. The two families lived at 1928 Leland Street in the Black Bottom; the Pooles paid $20 and Thomas $19 per month.[27] Three adults and seven children dwelled in a single-family home. While this was not unusual for 1930, the Poole children were the only ones on their block (populated with youthful migrants from Georgia and South Carolina, as well as European immigrants from Poland, Germany, and Italy) who did not attend school.[28] In all probability, nine-year-old Emmanuel's efforts to gather food for the family took precedence over formal schooling. Eight-year-old Ethel also assisted her mother with the three younger siblings. At times Clara must have felt that the only people she could count on were her older children. It is possible that she had begun to personally educate her children, since she later became an advocate for home schooling.[29] At this point, however, it is not clear if the Poole children were able to read and write.[30]

An exasperated Clara may have shared her dire concerns with her in-laws, Mariah and William Poole, who lived at 4182 Dubois Street. In Georgia they had rented farmland, but in Detroit William worked for the city as a street cleaner. He was sixty years old in 1930 and headed a household that included his wife; his seventy-five-year-old mother-in-law, Peggy Taylor; two sons, James and Herbert; and three boarders from the extended Poole family. The house was packed with family members who worked in the auto-body industry as spray men and sanders.[31] Did Clara divulge her private affairs to Mariah and Peggy? Did they possibly share their own stories of devotion and letdown related to their husbands? William was a self-proclaimed Baptist preacher (who lacked a substantial church following). Perhaps he encouraged Clara to find solace in the church, at the center of a circle of healing prayer.

Perhaps, too, it was because of William's ministry that Elijah was fascinated with religion. Acutely aware that his addictions compromised his marriage and constrained his family, Elijah wanted to be "a better man."[32] In fact, he confided to his mother that he had "always longed . . . to teach religion or preach."[33] Elijah believed that this was the only way he would "look like success."[34]

In Detroit the most prominent black pastors, such as Robert Bradby of the Second Baptist Church and Reverend William Peck of Bethel A.M.E., had large congregations and connections to Henry Ford. Indeed, many people joined their parishes with an eye to obtaining a job at Ford.[35] These pastors were community leaders, and the tithes and offerings from their flock kept them financially solvent. But even an unlettered, jackleg preacher dressed well, drove a car, and fed his children.[36] Elijah visualized achievement within divine terms; but his aspirations caused an inordinate amount of pressure in Clara's secular world. She remained unable to disentangle her suffering from his failures; Elijah's pitiful head-of-household performance undercut every dream the young Clara might have had for her family's life. Diminished dreams, however, can make room for new imaginings. Soon an unexpected offering would attract Clara's attention, filling with hope the space where dejection, heartache, and disappointment in an unsettled husband currently resided.

Fard and the Allah Temple of Islam

In the fall of 1931, Clara went to hear the teachings of a man named W. D. Fard, the founder of the Allah Temple of Islam (ATOI).[37] Attending a Fard meeting, which could easily last up to six hours, had to remind Clara of an all-day holiness service.[38] Yet Fard certainly did not look like your average Pentecostal preacher. He was not black, nor did he look white. She had seen a variety of peoples in Michigan (Italians, Greeks, Poles, Hungarians, Slovaks, and Russian Jews), but Fard's speaking voice lacked their accents.[39] Clara's brother-in-law, Willie, and his wife, Addie, had attended a meeting previously and shared what they had witnessed. They probably told her that Fard was of Arab descent. Clara was likely willing to listen to their observations because they divided their provisions with her and the children. They had carted supplies, "food and whatever [was] needed," from their home in Hamtramck, about two miles from the Black Bottom, recalled Elijah Muhammad Jr.[40] Willie, who worked as a painter in a paint shop, and Addie, who worked in a hotel as a maid, had picked up Elijah's slack.[41]

It was in Paradise Valley, the commercial and entertainment district for African Americans, northeast of downtown Detroit, that Willie and Addie had first seen Fard.

But Fard had peddled his way into the homes of poverty-stricken black Detroiters, now numbering 120,000, in the summer of 1930.[42] "He came first to our houses selling raincoats, and then afterwards silks," recalled Sister Denke Majied (formerly Mrs. Lawrence Adams).[43] Residential and commercial segregation provided an incubator for black-owned businesses and pushcart peddlers. Syrian and Lebanese men dominated the peddling profession.[44] Fard's vending cart illustrates the crossroads between the movement of cash, commodities, and religious ideas in the informal economy.[45] While the majority of the Syrian and Lebanese men were Christians, "five to ten percent were Sunni or Shi'a Muslims."[46] Detroit is noted as having one of the oldest Arab Muslim communities in the United States.[47]

Fard's followers remembered him introducing himself to a gathering of African Americans by saying: "My name is W. D. Fard and I came from the Holy City of Mecca. More about myself I will not tell you yet, for the time has not yet come. I am your brother. You have not yet seen me in my royal robes."[48] Hearing a man who looked like Fard declare that he was a "brother" must have surprised Clara and others in attendance. A few may have quickly gathered their belongings, shaken their heads, and proceeded to an exit. Others perhaps looked askance, raised an eyebrow, or smothered a snickering laugh. Clara may have flinched, but she stayed, refocusing her attention. It was rare that she had time away from the children, and surely her husband would ask her when she got home what the speaker had said. A halfhearted answer might prevent him from supporting her desire to attend another lecture. One can picture Clara with her shoulders leaning forward, her arms wrapped around her middle, physically and mentally folding herself into the service. Here was a man who said he was a "brother," and Clara had to fully listen to understand how this was possible.

Fard explained his brotherhood in a captivating revisionist narrative, teaching that "the black men in North America are not Negroes, but members of the lost tribe of Shabazz, stolen by the traders from the Holy City of Mecca 379 years ago."[49] All her life Clara had been identified as a Negro, a racial marker that had been nonnegotiable. But Fard's statement opened her to redefinition. The oppression that went with being a Negro — slavery, rape, sharecropping, debt peonage, lynchings, police brutality, unemployment and inadequate schooling — what human being would not want to be liberated from this horror? Fard's words, gestures, and facial expressions all combined to give Clara the possibility of rejecting what had been placed on her as a Negro woman.

Fard (later Master W. D. Fard Muhammad) was a mysterious man, and he continues to baffle scholars. He is shrouded in myth and slippery facts, and the Federal Bureau of Investigation (FBI) has attributed more than fifty aliases to him.[50] Despite his significance, most of what we know about Fard has been ascribed to him by others after his 1934 disappearance from Detroit. To separate fact from fiction and more fiction tests reasoning skills in this realm of contradictory and inconclusive stories. The information we do have has been filtered through so many sieves that it is nearly impossible to ascertain authorship. Thus Fard's archival voice is faint, barely audible, even for the most astute listener. But it is this voice that transformed the spiritual identity of Clara and thousands of other black southerners living in the urban North, giving them new memories of who they were and new possibilities of what they could be.

The ATOI can easily be seen as just another extremist offering to the already cluttered public life of the Black Bottom during the Great Depression years. Yet Fard's teachings enabled his understanding of Islam to move with dynamic vitality under the future leadership of both Elijah (Poole) Muhammad and Malcolm X.[51] What is at stake in knowing Fard is not only his particular Islamic vision for the ATOI but also how Clara and Elijah came to understand their role in its advancement.

Clara had listened to a truckload of preachers, but Fard knew more about the Bible than all of them put together. He captivated his audiences by teaching "like a man who was on the scene" with biblical prophets like Moses. His oratory sounded "like he had witnessed" Daniel in the lion's den and other biblical events.[52] Teaching "the truth" from this vantage point, Fard substantiated his authority to minister and introduce new genealogies of knowledge. "By the sweetness of [his] tongue," Fard's oral teachings represent the fluid interconnectiveness of story-telling, religion, and community knowledge.[53]

Now in 1931, living in the overwhelmingly white suburb of Hamtramck to be near her supportive in-laws, Clara went to an ATOI meeting back in the Black Bottom whenever the opportunity presented itself.[54] Each time she learned something different, because the loquacious Fard was conversant on a range of topics, from poisonous foods to scriptural interpretation.[55] But his creation lessons may have been the most startling to Clara. Fard claimed that black people were the "original" people on the planet who ruled from "East Asia." Anchoring the origins of African Americans in a place other than Africa was a transforming message. With a mission to restore his followers' identity by building a modern black nation from a glorification of an "Asiatic blackness," Fard gave them a sense of communal purpose. In detaching them from the Western imagination

Mrs. Clara Poole

of blackness and encouraging a rejection of sub-Saharan Africa as a homeland, Fard failed to critique colonialist descriptions of black Africans as "uncivilized" and "backwards," but he simultaneously exposed the very real alienation that his followers felt as a result of colonialism, slavery, and Jim Crow.[56] Fard's teachings liberated Clara from this damning history, giving her a clean slate, a fresh start. Clara began to see how racist ideas translated into her everyday life. It was not her fault that she was financially poor and disenfranchised.

Linking African Americans to his East Asia and the "ancient civilization of Egypt and the Islamic culture of Arabia," Fard's origins story was most easily swallowed in small chunks.[57] Did Clara reflect on her formal education to think about this geographical landscape? The limits of her Jim Crow schooling, combined with Fard's enlightening teachings, presented a challenge to what she thought she knew about world history. But logic may have been trumped by feeling the first time that Clara heard Fard say the "so-called American Negro" was in fact an "Asiatic Blackman, the maker, the owner, the cream of the planet earth, God of the universe."[58] Her carriage had to have lifted with pride. Even if she was a bit unclear about the concept of the "Asiatic Blackman," she knew that cream always rises to the top. She wanted to move upward, and Fard's message helped her reimagine who she was. If she accepted that she was an Asiatic black woman, then she was so much more than Detroit and Georgia. Clara's desperate need to feel better about herself and her situation must have made her more receptive to a new creation story, even if the dots were not fully connected.

Fard's lessons produced an identity framed as a kind of diasporic blackness, even though only black Americans, or the "so-called Negro," as opposed to continental Africans, could actually embrace this God-given identity.[59] This is also why Clara could focus her attention on a man whose physical appearance belied his black-centered rhetoric. Somewhat bewilderingly, he explained the movement of people on the planet via the introduction of a scientist who had encouraged some of the Shabazz Tribe to travel. Members of the Tribe of Shabazz who migrated away from Mecca to experience "a jungle life" found themselves in current-day West Africa. Living in the midst of a rugged landscape eventually chipped away at their advanced civilization, Fard argued, and over time they fell out of touch with the Islamic cultural legacy of their foreparents. In the end, only a shadow of the purported Asiatic Blackman existed there, allowing "the weaker of himself to rule."[60]

If anyone knew about the far-reaching implications of a "weaker" self, it was Clara. She had lived with her husband's binges and was eager to believe that she and Elijah were "lost members" of "the original black nation of Asia, the

Tribe of Shabazz."[61] At each lecture, Fard's message appeared both simple and profound, and Clara and others comprehended it largely instinctively.

The Remaking of Elijah Poole

One fall evening in 1931 Fard asked the audience, "Anyone here in this hall know the little man who lives in Hamtramck?" It is unclear if Fard was fishing more generally or if he knew of Elijah, but the question would transform the future of the Poole family. Clara could have avoided the swivel of heads and the landing of curious eyes on her by ignoring the question. But instead, she answered, "Yes, he is my husband."[62] Maybe she was at the meeting with her sister-in-law Addie, who nudged her to reply. Or perhaps she feared that word would get back to her husband that she had failed to comment. We will never know if she extended her neck and shouted over adorned heads from the back of a crowded room or spoke softly from a seat in the front row as her gloved hands held a worn handbag on her lap.[63] Without knowing what her reply would yield — Fard's intentions could have been to embarrass or reprimand — Clara believed that she had a duty to acknowledge the question. She certainly could not have anticipated that her simple response would lead to a mighty call that eventually changed her family's religious commitment and lifestyle.

When Clara returned home from that meeting, she was more than excited. It would have been understandable if most evenings she gave her husband a rundown on the event — not only what Fard had said, but how many people had attended, and if the spirit of the gathering was high. On this day, however, Clara told Elijah that Fard wanted him "to go ahead and teach Islam and he will back [him] up."[64] Clara voiced Fard's sentiments, and her husband had little choice but to trust that she had got it right. Did he insist that she repeat exactly what she had heard? Was the seriousness of her voice enough to convince her husband that she had indeed correctly conveyed Fard's intentions? Given the recent past, having her husband recognized for something good must have made her heart skip a beat and brought a smile to her lovely narrow face. Elijah recalled that, probably for the first time in a long time, he felt "so happy."[65]

Clara became the vessel for the remaking of her husband when she transmitted Fard's permission to "teach Islam."[66] In short, what became the Nation of Islam was driven by a woman. By encouraging him to accept the call, she took the lead to redefine her husband as she also remade herself. Rather than waiting for Elijah to set the course, she sought a solution by attending a meeting without him. Her self-love, and the force of her family love, particularly her responsibility for her young children, led to a deliberate use of personal power. She would meet the main challenge that she faced: how to make her husband "look like success."

After Elijah had heard Fard teach several times in 1931, he returned home feeling like the messages had done him "so much good just to think about them."[67] By the end of that year, Clara watched her husband repeat the lessons at their home in the evening "from hours to hours" with the "poor brothers and sisters" getting an earful of what he had "learned and heard from Mr. Fard."[68] Teaching Islam gave her husband a higher purpose for his life. Clara knew all too well that being a good father had not been enough motivation. The possibility that a rebirth for her husband would save the family gave her a personal interest in making the ATOI a mainstay in their household. Together they had received Fard's lessons about the Asiatic Blackman and the Tribe of Shabazz. These stories were an emotional appeal to people who had suffered because of their Negro identity; they had particularly touched Clara and Elijah, whose desperation was extremely entrenched.[69]

It was Clara and Fard who helped make Elijah into a minister for the ATOI. During the bumpy course of their marriage, Clara had watched her husband search for a way out of despair by self-medicating with alcohol and gambling to secure a big pay check. He had joined the Prince Hall Masonry movement in 1924.[70] Elijah tried to surround himself with black men who were invested in the financial, political, social, and spiritual concerns of their communities. But personal character was a high priority for the Masons, and Elijah's lack of pedigree, combined with his drinking and gambling, kept him on the periphery.[71] He could hear only whispers, when he longed for intimate, stimulating conversation. During his journey to recreate himself, Elijah had failed to elicit affirmation from anyone in authority. But Fard and the ATOI were altogether different. When Fard anointed him as a teacher and a leader, Elijah got out of his own way, began to gain confidence in his gifts, and became determined to make a better life.

As for Clara, she too would find success in the transformation she helped unfold. Over time, her husband would gain affirmation in his role as a minister for the ATOI, and the finances of their household would become solvent. Like many other black women of the period, she wanted her husband to be held accountable as a provider. When she witnessed her husband's elated reaction to Fard's approval, she quickly understood Fard's power over him. Clara moved to harness that influence to her family's advantage.

How would their spiritual work for the ATOI manifest into a lifelong commitment? The following chapters engage this question, as well as how Clara and

Elijah internalized Fard's teachings. Because of her husband's prominence as a leader over the decades, it is much easier to come by information about Clara than about most women of the NOI. It is worth telling her story in detail, so we can lean on what we know about Clara to help illuminate the sources we have about other women who made the choice to remake themselves for the glory of a new nation.

A grandson recalled many years later that Elijah's "message was to try to save the black man's life" by lecturing on the importance of "doing for self, becoming an upright man, knowing that you are the best, and you are not a slave anymore and you are equal to or better than anybody else. You are the Original Man."[72] During the years of the Great Depression, Clara knew that no one needed to hear these words more than her own husband.

CHAPTER TWO

BUILDING A MOVEMENT,

FIGHTING THE DEVIL

The years from 1931 to 1934 were crucial not only for Clara Poole and her family but for the building of the Allah Temple of Islam (ATOI) in Detroit. As Elijah Poole — soon to be renamed Karriem, then Mohammed — was developing as a teacher and minister, Fard continued to introduce his interpretation of Islam to African Americans who were in need of something profound to believe in at the beginning of the Great Depression. The growth of his movement ignited suspicions among outsiders, and the ATOI faced both legal and political challenges. One such challenge — a thorough investigation in 1934 of Moslem families who refused to send their children to public schools — resulted in the Dillon report, a document that provides our best early window on the lives of women converts and their families. But to reach that report we must first understand the ways Fard's teachings generated both devotion among his followers and conflict with the larger community of Detroit.

A New Religion

In promoting his version of Islam, Fard deliberately set himself apart from the standard Christian dogma with which his listeners would have been familiar, but he also appropriated some of the most powerful and familiar Christian themes. He knew he had to convince African Americans to abandon a belief system that had brought them comfort and shaped their daily lives. As Christians, they prayed to Jesus before eating their meals and going to bed at night. They celebrated the resurrection of their Lord and Savior on Easter Sunday in colorful attire, and his birthday on Christmas Day with material gifts and mouthwatering meals. Protection from harm, a good job, a healthy body, a sound mind, tangible possessions, and life itself would all be considered the result of God's blessings through Jesus Christ. To discredit the religious convictions that influenced so many everyday practices required superior rhetoric, compelling evidence, and the promise of something more powerful; thus, when he invited Elijah Poole to teach with him, Fard created a comprehensive lesson plan demonstrating why his Islamic teachings eclipsed what his followers understood as their proper religion.

To teach with precision, Elijah Poole had to master Fard's "Actual Facts," "Rules of Islam," lessons and problems. They required intense concentration, largely due to the abundance of mathematical formulations. The Actual Facts numbered eighteen and were primarily arithmetic details linked to the planet earth. "The earth weighs six sex trillion tons (a unit followed by 21 ciphers)," for instance.[1] The Rules of Islam were ten questions connected to student enroll-ment. "Who is the Colored Man? The Colored man is the Caucasian (white man), or Yacob's grafted devil, the skunk of the planet earth."[2] Lessons were short statements and questions. For example, "What is his ownself? His ownself is a righteous Moslem."[3] A problem included, "A Sheep contains fourteen square feet. One-tenth of a square inch contains ten thousand hairs. How many will the fourteen square feet contain?"[4] Additionally, Fard instructed all followers to read works by Marcus Garvey, the cofounder of the Universal Negro Improve-ment Association (UNIA); Judge Rutherford of the Jehovah's Witnesses; Noble Drew Ali, the founder of the Moorish Science Temple of America (MSTA); and books on Freemasonry, which were "symbolic" and foretold the "coming of a new prophet."[5]

Reading literature and doing intricate mathematical equations with a lim-ited formal education is not easy. Clara, now known as Sister Clara, assisted her husband in his study.[6] She had more schooling than her husband had, and her education was more reflective of that of other black Detroiters. While the reported illiteracy rates in Detroit were low (3.2 percent of its 120,066 black cit-izens over the age of twenty-one were illiterate in 1930), calculating illiteracy is tricky due to the varying levels of functionality.[7] Fard's followers were uneven in their capacity to interpret the assigned literature and engage in other activities that assume literacy. Understanding that his listeners needed to be thoroughly schooled, Fard answered "quickly and fluently every question" with his divine revelations of "truth."[8] He ultimately convinced the Pooles and about eight thousand others in Detroit that his mission was to provide them a way out of racial misery, body ailments, and class suffering with a new faith.[9]

Fard proclaimed that his followers would experience good health and a pro-ductive life not through the blessings of a Christian God but by living within the laws of Islam as revealed in the "most authoritative of all texts," the Qu'ran, written in Arabic.[10] The laws of Islam required that followers not lie, steal, gamble, nor consume liquor or tobacco; that they try to eat only one meal a day, preferably vegetarian, and under no circumstances eat pork; that their homes and bodies be kept immaculate (five daily baths were expected); and that they not be idle nor engage in extramarital sexual relations. So-called Mission Sisters walked door to door during these early days, disseminating Islam as taught by Fard.[11] Yet only Fard was positioned to interpret the Qu'ran; converts relied on him absolutely for the truths he imparted. Fard explained the need for his new religion thus: "Me and my people have tried this so-called mystery God [Christian God] for bread, clothing, and a home. And we have received nothing but hard times, hunger, naked, and out of doors. Also was beat and killed by the ones that advocated that kind of God."[12] This total dependency on a master teacher would shape the nation of believers forever. Over time Fard's oration, which both appropriated and inverted Christianity, convinced his followers that he was a prophet.

Carefully aiming at the jugular of Christian faith — the afterlife — Fard patiently explored concepts of heaven and hell. He attracted adherents by repeating traditional preachers' warnings that hell was in the ground with fire and the devil; therefore, all should seek to prepare themselves for heaven in the sky with Jesus and the angels. After lingering on this familiar territory, however, Fard went on to denounce heaven and hell and explain that one did not have to "suffer to keep from suffering."[13] Heaven and hell were earthly conditions. Heaven consisted of freedom, justice, equality, security, peace, love, and happiness on earth. Being poor, hungry, illiterate, and having no job or political rights was living hell. The devil was not in the ground but all over the earth in the bodies of white men, who acted like devils.

In collectively calling whites "devils," Fard seized on a commonplace metaphor in black communities. His religious intervention was timely and attracted the attention of black people who understood that Jesus had been taunted and tempted by the devil for a season. On Sunday mornings, preachers conveyed, usually with a sense of anointed, holy-ghost gumption, how Jesus had said to him, "Get thee behind me, Satan."[14] The black preachers taught that God's word should be used against Satan: "Put on the whole armour of God, that ye may be able to stand against the wiles of the devil."[15] The "shield of faith" would protect one against "all the fiery darts of the wicked."[16] Thus Fard attracted converts by centering his rhetoric within familiar religious imagery.

But Fard went farther. Not only was he comfortable calling the white man a devil but he also interpreted his existence as a physical by-product of science gone wrong; all Caucasians were demonic by nature. In naming the enemy "devil," Fard turned the tables on white racists who had used that same dehumanizing language against African Americans. According to Fard, the white "devils" used "tricknology" to keep black people in a subservient state. Most of Fard's teachings included the shrewd form of a catechism: "Why does the devil keep our people illiterate? So that he can use them for a tool and also a slave. He keeps them blind to themselves so that he can master them."[17] Christianity had served to exploit black people. Fard's denunciation of the Bible became bolder over time, and he eventually described Jesus as an Islamic prophet and not the son of God.

Fard's lethal indictment against whites cemented a racial order that would also become a foundation in the Nation of Islam. And his heartfelt, raging anger against whites must have cushioned for some converts the blow to their love of Jesus. Yet just how they personally negotiated replacing a belief system is difficult to ascertain. We have some evidence in our information about Sister Clara, who, according to her son Wallace (born 1933), continued to sing Christian music as she practiced her Islamic faith. Wallace recalled his mother singing "whenever she was cooking or washing or whenever she was in a bad mood or something." He often heard her say, "Give me that old time religion, its good enough for me."[18] The singing of church songs suggests that Clara remained grounded in the traditions of Christian worship. Negro spirituals, healing music for the soul, encouraged emotional renewal along with what Islam offered. Clara's persistence in singing spirituals and hymns can be read as one way in which she managed to combine Fard's Islam with the familiar — and presumably comforting — Christianity with which she had been raised.

Sister Clara's account of her family's struggle prior to becoming followers of Fard suggests another way that traditional Christian thinking remained with her. In an article she wrote for *Muhammad Speaks* in 1967, she described their "lowest ebb."[19] They had five children at the time, Elijah was unemployed, and she also had difficulty finding employment "steadily," so that "there were times when we didn't have a piece of bread in the house, nor heat, water or even sufficient wearing apparel."[20] Still, she wrote that she came to understand her family's destitute circumstances as "Allah's work, but I did not know it then. Praise His Holy name forever."[21] Where Fard taught that it was the devil that kept black people hungry, poor, and jobless, not Allah, Clara retained the Christian belief that God does not place on anyone more than they can bear, and that suffering can be an instrument of God's — or Allah's — will, to bring people to a greater glory (in this case Islam). What was true for Clara was likely true for many other followers of the ATOI: their conversion was neither an instantaneous nor a complete rupture from Christianity. They lived within what one scholar has termed "a contained narrative of conflicting memories" and belief systems, wherein the old text never fully disappears.[22]

Institution Building

In building the ATOI as an organization, as with his ideological teachings, Fard drew on the familiar while making bold breaks with the past. For instance, to emphasize the newness of his vision and the commitment his version of Islam demanded, Fard required that his followers take on new names. He taught that a main feature of their Negro identity — the lie covering the reality of the Asiatic Blackman — was linked to the surnames that they had acquired from slavery. To counteract the violence and humiliation of their history, as well as to restore them to their "original" identity, Fard replaced their assumed slave names with Arabic monikers. This was the equivalent of baptism or a rebirth into the new faith, and to many it became an important symbol. After receiving her Arabic surname, Sister Rosa Karriem stated, "I wouldn't give up my [new] righteous name. That name is my life."[23]

By 1931, once he had enough of a following, Fard coalesced converts into auxiliaries — the Fruit of Islam (FOI) for men and the Moslem Girls' Training and General Civilization Class (MGT-GCC) for women. Revaluing the black nuclear family, Fard instructed men in the FOI to protect other followers and to be responsible breadwinners, while the MGT-GCC taught women how to cook, clean, and ultimately master the domestic sphere.

Meanwhile, Fard needed to turn his attention to building for the future.[24] It was likely in the Pooles' home, filled with children, their brown eyes beaming with light, that Fard saw the next generation of adult membership. Emmanuel remembers meeting Fard at home sometime in 1931.[25] His father introduced all of the children and taught them that Fard was their "savior," in another holdover from Christianity.[26] The three oldest children would take turns watching Fard's car outside while he was inside with their parents.[27] This proved to be a profound moment in the Pooles' relationship with Fard. Their six children under the age of ten, including a new baby (Elijah Jr. was born in 1931), would have captured the bachelor Fard's attention, especially since the average number of young children in the homes of his followers was three. How to school children properly in his faith, especially given the challenges of educating them in Jim Crow Detroit, was the final step in Fard's re-creation of the Asiatic Blackman. He established the University of Islam, an elementary and secondary school, in 1932.

The early developments of the University of Islam are difficult to resurrect. Two scholars believe the school started in the Pooles' home.[28] No archival documentation exists, however, to support this assertion. We do know that in this period Elijah Poole was on his way to becoming a favorite disciple of Fard, and, given her greater education, that Clara was by his side. Fard had made Elijah into a better man, to his wife's delight. How her husband's teaching would translate into financial support of the family was still unclear, but he was now sober and on fire to save African Americans from the clutches of historical distortions that secured and perpetuated white supremacy.

A Jungle Cult

Not everyone was so favorably impressed with the effects of the ATOI. Just how negative its reputation was in some parts of Detroit became clear when a scandal erupted toward the end of 1932. When Robert Harris, one of Fard's followers, was charged with murder, the ATOI was catapulted into the spotlight, where the religion was on trial as much as Harris.

Robert Harris was clearly deranged. He admitted that he killed James J. Smith in front of Harris's wife, their two small children, and twelve so-called disciples as part of the rites of his religion. *The Detroit Free Press* front-page story on November 22, 1932, happily took Harris at his word, reporting that Harris had "plunged a knife through Smith's heart as he lay on a makeshift altar" of a flimsy "packing crate."[29] The Homicide Squad investigated Harris's assertion and "announced that all of the evidence indicated its truth, and speculated upon the hold" that "the jungle cult may have upon certain ignorant elements of Detroit's Negro population."[30] Harris was the "king" and a professed member of the "Order of Islam" headquartered at 3408 Hastings Street, according to the investigation. Harris's brother, Edward, tried to set the record straight. He denied, the *Free Press* reported, that the "cult practices human sacrifices," and said, "It is operated by a man from Morocco, W. D. Fard, our teacher." Edward continued, "It is educational and historical. We learn about the black race, which goes back in its culture 66 trillion years."[31]

Unpersuaded by Edward Harris's reassurances, black leaders organized into the Detroit Council of Social Service in response to Smith's murder, to fight for the "welfare of their own people" by crushing the "hydra of jungle fanaticism which is preying upon more than 8,000 Detroit Negroes."[32] The ATOI's mission, particularly its separation from whites, went against the desegregation efforts of black political organizers. They pledged a "house-to-house drive to prevent any more ignorant element of Detroit's Negro population" from "joining the vicious cult."[33] At a town-hall meeting presided over by John C. Dancy of the Urban League, the new Detroit Council Social Services members vowed to combat the "sinister influences of voodooism" by conducting private investigations and giving their findings to Detroit police officers. "Big Wigs," white leaders in Detroit, often consulted Dancy any time a "problem that ha[d] to do with Negro people" arose, because the Urban League followed a plan of interracial cooperation. The league's leadership believed that bourgeois respectability, in the tradition of W. E. B. Du Bois's "Talented Tenth," combined with Booker T. Washington's Puritan work ethic and righteous Christian doctrine, would transform black people's lives and white people's perceptions of them.[34]

Dancy was often called on for intervention, as there were many passionate religious zealots and political pontificators in Detroit in the 1920s and 1930s, each determined to build a counterhegemonic lifestyle. Between the Masons, the Garveyites (UNIA), the Moorish Science Temple of America (MSTA), and Jehovah's Witnesses (Watchtower Bible and Tract Society), Black Bottom streets were lively spaces where individuals paraded their allegiance to movements with a distinct dress and strut. Indeed, a journalist for the *Detroit Saturday Night* newspaper declared in 1926, "It is not easy to begin the discussion of all the schools of religious specialization that exist in Detroit."[35] The black elite, under the umbrellas of the Urban League and the National Association for the Advancement of Colored People (NAACP), responded by offering minimal services and giving counsel on how poor folks should maintain, as one observer put it, "their homes and their surroundings, the importance of keeping their children in school, good deportment, how to dress, and so on."[36] But the stubborn existence of people who refused to internalize the benefits of integration both confused and embarrassed upper-class blacks. In fact, they found it a challenge to keep up with the numerous new adherents listed each year in the assemblies of the "Novel Philosophers," as they were called, and they counted on the reality that few remained committed over time.[37] The lingering persistence of Fard's followers, and their resoluteness, surprised and alarmed many Detroiters.

Following the Smith murder, prominent clergymen attempted to thwart Fard's power by preaching from their pulpits against what was termed the "sinister cult called Islamism," which they believed "preyed upon the more gullible members of their people."[38] Reverend J. D. Howell accepted some responsibility for the ATOI's growth, noting that "its fanatical teachings and barbarous practices" occurring "right in the midst of our religious communities shows weakness on the part of our church life. It shows a deplorable lack of contact between the upper and lower strata of society."[39] Howell concluded that sermon by calling the present situation a "war on ignorance" that was being lost.[40] Another pastor held that "the Negro race cannot, as such, be held responsible for the action and teachings of fanatics," and pointed directly at Fard: "Their Arabian leader is solely to blame. There must be quick and just punishment of those who come among us and for personal gain lead us astray."[41] The collective cry of the group was, "The Islamic 'Bible' and the Nation of Islam must go!"[42]

Detroit detectives' investigation of the alleged cult produced a raid on the room of "Wallace Farad, self-confessed leader of the group, in a hotel at 1 W. Jefferson Ave," as a local paper noted.[43] There they found hundreds of communications written with lead pencil on inexpensive notepaper, in almost every instance "unintelligible scrawls."[44] The letters were applications to change a "slave" surname to a "Mohammedan" one, and the Negroes were said to be willing to pay Fard for the service.[45] Officers also searched members' homes and confiscated materials.[46] The police confessed that they had known about the group for some time and appealed to the employers of members to warn against it, but employers seemed inclined to treat the "weird fanaticism" lightly and were loath to initiate "drastic" steps to stop it.[47] The prosecutor's office justified its lack of action to date, explaining that since "the group . . . does not call itself an organization or a religion, but a nation," it fell outside of governing laws.[48] Lastly, detectives reported that while "the bulk of the group's membership of 8,000 is made up of Detroit Negroes, many converts were gained in outlying districts of the City, such as Hamtramck, Highland Park and Mt. Clemens," which were all former centers for Marcus Garvey's UNIA and Noble Drew Ali's MSTA.[49]

Evidence in hand, officers arrested "Wallace D. Farad, an Arabian, who confessed himself supreme leader of the Detroit cult of Islam" on November 23, 1932, and sent him, Robert Harris, and another purported teacher, Ugan Ali, to the "psychopathic ward of Receiving Hospital for observation" in connection with the Smith murder.[50] With the goal of judging the sanity of the men, and whether Harris was "demented by the murderous teachings of cult leaders," they were jailed for two weeks.[51] A commission eventually judged Harris insane and sent him to the Michigan State Hospital for the Criminally Insane at Ionia. The justice system dealt with Fard by encouraging his "voluntary abduction from the city."[52] Persuaded to leave by two detectives, who probably used — or threatened to use — the violent tactics known to Detroit officers, he reportedly "seemed willing to go" and "said he would not return to Detroit again."[53] Fard left — but returned.[54]

From Poole to Karriem to Mohammed

The bad publicity around the Harris trial and the labeling of Islam as a "Voodoo cult" did not defeat the growing movement, and it certainly did not deter Clara and Elijah Poole. The teaching of the alleged truth was correlative with

Fard's Islam, and followers believed that the only way the devil fought truth was with lies.

The biggest lie was that the Asiatic Blackman was a Negro. The Pooles received the surname of Karriem from Fard in 1933. Elijah Karriem demonstrated that he was a budding student of "the prophet" Fard by sending letters to the editor of the *Baltimore Afro-American*.[55] Given Sister Clara's education and Elijah's dependency on others to read texts out loud, she more than likely transcribed letters that he dictated.[56] The mutually dependent relationship also meant that she both assisted him in interpreting the written world as well as interpreting his thoughts to that world.[57] Thus, as a team, they worked to lift the ATOI to new heights. Celebrating the presence of "the prophet," they encouraged readers to "come to Detroit, and hear for yourselves" and "be convinced that the prophet here is the only friend of lost brothers."[58] Performing "the greatest work for the American black people," they wrote, Fard teaches "us who we are, that we are not the foot-mat of the world, but the CREAM. He teaches how to live a clean and intelligent life."[59]

These letters powerfully suggest that Elijah, and by extension Clara, were working and thinking through their racial muck. And the Great Depression had unleashed a groundswell of discrimination. One of the most talked-about trials of the period was the persecution of nine young black men in Scottsboro, Alabama, for the alleged rape of two white women.[60] In a letter to the editor, Elijah articulated that the trial's conclusion gave damaging proof of the "wicked enemies of the black man," since the "nine poor lost brothers" were jailed even after one of their accusers recanted and avowed their innocence.[61]

As students of Fard's Islam, however, the Karriems saved their heaviest critique for preachers. Christian preachers — many of whom had condemned the new "nation"—were unable to properly translate the Bible, they explained, because it was "written in symbolic language," and only Fard could reveal "all of the hidden mystery."[62] In fact, Fard wanted to deliver his "lost brothers" from misinformed "preachers [who] are implicated in politics, directly or indirectly, and sell the people to the devils (the white men) at every election."[63] This letter concluded by stating, "Awake from that dumb teaching the white man gives you" and which the "So-called Christian preachers" propagate.[64]

After reading two *Afro American* articles that detailed addresses by W. E. B. Du Bois and Carter G. Woodson, Elijah felt compelled to offer his own commentary. Although he ignored Woodson's brilliant analysis of how the "slave trade [started] out as triangular" and Du Bois's solid thinking on the Great Depression, wherein he discussed that, in the United States, "the difference in color means a difference in economics and living," he found common ground on other issues.[65] Passionately driven by Fard's black-centered Islamic teachings, he seized on Du Bois's critique of ministers and Woodson's documentation of a ubiquitous blackness. Woodson had discussed the trail of "Negro blood" throughout the world.[66] Du Bois's statement that he did not "go to church" because he was "tired of listening to nothing, absolutely nothing," had shocked an audience filled with ministers.[67] Further, Du Bois had pointed out that he believed in "Jesus Christ and His principles of love, honesty, [and] truth," but "if ministers studied, kept in contact with the world, interpreted problems in light of religion and pointed out the ways of meeting them, men would have a different attitude towards the church."[68]

Merging both articles, Elijah stated that he had "read [Du Bois's] statement to ten thousand Moslems and they all gave him a cheer."[69] Extending Woodson's argument, Elijah declared that "Mohammed himself was a full blooded black man and also Jesus, Moses, Alexander the great, Napoleon the great, were mixed with black men's blood."[70] Confident in their knowledge, as taught to them by Fard, the Karriems proclaimed that Mohammad's "name is more sacred than [that of] Jesus," and that they could "prove to Dr. Woodson or any professor that the Mohammedans out-number the other religions, especially Christianity, more than eleven to one."[71]

With the assistance of Sister Clara, Elijah Karriem was moving up the ranks. By 1934, Fard had once again changed their surname from Karriem to Mohammed and had affirmed Elijah's teachings by granting him the title "Minister of Islam."[72]

Challenges to the University of Islam

Elijah and Clara were not the only Detroiters who continued to pursue their new belief system with fervor. Enrollment at the University of Islam soared in early 1934 as Moslem parents began withdrawing their youngsters in droves from the Detroit public schools. Just a year and a half after the Harris scandal, the University of Islam became the next site of a major controversy. Because Detroit's schools were losing state funds due to lack of attendance, its Board of Education attendance director, along with the state superintendent of public instruction, demanded the closure of the University of Islam, an "unregistered Negro school," at 3408 Hastings Street on the "grounds that it [was] a nuisance."[73]

A squad of fifteen policemen and truant officers raided the building, where they found two painted flags adorning the same wall: the flag of the United States and that "of 'Islam' red with a white star and crescent," with the words "justice, freedom, equality and Islam" in the corners.[74] The police confiscated an enrollment book listing four hundred students and pamphlets used as instruction books — evidence for authorities that the children were being taught "voodoo practices."[75] The books contained claims like these: "Mohammed killed 6,000,000 Christians in his time and put 90,000 heads in a hole. The Nation of Islam has 21,000,000 trained soldiers ready to take the devils off the earth."[76] After reading these materials, officials went beyond the nuisance charge and added "contributing to the delinquency of minors," based on allegations that the instruction was "subversive."[77] According to newspaper accounts, the "teachings would frighten and disturb" most Detroiters.[78] Certainly, teachings that elevated black people above whites threatened the status quo. In addition, it was also reported that none of the thirteen arrested instructors and officials, who included both men and women, had a teacher's license.

Although neither Sister Clara nor Minister Elijah Mohammed was arrested at the temple that day, Elijah was jailed the next day and also charged with "contributing to the delinquency of minors." The arrested Moslems refused to cooperate with the police, maintaining what a newspaper reporter described as "ironic silence concerning their Islamic cult."[79] When they refused to eat food that Islam prohibits while in the county jail, newspaper reporters and radio announcers poked fun at what they called a "hunger strike," describing them as "fanatics." But their fast ended when they were provided fish, cheese, and other acceptable foods.[80]

Two days after the raid, in support of their jailed brothers and sisters, close to five hundred ATOI followers marched on Clinton Street to the police headquarters.[81] Given that her husband was jailed, one can speculate that Sister Clara had joined the group of protestors, her small stature hidden by larger, more robust bodies. As the morning air reminded Fard's converts that the winter season had finally abated, they walked proudly in old shoes and their best, though still worn, clothes.

According to the reports in the *Tribune Independent*, officers responded to the ATOI marchers by "club[bing] women, as well as men," while "the demonstrators fought desperately with knives, sticks, brickhats, and all similar weapons at their command."[82] The "Islamites'" fierce defense of themselves clearly startled the officers, who quickly called in "police reserves" and "mounted officers" to release tear gas on the followers of Fard.[83] The confrontation made national news: *Time* reported on April 30, 1934, that after "15 minutes the melee was over [and] 13 policemen retir[ed] for first aid, [and] 41 rioters [went] to jail."[84] Given the severity of the police response, and the fact that numerous spectators witnessed the assault, the Detroit NAACP president, L. C. Blount, who was no fan of the movement, called in their attorney Herbert L. Dudley to investigate.

"Negro Riot Order of Islam Hearing in Court," *Detroit News*, April 25, 1934.
(Reprinted courtesy of the *Detroit News*)

Prominent African Americans believed that the increase in pupils at the University of Islam in 1934 meant a "resurgence of the organization which two years ago climaxed its activities with a murder."[85] But they did not want to see any black people, however led astray, become victims of police discrimination and harassment.

At the hearing the judge dismissed the charges of "contributing to the delinquency of minor children" against all the school's instructors and officials. However, he did press the charge against Elijah Mohammed, stating that as the "leader of the group [he would] have to bear the cross."[86] Elijah defended himself, saying, "I am not the leader, I am the minister."[87] But the magical aloofness of Fard, who would mysteriously disappear forever just two months later, in June of 1934, elevated Elijah Mohammed as the visible head of a burgeoning nation.[88]

By this point, some of the newest converts had never seen Fard, and only had a "second-hand revelation" of "the prophet," which no doubt contributed to his deification.[89] The details of this transitional period lack an archive, but Elijah Mohammed's words and deeds give the impression that Fard was controlling him and the group's operations.[90] For example, though it was now Elijah who charged the new members one to two dollars to change their slave name to an Islamic surname,[91] the fact that they were still receiving the new names through a baptism ceremony suggests that Fard still had control over the movement.[92]

(Later, under his own steam, Elijah Mohammed would institute the placing of an "X," for the unknown, in place of a new name.)

Whatever the truth about Fard, by now Sister Clara and her husband Elijah were becoming role models for converts through their dedication to growing the ATOI. Minister Elijah Mohammed flexed his increased status to others by publishing a four-page weekly newspaper, *The Final Call to Islam*. Sister Clara likely assisted with the first edition, on August 11, 1934, which includes Marcus Garvey's *Negro World* trademark of a front-page editorial by Elijah Mohammed, as well as an update on the Educational Department, also known as the University of Islam. The school had "old brothers and sisters that actually did not know how to add 4 plus 4," as well as children "far more advanced than the adults." Thus, the ATOI membership included children and adults, with varying degrees of formal education. These were the believers that Sister Clara and Elijah Muhammad were determined to teach Fard's Islamic vision.

CHAPTER THREE

ALLAH TEMPLE OF ISLAM FAMILIES

THE DILLON REPORT

As Elijah Mohammed's ministry grew, so did the expectations for Sister Clara, the minister's wife. During the 1930s she was the equivalent of the Christian "preacher's wife." The role of a preacher's wife at times proved isolating; these women often mourned the gradual deaths of their own talents.[1] Working for the ministry, their duties included playing the piano during services, teaching Sunday school, entertaining guests, accompanying their husbands on trips, being prayer warriors (praying incessantly and fervently), and most important, being examples for other women to admire.[2] The latter was critical for Sister Clara too.

Aware of the impact she could have by living visibly as an upright follower of Master Fard, Sister Clara's self-making was deliberate. She may have initially strived to emulate what she had witnessed among preachers' wives in the black church; after all, Master Fard did not have a wife that she could imitate. But the signature accessory of a preacher's wife, a wide-brimmed, outlandish hat adorned with feathers and rhinestones would have been inappropriate on an Islamic body. Clara had to figure out a more proper way to capture the attention of followers. Being gazed on and read in a particular light was fundamental for her legitimacy, as well as that of her husband.

Although attire was important, the avenue Sister Clara found to signal her devotion to other believers of this movement was the decision to have her seven children educated at the University of Islam. It proved no easy feat; as we have seen, the reception of that new school by the larger community was anything but welcoming. Even before the April 1934 raid, Detroit's Board of Health and the Board of Fire Commissioners had surveyed the Hastings Street Temple (which included the University of Islam) and eventually had the building closed later in the year.[3] While Elijah was able to relocate the ministry's regular meetings to the Masonic Temple, at 632 Livingston, on Sunday afternoons, the

University of Islam presented another challenge.[4] Lack of finances to secure a new site shifted the education of the children into private homes.[5] Sister Clara, as the minister's wife and a mother of school-age children, rose to the occasion. Her dedication took many forms, and on one occasion she responded to an officer who came to the home with the express purpose of forcing her children back into the public school system. She put her "foot in the door," recounted Elijah Muhammad Jr., and told the officer, "over [her] dead body."[6] Even when faced with legal harassment, Sister Clara stood firm, and her words and actions supported a belief that education constituted a life-or-death matter.

Sister Clara knew firsthand the drawbacks of poor schooling and wanted her children to avoid a stumbling death walk through life. Whether or not the University of Islam had its beginnings in her home, she remained involved with the NOI's schools throughout her life. In later decades, she made a priority of attending the University of Islam graduation ceremonies. She rewarded the graduates' efforts by bringing personal greetings and best wishes from her husband and giving money.[7] In turn, graduates presented her with bouquets of roses and granted her "the first honorary diploma from the University of Islam" in 1964.[8] In 1967 she went on record saying that "black children have a vast capacity to learn when a genuine interest is given their well-being by parent and teacher alike."[9] Even after she and Elijah were gone, when their son Wallace (Imam Warith Deen Mohommed) had taken over the leadership of the NOI, he honored his mother in the late 1970s by renaming the University of Islam schools the Sister Clara Muhammad schools for her "unselfish commitment and tireless efforts."[10] She had "watched over the schools for many years," said Elijah Muhammad Jr., perhaps as a teacher, to ensure that Muslim children received a solid education.[11]

Origins of the Dillon Report

Private religious schooling was not an aberration; Catholic and Christian education had long been a popular choice for African Americans of modest means. Followers of Master Fard, many now under the direct leadership of Minister Elijah Mohammed, took pride in sending their children to the University of Islam.[12] But city and state representatives described the Moslems as a group who refused to cooperate, and believed that their religion was a deviant cult out of harmony with society. They worried that, by the perceived exclusiveness of their associations, ATOI members put their children in harm's way; specifically, the authorities feared that the children would not only lack education fundamentals but also "would become maladjusted to social life as it actually exists."[13]

Many Moslem families indeed tried to conceal their private affairs. Defending their religious beliefs, which were loaded with controversial ideas, required covering up personal matters that could be additionally scrutinized or misunderstood. Equally important, who they were may not have been who they wanted to be. At stake for them was the possibility that they would be seen as poor Negroes, overflowing with human vulnerabilities, as opposed to superior Asiatic Muslims. Revealing their full selves could have opened them to further attacks from "unbelievers." No doubt a relative or nosy neighbor had already critiqued the benefits of knowing obscure mathematical equations or calling all white people devils.

After the raid on the University of Islam, when ATOI members kept their children in private homes rather than return them to public schools, they successfully evaded attempts by the Attendance Division and Public Welfare to discuss the situation.[14] Frustrated, but refusing to drop the matter, representatives concluded that if they studied the case histories of Moslem families receiving assistance they could better understand what was happening with the children. Similar to the preeminent black sociologist E. Franklin Frazier and cultural anthropologists at the time, social service providers believed that "family disorganization was a major problem for the Negro."[15] Although "disorganization" had not yet morphed into a "tangle of pathology," Attendance Division and Public Welfare officials commissioned a study to explore the inner lives of ATOI members. Their goal was to construct an "intelligent plan" to re-enroll the children into public schools before "adopting a policy of aggressive action" against the ATOI parents.[16]

Miriam S. Dillon, a woman who claimed to have studied cults in the Caribbean, was hired to investigate the Detroit "Moslem Cult."[17] Under the direction of Florence Picotte, Dillon was assisted by Helen McCrae and Barbara Brown, all members of the College Women's Volunteer Service of the Merrill-Palmer School.[18] The Merrill-Palmer School, a child-development laboratory in Detroit, created academic programs and trained social scientists in the field. Much of the social science in that period sought both to detail the particulars of experience and to outline universal norms. Dillon and her team would use behavioral psychology and the supposedly value-free tool of statistics to evaluate African American families on welfare in the Alfred District of Detroit (a black neighborhood on the east side), through the notes and histories kept by welfare caseworkers.[19] Like other professionals and academics who documented human behavior, the Dillon team was animated by the hope of producing rigorous science that would lead to an ability to control social behavior.[20] Their ambition was to pick apart the Muslim parents, locating presumed disorder and dysfunction, to reassemble them as people who would enroll their children back into public schools.[21] The end point reflected the 1930s shift in the social science community from interpreting behavior in terms of biology and nature and toward the belief that black people could be assimilated into mainstream American life.[22]

The Great Depression had forced numerous families to rely on state welfare assistance, popularly known as "the Dole." Detroit, experiencing the plummeting of the automobile industry, showed stunning need; the city purportedly accounted for more than "25 percent of all the public general relief dispensed in the United States in 1930 and more than 13 percent in 1931."[23] Certainly, many ATOI families were among those requiring help. Sister Clara and Minister Elijah Mohammed's daughter Lottie remembered that their family received support in the early 1930s. According to Lottie, one day the "welfare lady came to check on us," and her mother was "too proud" to say that they were in need.[24] Lottie's cry that she wanted "a piece of bread [because] I'm hungry" garnered some food from the lady.[25] Sister Clara then said, "Well, there's no use in getting any food. I got nothing to cook it on," because "I have no wood and no coal to put in the stove."[26] With big brother Emmanuel in tow, the "welfare lady" got them what they needed.[27]

Each family receiving welfare was assigned a caseworker. In Detroit, the social workers were said to be "87 percent female and also 94 percent white in 1936."[28] The Dillon study combed the Alfred District workers' case studies for the following information: the personal backgrounds of the families; the characteristics that made families receptive to the "teachings of the Moslem cult"; an objective understanding of the ATOI's practices; and the impact of the "cult" on the behavior of its adherents.[29] Collecting this information — so-called life histories — would allow the researchers to understand the effect of the ATOI on the personality of its adherents, according to their theories. Notably, no personal interviews were conducted for the thirty-five-page document. The lack of oral interviews fits squarely within the tradition of scholarship produced by prominent white social scientists who embraced the role of experts on black people, even though some had never spoken to one for their research projects.[30]

Institutions as Instruments for Social Control

One of the few contemporary African American caseworkers sheds an interesting light on the climate of welfare work. Beulah Whitby, hired by the Detroit Department of Public Welfare in 1931, reported that she "had a whole case load of Muslims because they didn't know what to do about them."[31] In 1931, caseloads were reputedly "as high as 300 to 400 per worker," but by 1935, they were reduced "to between 80 and 125."[32] As a "social investigator," Whitby let her "basic philosophy" shape her interaction with the Moslem families.[33] Whitby stated that she did not "believe in using relief to make a person do something," and "whatever influence [she] could muster, [she] did it to stop them [white authorities] from pressuring these people."[34]

Whitby's candid comments establish that harassment of ATOI families was routine. This harassment initially centered on their refusal to cash checks issued in their former, non-Moslem, names. Unwilling to acknowledge the religious transformation of Master Fard's converts, the Department of Public Welfare "wouldn't issue a check to 'Ali Bay [Bey]'or something like that" said Whitby.[35] Islamic names were a crucial marker of the Moslems' new identity, and Whitby said "these people would starve rather than" cash a check in their old name.[36] While Whitby herself did not understand why the Moslems "made issues really that didn't have to be," she was sympathetic and believed that "relief should be regarded as a right," and "let them be, 'Ali Bay [Bey],' or 'Mohammed.'"[37]

Whitby indicated that the Moslem families' declaration that "their children had to go to the University of Islam" proved another point of contention between them and Detroit's Department of Public Welfare.[38] Indeed, it was the sticking point that led to the Dillon team's work. The team exclusively calculated all data from the caseworkers' files, providing a statistical lens on thirty-five converts (Group 2). For comparison purposes a control group of ninety-nine southern-born, non-ATOI black families with case files in the Alfred District were pulled at random (Group 1).[39] Admitting that the study was "necessarily rough," the authors looked for trends, but "no item, however small or casual, was passed over lightly."[40] The researchers took special care with caseworkers' notations on the families' religious activity or practices. Ironically, some of the comments the Dillon team quoted to substantiate its conclusions give us fresh insights into the daily lives of the pioneer converts. A picture begins to emerge of how Master Fard's collective lessons had pushed his followers to rethink the hows and whys of a racist world — and spurred them to work toward a better life.

According to the Dillon report, in the matter of school attendance, the sample Group 1 initially showed more interest than the Moslem Group 2. After joining the ATOI, the Moslems displayed a great interest in education, but not in the public schools.[41] Acquiring knowledge was now more fundamental to their lifestyle, wrote the Dillon team, but it was according to their "own notions." They insisted "on sending their children to the 'University of Islam.'"[42] For the new converts, the University of Islam guaranteed the moral protection and future academic success of their children. One man said that public schools "do not teach freedom, justice, and equality," the words placed on the ATOI flag.[43] In other words, Muslim parents believed that Master Fard's teaching countered the national racist agenda of Jim Crow, which was reflected in Detroit's public classrooms.

Without a doubt, the education of African American youth in Detroit had long been infected with racism. During the Reconstruction era, the Detroit Board of Education offered white children twelve years of instruction and African Americans only six years.[44] The early twentieth century saw the influx of African American migrants, who initiated lawsuits challenging segregation; by 1928 the schools were integrated, but principals and teachers routinely mistreated black children. At this time, it was reported that "4.5 percent of the students in Detroit" were African American, "but only 0.6 percent of the teachers."[45] Setting the classroom tone, white teachers daily embarrassed and humiliated innocent African American children. One teacher in Detroit had them stand in front of the class and used them to "illustrate the physical characteristics of 'the Negro race.'"[46] Children returned home discouraged and distraught; yet open protest by parents and the few African American teachers against racism was both infrequent and dangerous.[47] As historian Stephanie J. Shaw explains, "Detroit was not Canaan," and with a depressed national economy, it "was neither the time nor the place to incite hostile race relations."[48]

The poor treatment and education of African American children propelled W. E. B. Du Bois in 1935 to ask, "Does the Negro Need Separate Schools?" He answered his own question by writing, "God knows he does," because "I am no fool; and I know that race prejudice in the United States today is such that most Negroes cannot receive proper education in white institutions."[49] Even African American educators who championed desegregated schools admitted there was "greater inspiration, greater racial solidarity, superior social activities, greater retention and greater educational achievement for Negro youth in a separate public school than in a mixed school."[50] Detroit's two-tier curriculum, one for "gifted children" and the other for "subnormal children," gave even further cause for concern. Taking the standpoint that purportedly gifted children should be trained for leadership, whereas the "subnormal" could be condemned to "a bread and butter existence," the Detroit Board of Education made a mockery of its own motto, "Equal Opportunity for All."[51] The unabashed animosity toward African American children in Detroit also resulted in teachers stating that "the greatest amount of retardation [was] found among the colored" children.[52] The causes of supposed retardation were linked to "late entrance and late progress." Not surprisingly, a high percentage of African American children were flunked or dropped out after grade six.[53]

The Appeal of the ATOI

It is easy to see why Fard's followers would want to protect their children from the demeaning racism of the public schools. The Dillon report provides us glimpses that they wanted more for their children—and for themselves. The public schools offered instruction in four major subjects—mathematics, the sciences, English, and reading—along with hygiene instruction, which included "toothbrush drills" and "handkerchief drills" (teaching children to place a hanky over their nose).[54] A Moslem child, Charles Jr., said to a relief worker, "Our school is about the same as other schools except they teach religion and don't allow vile language."[55] A clean vocabulary was in keeping with Master Fard's moral expectations, and one Moslem parent explained that he preferred the University of Islam for "his children because they teach girls not to fight and to stay away from boys; they have separate teachers for boys and girls; they teach brotherly love and how to stay out of trouble, detention houses, jails etc."[56] Here we see early support for gendered difference and thus the need for distinct lessons on how to be feminine and masculine.

But the University of Islam also differed from the public schools by including instruction in other subjects. For instance, students learned about the "planetary system," a "form of Astrology."[57] Though the Dillon report listed "problems" in an assigned schoolbook that discussed "celestial bodies" and "their distances from earth etc.," these teachings had a magnetic affect on the ATOI adults.[58] Brother Challar Sharrieff explained that "the very first time" that he went to a meeting he heard Master Fard say that "the Bible tells you that the sun rises and sets. This is not so. The sun stands still. All your lives you have been thinking that the earth never moved. Stand and look toward the sun and know that it is the earth you are standing on which is moving." Sharrieff concluded, "That changed everything for me."[59] And while the Dillon team was not concerned with the schooling of adults, comments included in the document showed a thirst for education among the converts, both men and women. Twenty-year-old Alberta said, "[I] will learn all about [myself] and how to live clean; also mathematics and other studies" at the University of Islam, and this is why she wanted to attend.[60] Another Moslem man who was "illiterate to be just barely able to read and write," said that "he is studying 'Arabian' as he expects to go to Egypt."[61] And a woman who said that she had heard family members talk about slavery and often wanted to know "who [my] ancestors were" declared "that the Moslems had instructed her about this."[62] Fard's followers clearly wanted to learn, and wanted their children to learn, concepts—"higher mathematics," astronomy, and new ancestors—that they had been denied due to the workings of "the devil."

Beyond the particulars of University of Islam instruction, the Dillon report got at the larger appeal of Master Fard's religion. One of the most telling features of the converts' files was their enthusiasm for the "cult." The Dillon team reported that "72% of the group appeared to be actively devoted to their cause."[63] The evidence for this conclusion mirrored Whitby's earlier assessment of their "insistence on the use of their newly found Mohammedan names" and "sending their children to the University of Islam."[64] Indeed, one woman refused her "Mother's pension"—a cash allowance given to women with dependent children whose fathers were either dead or unable to support them — rather than remove her children from the University of Islam. She said she "will not sacrifice [my] religion for anything."[65] The Dillon team explained that the comprehensive alternative lifestyle, located at a spiritual and material nexus, was one with "promises of assistance, racial recognition, security and superiority," and that it had made an "appeal to those most bewildered by their social difficulties."[66] How the researchers measured supposed bewilderment is unclear. Some social scientists who studied black life would classify anything that could not be quantified as emotional.[67] What is clearer is that the new faith provided a balm for the hurt and pain that ATOI adults had felt as race and class oppression beat them down, and it put an end to their dehumanization.

As believers, the ATOI adherents had internalized Master Fard's message that they were the cream on earth, entitled to all that it had to offer, and so were their children. The Dillon team wrote, "The servile attitude which has characterized the southern negro for generations was discarded and replaced by on[e] of superiority" among the Moslem group.[68] Using ATOI publications to glean further information about its philosophy, the authors surmised that Master Fard's "rearrangement of the historical race background in such a way to demonstrate not only the equality but the superiority of the black race" gave them "assurance" and a sense of "satisfaction" that they were "an important and superior people."[69]

The sense of superiority showed, according to the report, in the way Master Fard's followers maintained their distance from those they deemed unbelievers. Caseworkers noted that some of them withdrew from interactions with relatives and refused to live with non-Moslems.[70] One woman said, "[I] cannot associate with unbelievers."[71] Social contact outside of the ATOI rubbed against the notion that they were a chosen people. One Moslem man, for example, said that he did not want to send his children to the Green Pastures Camp for "colored children only," because "they belong to a *different* black race."[72] A caseworker wrote that another man "believes himself to be of a chosen race, the race of the 'original' men.'"[73] And yet another stated "that his ancestors are of Asiatic descent."[74] These reiterations of Master Fard's teachings, along with strict adherence to his other ideas, irritated the Moslems' neighbors and relatives, on whose statements the researchers relied substantially. According to these secondhand reports, about 25 percent of the group had some "problems" with relatives because they refused the responsibility of supporting non-Moslem children.[75] One Moslem couple said, "[We] think they are old enough [the children were fifteen and sixteen] to decide for themselves; then they must look after themselves."[76] Many friends and neighbors complained that the Moslems possessed a "superior attitude."[77]

For all their devotion to their new religion, though, the ATOI adults were not very forthcoming about the details. According to the caseworkers, 48.5 percent were "completely evasive" about their new faith.[78] This refusal signaled danger for the Dillon team, who were invested in portraying the group as a cult. When one man refused to sign his welfare check until he "obtained permission from the leader [unnamed] to do so," they saw support for their idea.[79] It was due to the influence of the leader, the researchers argued, that the Moslems became more evasive and defensive against any interference in their home life. Before embracing a Moslem identity, the group on the whole was "fairly co-operative (39.1% very co-operative; 46.3% fairly so; with only 14.6% unco-operative)," but after joining, they had "demands for specific things and an evasiveness about the details of their manner of living."[80] One can hear the level of suspicion this aroused in the Dillon team in their conclusion that no form of "physical resistance or violence" was advised and that the members were "without criminal or anti-social tendencies."[81]

The report also focused on employment and attitudes toward work. And here again we can glean information about the lives of ATOI members despite the document's negative conclusions. The Dillon team reported that, collectively, Master Fard's followers ranked socially and economically among the most "poorly adjusted" migrants in Detroit, which made them vulnerable to cults. Tabulations and comparisons between the sample group 1 and the Moslem group 2 indicate that while they had resided in the North for a comparable length of time, the Moslem group had "less formal education" than the control group.[82] Lacking education directly impacted employment, and, not surprisingly, the Moslem group was composed of a larger number of workers in "only the crudest kinds of unskilled labor," who also suffered more from irregular employment.[83] The authors correctly pointed out that advancing age (the median age of adults in the Moslem group was thirty-eight), difficult economic conditions, and discouragement explained some of the slight difference between sample Group 1 and Moslem Group 2. Nonetheless, they deduced that after becoming Moslem, Group 2's attitude regarding work had changed, and about

"41.5% . . . were perfectly satisfied not to work at all."[84] This conclusion appears to have been based on a lack of shame in not working that the researchers discovered in some Moslem subjects, which fed directly into racial stereotypes of laziness. Fascinatingly, one Moslem man said, "I assumes I'll be cared for."[85] And a Moslem woman told her caseworker, "She had worked and slaved for 398 years, so now is going to be supported; some one is going to give [me] bread for [my] children."[86] The possibility that these responses indicated a reasonable reaction to the history of slavery and debt peonage, or even a psychological coping strategy given the dearth of jobs — let alone that the "cult" might be creating an alternative ethic of interdependence and caring — was dismissed. The researchers concluded that the teachings of the Moslems "encouraged the idea that the white man owed the negro a living," thus breeding contempt among critics.[87]

Unexpected Benefits

Relief workers consistently noted "obstinate attitudes" among the Moslems with respect to food prejudices.[88] They "refused meal tickets" because of "food restrictions imposed by their religion."[89] One man said, "The kitchen is not for [my] family. A Mohammedan cannot eat meat as served in the kitchen."[90] A caseworker recorded that they "eat but once a day, besides coffee in the morning."[91] Master Fard encouraged his followers to eat a traditional Islamic diet, with absolutely no pork and all "intoxicating liquors . . . tabooed."[92] Yet he added some interesting twists, most specifically the one meal a day: "over eating [is] greatly frowned upon."[93] Combining "chance comments" about food from the caseworker's files with information gleaned from an ATOI pamphlet, the Dillon team reported that "in the opinion of the leader," it is because of "excess [body] fat" that many people have "physical and mental sluggishness," causing physical ailments.[94]

Despite the caseworkers' annoyance and their own suspicion of "the opinion of the leader," the Dillon team's assessment revealed that Master Fard's diet and health teachings positively impacted his followers. The general physical conditions of family members was "slightly less favorable" among individuals prior to becoming Moslem when compared to sample Group 1. Home cleanliness before becoming Moslem was "somewhat inferior" to sample Group 1 as well. After becoming Moslem, the group improved in both of these areas. The researchers were wary of certain claims made by converts. One Moslem man said, "If you live right you won't need [doctors]."[95] One woman convert added, "One's well-being depends on one's state of mind."[96] They were no doubt echoing Master Fard's teaching that sickness could be conquered with a proper diet.

The researchers noted that this could be a damaging teaching; for example, one man's body had substantially deteriorated, yet he "claimed to be in perfect health."[97] But these were exceptions; overall, the authors concluded, "one effect of the Moslem Cult is to better the standards of hygiene" and health "among its members."[98]

Another area that showed noteworthy change among the Moslems was their family home life. The "cult has a tendency to improve the stability of the family rather than break it down," wrote the Dillon team.[99] Wives and husbands "worked together with complete agreement." Equally significant, if there had been a separation or daily quarrels prior to joining the ATOI, the individual who had become Moslem was the one "to smooth things over."[100] This observation counters the idea that Fard's followers were totally intolerant of unbelievers. Perhaps the hope of converting a spouse by example factored into their decision to work things out. Still, how the unbeliever behaved would certainly influence the interaction. The researchers punctuated that if one "disagreed with their religious theories," he or she was rejected.

Additional remarks about home life reveal Master Fard's encouragement of large families and the support ATOI members extended to one another. Culling from caseworkers' files, the researchers pointed out one couple who had separated before the woman joined the ATOI, apparently because she did not want more children. After becoming a Moslem, she believed that "if her husband would come back now (she is sure that their relationship would be 100% better)," wrote the caseworker.[101] Maybe she was now willing to have more children because, as one man is reported to have said, his "religion [was] opposed to any form of birth control; let nature take it course."[102] Or could she have decided that in the context of her new religion, more help was available? Families would not suffer because "Moslems help each other," noted a caseworker.[103] Another Moslem indicated the importance of extended family and said "that i[t] is contrary to rules of Moslems to take money from 'Brothers' for food and room rent; they must share with each other."[104]

Finally, "moral attitudes and behavior" also "improved noticeably" in the Moslem group.[105] One man is reported to have said, "Everything would be all right if people followed the golden rule. Most people do not, but . . . that is no reason why I should do wrong."[106] A relief worker detailed the conversion testimony of a female stating that "she is now a changed woman," which highlights the overall transformation that many of Master Fard's adherents experienced. "She does not run around with men; does not drink whisky; she is a respectable human being, and knows that she is clean."[107] Being clean, on the outside as well as within, was proof that the Moslems took their religious instruction regarding appropriate appearance and behavior, support for each other, and diet and hygiene seriously, and they showed pride in living within the parameters of Master Fard's Islam.

The Dillon Report's Conclusions

For all the effort that went into the Dillon report, it reached surprisingly tame, almost anticlimactic, conclusions. In part, the researchers were faced with a conundrum: had the relief workers whose files the Dillon team studied believed any true harm was being done to the children of Moslem parents, they could have removed the children from their homes. While children were more usually taken because their mothers were labeled "immoral" because of their engagement in "illicit leisure businesses," caseworkers could have exercised a vague "unsuitability" option had they elected to remove children from Moslem homes.[108] However, despite the ATOI members' demands that their new Muslim identities and the particulars attached to their religion be respected, no record exists of any of their children being removed. Perhaps the relief workers felt that the children were well cared for in Moslem homes, as all evidence pointed in this direction. Or, even though relief workers may have been frustrated, their personal employment depended on dispensing aid along with "the regulations that accompany it."[109] Already under pressure from business professionals critical of using welfare "for solutions to the economic downturn," relief workers faced hostility from the private sector, who claimed their work was "creating dependency."[110] This complicated terrain, compounded by relief workers' desire to work, certainly influenced their choices not to make the Moslems' children wards of the state.

After considering all the evidence, the Dillon researchers argued in the conclusion to their report that the ATOI home schooling would eventually die out, and thus no action need be taken. Believing that parents would grow tired of their children's "continual annoyance" in "small quarters day after day," they would, the authors stated, "return them to the public schools in self-defense."[111] Given the researchers' detailed analysis that the Moslem parents were passionate about their children learning the "truth" and keeping peace in the home, their conclusion seems rather odd. In fact, only an unfounded projection — that the children were ill-mannered and out of control — could substantiate the researchers' prediction that the Moslem parents would eventually lack the patience to educate their children. The Dillon team was no doubt swayed by certain dominant ideas about poor and working-class black children during the 1930s. In the words of historian Daryl Michael Scott, it was believed a child witnesses violence and "is also the object of the violent behavior of his parents. His own behavior will be impulsive, and the family as a socializing agency will have little influence on his conduct. He becomes a person seeking only the satisfaction of individualistic impulses and wishes."[112] Moreover, during this period, as Khalil Muhammad has shown, northern progressives connected black criminality and "peculiar forms of immorality" to the "absence of environmental intervention."[113] No wonder the researchers instructed representatives from the Attendance Division and Welfare Department to ignore the "irritating [b]umptiousness" of the Moslem "cult" and assist in the "underlying economic and social problems of other negro families of the same class," so that the "movement may not spread."[114]

In suggesting a passive solution, the researchers believed that the "whole movement will wear itself out in a short time."[115] The "cult," the Dillion team explained, would not survive the next generation because the "abstemious, almost puritanical requirements in the way of life" cannot "be adhered to by any large negro group over a period of many years."[116] The prevailing viewpoint during the interwar years was that the black family had low morals.[117] Here again, racial myths of promiscuity and lewdness clearly factored into the researchers' assessment of Master Fard's followers' inability to live clean. Perceptions that the cult lacked "continuity of purpose, an intelligent leadership and support, and a considerable amount of worldly goods" informed the researchers' conclusion that the group would "fall down with its own weight."[118] For the Dillon team, Master Fard's teachings were more "fantastic than fanatical."

What the Dillon team missed, but the caseworkers' reports still allow us to see, is that whatever its shortcomings, Master Fard's ATOI provided a compelling alternative to the racism and economic deprivation that had long gone hand in hand with traditional Christian teachings and the state-supported education system. The power of Master Fard's Islam in the lives of his converts reveals the forcefulness of what scholar C. Eric Lincoln calls "spiritual inventiveness."[119] According to him, Master Fard had "sense[d] out and [gave] dramatic verbalization to the most private yearnings of his followers, sometimes before even they themselves [were] fully conscious of what it is they want[ed] or need[ed] to enhance their lives with accomplishment or meaning."[120] Joining Master Fard's movement, his converts were given direction on how to receive the highest level of earthly satisfaction. No longer perplexed about their future, they embraced a new religious identity providing a fulfillment that went beyond conventional understanding. Master Fard offered his followers a new way to think about themselves and the reasons for their oppression — and new ways to take control of their own lives.

CHAPTER FOUR

CONTROLLING THE BLACK BODY

INTERNAL AND EXTERNAL
CHALLENGES

T he conclusion of the Dillon report that Master Fard's religious movement would die out because it lacked "continuity of purpose" is fully
contradicted by its steady growth in the ensuing decades. Before his
disappearance, Fard had established two additional temples, in Chicago
and Milwaukee. (According to his numerical designations, Detroit became
Temple No. 1, Chicago Temple No. 2, and Milwaukee Temple No. 3.) These
would be added to by Elijah Mohammed as the membership grew to its highest
peak in the early 1960s.

Unfortunately, we have few archival traces about women's participation during
the roughly thirty-year period between the Dillon report and the 1960s. Still,
there are critical moments when women's private worlds spill over into the public domain prior to 1960. The late 1930s present a particular challenge, but we
have two interesting lenses through which to view the growth of women's commitment to their new nation: an article in *The Final Call to Islam* by Reformer
Burnsteen Sharrieff and a 1935 legal challenge in Chicago that resulted in the
jailing of twenty-four ATOI women. Each of these adds to our understanding of
what was required of women to remake themselves.

Sister Burnsteen: Reforming the Moslem Body

Burnsteen Sharrieff acted as personal secretary to Master Fard from 1932 until
his disappearance in 1934. Born on July 14, 1915, in Robinsonville, Mississippi,
Sharrieff was still a toddler when her parents migrated to Detroit in 1919. Just
over a decade later, after attending several meetings at the 3408 Hastings Street
temple, her family joined the ATOI movement in October 1932. Although Sister
Burnsteen's full conversion narrative resembles Zora Neale Hurston's descrip-

tion of "a lost ball in de high grass," meaning that it is hard to find and follow, her lifelong commitment to Master Fard's Islamic mission is legendary.[1] She was just eighteen years old in 1934 when arrested with others in the raid at the University of Islam in Detroit.[2] She also traveled with Fard to Washington, D.C., Cleveland, Milwaukee, and Chicago as he taught and prophesied. Her mission was to scour the midwestern landscape, fishing for potential converts to the ATOI. Back home in Detroit, she typed Fard's Lessons.[3] As a single young woman sojourning with a man whom journalists disparagingly called a "voodoo cult leader," she undoubtedly raised the eyebrows of finger-wagging critics — perhaps even black clubwomen, whose signature cause had been the protection of vulnerable females from nefarious men.[4] Yet Sister Burnsteen was not dissuaded from her chosen career.

Although there were other women followers who might have been eager to do the same work, Sister Burnsteen seemed perfectly suited to the mission. She had proven on a number of occasions that she had the skill set and demeanor to meet organizational needs. In a pamphlet privately published by her family, Sister Burnsteen notes that she was an excellent typist, "95 words per minute with 98% accuracy."[5] Given the dearth of primary material on Sister Burnsteen, this pamphlet is important, even though we are not told how the memories were captured. (Another source suggests that she corrected Master Fard's grammar as she typed his Lessons.[6]) Second, her academic abilities were comprehensive. She recalled, "I graded letters (which everyone had to write for a Holy name), helped those who could hardly write by taking their hand and guiding it, giving them writing exercises until they could write on their own."[7] Third, she was a tireless worker who "never complain[ed]" to those in authority over her.

Sister Burnsteen developed a reputation for doing the behind-the-scenes work required to build a budding movement. Master Fard rewarded her steadfast devotion. She proudly remembered, "of the 9 First Laborers chosen by Master W. D. Fard I was the only female Laborer."[8] Yet their relationship had its downside. Sister Burnsteen remembered feeling the sting of humiliation on more than one occasion. Her days were largely filled with long hours of typing "Lessons and Facts" and tearing them apart for distribution. One time she "neglected folding and creasing them to tear smoothly," and Master Fard reprimanded her by saying, "Let me show you how to tear paper." He then took a sheet and creased it using his thumbnail. Sister Burnsteen recalled that he then "pressed [her] face down close to the paper and slowly tore it apart asking [her] over and over, can you see it?" Each time she replied, "Yes Sir." Or, said Master Fard, "you can do it like this." At this point he placed a folded sheet of paper between his clinched teeth damping it with saliva and tore it evenly.[9] As her "eyes were

Reformer Burnsteen Sharrieff, 1932.
(Courtesy of Nur and Median Mohammed)

all filled with tears," she sat at the typewriter and thought, "No one is for me." At this point Sister Burnsteen believed Master Fard read her mind, as he had before, because he "smiling and gently" said to her, "I'm for you and if I'm for you, who can be against you. I'll walk the water for you."[10] Here again, we have another powerful Christian image evoked by Master Fard.

Fard gave Burnsteen the title of Reformer, a name that ironically conjures up the Progressive (1890s-1920s) agenda of assimilation, the elimination of corrupt political power, and moral reform. Master Fard's use of the term seems to constitute another example of him strategically taking the familiar and infusing it with new meaning. His Islamic movement was dedicated to reforming African Americans who had been "led astray into different denominations of Christianity, which [was] one of the devil's strongest and most powerful plans of 'trick-nowledgy' he had to use on the black man," wrote the recent convert Dorothy Lewis.[11] It was through the leadership of Reformer Burnsteen, and others selected by Master Fard, that the "lost-found" brothers and sisters of Asia found living in "the wilderness of North America" could be redeemed.

In her later recollections, Sister Burnsteen describes not only how they fished for followers but also the establishment of a new spiritual home (temple) for Master Fard's "lost-found" Islamic converts in the Windy City. Believers gathered outside of the temple as well. Reformer Burnsteen remembered that every Tuesday they had a Moslem-only picnic. They "danced, played games, especially baseball," and would win prizes. Master Fard would even dance the waltz with a glass of water on his head and told believers that "the waltz was original music."[12]

Surprisingly, the only piece of writing we have from Reformer Burnsteen during the time she worked with Fard alludes to none of this. In an article published in *The Final Call to Islam* in August 1934, she focuses squarely on Master Fard's dietary dictates. "Reduce and Be Cured of Your Ailments" introduced to readers who were not converts the Moslem Girls' Training and General Civilization Class (MGT-GCC) and the Fruit of Islam (FOI). The MGT-GCC, she explained, was "set up by Master Fard Mohammed, for women and girls only." All participants were required to maintain a "standard weight of 120 lbs. and not over."[13] (The FOI mandated a "standard weight of 150 lbs. and not over."[14]) Through her attendance at the MGT-GCC classes, Reformer Burnsteen wrote, she "learned that most of the bodily ailments are directly or indirectly traceable to overweight."[15] She recounted all of the possible problems associated with fat, including inactivity, constipation, diabetes, heart trouble, high blood pressure, cancer, and Bright's (kidney) disease, and admonished the reader, "Sister, quit digging your grave with your knife and fork!"[16]

But what is most striking in the piece is her harshness toward overweight women. For instance, she discusses the "unjust" behavior of "a real overweight person (fat person)," who usually weighed at least "200 pounds."[17] Reformer Burnsteen asserted that the heavy woman "breathes more, eats more, takes more room and in other words is a complete nuisance to the normal one."[18] After the overweight woman "has robbed you of the fresh atoms from the air," Reformer Burnsteen explained (citing that on average one inhales "3 cubic feet of air per hour"), the physically fit woman is left to breathe "stale and lifeless" oxygen.[19] Essentially, obese women caused others in their midst to suffer.

Reformer Burnsteen explained that obesity "was caused by the devil (white man)," who encouraged excessive weight and consciously "disfigured us from our original selves in every way imaginable."[20] Her harsh descriptions of African American women's bodies as "badly disfigured and deformed" were paired with the comment that "we were once all beautiful." The contrast between obesity and Reformer Burnsteen's description of "perfect forms" suggests the use of fat as an indisputable moral sin; bodily traits produce visible, unmistakable evidence of the correctness of one's religious practices.[21]

Clearly, women believers' self-fashioning as Moslems required a personal engagement with their own bodies. An important concrete example we have of this is Sister Clara. Certainly, Master Fard's dictates played an important role in Sister Clara's image as her husband became more prominent in the movement. Her consistently trim physique was considered praiseworthy; her petite body was presumptive evidence that she lived according to Master Fard's nutritional rules.[22] Granted, this may have been easy when food was scarce during the Depression, but even in later years, when food became tantalizingly abundant, Sister Clara physically remained a flattering portrait for Islamic womanhood. Her body was understood to be a physical representation of what an Islamic woman ought to look like.[23] We do not know if maintaining a light weight took effort on her part. What is clear is that she was affirmed for it, and thus in those early years helped launch a symbolic aesthetic practice.

Feminist scholars have pointed out that the body, and the female body in particular, has been the principal "target of controlling and reforming systems."[24] Whether or not it was intentional on Master Fard's part, his maximum-weight requirement echoed prevailing Western notions of "fat and the un-civilized body."[25] According to Amy Ardman Farrell, by the 1920s, "the moral outrage against fat" had "everything to do with the construction of whiteness and the racial identities of white 'mainstream' Americans and Britons."[26] Fatness had become a marker of a primitive body. Indeed, a noted physician of the time, Dr. Leonard Williams, explained that only "men of 'savage tribes' preferred women who were fat and round."[27] Fatness wrapped undesirable racial bodies; hence, white women, says one analyst, had to fight the "tendency to gain weight because they knew that fat women were 'repulsive sights, degrading alike to their sex and civilization.'"[28]

On the one hand, then, by counseling his converts to maintain a lower body weight, Master Fard steered them away from "representations of racial inferiority —the fat mammy, the jezebel figure with protruding buttocks, or, in contemporary American life, the image of the fat (and over-sexed and over-fertile) black [1970s] 'welfare queen.'"[29] On the other hand, his critique of fleshy bodies as morbid—given full expression in Reformer Burnsteen's article—supported racist perceptions and added another dense, prickly layer to his remaking of the so-called Negro. Even so, his female followers likely strove to meet the 120-pound requirement. For them, chiseled bodies were an outward trademark of moral character, observable proof that they had rejected the devil's damaging cellulite body.[30] A fit physique was seen as a sterling receptacle in which to inculcate advanced thinking about the world and to store the new spiritual self.

But why was Reformer Burnsteen so preoccupied with the body weight of

African American women? Were there great numbers of overweight African American women "stealing the oxygen" from their smaller sisters? The best-known photos of the Depression years capture starving Americans, particularly destitute white women surrounded by their undernourished children.[31] When African Americans from this period were photographed — for example, in images taken by photographers who worked for the Farm Security Administration (FSA) and the U.S. Department of Agriculture (USDA) — they, too, look lean.[32] Notably, however, the senior women, usually surrounded by gloomy-faced, watery-eyed children wearing tattered clothing, seem particularly large by comparison. Their upper bodies are bosom heavy (probably a result of nursing), their lower bodies proportionally stocky.

But photography, even documentary photography, can be misleading. Therefore, to understand what might have been true of Master Fard's female followers requires going beyond these visual impressions. To get a more accurate understanding of the nutrition and weight of most African Americans during the Depression years, we need to take a closer look at the limited evidence available to us of what and how people actually ate. By employing an insightful reading of the Works Project Administration (WPA) ex-slave narratives, historian Stephanie J. Shaw provides details on aging African Americans, many of whom suffered from hunger during the 1930s. One informant, Elias Dawkins, spoke about "having been so hungry that he had once eaten animal waste."[33] Lack of food and poor nutrition is why Andrew Boone, another informant, said, "It's all hard, slavery and freedom, both bad when you can't eat."[34] The repeated hunger reported by formerly enslaved elderly people raises the question of whether one can be both hungry and obese. The answer is a resounding yes! But over time the body responds with weight loss.

Further knowledge about what African Americans ate can be drawn from cookbooks, memoirs, and fictional accounts of the time. In addition, the small sample of dietary studies recorded by the USDA Office of Experiment Stations, surveying the food habits of African Americans in rural Mississippi, Texas, Georgia, South Carolina, Alabama, and upstate New York, expands our knowledge of what African Americans consumed. Several years prior to the Depression it was reported that "the average Mississippi housewife is more apt to spend her time or money on a cake or pie than she is on a salad. In fact, potato salad is the only salad in general use among our rural people."[35] At the start of the Depression, in 1929, the diet of families in Georgia consisted, according to one analysis "too largely of highly milled cereals, fats and sweets, and too few fruits and vegetables."[36] Moreover, everything seemed to be flavored with molasses, especially during the winter months, when large portions of pork, bread, and syrup were consumed.[37] Yet by the third year of the Depression, in 1932, changes in agricultural conditions were evident and, says one contemporaneous report, "the negro dietaries were, on the whole, less adequate, less costly, and simpler than the white dietaries," even as African Americans continued to burn calories working in the fields.[38]

African Americans who had migrated to the North and Midwest, once used to growing some of their own food, now relied heavily on shopping, spending more of their income on food.[39] An upstate New York study, one of the few that includes the weight of adults at an average of thirty years of age, reported that the women "tended to deviate from 'normal' [meaning they weighed more and not less] more often than did the men," and that the "percentage of females who deviated from normal weight increased with maturity."[40]

Finally, an analysis of Body Mass Index (BMI) trends provides the best insight. When comparing white women and men with their black counterparts, "black females were often 30–40 years ahead of the other three groups in reaching the level of obesity in a particular decile."[41] Still, while obese African American women certainly existed in the 1930s, BMI evidence indicates that they would have been in the minority. If a woman was born in 1895, the generation of Sister Clara, she had a 10 percent probability of obesity during the Depression years. If she was born in 1905, the percentage increased to 20 percent. If she was born in 1915, the generation of Reformer Burnsteen, she had an approximately 25 percent chance of being overweight in the 1930s.[42] This gradual increase may explain why Reformer Burnsteen focused so adamantly on warning her sisters away from overeating. Yet during the 1930s, with the decline in income and people eating away from home less frequently, the rate of fluctuation in body mass decreased.[43] Thus, during the Depression, people stopped gaining weight as rapidly as they had been before those years.

What was at stake in producing a plausible fiction of an obesity epidemic? Master Fard advocated eating sparingly at a time when in fact there was little opportunity to do otherwise. "We Moslems," wrote Reformer Burnsteen, "go some times 48, 72, 96 and more hours without food, taking a hot bath daily and plenty of exercise. This is good for us, because it helps the thinking faculties and also prolongs our lives."[44] Hunger pains, so common during the Great Depression, were thus transformed from an unwanted state, which one was powerless to alter, to a noble bodily means for self-improvement. In addition to taking the shame out of hunger, advocating thinness served two important ATOI purposes: creating distance from the "large" and "ugly" body seen as both "uncivilized" and unhealthy; and providing a motif to make known one's upward mobility.[45] It was these purposes that were served by the MGT-GCC class to which Reformer Burnsteen referred.

Chicago: Proudly Jailed Women

If Sister Burnsteen's exhortations in *The Final Call to Islam* emphasize weight control as a paramount characteristic of the Moslem woman in the 1930s, a different picture emerges from a notable event that rocked the members of Temple No. 2, the spiritual edifice in Chicago. On February 24, 1935, Sister Rosetta Hassan was riding a Madison Line streetcar with her nine-year-old son Zack Jr. when a fight broke out between Zack Jr. and the son of Athenasia Christopolous, a nonbeliever. The mothers intervened and quarreled over whose son was the aggressor. Pushing and shoving ensued, and Christopolous's eyeglasses flew from her face. Christopolous sought a warrant against Sister Rosetta, accusing her of breaking her eyeglasses. A hearing was scheduled to examine the charge before a warrant could be issued.

Whether or not Christopolous was motivated by fear of or distaste for the new religion taking root in her city, Moslems responded as a community. Sister Rosetta arrived at the hearing accompanied not only by her husband, Brother Zack, but by more than forty ATOI members, who saw "the trouble of one as the trouble of all."[46] After listening to both sides, Judge Scheffler declined to issue a warrant.[47] At that point Brother Zack Hassan said, "It's all right, now, let's go." Then, according to the *Chicago Defender*, "the entire band rose with military precision (such military procedure is a part of their ritual) and started marching to the rear of the courtroom."[48] As the ATOI members, the majority of whom were women, stepped in unison, they "became intermingled" with other detained African American women. When a bailiff aggressively attempted to shift their direction, a "cultist woman" reportedly shouted at him, "Take off your glasses and I'll whip you."[49] Other ATOI converts then seized chairs and began battering the police with their fists and feet. The police, in turn, drew their revolvers. By the end of the melee, a police captain had died from a heart attack triggered by the excitement, and two ATOI members, King Shah and Allah Shah, had been wounded by gun shots. In all, forty-four people — seventeen policemen, seven bailiffs, and twenty ATOI members — suffered injuries.

Forty-three of Master Fard's followers were arrested and held for inquiry. Of the group, seven women were featured in a police lineup photo published in the *Chicago Tribune*. This is one of the few photos we have of Moslem women at the time. Wearing modestly stylish hats and dark-colored long winter coats, some of which were trimmed with elaborate fur, suggesting wealth in the midst of the Depression, the women looked regal and daringly proud.[50]

This courtroom scene is important for several reasons. First, these ATOI women had fought against white men with loaded guns. The ATOI men had proven equally assertive. Indeed, it took more than one hundred policemen,

Police lineup photo of seven followers of Master Fard after their arrest for rioting.
Left to right: Lennie Ali, Lennel Cushman, Georgia Jordan, Anna Bell Pasha,
Hattie Majie, Mary Gold, and Mary Ali, who are among the forty-three
women and men arrested and facing possible murder charges.
(Reprinted courtesy of the *Chicago Tribune*)

bailiffs, and court clerks, who struggled for close to an hour before all of Master
Fard's followers were "whipped into submission."[51] In this instance, clearly the
women's belief that it was their duty to support and defend a fellow member,
even if that meant fisticuffs, trumped any acquiescence to the dictates of appropriate feminine behavior. One woman is reported to have sung "Who's Afraid
of the Big Bad Wolf?" to taunt the officials.[52] The ATOI women were defiant.
At the same time, their injured heads and bruised bodies made clear who still
held absolute power.[53]

When the news came that forty-three ATOI members had been arrested, a
shock wave blasted through Temple No. 2, located at 3743 South State Street.
Five of the several hundred members who attended regularly scheduled meetings on Wednesdays, Fridays, and Sundays went directly to the police station.
They too were arrested when they allegedly protested after being ordered to

vacate the building.[54] Minister Elijah Mohammed, who had left Detroit in the midst of a leadership battle after Master Fard's 1934 disappearance, was identified by newspaper reporters as the "head man" of Temple No. 2.[55]

The next day in court, only Elizabeth Sheriff was allowed to testify. It is unclear why she was chosen. Perhaps she was the highest-ranking member. Or maybe the other women considered her the most articulate. The court could have also simply selected her. She explained, "We were through and ready to leave. We didn't know which door to leave through and started toward the rear. If the bailiff had directed us to the right door we would have left and nothing would have happened. Instead of that he began pushing us around and trying to force us to sit back down."[56] During the cross-examination, Sister Elizabeth was asked if she was aware that the judge was on the bench and therefore all in attendance had to be properly dismissed. Sister Elizabeth admitted that she had seen the judge but retorted, "I see no reason why a person or persons were not entitled to leave after their business had been finished."[57] In the face of her defiance, Municipal Judge Edward Scheffler jumped into the questioning of Sister Elizabeth by asking "if her society believed its laws superior to the laws of the state," and she replied, "No," adding, "We obey your laws."[58]

What happened next indicates that the judge was using this incident to teach the purported cultists a lesson — perhaps revealing the suspicion in which the larger community held them. After excusing Sister Elizabeth from the stand, Judge Scheffler gave the ATOI members instruction on their motto of justice, freedom, and equality. He admonished, "The constitution embodies the principles of freedom, liberty, and equality for all, but no individual has the right to interpret these terms in that instrument. That right is reserved to the courts alone. If every person were to interpret those words in his own manner there would be nothing but disorder and rioting."[59] He found the ATOI members guilty of contempt of court and sentenced sixteen of the men to six months and twenty-four women to thirty days in jail.[60]

Doing time in Chicago's Cook County Jail, or next door in the older Bridewell, Chicago's House of Corrections, was not easy in 1935.[61] Although Cook County had been built in 1895, by 1910 it had been condemned by the International Prison Congress as "one of the worst jails to be found anywhere."[62] It was described as "an overcrowded, insanitary, disease-breeding place."[63] It was not uncommon to find five men hemmed into a one-man cell that they were forced to occupy twenty hours a day in the 1920s.[64] Despite these disturbing facts, four bond issues for an improved jail had been defeated by Chicago voters. We can assume that conditions were slightly worse by 1935, since the economy had imploded and the "so-called war on crime" that had started in Chicago in 1933 had increased the jailed population sixfold.[65]

There were five lock-up police stations scattered across Chicago that held women, but the County Jail was different. Described as a "moral mud bath," the Women's Quarters were small, with thirty-one cells and two "bull-pens," common areas designated for recreation and meals. Each cell was "eight feet, four inches long, six feet wide and seven and a half feet high, containing 375 cubic feet."[66] One visitor observed that the "cells can without exaggeration be compared to stalls for animals, and at that to the neglected stalls that might have been found in country districts at least a half century ago."[67] The parameters provided poor air space —"a third less" than is sufficient for one person.[68] With the influx of twenty-four ATOI women, the jail was crowded far beyond its capacity, forcing the women to live two, three, or maybe even four in a cell.

In addition to discomfort, jail conditions posed a direct threat to ATOI Islamic teachings about cleanliness. Prior to going to jail, the women would have bathed daily, sometimes multiple times within a twenty-four-hour period. Cook County Jail had no reported schedule for bathing. Nor were there adequate provisions for sterilization to destroy disease-producing germs; the linen was washed only once a week, so that the same sheets were often used five or six times by rotating prisoners.[69] Finally, because women with tuberculosis were not segregated, opportunities for the spread of infectious disease were tremendous.

The ATOI women would also have suffered in terms of their dietary requirements. The jail breakfast, a large cup of coffee and bread, was in keeping with their morning ritual.[70] It was the midday meal, which consisted principally of stews, they must have dreaded the most.[71] The food was poorly prepared, and many prisoners of all descriptions refused to eat it, generating excessive waste estimated at "between two and three tons every week thrown into the garbage."[72] For the ATOI women, it was not just a matter of taste but of the indecipherable ingredients in the stews. We do not know exactly what had been given as a dietary guide by 1935, but we know from Reformer Burnsteen's article that eating habits were already under scrutiny in the MGT-GCC meetings. A later publication, *How to Eat to Live*, specified that Nation of Islam members should not eat field peas (black-eyed, speckled, red, brown), kale, collard greens, corn bread, beans (accept for the small navy), fried meats, sweet potatoes, white potatoes, white bread, cat fish, or the blasphemously forbidden pork.[73] It is likely that at least some of these food proscriptions were already in place by 1935, and that the jailed women were faced with either eating forbidden rations or going hungry. Did the women stir the stew, smelling its contents, looking at the bits and pieces of scrap meat in an attempt to figure out if it was pork? Or, might they have taken each day as an opportunity to fast, demonstrating their religious allegiance when the meal was too disgusting for consumption? Their supper was a soup, which once again put them in the position of having to evaluate and possibly turn down another small meal.[74] Even apart from dietary issues, rancid food forced the majority of all prisoners to "spend $3.00 to $6.00 a week" at the jail store.[75]

On some days, filth and repulsive food may have been the least of the ATOI women's worries. In the southern jails, women were racially segregated, but in Cook County they were not. No demand existed for a "color line," because difficulties between the colored and white women offenders went unreported.[76] Believing that they were indeed superior to the officers and other offenders, the ATOI women would have had no problem keeping to themselves. Nevertheless, institutional racism marked this space, and in many jails privileges were given to favored prisoners, while others were bullied and suffered persecution.[77] Because the women had been involved in a courtroom incident that had resulted in the death of a police captain, some members of the police department had wanted them to be charged with manslaughter.[78] Resentment against the ATOI women, whom some officials believed to have been lightly punished for a horrific crime, could have surfaced in subtle forms of retaliation. Perhaps on some days the officers refused to let them leave their cell for the assigned four-hour bull-pen recreation. Moreover, a push here or a shove there by the officers, of course while performing their duties, could keep the ATOI women in perpetual fear of an escalation of violence against them. Even though the women were capable of physically defending themselves, as the courtroom scene had demonstrated, they had to wonder who would respond to their cries in jail. Lastly, it was not uncommon for women in jail to be patted down by men, because the Chicago Police Department had no more than thirty policewomen during the 1920s. We can be sure that inappropriate touching was used to both humiliate and degrade the women.[79] Panic, as a natural reflex to a frightening situation, likely surfaced every time a man entered the Women's Quarters.

Thirty days in the "idle house" surely tested the ATOI women's faith.[80] Generally idleness was known to encourage prisoners' "plotting and doing things that mentally, morally and physically destroy" them.[81] During their limited four hours a day of recreation in the bull pens, the women could read (although the jail provided no reading materials), talk, or play cards.[82] These were privileges women in prison were denied. Historian Cheryl Hicks points out how women in the New York State Prison at Auburn were not allowed to talk or smile, and "any form of greeting between [them was] considered immoral, evidence of what is termed 'lady love' and promptly punished."[83] Fortunately, the ATOI women could communicate without fear of an infraction. So, how did they use bull-pen time? Did they try to replicate their MGT-GCC meetings, or did they find other ways to transform their confinement into a deeper commitment to Master Fard's Islamic teachings? Perhaps they shared their frustrations at being away from their husbands and children, or aired resentment that Sister Rosetta Hassan had not been jailed, even though she had been the catalyst for their being in court in the first place.[84] And at the end of the allotted reprieve outside their cells, when they were shuffled back into those spaces that lacked natural light and ventilation, how did they react to pleadings and pitiful appeals from the drug-addicted women in jail?[85] Perhaps it touched their souls to hear the suffering of others. Or, since the majority of offenders were white women, did such pleas underscore for the ATOI women how uncivilized the "devils" really were?

Persecution can sometimes have the opposite effect of its intent, inspiring a more profound commitment to one's original purpose. Many of the ATOI women emerged from jail more ardently committed to their Islamic life. On leaving, they were no doubt a tad thinner (bringing them closer to the body image encouraged by Reformer Burnsteen); more significant, one can surmise, a stronger devotion to one another bound them together and to their Islamic mission.

The two aspects of ATOI women's experience this chapter has examined — their cultivation of a particular spiritual body type and their tough determination to stand up for themselves, each other, and their faith — were inspired by Master Fard's early leadership of the nation. By the time of the courtroom brawl, Master Fard was gone, and Minister Elijah Mohammed's leadership at Temple No. 2 was becoming more pronounced. Elijah had his own views on the role of women in his budding Nation of Islam. While Master Fard had encouraged "Mission Sisters" to walk the streets disseminating his religion, Minister Mohammed believed that women should not "fish" like men. Over time, he simultaneously restructured and restricted the public duties of women. The mere physical presence of women was to convey serenity and femininity, as opposed to outspoken defiance. This was meant to attract both men and women to seek membership. Yet unbeknownst to Minister Mohammed, his plans to confine women to the domestic sphere would be entirely derailed a decade later by the onset of World War II.

CHAPTER FIVE

WORLD WAR II

WOMEN ANCHORING THE
NATION OF ISLAM

W omen in the Allah Temple of Islam (ATOI) took on new, if tempo-
rary, prominence during World War II. In the early 1940s, with the
country at war and concerns about security dominating the national
stage, the FBI, under J. Edgar Hoover, unleashed an entourage of
agents to squash "Foreign-Inspired Agitation among American Negroes." Believing "that Japan ha[d] sought to capitalize upon the legitimate grievances of
the [N]egro" and was currying favor by "asserting [that] both are 'dark races,'"
Hoover ordered his criminal division to infiltrate and report on various allegedly
pro-Japanese organizations, including the ATOI.[1] This chapter uses some of the
testimony gathered by the FBI to paint a picture of ATOI meetings during this
period, details the teachings that led the FBI to deem the ATOI subversive, and
shows how the ensuing raid on the Chicago Temple in 1942, which led to the
arrest of seventy members, also created the conditions for women in the organization to move from the margins to the center of leadership.

Inside the Chicago Temple

Working together over the course of several months in 1942, the FBI and the
Chicago Police enlisted several African American men and a few women to
report on ATOI meetings. While we have no independent verification of these
reports and therefore cannot confirm the extent to which they fully or accurately
represent what was actually said at the meetings, they nevertheless shed some
light on both the themes and concerns addressed by the ATOI leadership during
this time, as well as on the overall structure of those meetings. Ruth Coleman
worked for the Chicago police and attended several meetings. Much of what
follows here is drawn from her testimony for the FBI.

According to Coleman, the doors opened for a typical Sunday meeting promptly at 2:00 P.M., and each visitor (non-member) had to tell the guards stationed at the door who had invited them.[2] Clearly, the ATOI was aware of the threat of infiltration. These same guards physically searched the men and removed any article they deemed inappropriate, particularly knives and guns. Although there were no weapons in the temple (only wooden rifles used for marching drills), Coleman reported that the ATOI women had told her that the men had guns at home.[3] Women visitors were thoroughly searched by female members.[4] Coleman claimed that she "was made to take off everything she wore" and that her "pocketbook and identifications cards" were "kept and handed to her after the meeting."[5] During her inspection she observed that one woman who had the smell "of wine on her breath" was sent home.[6] Following her intrusive pat-down, Coleman was directed to go into the women's waiting room prior to entering the hall.

Coleman's testimony gives us a picture of the waiting room as a place that provided the women at the Chicago ATOI some autonomy from the men. It was both an informal teaching zone and at least a somewhat safe place for conversation. Here the sister captain, the highest-ranking woman in any ATOI temple, who gave instruction to other women at the MGT-GCC classes and was generally respected for her memorized knowledge, had another forum for leadership. Among the other women, Coleman heard a range of conversations that moved between fact and fiction, hope and desperation, but that ultimately consistently concerned racial justice.

Most important for J. Edgar Hoover's purposes, Coleman reported that Chicago's sister captain taught about Japan's foreign minister, Shigenori Togo. The sister captain claimed that "TOGO had resigned his position in the Japanese cabinet in order to come to the U.S. in disguise. When he arrives here he will campaign among the colored people in order to combine their forces and start an internal war here."[7] She also asserted that "the Japanese armed forces are releasing all their colored prisoners. TOGO advocates the freedom of all the darker races."[8] If Coleman's account is accurate, it not only echoes what Hoover feared but also reveals that the sister captain's teachings were actively engaging and linking international political affairs to the aims of the ATOI. It seems ironic that the sister captain zeroed in on Togo, who had always leaned in the direction of international peace.[9] Nonetheless, she saw Togo as an ally to the ATOI. Although her analysis may have been passed to her from male leaders, she owned it, situating her dynamic religion within a destabilizing political climate. Togo had essentially disappeared from public view after resigning his position on September 1, 1942, but for the sister captain, even his absence represented a hidden advantage for the ATOI. She wrapped up her political commentary with a postwar prediction: "The black race and the white race will exchange places" in terms of importance.[10]

The sister captain's political beliefs were reinforced by Sister Mary 2X, who professed in the women's room that soon the brothers would take "over the government and then we could rest and have everything we needed."[11] "Ghandi [*sic*] and his followers are Moslems," she said, and they are all on a "rampage," which provided further evidence that the time of victory was near.[12] Sister Mary 2X also disclosed that of the fifty female members at the Chicago temple, several were working as domestics, but most "are on relief," and a few had been recently evicted from tenement houses.[13] Clearly, the followers continued to rank among the working poor, still scrambling to make ends meet. Like the sister captain, Sister Mary 2X seemed convinced that the war momentum had shifted toward the ATOI vision of justice.

Once in the hall, which was designed like a theater and seated about two hundred, all first-time visitors were escorted to the front row.[14] This may have been a way to extend appreciation for their interest in the organization by giving them the best seats; at the same time, the gesture ensured that they could be watched during the program. The meeting was called to order promptly at 2:30 P.M., with an opening prayer led by the minister and repeated by the membership.[15] The minister then presented lessons from among Master Fard's series of thirteen, in Fard's original words. The male informants stated that these lessons "made no sense."[16] Only full-fledged members claimed complete understanding of these mysterious and metaphorically difficult ideas.

During the lesson instruction, the minister (usually Minister Linn Karriem, formerly Henry Burton, Henry Freeman, and Linn Freeman) sometimes shared the stage with the sister captain. For example, on one occasion she read Lesson No. 2, which concerned a woman who had "terrific headaches, misery in all of her bones so much so that she was unable to walk to the store" and died at the age of forty-seven.[17] After reading lesson No. 2, the sister captain stated that only approved individuals who were invited back to the temple on Thursday night would receive an explanation of this Lesson. When Coleman attended that evening meeting (most likely an MGT-GCC class) and questioned the sister captain about Lesson No. 2, she was told that since she "was very much interested in the teachings of the Moslems, [she] should know at least part of the meaning of the lesson. This lesson states in effect that I am a slave and cannot do what I please."[18]

After the lessons, the minister began his lecture. Again, this was most often Linn Karriem, but when Elijah Mohammed (whom Karriem sometimes called "an apostle"[19]) was in town, he gave the lecture. The lectures could be three to four hours long. Mohammed would introduce family members and provide many "illustrations and instances" to keep the attention of the audience.[20] Topics ranged from instruction on proper Moslem behavior to the differences between Fard's Islam and Christianity to political observations and judgments. If anyone fell asleep during the lengthy lecture, he or she was told by the guards (who rotated their positions every thirty minutes) "to go and wash their face."[21] At the conclusion, the minister in charge gave those in attendance mathematical Problems to be solved, with "the winner getting a prize of $10.00."[22] The sister captain followed the excitement of money being awarded with the temple announcements.

The final portion of the meeting belonged to Sister Pauline Bahar, the national secretary for the ATOI (formerly Pauline Hatchett, Pauline Burton, and Pauline Freeman—she and Minister Karriem were married). Sister Pauline stood out among the female members for her authority. Her distinction was even borne out by her clothing: on one occasion all of the women members were dressed in white, but she reportedly wore a "lavender dress" and carried a "brief case."[23] Though her portion of the meeting—membership and financial details—could be seen as mere housekeeping, she usually began by talking "about the goodness of Allah" and how "all other churches were the devil's churches."[24] Sister Pauline informed the audience that a form had to be filled out by each prospective member, and that they would receive a card after it was approved. The membership card, explained Sister Pauline, "entitled the holder to admittance to the Moslem temples located in Milwaukee, Detroit, Washington, and New Jersey, [and] in an unnamed place."[25] When one informant inquired about his membership, he said Sister Pauline notified him that he was "being investigated and that if everything turned out all right, [he] would be given [his] true name plus a card showing membership in the Islam Order."[26] All "new members were asked to raise their hands" if they had "any questions they wanted to ask."[27] The FBI informants reveal neither the nature of the questions asked nor who replied to the queries, but this moment appears to have been the only time that a dialogue occurred between the audience and the leaders in the hall.

It was consistently reported that the meetings were "well under the control of the minister or leader and also a secretary," Sister Pauline. When the minister was unavailable, the leader was the brother captain, head of the FOI, and the meetings took on a testimonial style of followers proclaiming their faith.[28] Periodically, when the minister was gone, Sister Pauline gave the Lesson about the woman who suffered from high blood pressure, heart trouble, rheumatism, and swollen joints who died at the age of forty-seven.[29] It seems that Sister Pauline was the mainstay at each meeting, and she "kept all of the records and read several announcements concerning the financial condition of the organization."[30] Coleman reported that Sister Pauline requested a $3 donation from her and said that it was to be "used for the burial of the members and also for doctor bills in case the members became sick."[31] A monthly donation of a minimum of $1 was also required of converts.[32] Finally, Sister Pauline distributed "plain envelopes" for donations for "emergency purposes"—a frequent need, given the rotating incarceration of members.[33] In fact, she was on "duty at the temple" daily from 1:00–2:00 P.M. for the express purpose of receiving emergency contributions.[34] Gracious and appreciative, Sister Pauline concluded her portion of the meeting by saying, "We sincerely thank you again for your good nature. May Allah forever bless you."[35]

The meeting ended at around 6:00 P.M., with a prayer and instruction to the attendees to depart in groups of three and four.

Subversive Teachings

The FBI found plenty in the ministers' lectures to confirm Hoover's suspicions. On at least one occasion, Minister Karriem said, "The devil tries to make you hate the Japanese, but the Japanese are your brothers and sisters."[36] The "Asiatic race" included all "darker races, even a certain class of Jews, but not all Jews."[37] He declared that "the devils" would not win the war and that they had been "lying about how many ships are being sunk."[38] President Roosevelt was "an old lying devil" who withheld "equal rights" for black people. In fact, in line with Fard's origins story, "The white devil is nothing more than a two-legged stinking dog" who had been "grafted from the black man." Additionally, Minister Karriem talked about "lynchings, evictions of black people, beatings, and other misfortunes."[39]

Meanwhile, one of Elijah Mohammed's lectures, "The Difference between the Christian Church and the Moslem Temple" suggested that the U.S. flag was not worthy of allegiance. This lecture was accompanied by an image of the flag, a drawing of a man lynched underneath the flag, and the word *Christianity* written below the hanging. To the right of this image was the Islamic flag.[40] Critiquing the flag of the United States, Mohammed said:

> The white that you see, and notice that you don't see any black anywhere on it, represents the white race, the red represents the blood that they lost keeping it for the White Devils alone, the blue background [and] white stars represent justice for the Whites[—] not the red men or the Black men but only for the White Devils. Why should they show you any justice? You know they won't show you any equality[;] if you think that[,] go down

to one of the big hotels and tell them you want to get a room there and see what happens to you. Or go down in the deep south and walk on the streets with a white woman. The first thing you know you will be right here [pointing to the picture of the lynching].[41]

Mr. Mohammed said that President Roosevelt "isn't, in fact, doing anything to prevent the lynching of the colored people." He continued, "The President pretends he is your friend and helping you, but he doesn't do anything about mobbing or burning you."[42] (Minister Karriem repeated this message in a lecture of his own, stating, "You are taught to honor Old Glory, the stars and stripes but it should be the scars and stripes as you get scars and stripes all over your body from Christianity."[43]) Under the flag of Islam, on the other hand, there "is no mobbing, lynching, or burning of black people," claimed Mohammed.[44] Moreover, he argued, "You're under the Sun when you're there in the middle of prosperity."[45]

When talking about World War II, Elijah Mohammed announced that the "Japanese will win the war because we have been fighting so long to rid the earth of the white man."[46] The white man had

injected himself into every small place on this earth, and he had exploited the earth for himself. He had set himself up in every part of the earth and had taken the richness for himself, giving none to anyone but himself. He had kept the colored people, the English people, and other inhabitants of the earth in slavery for hundreds of years and he had worked them and had taken all of their possessions and gave them nothing but this man called Jesus and a home in the sky promises after death; but nobody has ever returned to tell them. Yet they can believe in the white man.[47]

The FBI took particular interest in another topic discussed by Mohammed, that of the "Mother Plane." Fard had taught that the Mother Plane, a spaceship envisioned by the biblical Prophet Ezekiel as "the wheel," would remove his righteous followers from earth during the "Judgment, Armageddon, the fall of America, and the second hell."[48] By early 1941, historian Claude Clegg explains, Elijah Mohammed had taken up this theme, lecturing that the Japanese would use the Mother Plane to cross the Pacific Ocean, thereby becoming part of that coming era "when the white devils will be destroyed by dark mankind."[49] Sister Pauline, when later questioned by the FBI about the plane, described it as being "one-half mile wide, and one-half mile long, able to travel from 350–400 miles per hour."[50] This airplane, whose "blueprints" had been "buried in Mecca" many "thousands of years ago" held an additional "1500 small planes." On each little plane there were "three bombs, weighing 2000 pounds," said Sister Pauline.[51] When the bombs exploded, they had the capacity to "cast up mountains one mile high."[52]

As the authorities brought increasing pressure on the ATOI and rumors began to circulate that outsiders were in their midst, the heat began to be felt in the meetings. Minister Karriem was convinced that a "Moslem had been talking too much because the devil knew everything that took place in the temple."[53] He advised that if people "keep on talking and telling the devil what happens in the temple, someone will be killed." Slaying was justifiable, said Minister Karriem, because "anytime a Moslem goes out and talks, something ought to happen to him. It won't be long before Moslems will have a chance to whop some heads."[54] Mr. Mohammed issued a similar warning, saying, "The devil has hired some detectives of our own race to spy on us. If we can, we must convert our brother, and if we can't, we will get rid of them from the planet earth. The devil has not done any good for any black people. Don't talk too much. Insult them."[55] Threatening the lives of and seeking revenge on individuals who "talk too much" came in direct response to the knowledge of infiltration and would become a feature of ATOI and later NOI religious culture. In fact, the convert Ella Lewis told an informant that she was "afraid to quit" because she had heard that members who leave "have been killed."[56] Coleman reported that a woman who "was expelled" soon thereafter "died."[57]

Raid: Seventy Men and Sister Pauline

After months of investigation, on September 21, 1942, FBI agents, with assistance from the Chicago Police Department, raided the temple at 104 East Fifty-first Street. Over two days they arrested seventy members and seized documents, including — according to a report in the *Chicago Daily Tribune* — "a blackboard with a blueprint of the Mother Plane."[58] The only woman lassoed in the feverish roundup was Sister Pauline.[59] As Minister James 3X (Anderson) recalled, "The police did not 'molest' the women who were present at the Temple";[60] Sister Pauline was taken into custody the next day by three special agents at her home at 6117 Rhodes Ave.[61] Signing her name to all correspondence and keeping the records at her home placed Sister Pauline at the epicenter of the FBI's investigation of persons who reportedly "advocate[d] direct alliance with Japan."[62] Although several newspaper reporters described her as having a "passive" role and "only a small part in the organization," she would be one of only three people charged with sedition.[63]

The seventy men arrested in the raid on the temple, including Minister Karriem and Elijah Mohammed, were charged with failing to register for the draft, as required by the Selective Service Act of 1940. Of those, seven were released because they had in fact registered prior to their arrest. Sixty-three men, however, stood firm in their commitment to Fard's Islam, which was critical of military service, and pleaded guilty on arraignment for failure to register. They were held in custody due to their inability to post bond at $5,000 each, and all were interrogated prior to sentencing.[64]

This was the second time Elijah Mohammed was charged with draft evasion. He had been arrested earlier in the year in Washington, D.C., and made an initial courtroom appearance in July 1942. Sister Clara was able to post bond on July 23, after her husband had languished seven weeks in the District Jail.[65] That case had yet to come to trial when he was apprehended again in the Chicago raid.

The questioning of the sixty-three men who pleaded guilty after the September raid revealed "a series of queer quirks in the doctrines of the cultists," according to an article that appeared in the *Chicago Defender*, which provides us with an unexpected window on how the ATOI was growing.[66] Particularly interesting is the situation regarding the assignment of new surnames on conversion. One man who identified himself as John X caught the newspaper's attention when he explained defiantly to the court, "Anderson is my last name, but that is only a name YOU gave me. Such family names are the names of former slave-owners whose human chattels assumed their masters' name upon regaining freedom. We don't recognize them except as an insult."[67] As we know, this was not a new practice. But now, the majority of the men refused to give a surname other than the letter X. Once Fard was no longer available to assign new surnames, new converts were instructed by Mohammed, who had taken charge in his absence, to use the letter to signal the unknown.[68] The prevalence of the X surname thus underscores the success of Mohammed's efforts at fishing, and the dropping-off of Fard's pioneering followers from his leadership. When Brother Zack Hassan (the husband of Sister Rosetta, whose 1935 court appearance ignited the chamber brawl) was sentenced for draft evasion after he stated, "I registered with Allah," he was in the minority of jailed followers with an Islamic surname.

At the conclusion of the questioning, of the sixty-three men who had pleaded guilty, twenty-five were not prosecuted because they were over forty-five years old.[69] Of the thirty-eight who were indicted, thirty-two pleaded guilty.[70] Federal Judge John. P. Barnes "cracked down" on the latter and sentenced them to three to five years in the penitentiary.[71] The jury trials for the remaining six men (including Minister Karriem and Elijah Mohammed), who pleaded not guilty, took place in the District Court of Northern Illinois in April 1943 and were speedy because the men refused to "take an oath but instead they faced the direction of Mecca and mumbled the Moslem [Islamic] equivalent of I do."[72] They all received three-year sentences for refusal to register for Selective Service.

Sister Pauline's legal tribulations followed a different course. The documents that trace her experience, including her investigation by the FBI Chicago Field Office, fill in this important woman leader's life story. She was described as having "medium brown skin" with a slim build of "5'7" and "weighing 118 pounds." Her physical stature therefore met the requirements demanded by Fard and taught at the MGT-GCC classes. She was said to have worn a "turban and long dress which reach[ed] to the ankle."[73] Though we will never know if Sister Pauline was badgered by FBI Agents, it was reported that she "freely and voluntarily" made a statement that included the following facts.[74] Born on March 17, 1903, at West Point, Georgia, she had married Minister Linn Karriem there. They migrated to Chicago in 1927 and had no children. She had joined the ATOI in 1934, after her husband, and had served as the secretary of "the nation of Islam" since 1937.[75] All three of her brothers — Raymond Sharrieff, Alphonso Pasha, and Kasskar Ali — had been arrested for Selective Service violations. Two of her sisters were also members, Thelma Yacob (Thelma Walker) and Anna Yacob (Anna Hatchett). It is interesting to note the surname of Yacob, given the history of Fard's theology, which named an evil black scientist, Yacub, as the one who engineered the white race.[76] With the exception of one sister who continued to live in West Point, all of Sister Pauline's siblings followed Elijah Mohammed, who was now known as the "prophet of the Moslems."[77]

As the national secretary, Sister Pauline had attended nearly every meeting and collected money from the members and visitors.[78] The funds were used to defray expenses, "the rent of the Temple, the upkeep of Elijah Mohammed and his family and of my husband and myself."[79] Additionally, Sister Pauline gave "the new members the letters which they addressed to the Temple in order to obtain their original names,"[80] the same duty performed by Reformer Burnsteen Sharrieff in Detroit years earlier. She filed the letters, "awaiting the return of W. D. Fard, who is Allah."[81] Up to the present moment, she affirmed, "no original names have been given out," and those whose letters have been accepted are "allowed to use their first names and then the letter 'X.'"[82]

Sister Pauline was hardly passive in her questioning. Although the authorities were primarily interested in her alleged sedition activity — encouraging men to evade the draft — she reversed the direction of the interrogation by setting "forth the teachings of Allah." She frustrated the interrogators by repeating Fard's doctrine that black people were Asiatic and that "the black man is the original

Mrs. P. Bahar   Elijah Mohammad   Linn Karriem

"They're among 80 in Chicago Accused of Sedition to Defeat Draft Law," *Baltimore Afro-American*, October 10, 1942. Left to right: Mrs. P. Bahar, Elijah Mohammad, and Linn Karriem. (Reprinted courtesy of Afro-American Newspapers Inc.)

man[,] and the white man has been grafted from the black man six thousand years ago by Yacob."[83] Additionally, she explained that "the white man was also called the devil and was given power to rule for a limited period of time."[84] The crisis of World War II, she stated, was evidence that "this time is now about up."[85] Sister Pauline further told investigators, "The black people have 7 1/2 oz. of brain compared with the 6 oz. brain of the white devil."[86] (Mr. Mohammed's religious instruction had not deviated from Fard's, and therefore memorizing mathematical equations and data continued to be prominent among the membership.)

Although Sister Pauline was released after her initial interrogation in September 1942, one month later she was charged with sedition, and a bench warrant was issued for her arrest on November 2, 1942. She, Mohammed, and Minister Karriem — the three presumed leaders of the ATOI — were jointly charged with two felony counts: first, obstructing "the recruiting and enlistment service of the United States" by "willfully making and uttering" certain "statements to a large number of individuals assembled at a meeting" of the ATOI in Chicago; second, "attempt[ing] to cause insubordination, disloyalty, mutiny, and refusal of duty in the military and naval forces of the United States."[87] Bond was set at $5,000 each for Sister Pauline and Minister Karriem, and $10,000 for Elijah Mohammed.[88] Sister Pauline filed a not-guilty plea in January 1943, and thirty days later she was finally bailed out of jail when her bond was reduced to $2,500 and Henrietta Davis secured it with her property.[89]

How dangerous was Sister Pauline to the U.S. government? How important was it that she had allegedly told ATOI men: "Don't register for the draft"; "you should not serve under the American flag"; "you should not take up arms against the Japs"; "the Japs are not our enemies"?[90] Federal authorities called her a "top leader of the cult" in the fall of 1942. But, oddly, at a hearing in May 1943, the authorities dropped all charges against her, along with the sedition charge against Karriem and Mohammed.[91]

As far as the two men were concerned, it seems clear that once the government had them in custody for draft evasion, pressing further charges ceased to be a priority. Sister Pauline is another story. We will never know for certain all the factors that prevented prosecutors from pursuing their case against her. We do know that when Sister Pauline was jointly indicted with her husband and Elijah Mohammed, the FBI reported that her case was the "weakest." Of the three, in her case there was "no proof" that she had "made any sedition statements," rather than only performing her duties "as secretary of the organization, taking care of correspondence, soliciting membership, and taking an active part in each meeting."[92] Moreover, FBI officers stated that Sister Pauline had "undoubtedly acted under the guidance and influence of Linn Karriem."[93] Was this the whole truth? Or is it possible that prosecutors feared that the trial of Sister Pauline, the lone female defendant, could catapult her into the role of martyred heroine for the ATOI? Or that government authorities could not imagine that she, as a woman, had performed her duties independently of her husband, no matter the evidence? Whatever the reasons, Sister Pauline's case was dismissed and she went free in May 1943.[94]

A Changing Picture of Female Moslems

One of the unforeseen effects of the legal assaults on ATOI members in the early 1940s is the light it shed on how women were expected to dress and comport themselves. Some of this evidence comes literally in the pictures published in Washington and Chicago newspapers, some from the comments and teachings of the male leaders of the group.

According to the reports of FBI informants, ATOI ministers often asserted that Christian preachers "drank, smoked, rode around in big cars and went with every attractive woman in the church that they could," echoing pervasive stereotypes of Christian clergy.[95] But Elijah Mohammed also charged that "the women in the Christian churches would dress in such a manner as to arouse the passions in the minister[,] thus taking his mind off the sermon and causing him to wonder when he could see that sister."[96] Moslem women, by contrast, "keep themselves well covered in order to keep men from admiring their forms and to resist temptation."[97] Thus women's dress was becoming a key way to distinguish the new religion. But this change was not necessarily smooth; an informant also noted that there was concern about the initiation of female members, and thus "two sisters from the Temple #1," Mohammed explained, were going to take new women members to Detroit to "attend a training school."[98]

In 1935, Moslem women had often worn stylish hats, below-the-knee dresses, and fancy coats. Seven years later, when in public, believers wore ankle-length satin gowns and "matching shoes"; they were "bedecked with jewelry," and their hair was fully covered.[99] Although their homemade attire varied in terms of color and decorative details, such as ribbons and buttons, the women were easily identifiable as ATOI members.[100] The "Islamizing" of their bodies, Edward E. Curtis has argued, substantiates that the movement was "both highly religious and political at the same time."[101] Thus, when Elijah Mohammed later recalled the gathering at his July 1942 court appearance, he said, "When we were in Washington, the court room was filled with our sisters in their beautiful robes of white and green. They caused no little excitement. If 50 of our group could excite them this way, what would happen if 200,000 would storm the Capital?"[102] Similarly, at the sentencing in October of the Chicago brothers who pleaded guilty to draft evasion, the newspapers noted that their supporters were "garbed in ceremonial robes" and described by some reporters as "educated and cultured folk."[103]

Appropriating an Islamic world through dress created a strikingly "privileged opposition" to Christianity; and during World War II, authorities interpreted it as additional evidence of un-American behavior.[104] But what did it mean to the women themselves? Wearing clothes that hid their outer selves protected them from roaming eyes on their body parts, visual assaults that plagued the lives of women after puberty. Within this aesthetic boundary were Fard's rewards and cautions about the world.

As always, we have more evidence about Sister Clara than anyone else. When she posted bail in Washington, she wore what was described as her "Islamic costume with white flowing veil and full skirt."[105] Her robes were captured by a Washington *Evening Star* photographer — and so was her steely facial expression. She looked directly into the camera lens, appearing both in motion and

Sister Clara Mohammad,
"5,000 in Cash Donated to
Free 'Mohammad,'" *Evening
Star*, July 24, 1942. (Reprinted
with permission of the D.C.
Public Library, Star Collection,
© *Washington Post*.)

standing still as the hem of her skirt dragged the ground. She clutched a bag
that had held five thousand dollars in small bills, which she had unrolled in
the criminal clerk's office earlier in the day.[106] This was not the first (nor the
last) time that Sister Clara had bailed out her husband, but photos of her doing
so are rare. Still weighing only about 100 pounds (she had given birth to her
eighth and last child, Akbar, in 1939), Sister Clara's petite frame is swallowed
within the draping layers of her dress. With the exception of her headpiece, a
close-fitting turban-styled hijab, her entire outfit looks oversized and heavy. On
the one hand, she seems to be hiding inside her clothes. One might suppose
that she felt overwhelmed and worried about the future. On the other hand, her
exposed face looks determined and proud. Modesty of dress did not necessarily
indicate spiritual meekness.

Two days later, when Sister Clara appeared in the district court with her
husband who pleaded innocent to the charge of failing to register for Selective
Service, she wore a "scarlet red flowing robe"—it was both her husband's favorite
color and a statement that she too was being persecuted.[107] By contrast, the other

six ATOI women in court were clad in white. As we saw with Sister Pauline, clothing could either assimilate or distinguish women as individuals.

Women and the ATOI Leadership

With much of the active male membership incarcerated from the early to the mid-1940s, it fell to the women to keep the movement afloat. Sister Clara, who had for years lingered on the organizational periphery, was flung into the leadership circle. The need to stabilize the embryonic Nation of Islam seemed to fall squarely on her shoulders.[108] Sister Clara "took hold of the reins and actually ran the community in her husband's absence," their son Wallace recounts.[109] He additionally described her work as "correspondent, consultant and adviser to all the leaders in matters of duty and responsibility." Many writers have attested to Sister Clara's importance during this period.[110] The lack of archival evidence makes it difficult to know just how she fit into the organization's ongoing framework, but we can draw on what records do exist to speculate on just how she and other women of the ATOI filled the gap left by the incarceration of their male leaders.

In one sense, Sister Clara had been on her own well before 1942. From 1935 onward, her husband traveled extensively and lived for various periods in "Baltimore, Washington, D.C., Boston, Providence, New York, Newark, Hartford, Bridgeport, Philadelphia, Pittsburg, Cleveland, Columbus, Dayton, Cincinnati, and Atlanta. During this time [his] family remained in Chicago and [they were] supported by voluntary contributions from the Moslems."[111] Moreover, for years Sister Clara and her children had experienced harassment from authorities. When warrants were issued for Elijah Mohammed's arrest, agents would go to his home and question his wife and their children. On September 3, 1942, an agent, under the cloak of rent inquiries, approached Sister Clara, and it was stated she was "reluctant to give any information concerning the occupants of the house."[112] It was often noted in the resulting FBI reports that "all [household members] were extremely non-cooperative and belligerent to the Agents and [N]egro officers present in the home."[113] Ironically, with Elijah's incarceration, she now knew exactly where he was, and it was obvious to all why he was powerless to provide for his family. Receiving support from other women who were also financially strapped because their husbands were jailed may have actually given her a greater sense of community.

Although Sister Clara's leadership continues to loom large in the Nation of Islam narrative for the World War II period, FBI records place Sister Pauline at the helm. (Even after the raid, the FBI managed to keep a confidential informant among the women in Chicago.[114]) Sister Pauline had read the writing on the wall after the initial police raid and had vowed to the membership that "the white devils are trying to get rid of the leader, but if they succeed we will nevertheless continue our meetings."[115] Along with the older men and their children, who were reported to have been "well trained in the manner of answering the password and saluting in the Islam fashion," the women kept on meeting.[116] In July and August of 1943, it was reported that the wives of the incarcerated men were gathering in their homes under the leadership of Sister Pauline,[117] though Mohammed was still identified as leading "the activities of these women from" the federal penitentiary.[118] During this period, it seems clear that a tag-team effort between Sister Clara and Sister Pauline provided direction to a host of women who were equally committed to practicing their religion.

Finding a permanent place that could serve as a temple in Chicago was important for the women. Sister Pauline attempted to secure the old location at 104 East Fifty-first Street, but the owner refused to rent to them after the massive raid.[119] Even without a formal meeting place, by August of 1943, between twenty-five and thirty women were meeting on the first floor of a four-story private home. The women had arranged the large room to resemble, it was said, "the manner of a Temple."[120] They continued to wear their official regalia to the meetings, and neighborhood boys would tease them on the streets because of their "peculiar costumes."[121] Without the presence of the men, the women appear to have been more vulnerable to the boys. Most of the time they ignored the disrespectful youth, but one day a sister retorted to a boy that "the Japanese would take care of him and his kind."[122]

Generally, the women exercised caution while Elijah Mohammed was incarcerated and the leadership was in their hands. They were aware that their group was still a government target. At one point, Sister Viola 2X unwittingly told the informant that "no new members are being accepted" at the present time and that they were "being very careful to obey the laws of the United States." But Sister Viola 2X did assert that their religious movement would "remain intact through its women members until the release of" Mohammed and the other persecuted men.[123]

The federal government believed that the activities of the women, which were described exclusively as "holding meetings," justified its refusal to return property seized at the time of the temple raid, despite a request made by the ATOI attorney Richard E. Westbrook. The government had seized forty cartons of "voluminous reports, correspondence, financial records, minutes of meetings," and other materials such as "pictures, flags, blackboards, wooden guns, swords, and banners."[124] Assistant U.S. attorneys John Owen and William Connor reasoned that "returning the property would be considered tantamount to Government approval of the organization to continue to function."[125]

Although we do not have records detailing how the women conducted their meetings, one can imagine that they continued to follow the prescribed structure of prayers, lessons, and lectures. The sister captain's and Sister Pauline's duties may have expanded, and perhaps after visiting her husband, Sister Clara would return with an inspiring message. Equally significant, the women could have continued to fish. Some time before his arrest, Elijah Mohammed had given his approval to women recruiting new members by witnessing to family, rather than strangers. An FBI informant had reported, before the raid, the example of Daisy. After Daisy joined the ATOI in Chicago, she visited her aunt Dora Grant in Oplike, Alabama, and shared her new religion. On returning to Chicago she maintained contact with her aunt, who eventually "joined the temple by correspondence with Daisy in Chicago."[126] Sister Dora and her husband moved to Chicago in October 1941, and Dora began to use the surname X. Sister Daisy's selective fishing was acceptable to Mohammed. Without going door to door to witness (which Mohammed believed put them in harms' way), the women could certainly have continued to reach out to new converts.

With much of the male leadership jailed, another appropriate fishing site for women soon included the prisons. During his incarceration, Mohammed began to channel his conversion efforts among the convicts and encouraged members on the outside to expand the ranks by writing letters to specific prisoners. Malcolm X (Little) was one of the recipients of such letters while he was jailed in Massachusetts's Norfolk Prison Colony. In fact, in 1950 he wrote to Sister Henrietta, "the Sisters in Detroit have written to us more than the Brothers there have. Tell the Brothers shame on them!"[127] One cannot exaggerate the power of a personal letter received under such circumstances; isolated from loved ones and craving close association, prisoners were undoubtedly receptive to and grateful for these messages from caring strangers.

The writing of these letters was likely meaningful for the women as well. The process of sitting at a table for the deliberate purpose of composing a handwritten letter would have allowed them to connect with their religious devotion. Certainly the precise and exacting nature of the written word had been drilled into them from day one of their official membership in the ATOI. Every individual had to submit a handwritten letter accepting Fard's Islamic teachings. Each letter was evaluated for penmanship and returned if there were any grammatical or spelling errors. Many members reminisced about how many times they had had to rewrite their one-page letter. (Malcolm X states that he drafted his first letter "at least twenty-five times" before sending it off to Elijah Mohammed.)[128]

The letters crafted by the women to the jailed recruits no doubt evidence a range of writing skills. While a sample of a good letter may have been shared at a meeting, over time the most gifted writers probably developed a persuasive personal style. A sister's character and a spark of her former self may have seeped onto the page, intermingled with her deepest religious understanding. Malcolm X reflected that it was because of writing letters while in prison that he "happened to stumble upon starting to acquire some kind of a homemade education."[129] In all these ways, letters speak to the role of literacy in the black freedom struggle.

We do not know how many women stayed the course during this challenging period, but a leading minister declared that on Elijah Mohammed's August 1946 release, national membership was about one thousand.[130] Despite this drop in overall membership (Detroit membership during the early 1930s peaked at eight thousand), some women clearly remained committed to the cause throughout, writing letters and attending meetings. As the women arrested in 1935 survived their own jail time, they would survive their male leaders' incarceration as well.

[CHAPTER SIX]

FLEXING A NEW WOMANHOOD

The women who kept meeting through the early 1940s made possible the transformation of what had been the ATOI into a nationwide Islamic movement, now officially named the Nation of Islam (NOI). The four temples that had been established by 1945 (Detroit No. 1, Chicago No. 2, Milwaukee No. 3, and Washington, D.C., No. 4) provided fertile ground for steady growth under the leadership of Elijah Muhammad, who embraced a new spelling of his name as he led in Chicago.[1] (Detroit, the original head-quarters, proved an uneasy place for Muhammad; although it had been more than twenty-five years since Fard's disappearance and the resulting scramble for power, tensions continued to fester between Muhammad, his brother Kallot, and other pioneers.) By 1955, there were fifteen temples, and by December 1959, there were fifty, in twenty-two states (though only one, Temple No. 15, Atlanta, was in the South).[2]

The NOI's expansion owed something to the ways in which its teachings converged with the political and popular culture of the 1950s. Shrouded in esoteric secrets and the surveillance of its members, the NOI had always been obsessed with conformity of belief and securing its borders — obsessions it shared with McCarthyism and fears of communist infiltration. The vacuum created by the persecution of progressive thinkers only strengthened these attitudes.[3] Equally significant, post–World War II popular culture was consumed with sightings of unidentified flying objects (UFOs), such as the purported remains of an extra-terrestrial "flying disc" in Roswell, New Mexico.[4] The NOI's Mother Plane and its teachings about Armageddon fit squarely within Cold War fears.[5]

Women who converted to the NOI in the 1950s were surrounded by the fe-male elders who had built and maintained the early movement, such as Sister Clara Muhammad, Reformer Burnsteen Sharrieff, and Sister Pauline Bahar. The female leaders who were both pioneers and officers encouraged, corrected, chastised, and loved their Nation sisters. Their new religious environment in-cluded not only Elijah Muhammad's Islamic teachings but also his day-to-day

monitoring of followers via temple ministers, sister captains, and brother captains. Hierarchy and surveillance reinforced the potential for the leadership
to discipline and exert social control over the believers. This same apparatus,
however, produced a NOI religious identity that, in theory, shielded women
and their children, from Jim Crow violence and the harmful stereotypes that
plagued black womanhood.

It is important to underscore the phrase "in theory," because in practice, the
same conditions could reinforce harmful elements of patriarchy, such as domestic violence and domination. During this period we have not only documents
demonstrating the sometimes harsh patriarchal rhetoric of Nation ministers
(with Malcolm X being most prominent in the archive) but also the first archival
evidence of problems within the community.

For women, then, the tension between the oppressive and liberatory aspects
of NOI membership continued. By considering a handful of women active
during the 1950s, both new converts and longer-term members, we can explore
the different ways women negotiated the contradictions in their remaking for
personal betterment and nation building.

The MGT-GCC

Each temple was led by a local minister, secretary, sister captain (for the Muslim Girls Training and General Civilization Class, MGT-GCC), and brother
captain for the Fruit of Islam (FOI). The ministers (whose living expenses were
paid by the NOI) and FOI captains were all male, the MGT-GCC captains
were all female; both men and women could serve as secretaries.[6] They worked
together to create a holy space wherein visitors quickly understood the difference between an acceptance of "their own"—that is, other believers—and the
"dead world," which is how they described the outside.

For women, the MGT-GCC constituted the primary site of remaking. The
MGT-GCC classes offered women and girls "proper Islamic upbringing and
adequate instruction in everything a Muslim girl or woman ought to know."[7]
The MGT-GCC had a military structure. The highest-ranking officer was the
sister captain, who received a small salary and had access to a transportation
fund. Under the sister captain were her first, second, and third lieutenants, secretaries, and squad Leaders. Together these officers guided and drilled converts
on diet, prayer, dress, household responsibilities, and motherhood. Overall, the
MGT-GCC classes were dedicated to the importance of women conducting
themselves at all times with proper charm and grace, and with the respectability that these traits encouraged. Cultural refinement was believed to broaden

women's knowledge and wisdom of the world — to the point where they no longer wished to take part in the demeaning "sport and play, filth and evil of the white man's society."[8]

As during World War II, Muhammad sent instructions to the temple minister, who gave them to the sister captain, who in turn taught the women. The military structure reinforced the idea that MGT-GCC women were "soldiers for Mohammed." Sometimes they would get to hear their leader directly. In May 1958, for instance, female representatives from twenty-two temples gathered in Detroit under Muhammad's guidance to celebrate the twenty-sixth anniversary of the MGT-GCC. They were overjoyed when he provided a lecture on the subject, "The Founder of the Class, W. F. Muhammad," and apparently hung on every word.[9]

Not everyone was so impressed with Elijah Muhammad as a speaker; when Dorothy and Allen Donaldson, cousins of Minister Malcolm X, heard Muhammad's public lecture at the John Hancock Hall in downtown Boston that same year, they were shocked by his "little squeaky voice" and the way he "stumbled" over elementary words and "made big errors in pronunciations." To the untrained ear, Muhammad's teachings could also be "hard to follow."[10] But the NOI crowd encouraged him, saying things like "It don't matter how you say it, dear holy apostle, just say it";[11] and "Take your time, dear holy apostle, take your time."[12] They modeled a correct attitude toward their leader. Minister Malcolm, who followed his teacher on stage that evening in Boston and whose influence in the Nation was growing, put any criticism in perspective by saying, "had the Honorable Elijah Muhammad come to Boston and spoken in pear-shaped tones, like a white man, and his lips had what we consider proper shape, we would have listened to him. But since he didn't — he talked just like we talk — that's why we didn't want to listen to him."[13]

Muhammad may have had some linguistic hiccups, but he had come a long way as both a teacher and leader of the NOI. In 1958, he owned two apartment buildings estimated at twenty-five thousand dollars, a family home, a bakery, a grocery store, and a 160-acre farm in Michigan.[14] The wealth was material evidence that his converts believed his teachings — and followed his instructions to send money for the support of his family and for nation building. Moreover, Muhammad's material plenty seemed to show what was possible for new converts. Even his wife, Sister Clara, had her own Cadillac purchased in 1956.[15]

Meanwhile, most of the time it was the sister captain who set the tone for the MGT-GCC class. After offering a welcome, she would teach new converts using a script that included the following:

So our Saviour Himself has called you into this class (M.G.T. and G.C.C.) to reform you from the unrighteous, and uncleanliness of this devil's wickedness and adulterour [*sic*] generation: So that our Saviour Allah will sit you in Heaven at once, and Destroy those who have destroyed you, and to reform You, Means that you must be willing to forsake the ways and teaching of the devil's Caucasians and accept the Teachings of your own original Nation of Islam from the Mouth of Almighty God Allah through His Servant and Apostle Elijah Muhammad.[16]

The MGT-GCC women were told to "forsake anyone that does not Love and Obey Allah and His Apostle. Whether it be their Fathers and Mothers, brothers and sisters, husbands or wives, or their children."[17] Anyone who was not a member of the NOI was in "the grave"; new friendships with other believers, who were committed to being "civilized" and not "ignorant," sealed one's conversion.

The women received a fifteen-point list of "evils" that "must be forsaken by all that accept Islam and enter this class (M.G.T. & G.C.C.)":

#1 Clean internal and external at all times.

#2 Do not use tobacco in any form.

#3 Drink no Alcoholic beverages (intoxicating drinks).

#4 You shall not tempt Men with your beauty in any form, by displaying nudist parts of your body. Hair, Bust, Legs, back and hips, singing love songs, enchanting looks, walking, sitting or lying down.

#5 You shall not wear tight form fitting clothes in public, for the Ignorant dress in such manner to tempt men. No short dresses, no short sleeves, no low neck garments that will show your chest or breast. Wear no high heel shoes, for they are against good health. Go not bare leg in public in no season of the Year; for this the ignorant and Savages do.

#6 You should not use make up such as, face lotion, paints, long nails, beyond what is necessary for a shapely finger. And do not use hot irons on your hair, they do more harm than good. Devil made greases, and bleaching creams. You are Natural beautiful without make ups, Stay away from devils places of amusements, Pictures shows and dances.

#7 You should wear an over garment in the Temple of Islam that you may be known, and also a head covering of the same Material, or suitable Material. The material should be in such colors as, white, green, or Red whatever color that is most desired by the Class.

#8 You shall eat such foods as Allah commands us to eat. And all adults should not eat over one meal a day, and your children should not eat over two meals a day. Touch not the swine flesh, nor let anyone live under your roof with you that use this poison animal flesh. For Allah shall destroy all the wilful swine eaters.

#9 Commit not Adultery. Go not near to it.

#10 Kill not your children to cover your own shame of the act of adultery. Not for the fear of hunger, Nor destroy the seed of the womb.

#11 The Students in the M.G.T. & G.C.C. shall be trained into the knowledge of general house keeping. The Muslim Woman can study other Science, and do other clean work. How to cook, sew, House Clean, read, write, speaking the languages in their proper terms.

#12 You should not marry Non-Muslims until they believe as you believe, nor marry one that is not a member of your own Nation. A righteous Muslim cannot love one who say they love You, but do not love Allah and your religion Islam.

#13 You shall not stare at beautiful men, lest they will turn your heart into unclean thoughts. Cast down your looks and look not upon them. Nor listen to their love songs, or any other sign of charm.

#14 You shall keep up fasting for fasting keeps you from evil, and gives you good health. If you want to marry and cannot find a Husband of your choice, then keep chaste until Allah gives you. For Allah knows what you keep secret and what you manifest. Keep up prayer and give Charity.

#15 Obey Allah and His Apostle, and be Obedient to those in authority over you, as long as it doesn't conflict with the Principals of Islam.[18]

Ultimately, Nation women pledged to be honorable; to keep themselves physically clean (inside in terms of abstinence from alcohol and tobacco; outside in terms of baths and attire); to understand that their bodies were personal temples and should not be used to entice men, to fornicate, or to have abortions; to commit to mastering the domestic sphere in terms of cooking, cleaning, and sewing; to be good mothers and wives; and to serve Allah, the God of Islam, as taught to them by Elijah Muhammad.

Sister Captain Burnsteen Sharrieff

The sister captains themselves were closely supervised, and were held to the highest standards. If a sister captain was late more than two times without a "legal cause," she was subject to thirty days' time out (suspension from the temple) or possibly removal from the position. Though Muhammad told them to always teach with courtesy and compassion, one can imagine that the fear of not doing well — perhaps combined with a relishing of their power — sometimes made these women treat those under their authority with a strictness bordering on harshness.

For instance, though the NOI rules about dress were clear, some older sisters took license and would go to the temple "as they go any place else. They don't seem to be trying to do that which is towards dressing correctly."[19] Sonsyrea Tate recalled the sister captain in Washington, D.C., sending women home if their uniform was not "clean enough." "She'd talk about the woman in front of everyone. And sometimes, instead of sending the woman home, she'd take her in the bathroom and talk to her until she cried, then make her go back to the group with a tear-stained face."[20] If a sister came into the temple with her hair coming through her headpiece, the sister captain would tell her, "Sister, you know this is not something you carry in your purse and throw on your head once you get in the Temple."[21]

Sister Burnsteen Sharrieff, who was formerly identified as the Reformer and had served as Fard's secretary, was the sister captain at Detroit's Temple No. 1. Burnsteen had more than twenty years in the Nation, and likely added her own thoughts to the MGT-GCC teachings in Detroit. When instructing women on the NOI's holy flag demonstration, she explained that "the original man chose the Sun, Moon, and Star, the best by which to represent himself."[22] Yet when she discussed the moon, Sister Captain Burnsteen feminized it, writing,

> The Moon gives off poison every night or 24 hours; the woman gives off the unwanted blood and womb lining every month varying from 24 days sometimes to 31 days. The Moon attracts the water. The woman attracts the man. The man contains the life (water meaning civilization). The woman has something the man desires (companionship etc.) therefore being unlike she attracts the man and she grows the civilization after it has been planted by the man. So does the moon feed the vegetation over night. The civilization is nursed, in a dark world, by the mother in her womb, thus in line with the Moon feeding the vegetation over night (darkness). She, during pregnancy, has a lot in common with the solar system.[23]

At the same time, Sister Captain Burnsteen continued to hold fast to her now legendary, uncompromising position on body weight, and this led to her "correction" by Elijah Muhammad himself. In her zeal, she sometimes assigned overweight sisters who failed to reduce their weight a thirty-day ritual of writing, "I AM CARELESS, THEREFORE I CANNOT SEE MY OWNSELF FOR I HAVE GAINED WEIGHT INSTEAD OF LOST."[24] Their writings were sent to Muhammad, by the Temple secretary. Additionally, Sister Captain Burnsteen would ask the temple minister to give the sister timeout. Her dismissal pattern required Muhammad to send her a letter of clarification. Although he, too, had warned Nation women, "Do not let me catch any sister other than her ownself in regards to living the life and weighing properly," he wrote to Sister Captain Burnsteen, "as long as a person remains within 5 or 10 lbs. or say anything under 10 lbs. over their proper weight they should not always be punished; especially if they have passed the age of forty (40), because lots of times they increase in weight beyond 40."[25] Muhammad also recognized that teens varied in weight due to irregular growing patterns. Even the two hundred–pound woman that Sister Captain Burnsteen had no tolerance for in the 1930s garnered a level of sympathy from Muhammad. Certainly, "we want to reduce" one who "is say 200 lbs.," but it should be done "according to their statue [*sic*], and if she can take away 50 or 60 of these pounds within a couple of years, that is doing fine." Finally, Muhammad stated, "Again, if one is 125 lbs. and we think they should weigh 118 or 120 lbs. if they remain at the same weight of 125 lbs. for a while, then we are not justified in throwing them out of the Class for just a few lbs. over weight, especially when they are new to the proper weight."[26] Closing his letter to Sister Captain Burnsteen, Elijah Muhammad stated that he wanted her to "observe these rules." Indeed, when she was concerned about a sister's weight, it was "proper on [her] part to send" him "their weight before dismissing them from the Class."[27] Sister Captain Burnsteen was an enforcer who had to be reigned in privately by Muhammad.

How did someone like Sister Burnsteen affect recruitment? The Detroit temple, like the others, continued to grow. When Sister Sara joined in 1959, she had to recite the lessons for a year in front of Burnsteen Sharrieff—but this did not in any way dissuade her. Sister Sara was introduced to the Nation by her husband, Sammy, who was raised in a family of pioneer followers of Master Fard in Detroit. Sara recalled that her husband had told her that he "had seen God when he was a child."[28] Sammy had been suspended by the temple close to fifteen years earlier and gone into the military.[29] One day Sammy came home with a copy of the *Pittsburgh Courier* and showed her an article by Elijah Muhammad. After reading the piece, Sara asked her husband, "Why are you not with those people?" Sara had been raised in a Christian home, but what she had read sounded more like what her parents had taught her. She especially liked the statements "you can accomplish what you will" and "do for self"—

the former, Marcus Garvey's watchword during the 1920s, had been reintroduced to another generation of African Americans by the NOI.

Soon thereafter, Sara, accompanied by a female neighbor, took their five children to 5401 John C. Lodge, Temple No. 1. The next time she went she took her husband. When they arrived, the brother at the door would not let Sammy enter the temple, because he had not cleared himself. Though Sammy had not been back for a decade and a half, the brother knew him and told him that he had to be cleared by the minister.

Temple No. 1 was in transition in 1959 and had only about thirty-five active members. Sister Sara heard a variety of ministers speak, including Malcolm X, who was "good but flamboyant." She preferred Minister Wilfred, Malcolm X's brother, because he was a "down-to-earth Brother," and, in her opinion, "more easy." Muhammad selected Minister Wilfred to serve Temple No. 1, but in the meantime Sara also heard Elijah Muhammad himself on occasion. Sister Sara recalled one lecture in which Muhammad talked for hours, and she was mesmerized. One woman, Sister Sara said, "sat with her mouth open out of astonishment."[30] Sister Sara was convinced that the NOI was right for her family and wrote her letter following the "sample," without any mistakes and mailed it to Chicago. In return, she received instructions and student enrollment.

With a pioneering role model to emulate in Sister Captain Burnsteen, Sister Sara learned her lessons well. She enjoyed wearing her uniform to the temple; Sister Sara "thought she was dressed up" and "felt good."[31] Moreover, Sister Sara appreciated that all the women came together for MGT-GCC on Thursday nights, because she found it helpful to learn from the older women. They were divided by age for domestic activities (division A was teens to age thirty, division B was women thirty-one years to forty, and division C was women forty years and older) and took turns providing demonstrations for one another.[32] Sister Sara looked forward to Thursday night, and like other women, she brought her children and they would often play together.[33] At times, Sister Clara envied the rank-and-file women and told them they were "lucky" that they could bring their children out with them to the MGT-GCC meetings, because "her husband would not [have] let her."[34]

As the NOI increased its membership, Sisters Lottie and Ethel, the Muhammads' daughters, took a more active part in the day-to-day management of the nation. During the 1950s, Sister Lottie "was over the women" at the Chicago temple, and she shared with her father that "these are educated people coming in here now."[35] Having received education in vocations and trades, which enabled them to hold down higher-paying positions, the women sought answers to questions that Sister Lottie did not fully understand herself. She told her father, "Well Daddy," a "Lady, she looked at it [Fard's picture] and she said he looked like a white man, and she was wanting [*sic*] to know who he was." Sister Lottie hesitated in her response, because she had never heard as a child Fard say that he was "God." Sister Lottie did not want to go against her father's teachings, but at the same time, she did not feel comfortable revealing her own knowledge. Fully understanding that the woman's question was going to become common-place, she asked her father, "Daddy, what should I have said?" Muhammad replied, "Just tell them that that's your father's teacher."[36] Clearly, Sister Lottie's simple explanation was enough for some women, because the female member-ship in Chicago multiplied.

Sister Thelma X

While the stories of Sister Captain Burnsteen and Sister Sara in Detroit are mostly focused on the NOI as a religion, another female member was more concerned with what Elijah Muhammad's teachings could tell the external, political world. Sister Thelma X Muhammad, who identified herself as the edi-tor of her own magazine, *Truth*, explained that her purpose was to provide "an understanding of the true meaning of integration."[37] *Truth* featured provocative articles such as "An Asiatic Grandmother Speaks for the Negro Children and Offers Her Solution to the Little Rock Problem of Integration" and "What Good Is Your Son's Diploma Hanging on the Wall While He Is Hanging on The Limb of a Tree?"[38] While Sister Thelma X's historical footprint is limited — only one partial issue of *Truth* survives — she provides a unique example of a Nation woman claiming her own voice, owning her political opinions (which followed those of the NOI), and, indeed, producing a small but significant archive.

Our early information about Sister Thelma X comes via the FBI's World War II surveillance files. Also identified as Thelma X Hunter and Thelma X Dona-hue, she lived in Milwaukee in October 1942 with her fourth husband, Minister Baker X Donahue. They used their apartment to hold temple meetings, and Minister Baker X was identified as "a principal leader of the Moslem group in Milwaukee."[39] According to informants, Sister Thelma was 5'6", and her beauti-ful brown skin and "black kinky" hair magnified her "maroon" eye color.[40] The files also note that she tipped the scale at 140 pounds — certainly beyond Sister Captain Burnsteen's liking! Minister Baker X was indicted in the Selective Ser-vice case against the ATOI on September 16, 1942.[41] Sister Thelma X relocated to Chicago thereafter and continued to carry out the temple teachings.

In the few pages of *Truth* that survive, we see Sister Thelma X engaged in an all-out war against desegregation. She commanded her readers to "**STOP BEG-GING**," which results in "unnecessary trouble," and "**STOP FIGHTING**," because the result is "garbage, pure garbage: HAVE YOU FORGOTTEN SO SOON EMMITT [Emmett] TILL'S LYNCHING!"[42] (Till was a fourteen-year-old youth murdered on August 28, 1955, in Money, Mississippi, for allegedly whistling at a white woman; his mother, Mamie Till-Bradley, insisted on an open-casket funeral, which galvanized civil rights activists' efforts against violent Jim Crow segregation.) Focusing on the push to desegregate public schools following the Supreme Court's 1954 *Brown v. Board of Education* decision, Sister Thelma X described how preachers are "telling us to get ready to DIE, when he is encouraging INTEGRATION IN THE SCHOOLS."[43] In fact, she asked, "Why doesn't he attend schools in Little Rock under guns, knives, threats, and mob LYNCHING PEOPLE?"[44] She claimed a superior insight for herself, saying that this unnamed preacher "needs some schooling himself, as you will see when I am finished opening your eyes."[45] And in a language that mirrors that of the most gifted NOI ministers, Sister Thelma X details how black politicians and preachers resemble each other in doing the white man's bidding. The main reason that these men failed to see their enemy was because "the educated, of our kind, are so proud to be seen in the presence of white people."[46]

Sister Thelma X was incensed by "dumb Negro[es]" posing the question "What difference does it make, who you marry?"[47] Sister Thelma X's responded, "If the Chinaman felt this way where would the Nation of Chinese people be today? If the Japanese man or woman felt this way where would Japan be today? If the white man felt that way, where would the white race be today? Can't you see who is the FOOL?"[48] Lynching was unequivocal evidence of how far the white man would go to keep his race white, argued Sister Thelma X. But "the Negro doesn't give a DAMN, anything can have his babies and his women. We women have no protection from our men," she cried.[49]

Protecting black womanhood had always been a feature of Master Fard's Islam, but under Elijah Muhammad it had moved into the center of his Islamic teachings. Sister Thelma X had thought seriously about the mistreatment of black women and had formulated her own theory of who was the black mother's chief enemy.[50] For her, it was "Jewish mothers and women kind who are the real traitors, double crossers and creators of the murderous feats and ideas to destroy Negro children while we take good care of Jewish children."[51]

Sister Thelma X's anti-Jewish stance was largely driven by the figure of the Jewish slumlord who loomed large on Chicago's South and West sides. By the 1950s a prosperous group of Jews had begun to "work the system" as landlords and merchants, egregiously overcharging black people for housing.[52] Historian

Beryl Satter documents that "a significant proportion of exploitative contract sellers were Jewish."[53] Regularly turned down by home mortgage banks, black people used the so-called contract system in Chicago. Land contracts, "articles of agreement for warranty deed," exposed black people to legal yet grossly exploitive tactics.[54] Even after turning over a hefty down payment that did not truly reflect the value of the property, purchasers were then treated like renters, and if they missed one payment, swift eviction procedures followed. Black people wanted home ownership, and by the late 1950s close to 85 percent of their homes were purchased by this system in Chicago.[55] Few, however, were actually able to keep them. Legions of stories connected to Jewish businessmen and lawyers swindling black people filled local newspapers, and by the early 1970s, Jews were noted as "the most ruthless slumlords in Chicago."[56]

Sister Thelma X had worked for a number of Jewish women who had told her that they supported integration, probably assuming that she was in with the civil rights movement.[57] Given her already negative view of Jews, this led Sister Thelma X to conclude that integration was a calculated plot for the benefit of Jewish children, and she was determined to make known the "Truth."[58] Her truth marked Jews as the collective white enemy, largely because of their financial power in Chicago.

Although we do not have information about Sister Thelma X's formal schooling, she clearly had immense confidence in her knowledge about Jews, gentiles, and the Bible. She was grounded in temple teachings and used her live-in maid experiences in Jewish households to substantiate what she had been taught in the temple. For example, she recalled how one youth slept nightly with her bulldog to keep "her stomach warm."[59] This behavior — which kept Sister Thelma X changing sheets to keep the bed smelling clean — disgusted her and seemed to confirm NOI lessons about white people "crawling around like any other animal on [their] hands and knees in the hills and caves of Europe less than 5,000 years ago, while our black people were living the life of intelligent people, going to school and attending colleges that you can't enter."[60] She declared that Jews "are more animal than human" and that "these people should be back in the caves where they came from."[61]

As a female she was unable to serve as a NOI minister, but Sister Thelma X had internalized a leadership agenda and was bent on promoting it. She felt that it was her duty to travel throughout the United States with the revelation of Allah, who is "God and he is black, and he will fight and save our children at any cost to your entire race, Jewish mothers and their children."[62] She had kept notes on her interactions with Jewish women and planned to feature them in a book. In the spring of 1959, she took a leave of absence from working as a maid in a private household to assist her daughter and grandchildren. When she realized that she had misplaced her synopsis, she wrote a letter dated April 3 to her Jewish employer, opening with, "I might have left [my notes] in the maid's room, under the sheets in the drawer," politely inquiring, "Would it be asking too much if I ask you to get it and put it away for me please."[63] But there the niceties ended: Sister Thelma X went on to unleash her harsh critique and directly indicted all Jewish women for wanting integration for "the benefit of [their] children, and destruction of all others, non-Jewish."[64] Believing that her employer could not function without a maid, she wrote, "If your next maid is a Negro woman or a gentile woman she will by then have received a book written by me (a maid) and this will enable her to see you and other Jewish women for what you really are."[65] Sister Thelma X had no doubt that her book would be published and indicated that she had remembered every thing she had written but wanted to refer to her notes to save time.[66]

Yet Sister Thelma X continued to work in Jewish homes. She needed the income, but also, it seems, she took this work as an opportunity to learn their alleged secrets. On one occasion an employer handed her information that Sister Thelma X had planned to use against her in the next issue of *Truth*, where she mocked, "you gave it to me with a big Jewish smile, hope you can take it with a smile . . . an Asiatic smile in the name of Allah and his chosen Messenger," Elijah Muhammad.[67] Another time, an employer told her "exactly what kind of integration Jewish lawyers had in mind," and this "was news to" her.[68] She shared with her readers that she was able to work in the midst of the "enemy" by making them believe that she "worship[ed]" them, asking "questions stupid-like" and "wear[ing] smiles."[69] Wearing "the mask that grins and lies" to white people, Sister Thelma X followed in a tradition spelled out poetically by Paul Laurence Dunbar; she had "racial fire" and had mastered concealing her whole self from "devils."[70] She made it clear that it was a performance, writing that her smiles were "for [her] benefit, not [the employer]."[71]

Sister Thelma X enjoyed intellectual jousting, and it is difficult to measure if she was more anti-Semitic than others or only more vocal. She describes an instance where she impressed a Jewish merchant with her personality she "played it cool."[72] It did not take long for her to manipulate the situation by affirming his importance, and she eventually asked him who gave the world Christianity. He quickly replied, "Jews." Sister Thelma X, "smiled" with the rejoinder, "Why Jews?" He answered, "Only the Jews knew what to give them." At this point Sister Thelma X observed, "if this is true and you gave us a God and a devil, two men, then which one is God and which one is devil?" It was amusing for her to see this Jewish merchant allegedly "so twisted trying to keep from telling [her] the truth that he ended up telling [her she] was of God which was saying God was black."[73] The merchant was taken in by her intelligence and pressed to know what college she had gone to, which she divulged to him.[74]

In her magazine, Sister Thelma X blurred the boundary that prohibited women from holding ministerial authority. The Bible was the primary text engaged by Nation ministers, and Sister Thelma X took it on in an issue of *Truth* that featured the title "Queen Thelma VS. King James-Version" on its cover.[75] She repeated the NOI understanding that a black scientist, Yacub, "grafted" the white man from "60,000 black people" over "600 years" ago on the "Island of Pellan."[76] Yacub was the Bible's Jacob, and Pellan was Patmos. She also wrote that it was Elijah Muhammad who had the "PATIENCE OF JOB," for he had waited for the black man to "WAKE UP FOR 27 YEARS." Finally, making connections between Lazarus and black people, Sister Thelma X told her readers, "THE BIBLE WAS SPEAKING OF YOU WHEN IT READ THAT LAZARUS IS NOT DEAD HE IS ONLY SLEEPING." In concluding, she wailed, "WAKE UP MY SISTERS AND BROTHERS HOW LONG DO YOU WANT TO REMAIN ASLEEP."[77]

Sister Thelma X's zealous writings bring home that she was not a passive, acted upon, woman. Quite the contrary. She wrote, "I RESERVE THE RIGHT TO SPEAK FREELY AS I THINK, AS LONG AS I AM TELLING THE TRUTH."[78] Passionately devoted, Sister Thelma X was both a typical and an atypical 1950s NOI woman. She was typical insofar as she was against political activism (even if still highly opinionated about politics) and was willing to be taught by others whom she believed to be divinely informed. But she stood out from the masses of Nation women by making public her investment in Muhammad's race-centered Islamic teachings.

Sisters Louise Dunlap and Ernestine Scott

Sister Thelma's invective against integration was right in line with the NOI's black separatist practices, but by the mid-1950s, both were completely out of step with mainstream African Americans' political struggles to desegregate America. Nation members were told to avoid civil rights endeavors, not to register to vote, and not to engage in demonstrations or civil disobedience.[79] Yet somehow in early 1957, Louise Dunlap and Ernestine Scott boldly decided to sit on a bench in the whites-only section of a Flomaton, Alabama, railway station. They were en route from Florida to attend the annual February NOI Saviour's Day (the birthday of Master Fard Muhammad) Convention in Chicago; Flomaton was the Louisville & Nashville (L&N) Railroad transfer point. There, less than a mile from the Florida border, the two NOI women sat well before the 1960s sit-in movement. Perhaps they had reflected on what they had heard in the temple and internalized a language capable of spurring resistance.

Riding on the well-known passenger train, the L&N Railroad Humming Bird, which was decked out in its "confederate gray and yellow" colors, Sisters Louise and Ernestine began their journey from Elgin Air Force Base in Florida.[80] They had traveled only seventy miles of a nine hundred–mile trip to Chicago when the train stopped at Flomaton, a tiny town (5.3 square miles) known for its bustling railroad station.[81] The women made an exit holding a railing that "divided the stairs on the train, one side of the railing for white passengers, the other side for colored, so the soles of their shoes would not touch the same stair."[82] Passengers were continually segregated in Dixie despite the 1955 Interstate Commerce Commission (ICC) federal law banning racial segregation on buses, trains, and in waiting rooms. In the case of Sister Louise, who was twenty-six years old, and Sister Ernestine, two years her senior, we will never know if their sitting in an area designated for whites was a calculated step to test the law or a spontaneous impulse to demonstrate their humanity. But we do know their action took great courage.

Sisters Ernestine and Louise must have had an engrained understanding of how segregation worked. Living in Florida, they had seen the "white" and "colored" postings that littered the state all their lives. They faced racial discrimination at every public place off the Elgin Base; when they mailed their letters, it was at a colored post office window; and, if they had children in the public school system, it, too, was segregated, because not a single Florida educational institution was racially integrated during the 1950s.[83] The southernmost state's brutal enforcement of Jim Crow was as legendary as its sandy, segregated beaches. According to Jefferson Elliot, a special investigator for Florida's governor, in 1950 there "so many mob executions in one county that it never had a negro [*sic*] live long enough to go to trial."[84] This horrific violence kept most black Floridians in a perpetual state of fear. Surviving in the Sunshine State, as in Georgia or Mississippi, meant being keenly aware of one's surroundings, especially when traveling away from home.

As Sisters Ernestine and Louise prepared for their trip to Chicago, they might have perused a copy of the immensely popular *Green Book*, the "Negro Motorist" guide published yearly from 1936 to 1964 by Victor H. Green, a former New York City postal worker.[85] The travel book listed hotels, restaurants, boarding houses, beauty and barber shops, and other establishments in each state that served African Americans, to minimize Jim Crow travel difficulties, embarrassments — or worse.[86] Green hoped that one day he could suspend the publication, "when we as a race will have equal opportunities and privileges in the United States."[87] Sisters Louise and Ernestine had been taught to believe that Green's dreams of social equality resulted from misguided thinking; as Nation women they imagined themselves superior to whites. Their act of sitting in demonstrated the human dignity and self-respect fomented by two Asiatic black women.

Sisters Ernestine and Louise's action ignited a call to the police station, where Chief C. C. "Red" Hemby responded. Chief Hemby was noted for his experience in law enforcement. After serving at nearby Atmore, another railroad town, Hemby had accepted the offer to head Flomaton's police department. Bespectacled, portly, and slightly jowled, he looked much older than his peers.[88] But working at Atmore had prepared him to enforce segregation in Flomaton. The railroad station was in the heart of town, and its agents would flagrantly violate federal law by summoning "the police to arrest some colored persons . . . who happened to select seats . . . reserved for whites."[89] Hemby and other officers would respond according to racist customs.[90]

As Hemby approached Sisters Ernestine and Louise, they would have had to tilt their heads up to see the face of the man looking down on them. They would also have seen his gun, club, necktie, badge, and captain's cap when he ordered them to vacate.[91] But unbeknownst to Hemby, the women were not alone. Minister Joe White and Brother George Allen of Pensacola, Florida, were also on their way to the NOI convention. Although Minister Joe, twenty-nine years old, and Brother George, twenty-five, were not sitting in the white-only section, they "protested" against Hemby's demand for the women to move and physically confronted the captain.[92] Hemby said, according to newspaper reports, that the "two men jumped him from behind and beat him with his own billy club" when he attempted to "remove two Negro women from the white waiting room."[93] In the midst of the alleged "mauling," Hemby struck Minister Joe on the head with his gun and was able to keep both men at bay until backup patrolmen arrived. Jailed at Escambia County, a notorious lockup station, Minister Joe and Brother George were placed in segregated cells.[94] They were charged with "assault and battery with intent to kill" Chief Hemby.[95]

With bail set at $2,000 each, the men immediately turned to the NOI leadership, and Minister Malcolm X was sent to Alabama to handle the situation. It was not unusual for Minister Malcolm to bail brothers out of jail, though he tended to work far more outside the South.[96] Flomaton was in uncharted territory for the NOI, whose lone temple in Dixie was No. 15, Atlanta. Minister Malcolm worked with J. L. Le Flore, head of the Non-Partisan Voters League and director of the Public Affairs Research Committee, who had documented

"We Must Protect Our Most Valuable Property, Our Women." Nation of Islam
meeting, Washington, D.C., June 25, 1961. (Eve Arnold, Magnum Photos)

abuses at Flomaton's transportation facilities.[97] From a distance, NOI members
would have placed Le Flore in the dead-wrong integrationist's group, but in the
belly of the beast, "where the devil is not afraid to let you know that he is the
devil," they understood the necessity of working with activists.[98] Le Flore made
an investigation of the incident, and Brother George accepted his offer to secure
his release as Minister Malcolm paid a lawyer for representing Minister Joe.[99]

Brother George and Minister Joe were acting as good NOI men, protecting black women in the service of Allah. Indeed, when Minister Malcolm recounted the Flomaton incident to a NOI audience, he zeroed in on how the
men "wouldn't allow anybody to talk to his woman in the manner in which the
white man had spoken and as a result a fracas was started in which the black
man disarmed the policeman with the help of Allah."[100] But the men's actions
also abruptly shifted the focus away from Sisters Louise and Ernestine's bravery.

Sisters Ernestine and Louise, who felt entitled to sit where they pleased, became the object of the account. In effect, their female agency was usurped by
men. Although the women were no doubt questioned by someone in the NOI
about what had happened, they too may have agreed to privilege the men's actions above their own given the emphasis on the defense of black womanhood.

Since no charges were filed against Sisters Ernestine and Louise for their gutsy actions, which touched off the fight, their courage was eclipsed and even their names disappear from the historical record.[101]

The Challenge of Fishing for Women

During the same years that Sisters Louise and Ernestine, Sister Thelma X, and Sister Captain Burnsteen were finding ways to flex their wills within (or despite) the NOI's prescribed roles for women, one of the Nation's most spellbinding public speakers was having significant trouble attracting new female converts. Minister Malcolm X, hammering on the protection of black women, repeatedly appealed to his audiences' sense of grievance over historic abuse. For example, at the Chicago temple in 1957, he said that "during the time of slavery, pregnant women were forced to work in the fields almost to the point of delivery, and the women who did not keep up their work, were whipped."[102] At the end of his lecture, eleven men responded to his membership call, "but no women."[103] Minister Malcolm then "made a special appeal to the women visitors with negative results. He told them that they were welcomed and emphasis [*sic*] the protection they would receive if they became members."[104] At each lecture, all the women in attendance would stand up when he asked, "How many believe what they have heard?" But to his surprise "never more than an agonizing few" would stand up "to follow the Honorable Elijah Muhammad."[105] Given that he was one of the more "persuasive speakers" in "the whole Moslem movement," Minister Malcolm's inability to convert women at the same rate as men deserves exploration.[106]

Despite Minister Malcolm's emphasis on how the "beautiful black woman!" deserved shelter and respect, his lectures painted an unflattering portrait of those for whom he was "fishing."[107] At the Philadelphia temple in 1957, Minister Malcolm spoke at length about how "our woman has been the greatest tool of the devil" and "is the one who hesitates to accept our teachings."[108] As evidence he cited the lies that black women tell their children: crediting Santa Claus, "a fat white man," rather than the father for Christmas gifts, which teaches children to "love the white man and have contempt for you [the black man]"; telling children that the "stork brought them into the world rather than him"; teaching them that God and angels are "all white." Finally, the black woman "is the one who supports the preacher, and there is sin in the church more than outside the church. No wonder our children do not respect their parents," said Minister Malcolm.[109]

Moreover, pushing only slightly beyond degrading stereotypes of the licentious black woman, Minister Malcolm pointed to their alleged lustful behavior. In fact, he believed that the NOI's "moral code and discipline was what repelled" black women the most.[110] He argued that living in "a society dominated by sex" had produced an "unreal" relationship between men and women.[111] Using her body to seduce men, the black woman "shave[s] off [her] real eyebrows only to paint on false ones, takes lipstick and paints on a false mouth," and "with paint and powder achieves a false face."[112] This "unreal" body arouses an unnatural gendered interaction — or, as Minister Malcolm bluntly explained, "woman has led man into evil and the one she was created to serve became her slave. She rules him entirely with her sexual appeal, her clothes designed by man to accentuate those portions of her body related to sex, and when he fully dresses she undresses. She has departed entirely from the real to the unreal."[113] In a lecture finale, Minister Malcolm instructed the Nation men not to be "weak" for black women. "Do not sit in her house talking to her alone or you will lose your reward. She will tempt you but you must be strong. . . . You who are weak will surely be destroyed in the fire that is about to rain on North America."[114]

All of this seductive behavior, Minister Malcolm taught, went back to Adam and Eve in the Garden of Eden. Like Christian ministers, he used biblical stories to charge women with being both "weak and wicked, and like the snake, sneaky."[115] But Minister Malcolm, went further than Christian preachers to link the black female seducer with the white male devil. He explained,

> Ever since [the] time of the enemy began, the white man has been able to influence the black woman. She in turn influences you and your children. She is the only teacher of your children and she teaches them to look up to the white man and look down on you. She leaves the home every day to work for him while you and your children are uncared for and she is the boss of the house because the white man has given her the knowledge to do so. The trickiest [pair] in existence is the black woman and the white man.[116]

United in deceit, "the saying is the only ones free are the white man and the black woman," proclaimed Minister Malcolm.[117]

A black woman hearing a high-ranking NOI minister argue that she was in cahoots with the devil would find the claim disconcerting, to say the least. Nation women did not take this accusation lightly. They wrote to Elijah Muhammad complaining that Minister Malcolm "talked so hard against women."[118] Certainly it is hard to imagine a female visitor being convinced to join the NOI if this was all she heard.

To be sure, Minister Malcolm said his purpose "was not to condemn them, but to have them understand their position as helpmates to their husbands, and [to] stop trying to rule him; for in doing so they only lead him to destruction. They are to be the mothers and properly rear the children and take care of the home."[119] This vision of family life echoed the fictional households that surfaced nightly on television during the 1950s, in which a happy white housewife had a hardworking husband who made her fairy-tale world possible. (Often the household also included a compassionate black maid.)[120] And Minister Malcolm did also exhort Nation men. He said, "Do not call yourself a muslim [*sic*] until you are working [,] trying to be independent. . . . You should own your own home and your own business, then you can say you are a muslim." Additionally, "If you are making $35 a week you cannot have the respect of your wife. . . . Do not ask that sister to marry you if you cannot take care of her."[121]

Minister Malcolm was genuinely concerned about low NOI female membership; he fretted, "there is something very wrong that sisters are not joining."[122] But instead of considering how portions of the NOI teachings might have been offensive to black women, Minister Malcolm found fault in the Nation women and complained about their failure to recruit new members. "The brothers are bringing in lost founds and the sisters are not," he remarked.[123] At a 1956 Philadelphia temple gathering, he accused the NOI women of being mean-spirited. "Sisters must become more friendly," he exhorted; "I noticed tonight that they were not sitting next to each other. When you come in here and see an empty seat beside a sister, sit there."[124] Calling for a new MGT-GCC in Philadelphia, he upbraided the sisters and threatened to suspend them. He said, "I'd rather put all of the sisters out for bickering and go out and get a lot of prostitutes. That sounds harsh but I cannot stand this disunity." [125]

Minister Malcolm did not have the same problems at his own Temple, No. 7 in Harlem — perhaps because he himself was an important draw. Malcolm X had converted to the NOI while he was in prison. On his release, Elijah Muhammad had assigned him the charge of organizing a temple in his former stomping ground, Boston, Mass. Proud to have been promoted to the coveted position of minister, Malcolm worked hard to establish Temple No. 11 and brought his relatives and acquaintances into the NOI by 1953. Among these was his former girlfriend, Sister Evelyn Williams.[126] Malcolm's half-sister Ella had introduced Evelyn to him before he had converted to the NOI, and she was a frequent visitor while he was incarcerated (1946–1952). When Muhammad transferred Minister Malcolm to Harlem in 1954, Sister Evelyn followed.[127]

As an unmarried woman, Sister Evelyn, would, in theory, have no unchaperoned contact with men at the temple. The Nation's ultrapuritanical code of sexual morality followed the tradition of Muslims throughout the world. Single men and women had to follow strict courtship procedures (directed by the MGT-GCC and FOI Captains). Assistant Minister Benjamin 2X (Goodman, later Karim) of Temple No. 7 stated that only after marriage "were the brother and sister allowed to be in each other's company without a chaperone — not in anyone's home, not in the Temple, not in a restaurant or any other public place."[128] Sister Evelyn knew the rules, but Minister Malcolm continued to be smitten by her.

In 1956, Minister Malcolm asked Sister Evelyn to marry him, and she accepted.[129] However, several days later, he rescinded his proposal. In hindsight, he wrote, "And for anyone in any kind of a leadership position, such as I was, the worst thing in the world that he could have was the wrong woman."[130] He understood the problematic nature of his indecisiveness and later wrote to Elijah Muhammad, "Sister Evelyn is the only one who had a legitiment [*sic*] beef against me . . . and I do bear witness that if she complains she is justified."[131] He was under intense pressure "from all sides about marriage plans," but Muhammad wanted him to "stay single."[132]

Sister Betty X

Minister Malcolm worked hard to establish Temple No. 7 as a thriving unit. By comparison with the women he had chastised in the Philadelphia MGT-GCC, he bragged, "the sisters in New York are in complete harmony and are progressing while helping to rise up the dead."[133] Membership drives, which included "fishing contests," were employed to bring potential female converts to temple lectures. The inclusion of Betty Dean Saunders into the MGT-GCC sisterhood offers a perfect example of how the New York sisters took their fishing duty seriously — and of the ultimate drawing power of Minister Malcolm. Betty's journey began at a dinner party hosted by a member of the Harlem MGT-GCC. Betty always describes her simply as "a nurse's aide."[134] Unnamed, but pivotal to Betty's conversion, this sister was fishing in the way encouraged by Minister Malcolm and his teacher Elijah Muhammad. She had worked in the Bronx's Montefiore Hospital, which was connected to Betty's Brooklyn State College School of Nursing; this allowed her to observe the making of professional women.[135] Betty gave the impression that she was not aware of being evaluated by this sister prior to the 1956 invitation.

Being friendly and upbeat was an important quality for Nation women; their disposition had to be charming to signal to other women the gratification of NOI membership. The unnamed sister was comfortable enough in her assessment of Betty to invite her to share a meal. Nation members did not break bread casually. "The food was delicious" recalled Betty; "I'd never tasted food like that. It was seasoned with corn oil, margarine, onions, garlic, celery, green pepper and chives — just all sorts of good things."[136] Unbeknownst to Betty, but clearly on the agenda of her sister host, the mouthwatering meal concluded with an invitation to Temple No.7. Betty recalled, "Now, how are you going to sit and eat all that food and say 'no'?"[137]

The sister who had fished for Betty really wanted her to meet "her" minister.[138] Laying claim to Malcolm X as her personal minister resembled the way Christians might honor their pastors and vicariously bask in their power. But Minister Malcolm was not there that night, and Betty remembered that she had wished the lecture "would be over any minute."[139] Betty's host was surprised that she had not responded to the membership call. Betty explained to her that "number one, I was not familiar with the philosophy, and number two, my parents would kill me if they knew I joined another religion and gave up being a Methodist."[140] Unmoved by Betty's answer, the sister said, "Just wait until you hear my minister talk," because "he's very disciplined, he's good-looking, and all the sisters want him."[141] Even Minister Malcolm admitted that "in almost every Temple at least one single sister had let out some broad hint that she thought I needed a wife."[142]

Ironically, the desire that Nation women expressed for Minister Malcolm speaks to the same charismatic aura of powerful men and authority that has so often led Christian women to a romantic interest in their pastors — which NOI teachings so condemned. Perhaps the sister's description of Minister Malcolm piqued Betty's interest, though in later recollections she offers only the admission, "Well, if I was going to go back to her house to eat, which I really wanted to do, I would have to go to this place to listen to her minister [at] Temple Seven."[143]

Not missing a beat in the fishing ritual, the sister brought Betty back to the temple and was excited to "whisper" in her ear, "The minister is here."[144] Betty recalled thinking, "Big deal. But then I looked over and saw this man on the extreme right aisle sort of galloping to the podium. He was tall, he was thin, and he was galloping, it looked as though he was going someplace much more important than the podium."[145] As Minister Malcolm mounted the rostrum, Betty found herself sitting straight up and "was impressed with him clean-cut, no-nonsense."[146] Betty instantly felt a connection and was "struck" when he removed his eyeglasses; she thought, "Oh, my God — hurry up, please put your glasses back on![147] Minister Malcolm may have appeared handsome to some Nation sisters, but Betty saw a "malnourished" man. "He was rhiny," thin-faced, and clearly "overworked."[148] After he cleaned his dark-rimmed glasses and put them back on, Betty thought he looked "a little better."[149] Unable to recall the essence of his lecture that night, Betty did "remember thinking I'd better not get close to him in case he could read minds too — I would be in terrible trouble!"[150] Why she believed the thoughts swirling in her head were "terrible trouble" may have had something to do with her desire to feed Minister Malcolm "some liver, some spinach, some beets and broccoli" because "he needed care" and she was "thinking that maybe [she] was the person to help him."[151]

Betty was formally introduced to Minister Malcolm at the conclusion of his lecture and he said to her, "Will you be back? We'd love to have you."[152] Betty does not share her reply to him; she was certainly "impressed" but did not "understand the philosophy."[153] Minister Malcolm had not reeled Betty into the NOI fold.

Completely understanding that successful fishing required tenacity, the Nation sister would look for Betty at the hospital and repeatedly asked her, "Are you going to the Temple?" With no desire to return, Betty would shut down the invitations by saying that she was "on duty" or "give some other excuses."[154] Everything changed, however, when Betty ran into Minister Malcolm at a dinner party in Brooklyn. Certainly she recognized him; but she recalled that he had also recognized her, and asked, "Sister, how are you doing?" She gave the standard reply of "fine," but he saw through her and said, "Are you sure? . . . Because you look worried." She told him that she "was not worried," but then they "started talking."[155] Betty shared her experiences at Tuskegee Institute and the hostilities she had encountered while living in Alabama. This conversation transformed Betty in a way that Minister Malcolm's public lecture had not. She remembered, "Malcolm was the first adult that I met who helped me face the discrimination I experienced in the South. Everyone else, including my parents, didn't want to discuss it. It was like bad manners to discuss it. It didn't exist, and if you didn't talk about it, it would go away. I wanted to go back to be able to talk to him."[156] Minister Malcolm had given Betty "a history lesson" at that dinner party, and she began to see herself "from a different perspective."[157] She also began to attend the general meetings at Temple No. 7 on Sundays at 2:00 P.M. to hear more from Minister Malcolm.

Minister Malcolm was known for saying that "everything he had learned came from the Honorable Elijah Muhammad," but Brother Allen (Donaldson, Hakim Jamal) "doubted that: no one could have taught Malcolm how to smile or talk."[158] Teaching from the Bible, Minister Malcolm replaced the emotionalism attributed to black preachers with rational thinking. He broke down the familiar, infused it with humor, and nudged his audience along with logical reasoning and love. For example, when talking about "those lying black preachers," he said, they "got us into their churches where we sweat and squirm around from the heat. Why do you think that they give you all those funny-looking fans with pictures of Jesus on them? They know that you are hot and they know they are not going to buy an air conditioner . . . a Cadillac, yes, an air conditioner for you, no."[159] And when talking about drug addicts, Minister Malcolm said, "We should all love ourselves and our brothers who can't yet love themselves." But at the same time, "The man who owned the dope factories, the man who owned the ships that brought the dope here to us, the man who owned the airplanes that flew the dope to us and to our children — he was nothing but a devil."[160]

Despite the indictment of black women that frequently filled his public lectures, Minister Malcolm could make respectful room for them to struggle with his ideas. At the end of one lecture, the audience was surprised when an angry woman, said, "Minister Malcolm, I don't care what you say, I'm a Christian, just like our Lord Jesus Christ. I only came here today because my sister told me about you. She said that I should hear you. Now I have and I'm sure that you are wrong about many things, but one question that I have is . . . who ever told you that Moses was black and Noah was black?"[161] The crowd hissed and booed the woman, but Minister Malcolm said, "Let the sister talk, most of you were in the same condition that she is now. She has a right to think what she wants to think and to try to gain a better understanding. . . . Don't any of you laugh at her again."[162] Minister Malcolm affirmed her by saying she had posed a "very intelligent question" and used the Bible to provide an answer.[163] It was in Exodus 3:16–17 that the illustration "leprous as snow," which means "white as snow," was a demonstration of a miracle, so "why would it be a miracle for a white man's hand to turn white? If his hand did turn white, as it says it did, and then turned again as his other flesh, this should simply mean that his hand returned to normal which, in order to be a miracle, had to be black. Not only that. We know that Moses was in Africa: it was he who took the Hebrew children out of Egypt's land, which is North Africa. He crossed the Red Sea, into Arabia, so Moses was African and –according to the Scriptures — black."[164] Although we don't know how this woman received Minister Malcolm's answer, she surely appreciated that he told the audience not to laugh at her, taking her question seriously, and she thanked him.[165] He was a gracious, captivating teacher who could anticipate and control his audience and fill a NOI temple beyond capacity.

When Betty joined the NOI by the fall of 1956, against her parents' wishes, she formally became Sister Betty X. She learned many of the same teachings that Nation members had memorized during the 1930s and 1940s. No longer on the "dead level," converts took pride in their knowledge and on being able to easily answer mathematical questions, such as "How much does the earth weigh?" or "How deep is the Pacific Ocean?"[166] Additionally, similar to those of Fard's pioneers, NOI members' chests lifted when they replied to the question, "Who is the Original Man?," answering, "The Original Man is the Asiatic black man, the maker, the owner, the cream of the planet earth, the father of civilization, and God of the Universe."[167] And on Thursday night at the MGT-GCC, Sister Betty X was further indoctrinated into the specific regulations and expectations of female membership. She embraced her new attire as well and even extended the length of her nurse uniform.[168] Her college education made her unique. Sister Betty shared her nursing skills with the women and eventually became a health teacher in the MGT-GCC class.[169]

Sister Betty X would also witness how the Nation kept its members under control. She had joined Temple No. 7 during a pivotal moment. In September 1956, Minister Malcolm conducted a series of trials before the entire temple membership. "Brother Adam and Sister Naomi, who'd admitted to the sin of fornication, were banished for five years. Sister Eunice, who had joined the Nation of Islam as a child, was charged with adultery."[170] Minister Malcolm asked Sister Eunice how she thought her husband, a "registered" NOI member in prison, felt about her actions. After hearing her response, Minister Malcolm told her, "Sister, I have no alternative other than to give you five years out of the Nation of Islam, during which I would advise you to fast and pray to Allah, ask him for forgiveness, ask your husband for forgiveness. . . . In no way can I show you any sympathy, pity, or anything, because you should know better." Lastly, Minister Malcolm charged FOI Captain Joseph (Gravitt, Yusuf Shah) with beating his wife. "You are charged with putting your hands on your wife. Guilty or not guilty?," asked Minister Malcolm. He replied, "Guilty." Minister Malcolm at this point said, "You know, as well as I, and better than perhaps most brothers here, that any brother that puts his hand on his wife . . . if it comes to my knowledge, automatically has ninety days out of the Temple of Islam."[171] While fornication was harshly punished when compared to domestic violence, these trials formed part of the NOI culture to maintain marital fidelity and religious morality. They also demonstrate the severe repercussions for breaking NOI rules.

Introducing Mrs. Malcolm X

From the moment Sister Betty laid eyes on Minister Malcolm, she had recognized that he was a "workaholic" and thought "that maybe [she] was the person to help him."[172] As Minister Malcolm evaluated her, she had already seen through him. Staying within the strict NOI rules, they never "dated," according to Sister Betty. Women and men would go out in groups, and at times, Minister Malcolm was included. He always insisted that Sister Betty sit directly behind him as he drove. Sister Betty never understood why, "until one day" she "happened to look up into the rearview mirror. I saw him looking at me. When he saw me looking, he smiled and I smiled back. That was as much as we could do."[173]

Minister Malcolm made his intentions known to Sister Betty when he began to ask her questions about her relatives and future plans after graduating from nursing school. Her height and age perfectly suited him, according to Elijah Muhammad's teachings. A woman's age should be "half the age of the man's age, plus seven."[174] Minister Malcolm also liked that she had a small family. He described in-laws as "outlaws" who could destroy a marriage.[175] Further, Muhammad thought that Sister Betty was a "fine sister."[176] When Minister Malcolm was in town, he would take her to dinner, always in the presence of another Nation brother. Sister Betty would drop all her responsibilities to accommodate his schedule. In addition to working at the hospital, she was also babysitting for physicians because her parents had refused to provide financial support for her schooling after she had joined the NOI.[177] At the hospital she frequently told her supervisor, "I've got to go," and the supervisor would laugh and ask, "Did that man come into town again?"[178]

Sister Betty became most attracted to Minister Malcolm's "nobility," and she was completely caught off guard when he phoned her from Detroit and directly asked, "Look, do you want to get married? . . . Are you ready to make that move?"[179] She "screamed," and later recalled, "I don't remember being that happy in my entire life."[180] They married two days later, on January 14, 1958. Unbeknownst to Sister Betty, the day before he had penned a letter to Muhammad, explaining, "My main reason for deciding to marry is that I saw where at least I was getting in danger because there were too many Sisters who would do ANYTHING [the word anything is typed in red] to trap me . . . and since I'm human, I decided the risk was getting too great to leave to chance. So I pray Allah I'm making the right move."[181] This helps explain why at a courthouse in Lansing, Michigan, no family or friends were in attendance. Even though Sister Betty and her parents were on good terms by this time and Minister Malcolm had relatives in Detroit, he insisted on no fanfare.[182] The day marked the first time Sister Betty had been alone with Minister Malcolm.

By eloping with Sister Betty, Minister Malcolm went against NOI tradition. Members were instructed to announce their wedding plans two weeks before in the temple. Instead, Minister Malcolm called Captain Joseph from Lansing and told him to go before the Temple No. 7 body and share that he and Sister

Betty were married. After making the announcement, Captain Joseph recalled, Sister "Evelyn jumped up screaming, hollering, and ran out of the temple, from the mosque."[183] Minister Malcolm received word of Sister Evelyn's emotional response to the news, and after a conversation with Elijah Muhammad, solved the crisis by having her transferred to Temple No. 2, Chicago, to work as a secretary.[184] Brokenhearted and fatigued from disappointment, Sister Evelyn had no real choice aside from leaving the NOI, which she had been taught was "the only group that really cares about you."[185] At home in Boston, she would be questioned and repeatedly asked, "What happened?" In Harlem, where word regarding her reaction had circulated, all-knowing eyes would meet her at MGT-GCC meetings—and she would have to look at Sister Betty. Chicago would provide a new temple home, and in the seat of NOI power, which may have also given her hope for a fresh start.

Sister Evelyn accepted, and Minister Malcolm later recalled that the Harlem MGT-GCC "just about ate up Betty," because they were so happy for her.[186] Minister Malcolm's half-sister, Ella, was also pleased with his choice of Sister Betty. She "was glad that he now had someone nearby who would see that he ate and slept properly."[187] Sister Betty accompanied her husband and sometimes, like other ministers' wives, represented the MGT-GCC without him. The FBI reports that from 1958 to 1960 she addressed affairs, meetings, and conventions in Atlantic City; Detroit; Dorchester, Massachusetts; Chicago; Hartford, Connecticut; New York; and Philadelphia.

Not all the women were pleased with Sister Betty's promotion within the Nation. The sister captain of Harlem wrote to Elijah Muhammad in June of 1959, complaining that Minister Malcolm had "caused trouble" by appointing Sister Betty as head of all the MGT-GCCs on the East Coast. The MGT-GCCs by 1959 had organized to showcase their creative talents at annual bazaars. They sold handmade washcloths and towels, aprons, children's clothes, ladies' blouses, and fine needlework items. Homemade pastries and preserves were top sellers.[188] Their efforts yielded extra money for themselves, for temple activities, and for the national headquarters in Chicago.[189] Sister captains took pride in their strong sisterhood and the authority they held over Nation women. The sister captain of Temple No. 7 felt Minister Malcolm had no right to replace her and wanted to find out if he had the power to do so.[190] Even with Minister Malcolm's position as the national representative for the NOI, he may have exceeded his latitude by advancing his wife. Muhammad stepped in and brought Sister Betty to Chicago during the summer months of July and August 1959. He invited her back with a personal phone call on October 1, 1959; he was impressed and wanted to further groom her for MGT-GCC leadership.[191] Finally, when the

Mrs. Betty Shabazz, "Intro-
ducing Mrs. Malcolm X,"
New York Herald-Tribune, June
30, 1963. (Photo by Morris
Warman; courtesy of Ronald
Warman)

New York Herald-Tribune reporter Ann Geracimos contacted Minister Malcolm
to write a story on the roles of Nation women, he believed that his wife could
"handle it very well," and Elijah Muhammad agreed.[192]

"Introducing Mrs. Malcolm X" was the title of the short piece published on
June 30, 1963. The interview took place at the Shabazz Restaurant of Temple
No. 7-B at Corona, Long Island. Although Minister Malcolm sat next to his
wife, Geracimos focused on Sister Betty. Clearly her husband's "nobility" had
rubbed off on her: Geracimos observed that "she acknowledged us impassively,
as a queen might treat a subject."[193]

Wearing white gloves and a sheer white veil over her hair styled with bangs
across her forehead, Sister Betty "refused to look anything but beautiful," recalled Ameenah Omar, the wife of Minister Malcolm's brother, Philbert.[194] She
also refused to answer questions about her past. Geracimos made it clear that
"Black Muslim women as a rule do not seek, or receive any publicity," and this
is why Sister Betty had not granted interviews. As Nation women, "their primary role is caring for their home and families, and obeying the moral tenets
dictated to them by Elijah Muhammad who stays mostly in Phoenix, Arizona,

through his daughter Ethel Sharrieff in Chicago, leader of the women's training program."[195] Sister Betty stated that "all of us try in some ways to copy her." But in 1963, Minister Malcolm and Sister Betty were still the celebrity couple of the NOI. And, in her role, Sister Betty "deferred to" Minister Malcolm repeatedly during the interview, wherein he recited his temple message that "a woman must be taught her role. And the man must be sufficiently equipped to create an income for the family to be given more respect and so respect himself."[196] Sister Betty's public role was in keeping with that of other Nation wives. They stayed in the background while their husbands navigated the public space.

Moving into the 1960s

As the Cold War isolated the United States and civil rights victories failed to fundamentally change black lives, the NOI became an appealing black-centered Islamic alternative community for frustrated and bewildered African Americans who lived for the most part outside of the South. Nation women had deduced that Elijah Muhammad's program was the answer to their plight. But occasionally, they defied the NOI expectation of a sequestered black womanhood. In Philadelphia in August 1960, women and girls marched in front of the Arena Theatre at Forty-first and Halsted, where Muhammad was scheduled to appear. Dressed proudly in white, they held placards "uplift our race! Muhammad."[197] This was one of the few moments where visuals captured NOI women participating in activities that mirror those of activist women. Their efforts helped to bring "a throng of 10,000 persons" to hear their leader.[198]

Individual women also sometimes showed boldness and visibility in their nationhood dedication. By 1961, no Nation woman in Chicago was bolder, or more visible, than Sister Thelma X Muhammad. Her indictment against Jews and her allegiance to "Msgr. [Messenger] Muhammad" had increased over time, and now she was a public voice for the NOI. She made her leadership plain by writing, "I feel that I am one of the more able members of this dynamic, breathtaking fast moving brain busting movement headed by the Hon. Elijah Muhammad and I am taking command."[199]

Apparently, Sister Thelma X's straightforward and, at times, audacious comments, made Chicagoans want to know more about her. Considering that she was the "best authority" on her "character," Sister Thelma X explained "what [made] her tick" to the readership of the *Chicago Defender*.[200] In a letter to the editor, she exposed her inner workings "for the benefit of the curiosity seekers who [were] inquiring about" her.[201] Proclaiming that she was "born with [her] own kind of education and [her] own kind of CIVIL RIGHTS," Sister Thelma X eschewed voting, because the process gave one's "CIVIL RIGHTS back to the white man everytime [*sic*] you give him your VOTE."[202] Clearly in tune with her own power, she declared, "I don't vote for anyone but myself which makes me my own president."[203]

Sister Thelma X's confidence in her intellect had tried the patience of others when she was young. Smart and equipped with a response for just about everything, "what she couldn't master [she] would put it down."[204] It was not until she tried the teachings of Messenger Muhammad, "so tiny, so tender, so fatherly," that she had a "CURE ALL pill."[205] Sister Thelma X declared, "I took this pill and added grandmother's teachings, the white man's arrogance, the ten commandments and what I was born with 'CIVIL RIGHTS' and began to make EDUCATED BOMBS and dropped these bombs on everybody regardless of race or religion and germs of every description began jumping for cover, disintegrating."[206] Interestingly, her self-description asserts her own knowledge (mother's wit, observation, Christianity, and intuition) as equally important to NOI teachings in her understanding of the world.

Sister Thelma X's letter sparked a fiery exchange with another *Chicago Defender* reader, James Allen — and one that pointed to the NOI's Achilles' heel as it approached its fourth decade. Allen wrote that he was shocked at the NOI's "gross stupidity" when it "allowed the leader of the American Nazi Party [George Lincoln Rockwell] to make a speech from its platform."[207] Given Hitler's crimes against humanity, Allen summed, "not even the leadership of the John Birch society could be that stupid" to invite Rockwell to speak at a public gathering. The rank-and-file members of the NOI were not at fault, but its leadership, wrote Allen. He urged the NOI leaders to "rationalize its doctrine or step down and let the more able members of the organization take command."[208]

Sister Thelma X, as emphatic as ever, opened her response to Allen with the question, "WHO IS STUPID??" It had to be Allen, who she was "quite sure [was] a Negro Jew trained Christian."[209] As a "so-called Negro" who wanted integration, Sister Thelma X asked Allen, "Itn't [*sic*] Mr. Rockwell a white man and why discriminate against him?"[210] To be clear, wrote Sister Thelma X, "Mr. Elijah Muhammad wants to keep our race black and we feel that Mr. Rockwell is determined to keep his race white."[211] But, the "mixed up race" also needs a leader and "we feel that you couldn't have a better one than the Hon. Mr. Rockwell and his Nazi party."[212] So, "Now that you feel that Msgr. Muhammad is too stupid to teach you we will step aside and let the Nazi party teach in a way that you can understand and he has our blessings. Beggars cannot be choosey, you take what you get."[213] Holding onto anti-Jewish rhetoric, even in light of Hitler's mass extermination of human life, Sister Thelma X and the NOI refused to stop identifying Jews as their enemy.

Allen believed Sister Thelma X and other NOI leaders to be misguided thinkers. He clarified, in "an open letter to Madame Thelma X," that he was a black "atheist and proud of it."[214] Moreover, he was "not enthusiastic about integration —when it finally comes—because it will not solve the economic problems of the Negro."[215] Highly concerned with Sister Thelma X's "confused thinking," he concluded his letter by encouraging her to develop her intellect through the "formal study of history, psychology, economics, political science, philosophy and anything else you can find."[216]

Although there is no public reply to James Allen from Sister Thelma X, one can imagine that she shrugged away the indictment. Nation of Islam members had been taught that their teachings and Lessons constituted an eclectic kind of "formal study," which well supported their belief that race mixing was "DEATH and DESTRUCTION" for black people.[217] But as the movement to desegregate America picked up national momentum, the NOI's arguments about so-called race mixing lost steam. How women in the NOI clung to its sectarian Islamic belief system in the midst of the changing culture of 1960s America will be the focus of the next chapter.

CHAPTER SEVEN

NATION OF ISLAM WOMANHOOD, 1960–1975

Jamesetta Hawkins was an unruly teen with a powerful singing voice. She dropped out of high school and began her professional career at the fragile age of fifteen. It was 1953, and for most of her young life she had been called a "Devil's child." Her mother, Dorothy, was a "Bad Bohemian," and her lifestyle, which included drugs and prostitution, had stigmatized Jamesetta.[1] But Jamesetta added her own fuel to the fire. She loved gutbucket blues, "devilish sounds," music that was "sloppy and sexy and easy as falling into bed."[2]

The Hawkinses lived in Los Angeles, and occasionally Dorothy would go to Temple No. 27 on West Jefferson Blvd. She thought the "Muslims were cool" and was "tight" with some of the "brothers."[3] Although she never converted, Dorothy talked about the NOI to her daughter. Jamesetta, known in the music world as Etta James, would eventually go beyond her mother's pattern of simply "hang[ing] out" at a temple and join No. 15, in Atlanta, in 1960.

Seven years in the music business, traveling the country in beat-up vehicles, living in raunchy motels, and eating fried chicken and greasy fries out of paper bags proved both exhilarating and exhausting for Etta. But her hard work had paid off. She was a rising jazz and blues singer, whose consecutive hits, which included the 1961 classic "At Last," made her a standout. Still, even though she was no longer "little churchgoing Jamesetta," her insecurities made her anxious and vulnerable.[4] One response was to channel the rebellious power of Dorothy, to shape herself as "a tough bitch called Etta James."[5] Filled with rage and an "I'm gonna do what I please, when I please" spirit, she had begun to increase her use of alcohol and added marijuana, heroin, and cocaine. She was an addict who nonetheless could also stay clean for months at a time, and, during one long stretch, she became a member of the NOI.

At first, Etta and her friend Abye would visit Temple No. 15 when they were "bored." Etta recalled hearing Minister Louis X (Walcott, later Farrakhan) there and being struck because he "could preach."[6] She zoomed in on the strong "anger and rebellious vibe of the teaching."[7] Although Etta did not agree with everything she heard, she needed the sense of racial pride. Her fair skin constantly reminded her that she did not know her biological father; being fully embraced as a black woman felt important to her; and the lifestyle of no drugs and healthy food made for a positive alternative. She had become an Eastern Star (Masonic female order) years earlier, so the more esoteric and astrological aspects of the teachings did not appear completely foreign to her.[8] Calling the white man the devil also gave her a "chuckle," and she became "superenthusiastic [sic]" after reading the pamphlets.[9] But, frankly, she wrote, it was those "fine-looking clean-cut Muslim brothers" who clinched her conversion.[10] She was young and unattached and wanted manly attention. For years, she had been drawn to men who had made her "feel safe," and the Fruit of Islam constituted the epitome of protectors.[11]

Etta James — who proudly called herself Jamesetta X after writing her letter to the Honorable Elijah Muhammad — had but a fleeting moment with the Nation of Islam in the early 1960s.[12] When she left Atlanta for New York and the legendary Apollo Theatre, she joined Minister Malcolm X's Temple No. 7, and enjoyed his emotionally stirring and candid testimony ("the cat inspired").[13] She fished, like all good NOI members, and may have had a hand in bringing Cassius Clay (later Muhammad Ali) into the fold.[14] But Sister Jamesetta never fully embraced what she described as the "strict doctrine."[15] Having built a career and a following, she had more confidence, options, and resources than many women. She enjoyed tasty food and would "sneak and eat pork."[16] She also never stopped wearing dresses with plunging necklines that hugged her shapely body while she sang sexually laced lyrics. Only her inner circle knew about her Nation membership, because her stage name remained Etta James.[17] Much later, Etta said that it was "something of a fad" for her; it was the "radical, the 'in' thing to do."[18]

A Radical Black Nation

Etta James was not alone in her attraction to Muslim men and the ideal of protection that Master Fard had set out earlier, nor in her fascination with radical black nationalism. During the 1960s, women continued to convert to and develop the NOI for seemingly different reasons: to secure the kind of traditional, stable family life Elijah Muhammad touted and to participate in the development of a new black nation. In the end, Muhammad's ideals for marriage proved difficult for many to achieve, and the sacrifices required from women were great. Some, like James, chose to leave the Nation; others found ingenious ways to work within the patriarchal system, indeed, to trump patriarchy for their own ends.

It is interesting to consider how the Nation of Islam, whose ministers maintained a mostly apolitical stance, morphed into an organization that was viewed by Etta, and so many others, as political and radical. The year 1960 ushered in a decade that alchemized the heart and soul of former "Negroes." The sit-in movement was ignited in February 1960, and the Student Non-Violent Coordinating Committee (SNCC) came into existence in April. The freedom fighters sought desegregation, and college students helped to shift the political strategies to include direct action against racist practices. Yet the NOI leadership remained critical of the civil rights movement, maintaining that separation and their black nation were the only path to real freedom.

In large part, the NOI gained a reputation as a radical organization because that was how the criminal justice system viewed it. Since the 1930s, the FBI and police departments in Detroit and Chicago had kept the temples under surveillance. By the late 1950s, the charismatic power of Minister Malcolm X had become of particular concern to law enforcement. In 1958, Johnson X (Hinton), a member of Temple No. 7, was beaten badly by Harlem policemen on April 14. Under the direction of Minister Malcolm, more than five hundred FOI surrounded the 28 Precinct Station where Johnson X was jailed. When Minister Malcolm "made a slight gesture" and the street was cleared in about three minutes, the New York City Police Inspector McGowan said to the New York *Amsterdam News* writer James Hicks, "No man should have that much power over that many people. We cannot control this town if one man can wield that kind of power."[19]

The authorities' inability to distinguish the Nation's mandate to defend itself — by any means necessary, according Minister Malcolm — from encouragement to initiate violence magnified the NOI's supposed threat. The police officer Lee P. Brown described the group in 1965 as "a black supremacist cult" and noted that its teachings included conceptualizing the police as an example of the white man's authority. Understanding the Nation's goals around the annihilation of white people, Brown argued that the FOI were willing to "kill a policeman," and there was much suspicion surrounding the deaths of officers in urban America.[20] Only lack of evidence kept Nation suspects out of jail, proclaimed Brown.[21] Further, and ironically, authorities in Alabama believed that NOI leaders were closely connected with the SNCC and Martin Luther King Jr.'s Southern Christian Leadership Conference (SCLC).[22] The tenor of the times tainted any pro-black group as political rabble-rousers, and the police and federal government imagined all kinds of unlawful conspiracies to dismantle their power.

But it is also true that the NOI's direct opposition to white supremacy was itself radical. This was the NOI's magnet, its black nationalist core. The NOI's lethal critiques of white power emboldened members to support and trust its leadership. As they joined temples (renamed mosques in 1962) around the country, they chose to accept a moral lifestyle and dedicate themselves to personal discipline.

Still, as we have seen, this moral lifestyle was largely rooted in traditional gender roles. The expectations for women remained highly demanding. Above all, each woman who entered the NOI, and who stayed committed for an extended period of time, had to answer the call to marry and to have children. Women were taught to be supportive housewives and good mothers. This meant, among other things, not practicing birth control. Elijah Muhammad believed that black women should not want to be liberated from having children; it was their duty to follow the biological laws of creation and reproduce the black nation. Further, women were expected to dress modestly and wear a headscarf. The exact teachings were that a "single sister could have a scarf on but once you got married you completely covered your hair with nothing showing at all."[23] Women's work also served to support their husbands and the Nation of Islam, rather than constitute a means of independence.

On the flip side, of course, men were instructed to both provide for and protect their families. The traditional patriarchal idea had always reigned supreme in the NOI; yet Elijah Muhammad patterned his notions of manhood and womanhood on a paradigm rarely financially achievable for black families. Class differences always influenced the possibilities and limits of attaining this goal.

Marriage

When Sister Belinda Boyd (later Khalilah Ali) married Brother Muhammad Ali (formerly Cassius Clay) on August 17, 1967, many Americans had their first introduction to a NOI woman. While Sister Clara Muhammad and her daughter Sister Ethel Sharrieff were respected and influential among NOI women, neither had the kind of public image nor photogenic currency of Sister Belinda, who graced the covers of *Ebony* magazine seven times with her husband, producing the first popular representation of Nation womanhood.

Sister Belinda was Ali's second wife. Devastated that his first marriage to Sonji Roi, whom he had wed in 1964, had lasted less than a year, Ali selected Sister

Belinda because "he just wanted a woman who was a good Muslim and would be a good wife."[24] She was seventeen years old when they married.

Sister Belinda had been raised in the NOI, though her family was not typical. Her father, Brother Raymond, was the first lieutenant of the F.O.I. for the Honorable Elijah Muhammad. Her mother, Sister Inez (later Aminah), worked in the temple as a security person, and as a companion to the "first lady" of the Nation, Sister Clara Muhammad. Smart and formally educated, Sister Inez also wanted to work outside of the home, and outside of the Nation. In a compromise that allowed her some latitude while still asserting his appropriate role as provider, Brother Raymond told her, "if you want to work you can, but you don't have to."[25] Sister Inez secured a job at an apparel store in downtown Chicago.

Through her parents, Sister Belinda had already been close to the Muhammad Royal Family. When her mother began to work, she gained her own unique access to their Chicago world. The Boyds needed childcare for Belinda, and Elijah Muhammad had offered a solution: "Bring your child [Belinda] to my house and she can be with my grandchildren."[26] Sister Belinda recalled that Muhammad had her "watching the kids and they were a little older than [she, which] was weird."[27] Sister Halimah Muhammad recalled that when her "grandparents [Clara and Elijah] had special events and dinners at the house [Belinda] would come and help us."[28]

Sister Inez and her husband had joined the NOI during the late 1940s, and both were noted for living "good clean [Muslim] lives" with "no hypocrisy."[29] They poured into their daughter Belinda those same virtues. Sister Belinda attended the University of Islam in Chicago from kindergarten to twelfth grade, and she loved her school. It was here that she first met Cassius Clay. Sister Christine Johnson, the school's principal, had invited him to an assembly after he had won the 1960 Olympic gold medal.

As he handed out autographed photos, Sister Belinda recalled confronting him with the questions, "Your name is Cassius Clay? Like mud? Like dirt?" She continued, "Brother, come back when you get a real name. Then we can talk."[30] Ten-year-old Belinda was deeply committed to the Nation's teachings.[31]

By the age of fourteen, Belinda was striking, close to six feet tall, with shoulder-length hair, almond-shaped eyes, cocoa brown skin, and a dazzling smile. It had been rumored for years that Clay was planning to pledge allegiance to Elijah Muhammad's teachings. As he prepared for his February 25, 1964, fight with Charles (Sonny) Liston, Sister Belinda saw him again and recalled giving him a poem. Any young man would have been taken by her beauty, and Clay had to notice that she also looked athletic, despite the Nation's teaching against sport

Heavyweight boxer Muhammad Ali flirts with Belinda Boyd in a Nation of Islam bakery shop, Chicago, Ill., 1966. (Thomas Hoepker, Magnum Photos)

and amusement. A self-described tomboy, Belinda enjoyed riding horses, playing tennis, softball, and basketball.[32] In another compromise with the strictest dictates of the NOI, she had learned these sports during the University of Islam's annual two-week vacation at the tail end of August. Like many Chicagoans who had migrated from Mississippi, her father would drive the family home, where the Boyds grew wheat, cotton, and watermelon. There at the family compound, Sister Belinda got to play by different rules: she "got to wear pants down there to ride horses and go fishing, and hunting." In Mississippi she "got [her] freedom," recalled Sister Belinda.[33]

Full of youthful energy and on the cusp of graduating high school, at age seventeen Sister Belinda worked behind the counter at a popular NOI bakery shop in Chicago. She wanted to work and had her mother as a role model. A stickler for providing excellent customer service, she outsold many of her peers because she took her job seriously. It was at the bakery that she once again saw the man whom she had scolded for embracing the slave name of Clay. All Nation members knew that he had officially confirmed his membership the day after the 1964 fight, and that their teacher and leader, the Honorable Elijah Muhammad, had given him the Arabic name Muhammad Ali. It would have been difficult for Ali not to notice Sister Belinda when he went into the bakery. He had a flirtatious reputation at the age of twenty-five, and she made him smile and laugh out loud.[34] Ali was soon smitten and visited the bakery so often that Sister Belinda mastered "talking and acting just like him."[35]

Apparently, Ali also appreciated the challenge that Sister Belinda posed. It was reported that she had "never been to a movie, never been out alone in the dark without her parents, never traveled by bus, [and] never smoked."[36] Belinda lived by the Honorable Elijah Muhammad's moral teachings as well, and remained a virgin until her marriage. Recalling her formative years, she said, "And you could talk about my mama and my daddy, but you better not talk about Elijah Muhammad."[37]

Sister Belinda and Ali's courtship shows her taking an active role as a female while still following a more traditional script. Ali's travel schedule made it impossible for them to have dates with the appropriate chaperoning by the MGT-GCC and FOI Captains. The telephone proved essential to their courtship. He would call her before some fights, and Sister Belinda recalled him saying, "You know, sister, a lot of people want me to lose because I'm a Muslim. What do you think?" Confident in herself and her religion, she replied, "Brother, God can't put you in top condition; that's up to you. Do your training, be dedicated, don't take any shortcuts. And if you do everything you can and say your prayers, Allah will help you the rest of the way. With his blessings, you can't lose."[38] Ali was encouraged by her and said, "Okay, I like those words; I'll whup this guy for you."[39] After he won, he called Belinda on the phone to tell her. Reflecting later on her attraction to Ali, Sister Belinda said, "We were similar, alike. When you want to go after something you go get it, you believe in something, you stick with it."[40]

Ali never asked Sister Belinda to marry him. "He told me," she said. Sister Belinda recalled him saying, "'You're gonna be my wife,' and she replied, 'Right,' and that was it."[41] The ceremony, like all Nation marriages, was conducted by a licensed representative of the state, who rarely was a temple minister. In their case, he was a Baptist preacher, and their wedding was private, with Sister Belinda wearing a traditional white dress, a lovely, cascading shoulder-length veil, and a simple strand of pearls. Ali was decked out in a black suit and Elijah Muhammad's signature bow tie. Herbert Muhammad, Ali's manager and handler, as well as the son of Sister Clara and Elijah Muhammad, served as the best man. The young couple married on August 17, 1967, several months after Ali had been stripped of his boxing license and heavyweight champion title because of his refusal to be inducted into the United States Army. Ali was Belinda's "first love."[42]

Muhammad Ali marries seventeen-year-old Belinda Boyd in a ceremony in his home in Chicago, August 18, 1967. Performing the marriage is Dr. Morris H. Tynes, minister of the First Church of the Master. At his left is best man Herbert Muhammad. (Associated Press)

During the first months of their marriage, it took Sister Belinda some time to get used to having a disposable income. She had been trained to sew her own clothes at the junior MGT-GCC classes, so felt no need to shop for them. The Philadelphia Minister Jeremiah Shabazz recalled an occasion when Ali gave her $100 to buy herself something nice. Unable to "figure out how to spend the whole hundred dollars," she "bought a tie" for her husband and several blouses for herself and had about $30 left.[43] Sister Belinda "never did get used to having money," said Shabazz.[44] Nevertheless, it was Ali's money that gave her the option of not working outside the home after marriage, or even for the NOI. Ali was Elijah Muhammad's traditional patriarch — provider and protector — and Belinda gave the public the impression that she was an ideally docile and submissive wife. During their honeymoon in New York and Boston reports claimed that "she never complains, and accepts her husband's decisions in everything, down to her clothes and jewelry accessories."[45] Sister Belinda had been groomed to believe that Muslim wives "stay in the background."

Sister Eula Foreman (later Waheedah Muhammad) was married the same year as Sister Belinda, but far from the spotlight that followed Muhammad Ali's every move. Though not raised in the NOI, Sister Eula, too, took Elijah Muhammad's teachings seriously. For her, marriage was less about a mutual attraction than a decision about where her life needed to go. She had been a member of Newark Mosque No. 25, for just one year before marrying Brother Herbert Hickman (later Musa Muhammad). Sister Eula had migrated to New Jersey from Roxbel, North Carolina, after graduating high school in 1966. Her two older sisters, Emma and Dorthoria, had joined the NOI in New Jersey in 1960 and 1961. When they returned to Roxbel for visits, they shared Muhammad's teachings with their North Carolina family. Sister Eula wrote twice for her "X" while still in high school, and occasionally her brother would drive the family to the nearest temple in Norfolk, Virginia. But Eula also felt attracted to the "bright lights and the fast life" in New Jersey. During the summer months, she would visit her sisters there, and she relished having indoor running water: dirt roads, outhouses, and outside water pumps were common in Roxbel. Sister Eula enjoyed life in New Jersey, having "things right at your fingertips,"[46] and was determined to move there to "learn what life [was] about." Still, relocation proved difficult. She was unable to find "good work," and the temptations were many. Sister Eula believed that "if it had not been for God's will for me to come into Islam I probably would have been on the streets somewhere" in New Jersey.[47] Going to the mosque regularly gave her a purposeful routine, because they "didn't give you a lot of time to be out there."[48] Sister Eula would come to credit the NOI with saving her life.[49]

When Brother Herbert pursued her, as the men were instructed to do, Sister Eula initially showed no interest. But with the encouragement of an older mosque sister, Brother Herbert persisted. The more experienced sister told Brother Herbert not to give up: "Ask her again to just go and have a meeting with her mother."[50] (By this time, Sister Eula's mother had also joined the NOI and moved to New Jersey.) Eventually, Sister Eula relented, and she and Brother Herbert were chaperoned at every turn. It did not take long for Sister Eula to think, "maybe that's what I should do"—get married—and "then I won't have to worry" about work, because she would be "able to stay at home."[51] They married in 1967 and had the first of six children in 1968. Elijah Muhammad's Nation required strong black families, grounded in gendered roles, and Sister Eula and Brother Herbert were serious about living up to his standards.

A *Nation of Working Women*

Both Sister Belinda and Sister Eula, whose husband was self-employed selling clothes and jewelry, were able to live up to Muhammad's ideal of male provider, female homemaker. It seemed reconstituting NOI families to resemble patriarchal upper- and middle-class households was the Honorable Elijah Muhammad's mission. But one of the biggest misconceptions of Nation women during this period — helped, no doubt, by the public image of Sister Belinda — is that they did not work beyond the home. Most black families in the 1960s and early 1970s, including those who populated the NOI's mosques, were working class, and economic conditions forced black women to labor both inside and outside of their homes.

For some NOI women, work for the Nation supplemented their husbands' earnings. The leadership approved these efforts — indeed, the Nation could hardly have gotten by without the women's work. Women toiled as secretaries for the NOI, sewed clothes in the Nation factories, baked pies and bread for Nation bakeries, cooked at the Nation restaurants, served as cashiers at the Nation department and grocery stores, taught school at the University of Islam, made fish byproducts for the Nation's Whiting H & G Fish Company, wrote articles for the Nation's newspaper, *Muhammad Speaks*, and performed countless other duties to build the NOI. We do not have records of how they felt about their work, but clearly they were not simply submissive homemakers.

Yet working hard for the NOI did not always guarantee a much-needed income. Sister Doris 9X (later Doris Shahrokhimanesh), who made fish sausages in a cold storage freezer for Mosque #26 (San Francisco), recalled that it was common to alternate paying the women. If the single women were paid one week, the married women would be paid the next.[52] The wages were low, and she never received more than $60 a week during the early 1970s, when a minimum-wage employee earned at least $64.[53]

Other Nation members, including women, were spurred by Mr. Muhammad's echo of Marcus Garvey's mantra, "you can accomplish what you will," as well as his own command that his followers "do for self" to establish independent businesses. Sister Sara Sharrieff (S. Alimah Sharif) and her husband Brother Sammy Sharrieff (Jalal Najjar Sharrieff) led the way in Detroit by opening Sharrieff's Department Store on Linwood near Mosque No. 1 in the early 1960s. Sister Sara recalled that initially a group of members pooled their funds for a store, but then "everyone backed out." Sister Sara "was determined to make it happen because [she] wanted something for [her] children to inherit." While

Brother Sammy worked full-time at a cement company, Sister Sara took charge of the store. Six days a week she sold coats, suits, consignment goods, shoes, jewelry, and candy for children who would pass the store on their way to school. Every evening after closing, she went home and cooked a large dinner for her family. They ate "a lot of bean dishes," and she made bread twice a week. A mother of ten, she had had five children before her NOI membership and five thereafter. Sister Sara said that initially "Minister Wilfred didn't think [she] would be able to do it because of the children."[54] With the support of another MGT-GCC sister, who would babysit her youngest children, Sister Sara managed her family store until it closed in 1971.

Still, not everyone had Sister Sara's desire, drive, or management acumen. Moreover, lack of financial resources limited the establishment of independent NOI businesses. These conditions spurred some women to seek employment outside of the Nation. For them, the best option in terms of acceptance from the NOI leadership was to perform work commonly understood as an extension of the domestic sphere. The enforcement of the Equal Employment Opportunity (EEO) legislation contributed to black women's possibilities to work beyond domestic service. A high school diploma opened the door to the secretarial pool. Nation women earned higher wages as secretaries, stenographers, and typists than domestics or those working for the NOI.

Women who ventured farther afield risked disapproval or obstruction from leadership. Sister Gwendolyn 2X (Zoharrah Simmons) worked for the National Council for Negro Women (NCNW) as the Midwest region coordinator for Project Woman Power. A former SNCC activist, Sister Gwendolyn 2X recruited and trained low-income African American women for social change. Though she lived in Chicago with her husband, Brother Michael (Simmons), traveling alone was an essential component of her work. Her territory included Cleveland, Elyria, and Rain in Ohio; Detroit; and Chicago. She would "sometimes run into a buzz saw" with NOI leadership, she later recalled, because to visit a mosque in a different city you had to apply for a travel letter. Brother and sister captains at each mosque questioned her activities. After she explained her job, she would often meet with resistance: "A lot of them had difficulty with it."[55] Sister Gwendolyn 2X, however, knew that she "had more leeway than other [Nation] women" because her brother-in-law was John Ali (formerly Simmons), the national secretary of the NOI. He represented the upper echelons of leadership, and Sister Gwendolyn 2X recalled that "word came down that this woman is different. This is her job and she has to do this."[56] In this case intervention from a male leader served as Sister Gwendolyn 2X's "protection." When "word" came from Brother John Ali, said Sister Gwendolyn 2X, that "they better leave me alone, they were going to leave me alone, believe you me."[57]

Family Planning

Sister Gwendolyn 2X challenged Nation leadership in other ways as well. For one thing, she never wore the MGT-GCC uniform, headscarf, or "anything that showed [she] was a Muslim or was with the Nation" while she worked.[58] Many of the women were Christians, and she did not want her religion to be "a deterrent" to her ability to organize women in these communities.[59] But she was not alone in avoiding the headscarf. It was common for Nation women to dress modestly, but many did not wear a headscarf at work.[60] Even women working at NOI jobs did not feel it was inappropriate to go to work without a headscarf. From Sister Belinda Boyd's photographs at a Chicago Bakery; to photos of women working at the Nation's Clothing Factory; to the principal-director of the University of Islam in Chicago, Sister Christine; to First Lady Clara Muhammad, a strong pictorial narrative of NOI women runs the gamut between sisters having no scarf, wearing a scarf stylishly to show a hairstyle, to completely covering their hair.[61]

There was yet another way Sister Gwendolyn 2X ignored core Muslim teachings. One reason that she could do the work she did was that she had only one child; during her five years of Nation membership (1967–1972) Sister Gwendolyn 2X used birth control.[62] In 1965, the Supreme Court protected married couples' right to privacy in using birth control. (Single women were legally denied the same choice.) But this legal right stood in stark contrast to Elijah Muhammad's teachings. He maintained that birth control was a scheme promulgated by whites to eliminate future black families. Indeed, when the Supreme Court's 1973 decision in *Roe v. Wade* legalized abortion, Muhammad named it a further plot by the devil to shore up the birth-control pill, which was not enough to stop all conceptions. It was a sign of the "fall of America." He and Sister Dorothy Wedad used the fact that many black women were victims of forced sterilization to further condemn family-planning methods. Sister Dorothy urged all black women to come into the NOI, because "tomorrow may be too late to save you from permanent sterilization by this beast."[63] In his book *Message to the Blackman in America*, Muhammad asked, "Who wants a sterile woman?," implying that no black man would.[64]

Despite Muhammad's invective against birth control, Minister Malcolm X, his most popular representative, agreed to have a conversation with Planned

Parenthood representatives in Harlem as early as 1962. This would later become significant in light of a future rift between the two leaders; Minister Malcolm X knew that rumors of sexual misconduct were scarring Muhammad's reputation, causing large numbers of followers to leave Mosque #2. Minister Malcolm X was determined to keep the Nation going and growing. His interview with Marian Hernandez, director of the Harlem Planned Parenthood Clinic, and the field consultant Wylda Cowles offers a more complex view of the intimate lives of NOI married couples than Muhammad's proscriptions. First of all, Minister Malcolm said that there was nothing in the NOI teachings "that would discourage members" from "practicing family planning."[65] He opposed "birth control" as a term and suggested to Hernandez and Cowles that their organization would be "more successful" if they gestured toward "family planning," because "people, particularly Negroes, would be more willing to plan than to be controlled."[66] Second, Minister Malcolm X gave the impression that Nation couples used either "the rhythm method or coitus interruptus." These were techniques that required discipline, said Minister Malcolm X, and "we are a disciplined people."[67]

At the close of the interview, Minister Malcolm X agreed to arrange for Hernandez and Cowles to meet Harlem MGT-GCC Captain Clotelle (Scott), opening the door for Nation women to be formally introduced to contraception. Minister Malcolm was apparently a bit unsure about the technical aspects of the rhythm method, which raised questions for Hernandez and Cowles about the "possibility of a discrepancy between theory and practice" in the NOI. He wanted to make sure that Nation women had the knowledge to plan their children.

In identifying Sister Clotelle to attend Planned Parenthood sessions in Harlem, Minister Malcolm X selected someone dedicated to changing the situation of Nation women. He had recommended her to Elijah Muhammad in 1958 to serve as the sister captain in Mosque #7. Sister Clotelle had become a believer in 1957 and brought to the NOI formal schooling in "tailoring, cosmetology and culinary arts" from Brainerd Institute in Chester, South Carolina.[68] The NOI women under her leadership were noted for being the "opposite of the myth that Black Muslim women were meant to be docile and unlettered and to 'just make babies.'"[69] She guided women on the importance of seeing themselves as "leaders, entrepreneurs, educators, property owners, informed mothers and wives."[70] During the 1960s and 1970s, Sister Captain Clotelle had the reputation of knowing "how to cement a family."[71]

Interviews with NOI women confirm that many did their best to employ the natural methods taught at the MGT-GCC classes, but they also indicate that women understood this to be a matter for their own self-determination. Sister

Hafeeza of Washington, D.C., recalled how she was told to extend the breast-feeding of her baby, count ovulation days, and to take her temperature.[72] But she also noted that having multiple births "like cattle" was not healthy.[73] Sister Mary Tarver, who lived in Syracuse, New York, said, "I wasn't taking any pills, and we tried the natural way, and then we used a condom."[74] Sister Beatrice Muhammad of Durham, North Carolina, said, "I wanted to try the natural way first, but you get to a point where . . . okay, every other year now I'm having a baby. . . . I need a little help."[75]

Reflecting on the NOI climate, Sister Beatrice recalled "sometimes people talked about it, and sometimes people didn't talk about it, but it's one of those things where you have to do what's best for yourself, because [sic] come down to it, you're the one who's going to have to shoulder the responsibility."[76] She believed that it was a woman's decision and that one had to consider her own health history to know her birthing "limit."[77] Insightfully reasoning that "a lot of these rules were written by men, and they are not the ones having all of these babies," gave her the wisdom to know that three children were her limit.[78]

Sister Ruth of Durham remembered that her MGT-GCC captain taught them "not to go through a lot of marriages, and not to have a lot of children . . . she didn't teach us just to lay up and have children."[79] Honoring one's body was an important lesson. This is why, Sister Ruth said, "they were on birth control. They were controlling having those children. Cause the majority that I know now, they might have had two or three children, or one."[80] Indeed, when Sister Eula of New Jersey relocated for a brief period to Birmingham in 1977, she was surprised by what "looked like the norm, that none of them had a lot of children."[81] Sister Eula said in New Jersey "breastfeeding was encouraged and that could be one way to keep yourself from being pregnant every year and that was about it."[82] Moreover, she was "told that it was un-Islamic to not go ahead and have as many children, as you possibly could. Because that was Allah's blessing for you."[83] A mother of six children, four sons (1968, 1969, 1970, 1974) and two daughters (1972, 1975), Sister Eula did not try to keep from having children, but even she, during her last pregnancy, "prayed the whole nine months" that her baby "would be a girl because then [she] knew it was Allah's permission for [her] to stop having children."[84] Coincidentally, the birth of her daughter in 1975 paralleled the New Jersey Supreme Court ruling in favor of Judith Ponter, who had challenged the policy requiring spousal consent for a sterilization operation, popularly known as tubular ligature. Exercising her constitutional right, Sister Eula returned to the hospital six weeks later and had her "tubes tied. I was like, this is it, I am done."[85] She agreed with Sister Beatrice that every woman knows her limit.[86]

Increasing Pressures

While women took their own approaches to family planning, when it came to financial planning, they had joined an organization that had promised their men would take responsibility. In fact, Sister Eula remembered that Elijah's Muhammad's "bottom line" was that brothers had to "take care of those sisters"— so "she will not have to work; she is to maintain the home."[87] A sister employed beyond the bounds of the Nation could theoretically signal to Muhammad, and others who agreed with his teachings, that her husband was falling short on his household responsibilities. Yet in other ways the Nation's requirements for men worked against the very promise it made. For instance, each man was responsible for selling copies of the *Mr. Muhammad Speaks* newspaper, which first rolled off the press in May 1960.[88] Despite their efforts, too many fell short of the Nation's goals for them; thus, the Nation leadership instituted a directive that required them to purchase copies first, and then work to sell them. On average, each man spent $60 a month with the hope of earning his cash back.[89] As Brother Benjamin 2X (Goodman) recalled, "the competition" to sell the newspapers became "fierce and the weekly payments a burden. Each week you'd see more papers stacked up in your closet. It was discouraging."[90] Unsold newspapers had to be kept in the home; as Sister Doris 9X of San Francisco recalled, "You better not throw them away because if they saw them in the garbage, you had to answer for that."[91]

In addition, families had to tithe and give a mandatory "donation" of $100 for the annual Saviour's Day Convention celebrated on February 26 in Chicago. The pressure to raise money fell squarely on the registered members.[92] "Work, work, work, work," echoed throughout the mosques. As Sister Doris 9X lamented, "you could never sell enough!"[93]

By 1974, the requirements for Nation men came into even more direct conflict with their duty to provide for their families. One Sunday in the San Francisco Mosque No. 26, Minister Jael announced, "Brothers, the Honorable Elijah Muhammad needs you to push his program. He wants you to give up the white man jobs."[94] Sister Doris 9X remembers him saying, "Do something for yourself. Walk, brothers. Don't worry about your families. Allah will provide for them."[95] With the roar of Minister Jael's voice, Nation men stood up from their seats and Sister Doris 9X could not believe that "they acted so proud to have the guts to walk off the white man's jobs."[96] She was shocked when her husband, Brother John 24X, stood up as well. And, she was confused when sisters began to pat her on her back and tell her that she should be proud of her husband's courage.

In the privacy of their home, Sister Doris 9X questioned her husband about his decision. His only response was that he was "doing [it] for Allah and the Honorable Elijah Muhammad."[97] He quit his bus-driving job to sell *Muhammad Speaks* and Whiting H & G fish, as well as to guard Minister Jael's home. Thirty days later bill collectors called asking for payments, and the family's home went into foreclosure three months thereafter. Sister Doris 9X's dreams of a stable home and a husband who would provide were going up in smoke after less than a year of marriage.

Sister Doris 9X and Brother John 24X had begun courting six months after her 1972 conversion at Mosque No. 26. He was tall, 6' 7", and when he first looked at her, she immediately lowered her eyes as she had been taught to do at the MGT-GCC class. She had the feeling that he would inquire about her to the brother captain, and he did. They were chaperoned by married couples and enjoyed functions with other NOI members at the mosque. Although their activities were supervised, and going though appropriate channels was still required, Sister Doris 9X remembers that they were given permission to join one another for dinner. Generally the interaction took between three and six months to determine a couple's suitability. In their case they married after eight months, on September 15, 1973, at the home of an older NOI couple. A Christian minister performed the ceremony. Sister Doris 9X explained that Minister Jael was not ordained and thus could only teach Elijah Muhammad's vision and the truth of Allah. They enjoyed their very first kiss at the conclusion of their vows, and their first sexual encounter happened on their honeymoon, a trip to Disneyland in Anaheim, California.

Sister Doris 9X was pleased that her new husband moved her and her daughter from a previous relationship out of their roach-infested Oakland apartment.[98] Brother John 24X had changed her life and she was happy. He bought a home in Daly City, San Francisco, the Southern Hills area, as a wedding gift and led their daily 5:00 A.M. prayer, the first of five. She was determined to put all of her MGT-GCC training to good use. Preparing one meal a day, she labored to make it tasty for her family. Sharing recipes with the other sisters expanded her dinner repertoire. She cooked fish loaf and dressing, bean soup, asparagus casserole, barbecued lamb chops, baked okra, corn pudding, and carrot pies. Additionally, she kept the house clean and made sure to take care of all of her daughter's needs before Brother John 24X came home.

But all of Sister Doris 9X's household management could not relieve her husband of overwork. Increasing the sales of *Muhammad Speaks* beyond the designated fifty, and other demands kept him, and many other Nation men, fatigued. Sister Doris 9X wrote, "By the time the wives see their husbands their ability to function with the family is long gone."[99] As Brother John 24X came home later and later, Sister Doris 9X put pressure on him to spend more time with her. But as she put it, "He gave one hundred percent to the Nation of Islam." When he quit his employment for the movement in 1974, she knew it was the final blow for her marriage.[100] The "welfare line had captured" her again.[101]

She wasn't the only one. A lot of NOI women were "leaning on the mother Nation [federal government]," said Sister Doris 9X, getting food stamps, having babies on Medicaid, and living in low-income housing.[102] Given Elijah Muhammad's teachings, a NOI family on welfare should have been an oxymoron. For many, welfare signaled utter dependence on the white man. Muhammad and his ministers admonished men to stand up and take control of their women and homes. Yet some of these same ministers told the sisters, "Whatever we can get from the white, blue-eyed devil is owed to us in one form or another."[103] Sister Doris 9X filed for divorce, which was finalized on May 8, 1974.

Trumping Patriarchy

The NOI did not frown on divorce. Elijah Muhammad's teachings were novel in this regard. Whereas in Shi'a and Sunni Islam it is extremely difficult for a woman to successfully sue for divorce, Muhammad wrote that if one was deserted by a spouse one should not worry but should "forget about them and pray to Allah to give you one better than that one. And, if you are a good Believer, He will."[104] Although it is impossible to figure out the divorce rate, the procedure was common.[105] Women understanding that they could opt out of a difficult marriage gave them room to reinvent their lives within the Nation—even if children could complicate the decision to separate. Although Sister Doris 9X considered that "my almighty Muslim Nation had failed," she did not leave the NOI after her divorce.[106]

Nation women who did not desire divorce had the other option of taking control without appearing to. Women were not supposed to be the leaders in their families, but often enough they had to break the rules of the patriarchy in order, ultimately, to support it. In other words, they learned to trump patriarchy.

Whether it meant shielding her husband from a direct confrontation about his not fully providing for the family or taking control to ensure family stability, trumping patriarchy was a choice a woman might need depending on whom she married and how he earned a living. Sister Eula, for example, was well supported financially. She was able to stay at home until her youngest began to attend school. This did not mean her life was easy: her husband's work kept him on the road for weeks at a time, leaving her to function for long stretches as a single parent of six children. When her husband was at home she was confident in what she knew, communicated with him in a direct style, and "made sure he pulled his share."[107] Sister Eula did not bake, and her husband knew he had to buy the family's cakes. She also did not sew, and because of her husband's occupation, he "knew how to shop."[108] She recalled that he would not only purchase the children's clothes but hers as well when she was having children.[109] She put effort into carving out a balanced household, and her husband appreciated what she did in his absence. And she gave herself a well-deserved motherhood break when she could, with no apologies: sometimes, Sister Eula remembered, "as soon as he walked in the door," she said, "I am leaving and I will be back in a little while."[110]

Sister Doris 9X was not so lucky. By June of 1975, a year after her divorce from Brother John 24X, she was preparing to marry Brother Mahad. Because Brother Mahad could not fully support Sister Doris 9X and her daughter, they agreed that she would continue to accept welfare. This seemed necessary to prop up his manhood, even if it proved a wobbly, three-legged stool. Two years later, in 1977, Sister Doris 9X alone was charged with welfare fraud, and she received a three-fold sentence: three years' probation, the payment of $4,799.48 to the welfare system, and six months in jail, all time suspended, except for ten days.[111] As she drove to the Redwood City Jail, Sister Doris 9X, thought, "If this was the price I had to pay for accepting less from a marriage in the Nation of Islam and hide the fact that some of the Muslim wives were suffering to maintain the honor of their Muslim husbands, so be it."[112]

Other women were able to trump patriarchy at less cost to themselves, building up the ego, the spirit, and the will of their husbands. Sister Belinda Ali stands as a powerful example. As the wife of an international celebrity, Sister Belinda knew that it was largely through her that Americans became introduced to NOI women. Although she seldom said anything publicly, photographers were drawn to her beauty. The press described her as a woman "who will never have to go to the beauty shop."[113] Acutely aware of her public persona, Sister Belinda understood that it was not her, but the entire black Muslim womanhood that the public gazed on. Her pictorial representation went a long way in terms of making the NOI a welcoming religion for women. Moreover, everywhere she and Ali went, their photos were published in *Muhammad Speaks*. Readers also wanted to keep up with Sister Belinda. When she became pregnant, it was announced in the newspaper and when she turned eighteen, a photo of her eating birthday cake with Ali was featured.[114] The birth of their first child, Maryum, on June 17, 1968, was also celebrated among the readership. Born in Chicago at the South Shore Community Hospital, their "plump infant girl" had her photos serialized in *Muhammad Speaks* "in response to numerous calls and requests for additional photos of Sister Belinda ['s] and Muhammad Ali's first baby."[115]

At times Sister Belinda felt the weight of being the popular image, yet because she was "not acting" in terms of living the life of a Nation woman, it eased the pressure. She knew that she needed to look a certain way: "Woman can be powerful at home, but in public, that's not the wife's way." But that did not mean she subordinated herself entirely. "I did the talking in the house."[116]

In the privacy of their home, Sister Belinda was faced with a husband unsure about his professional future after the suspension of his license. She recalled, "It was tough for him. He was depressed most of the time. He was unhappy. He did not know what the hell was going to happen to him."[117] How does a wife talk to her temperamental patriarchal husband when in theory he wields all the power? Trumping patriarchy meant using one's own ingenuity to manipulate social relations steeped in structured power. As Sister Belinda explained, "Manipulation is not always bad; it's a form of devotion, a form of power to help and inspire and give a man drive."[118] Essentially, trumping patriarchy disrupted the man-power landscape to secure enough authority for short-term leadership. Committed to keeping Ali on track for what was most important, his family, Sister Belinda initiated the "campaign to make him the people's champ so folks could get behind him getting his license back."[119] As Ali worried about going to jail, Sister Belinda "had faith that the boxing industry could not resist making money off him."[120]

Sister Belinda became Ali's unofficial publicist and circulated stickers and buttons sealed with his photo that she had made. Working like a campaign manager, she would get the attention of the press, including that of sports journalists Dick Schaap and Howard Cosell, on her husband's behalf. She kept their phone numbers in her purse and would phone them or send a note indicating where she and Ali would be. When the press was in tow, however, Sister Belinda had no public words. She consciously "didn't say anything. Sometimes, people would ask Ali, 'Does your wife speak English?' And he'd tell them, 'Yes, but she don't say nothing. There can't be but one big mouth in the family.'" "I liked it that way," claimed Sister Belinda.[121] Certainly, she was able to accommodate this public performance because of her domestic power and ability to trump patriarchy in the obliging spirit of maintaining their family.

Understanding that a steady stream of money was needed, Sister Belinda encouraged Ali to seize opportunities to speak at college campuses for an honorarium.[122] Although he was eight years older than she, Sister Belinda admitted that she "was a bit smarter than him and a little more educated, too."[123] Ali's early speeches largely consisted of him repeating Muhammad's dictates as published in *Muhammad Speaks* (for example, "What We Want, What We Believe"), and listeners described them as boring.[124] He complained to his wife that he also faced being called a "Nigger draft-dodger" at public talks.[125] At this point they had no money, and Sister Belinda knew that they had to make this work. She told her husband, "Brother, all you got to do is fight fire with fire. Next time, you go up there and someone heckles you like that, put him down."[126] She also offered, "I can write the speeches and you can speak the speeches."[127] She had the ability to tell a story with a good sense of humor. Sister Belinda's childhood friends Halimah and Wali Muhammad harkened back to the days that she "was always making things up," suggesting that "she would make a great writer" because she had a "great imagination."[128] Soon Ali was noted for giving fantastic lectures that still toed the NOI line. The engagements booked by Sister Belinda would earn $1,500 to $2,000 each.[129] Years later, when Sister Belinda recited a popular Ali poem on *The John Lewis Show*, the host remarked, "Ali, you have been fooling a lot of us like you were writing the poetry, now we know the real deal."[130]

On the lecture circuit the talks embellished a variety of themes, including the financial hardship that Sister Belinda and Ali were experiencing because he was unlicensed to box. He said, "My wife is such a good cook I never go to a restaurant. I give her twenty dollars for a whole week and it's enough for her. We can eat on three dollars a day."[131] Unbeknownst to Ali, however, his wife was using her college savings, which her parents had labored to squirrel away for her, to supplement his income during the blossoming years of their marriage.[132] Yet she "never let him know because [she] did not want him to feel bad as a man."[133] In practice, Sister Belinda and other NOI wives who learned to trump patriarchy had to closely read their husbands' dispositions to carefully guide how to make them responsible for their families without chipping away at their manliness. Thus trumping did not mean to completely topple patriarchy. On the contrary, it served Sister Belinda as an avenue to safeguard it.

In addition to sustaining their family and finances, Sister Belinda also had to step up to save their religious home. On April 4, 1969, it was reported in *Muhammad Speaks* that the Honorable Elijah Muhammad had suspended Ali for one year because of his plea that he wanted to box again to earn money. Ali already functioned as an exceptional member of the NOI due to his profession. Muhammad wrote, "This statement is to tell the world that we, the Muslims, are not with Mr. Muhammad Ali, in his desire to work in the sports world for the sake of a 'leetle' money. Allah has power over the heavens and the earth. He is sufficient for us."[134] Ali received a "Class C suspension." Because a husband and wife were considered one, Sister Belinda also suffered from the suspension. She had never been suspended, and although she refused to be "cut off from [her] parents" because she "would not listen to that part" and "nobody messed with me," it still felt like "torture."[135] She experienced the isolation from her friends and her inability to go to the mosque as a "death sentence."[136] Eventually, Sister Belinda wrote directly to Muhammad, stating, "If I had known that this man was going to do that, I would have never married him" and requested to "please be reinstated."[137] To her surprise, Muhammad agreed, and said to "bring your husband, too."[138]

Husband management became a lifestyle for Sister Belinda during the early years of her marriage. She walked a tightrope, taking control for fleeting periods to trump patriarchy, both as a form of self-preservation and in the service of perpetuating it.

It is important to note that Muhammad never suspended his son Herbert, who worked as Ali's manager and was the one trying to secure the fights.[139] Throughout the 1960s and into the 1970s, Muhammad's self-interest became more and more blatant. How the Royal Family fits into the story of NOI women is the subject of the next chapter.

CHAPTER EIGHT

THE ROYAL FAMILY

S ister Clara, the Honorable Elijah Muhammad, and their children constituted the Royal Family of the NOI. At one time or another, all of the children worked actively for the Nation. By their example and through their work, the whole family influenced the lives of women in the NOI.

For example, Sister Clara's two daughters, Lottie and Ethel, actively shaped how women experienced the NOI during the 1960s and 1970s. Most noted of the two was MGT Supreme Captain Ethel. In many ways, Sister Ethel modeled taking women's designated, gendered work to a higher, or at least more profitable, level. The mother of five children, she also is credited with starting the first NOI bakery, Eat Ethel's Pasteries, at Thirty-first Street and Wentworth Avenue in Chicago.[1] Her second husband, whom she married in 1948, FOI Supreme Captain Raymond Sharrieff, recalled that "she baked bread with her own hands without a mixer."[2] Sister Ethel also had the idea for the MGT-GCC clothing factory, which began in her home basement and eventually moved to Seventy-ninth Street.[3] Brother Albi recalled that "The M.G.T. in her time were into emulating Sister Ethel's walk, her talk, and her grace, she was very, very noble."[4]

In addition, Sister Ethel's daughter, Sister Sharon, recalled that she "worked quietly to influence her father's strict restrictions on women."[5] For example, Sister Sharon explained that her mother not only suggested that "her father relax dress codes that required headdress and jackets at all times" for women but she also "told women to walk beside the men, not behind them."[6] At rare moments she would even confront her father directly. When Sister Ethel's daughters were planning their weddings, Elijah Muhammad tried to seize the opportunity to showcase the NOI. He suggested a lavish double wedding at the Chicago mosque. Sister Ethel refused, reportedly arguing that she "did not desire to have them married on a 'wholesale' basis."[7] As a mother, she understood that her daughters' nuptials were important for their personal futures, not for the promotion of the NOI. She may have even reflected on her own marital choice. Sister Ethel had married young, without a high school diploma, and much like those of many Nation women, her first marriage ended in divorce.[8] Nonetheless, Sister Ethel, like all of her family, benefited from an increasingly unfair relationship to the Nation membership.

Sister Clara had first encouraged her husband to follow Master Fard in the hope that Elijah might find his way to financial security for their family. By the 1960s, their financial excess had spilled over and flooded the lives of their eight children.[9] The NOI had grown tremendously during a thirty-year period, and by "1961 increased tenfold—possibly reaching as high as 75,000 members."[10] Believers supported every aspect of its nation-building efforts by donating funds and patronizing its establishments. Money, however, flowed largely in a one-way direction—toward the Royal Family.

Sister Ethel and her husband managed many of the NOI's businesses. Noted for recklessly spending money and "thinking big," Sister Ethel in 1964 had planned to construct a $75,000 extravagant home in Chicago.[11] Further, she and Brother Raymond brokered the family's wealth. How much cash they received in Chicago on a weekly basis is impossible to document, but in February 1969, as the NOI prepared for the annual Saviour's Day Convention, all were shocked when Sister Ethel and Brother Raymond reported that they had been robbed in their home. Three gunmen, one of whom initially posed as a deliveryman, had entered the couple's "swank" South Shore residence at 6839 S. Cregier Avenue and took part in the "daring daylight robbery."[12] They targeted the palatial home at an opportune moment: the Sharrieffs were holding $23,000 in cash to be used to conduct transactions for the "family-owned firms."[13] The thieves bound Sister Ethel, Brother Raymond, their three children, and a maid, and forced Brother Raymond to hand over the money, business-related papers, and property deeds. After the gunmen escaped, the Sharrieffs called the local police and reported the crime. But the incident exposed the family's wealth and the opulence of their lifestyle.

By the early 1970s, the Royal Family had built five mansions for their personal use, "at a reported expense of $2 million" dollars.[14] Devout believers, too many of whom were eating bean soup daily because of poverty, had "donate[d] every extra cent possible" for the building of the nation to receive their reward of "heaven on earth."[15] They too wanted nice homes and fine cars but had followed Elijah Muhammad's economic program of delayed gratification. He had instructed believers not to consume "extravagant" food, not to buy more than "three outfits a year in excess of sixty-five dollars each," and not to purchase fancy cars, like his fleet of Cadillacs and Lincolns.[16] By living frugally, followers would come to understand that they did not need the trappings of material possessions. The glaring contradiction of Muhammad's leadership, selling a middle-class lifestyle but instructing believers to be satisfied with less while he and his family lived in excess, could only be collectively agreed on for so long. Over time, a good portion of the Nation's converts questioned how their financial contributions were spent, and a few even boldly articulated the concern to their immediate superiors, mosque ministers and sister captains. Unquestionably, the Royal Family spent out of control, and they knew "full well that we need better mosques, schools, [and] business of all kinds," wrote Sister Ruby Williams, a maid in one of Elijah Muhammad's homes.[17] Moreover, if the NOI businesses were "owned by the Believers," some rank-and-file women confided to a sister captain, then why were the key positions "held and operated by most of those of the First Family[?]"[18]

The financial disconnect between the Royal Family and its rank-and-file members was grotesque. At the 1974 Annual Saviour's Day Convention, Muhammad wore a jewel-encrusted fez purportedly valued at a staggering $150,000.[19] That same year, he also purchased a million-dollar jet exclusively for his travel.[20] The Nation was no longer a dinky Islamic storefront; by the 1970s, it was noted as the "richest black organization in American history."[21] Sister Clara and her husband's efforts and sacrifices had not been in vain. But as the NOI's undisputed leader, Muhammad told his followers to "wait until I pull you up."[22] He rationalized the class divides in his organization via conservative, accommodating, trickle-down economics. The postponement of earthly bounties, sweating it out with hard work and sacrifice for the larger nationhood goals, were mantras internalized by the membership for decades. He did not see a need to change it now.

No doubt this attitude had particularly severe effects on women in the NOI, who as wives and mothers were responsible for their family's well-being even as their husbands toiled for the Nation. But the situation took its toll on the Royal Family as well. Muhammad's wife and children may have had access to enormous wealth, but family members also had to submit to his religious and personal dictates to receive the benefits of his affluence.[23] His ironclad authority caused serious tensions, and some family members were "not speaking to others, for certain reasons," even as early as 1964.[24]

And then there was the question of who was family: by 1967, seven NOI women were mothers to Muhammad's additional thirteen children.[25]

Elijah Muhammad's Secretaries

Muhammad had to effectively communicate with male ministers and captains dispersed throughout the fifty-one different mosques in the United States. To execute his responsibilities, he had early on assembled a cadre of female secretaries to perform a variety of duties. The NOI had a contract with the Speed-

Elijah Muhammad and a secretary, January 14, 1972.
(Reprinted courtesy of United Press International)

writing Secretarial School in Chicago to train them.[26] The women, both single
and married, worked diligently for the Nation.

Anyone who worked directly for Elijah Muhammad recognized the appoint-
ment as a prestigious honor. Most of his secretaries lived in houses owned by
the Nation. The single ones might have rooms at his Royal Family mansion in
Chicago. The single young women who worked for him theoretically would
have had no fears of being abused or taken advantage of by men in the folds of
the NOI. Muhammad allowed only minimal contact between men and women,
especially unmarried individuals, and those under his direct supervision could
certainly count on the enforcement of courtship procedures by FOI and MGT-
GCC Captains. The Nation's ultrapuritanical code of sexuality aligned with the
tradition of Muslims throughout the world. Much of our knowledge of the secretaries' work conditions comes from Sister Betty 2X West, who was hired in 1967.
The secretaries' office was located on the fourth floor of Muhammad's royal
mansion in Chicago.[27] The door to the office was kept locked, she recalled, and
the women worked in seclusion.[28] Muhammad told them to refrain from "loose
talking" and to be serious so as not to delay correspondence. Sister Betty 2X

West was married, and her assignments included proofreading all mail for any grammatical and spelling errors.[29] Sister Valora Najeib served as Elijah Muhammad's personal secretary in 1967, and it was rumored that she was essentially running the headquarters by 1975, though Sister Betty 2X was still responsible for errors in Sister Valora's correspondence.[30] Additionally, Sister Betty 2X read out loud the *Muhammad Speaks* newspaper to Muhammad at the dining room table that doubled as his office.[31] The secretaries wrote pieces for *Muhammad Speaks* as well.[32]

One of the duties that fell to secretaries, including, by 1968, both Sister Betty 2X and Sister Valora Najeib, was answering believers' letters.[33] Generally, these asked similar questions regarding proper diet; how to fill out "Form 4," which allowed members to return after being given timeout; how to handle back issues of *Muhammad Speaks* that went unsold; whether sisters could be out at night for work or school (these requests were never approved); proper position for prayer; and how many questions should be recited at one time at the MGT-GCC and FOI classes.[34] Sometimes the mosque ministers and captains would reprimand followers who wrote letters directly to Elijah Muhammad. They viewed the letters as disrespectful of their mosque authority and occasionally dismissed followers about whose missives they learned. When Muhammad himself learned about the expulsions, he would sometimes remove ministers and captains. The secretaries had a standard letter for handling this situation: "Followers Have Permission to Write the Messenger [Elijah Muhammad]."[35] Muhammad shared confidential information with his secretaries, and some even believed that he could "read thoughts if he wished to do so."[36] Sister Betty 2X fondly recalled that Muhammad was kind and respectful, and how on one occasion he even made all of his secretaries a tasty bean soup.[37]

Nevertheless, well before Sister Betty 2X and Sister Valora were hired, scandal surrounded Elijah Muhammad's relationship with his secretaries. As early as 1954, members were astonished when a young woman who had served as his secretary in Chicago became pregnant. Muhammad judged her as unfit and isolated her from the Nation. In 1956, another unmarried young secretary in Chicago became pregnant. And in 1960, four of his secretaries were brought before the Chicago temple and placed on trial because they were unwed and pregnant.[38] Minister Malcolm stated that at these trials, "everyone at each time took it for granted" that the fathers of these children were non-Muslims.[39] But later it was established that the father all of these children was not only the same man, but Elijah Muhammad himself. In 1961, Sister Ola Muhammad, another teenaged secretary, gave birth to Kamal, who was the first son of Muhammad's children among the secretaries.[40]

Rumors about Muhammad's indiscretions with the secretaries circulated among the membership, but only in whispered tones. Alarmed at the hearsay, Minister Malcolm met with Muhammad in April 1963 in Phoenix, Arizona. He knew not to chastise his leader for immoral behavior. In fact, he encouraged Muhammad to present his actions to the membership as the fulfillment of a divine prophecy. Minister Malcolm linked the Messenger's actions to "David's adultery with Bathsheba" and "Moses' adultery with Ethiopian women."[41] Adultery was grounds for NOI dismissal, and Sister Supreme Captain Ethel had no problem banishing MGT-GCC sisters for the act.But since Elijah Muhammad was an apostle, Minister Malcolm believed that his followers would be able to accept his behavior if it was linked to that of other biblical figures.[42] In his autobiography, Minister Malcolm recalled that Muhammad initially responded positively to his idea, but later changed his position.

Historian Claude Clegg suggests several possible motives for Muhammad's extramarital affairs: the conquest of the secretaries may have given him a renewed sense of power in the face of opposition; they may also have been a response to his fear of mortality (advancing age and declining health), each one confirming his stamina.[43] Lance Shabazz, a devout supporter of Elijah Muhammad, seemed to point to the latter possibility when he said, "If he, in advanced age, recharged his battery with women who were supposed to carry his secrets (secretaries) to advance our Nation, so be it. If this is what he needed to sharpen and elevate himself for his mission, then I say Allahu Akbar."[44] Michael Kimmel argues that American men define their masculinity not as much in relation to women as in relation to each other. "Masculinity is largely a homosocial enactment. The evaluative eyes of other men are always upon us, watching, judging."[45] Muhammad's inner circle of male followers comprised of young, energetic men jockeying to prove their loyalty to him. In turn, he probably felt the need to constantly reinforce to them his authority and power. His relationships with his secretaries were a socially constructed way to perform and prove his manhood.

Aside from the secretaries themselves, the woman most affected by these indiscretions was Sister Clara. How much did she know? The FBI's electronic intercepts of Elijah Muhammad reveal Sister Clara's reaction to the early rumors. He stated to one of his advisors that she "asked me if I brought maternity clothes for my secretary," and that he had replied yes, "but that didn't prove anything."[46] Yet over the years Sister Clara became aware of his additional children. "Believe me she did" know, said her daughter, Sister Lottie.[47] Reports by the FBI indicate that all of his children by Sister Clara had "full knowledge" of their father's affairs, and Sister Supreme Captain Ethel "freely discussed them with her mother," but her "financial ties with her father [were] such that she would be fearful of any situation that might cause her to lose such backing."[48] Eventually the level of Sister Clara's frustration would lead to separate domiciles. Muhammad informed his advisor to explain to the membership that he lived in Phoenix, Arizona, and Sister Clara in Chicago because his doctors had advised him to be in a warm climate, and "that if Clara [was] here, there wouldn't be anybody in Chicago to run things."[49] Unlike Minister Malcolm, who appeared expendable, Sister Clara served as an icon for Nation women. Her reputation embodied all that was ennobled, and the Messenger could not afford to alienate her completely. If she had left the NOI, the organization's foundation would have been shaken beyond repair. Her departure would have signaled that Muhammad could not maintain his own household, which constituted the ultimate duty of a Nation man.

By July 2, 1964, the adultery rumors surrounding Elijah Muhammad were openly confirmed when two former secretaries, Sister Evelyn Williams and Sister Lucille Rosary (Karriem), filed paternity suits against Muhammad in the Los Angeles Superior Court. Sister Evelyn and Sister Lucille had been advised to do so by Minister Malcolm X.[50] Sister June recalled that "Malcolm was very bitter and he wanted me to go against the Messenger with him. He said if I got you, the Messenger will be very hurt."[51] Sister June's son, Abdullah Yaseem, showed a facial structure identical to that of his father and looked more like Elijah Muhammad than any of his sons by Sister Clara. Perhaps this is why Minister Malcolm believed that Muhammad would have been extremely disappointed had Sister June entered into the suit. In the end, she did not.[52]

Sister Lucille (thirty-three years old) and Sister Evelyn (thirty years old) had both worked for Muhammad in Chicago before moving to Los Angeles to file suit. Sister Lucille was nine months pregnant at the time, but had already given birth to two children sired by Muhammad: Saudi, born January 17, 1960, and Lishah, born October 13, 1961. Sister Lucille's paternity suit documented that the defendant, Elijah Muhammad, had "paid some support money to plaintiff for the minor children and said defendant does not deny that the minor children were fathered by him."[53] Initially, Sister Lucille said, she was "shocked" by Muhammad's advances.[54] Their sexual relationship began in November 1957 and lasted until about October 1963. Sister Lucille's attorney, Gladys Towles Root, had a reputation for being the "Defender of the Damned." She stated that her client was fearful of Muhammad and recounted in the suit that in 1959, he had told Sister Lucille that if she "made known the fact that he was the father" of her child, "some frantic follower, disbelieving [her allegations] would seek to kill" her.[55]

Sister Evelyn had only one child by Muhammad, Eva Marie, who was born on March 30, 1960. Her relationship with the Messenger had begun in August 1958 and lasted until June of 1964. As with Sister Lucille, Muhammad had paid child support in the past and did not deny fathering her child. She had also received threats from Muhammad that if she publicly disclosed his fatherhood "frantic followers" would murder her.[56]

There were legitimate concerns about the threats. Officials from Chicago had gone to Los Angeles in an attempt to keep the women quiet, but Minister Malcolm was more determined to get them, and their children, to see Gladys Towles Root. Brother Allen (Hakim A. Jamal), a cousin by marriage to Minister Malcolm, escorted all of them to the law office. At each turn "we were on the lookout for Muslims. They were there," he wrote.[57] The level of danger seemed intense, and after leaving Root's office, Sister Lucille said, "I really don't mind getting killed by those fools, but I don't want my children to become orphans. They can hurt me but I hope they don't hurt my kids, that's what worries me."[58] With sweaty palms, Brother Allen admitted that he was scared and "told everyone in the car that maybe they didn't mind dying but that [he] did."[59]

Minister Malcolm's resoluteness about assisting Sister Lucille and Sister Evelyn came from a sense of guilt. Sister Evelyn was a former girlfriend whom he had known before NOI membership, and he also knew Sister Lucille. He took full responsibility for converting both women to the Nation. As he explained, "I opened their minds for [Muhammad] to reach in and take advantage of them."[60] By encouraging them to file suit, he wanted to undo what he "did to them by exposing them" to the Messenger.[61]

Sister Lottie confirmed that Minister Malcolm had brought both women to her "father's house to be secretaries."[62] Unlike the others, they were not teenagers: Sister Evelyn was twenty-three and Sister Lucille twenty-six years old when they began their relationships with Muhammad. Their ages complicated the situation for some who believed that they had the maturity to consent. Some were also willing to ignore the unequal power arrangement: Muhammad was the Messenger of Allah, an apostle, and the source of their employment. Sister Lottie went further in sympathizing with her father: she believed that Minister Malcolm had brought the two women there to "seduce [my] father" and that the paternity suit was evidence that they had "turned" against him.[63]

In the suit, Sister Evelyn stated that Elijah Muhammad had "told us that under the teachings of the Holy Koran, we were not committing adultery and that we were his wives."[64] He may have married the women, "in his own way," Sister Lottie confirmed.[65] In fact, Sister Lottie "wouldn't doubt that he might have had a ceremony in private between the two of them, whoever they were."[66]

Under Islam, a man can take up to four wives if he can equally provide for them. Her father, Sister Lottie understood, "didn't have any limits, whereas the average man is limited to four, but in his particular standing in the community he was a leader, and so he could have as many as he could take care of."[67] But Zak A. Kondo correctly points out that "neither Elijah nor the NOI general body treated any of the secretaries like wives. In fact, the NOI isolated, excommunicated and/ or ostracized these sisters. Had they been treated like 'wives,' two secretaries probably would not have filed paternity suits against Elijah in July 1964."[68]

Both Sister Lucille and Sister Evelyn had appealed to the Messenger to increase their monthly support of $100 per child prior to the suit. But he instead cautioned them that if they went public, "one or two of his sons would stand in his place and take the blame."[69] After the suit, however, Muhammad pointed the finger at Minister Malcolm and publicly speculated that he might have fathered the secretaries' children. This charge was convincing to many because of Minister Malcolm's prior relationship with Sister Evelyn. Utilizing *Muhammad Speaks* as a forum, the Messenger simultaneously defended his own character and besmirched Minister Malcolm's reputation.

Muhammad was further able to divert attention away from himself by generating and manipulating a more explosive issue, the need to protect the NOI from hypocrites. The Qur'an states: "And when you see them, their persons will please you, and if they speak, you will listen to their speech; (they are) as if they were big pieces of wood clad with garments; they think every cry to be against them. They are the enemy, therefore beware of them; may Allah destroy them, whence are they turned back." Nation believers argued on behalf of their leader and threatened those who opposed him. Of course, the women and men who came to the defense of the secretaries did not have a forum like *Muhammad Speaks* in which to air their grievances. Some followers disgusted with Muhammad's behavior cast their vote against him by leaving the NOI. Others were fearful and stayed put.[70]

Interestingly, six days prior to Minister Malcolm's murder on February 21, 1965, he revealed how far he had internalized Muhammad's teachings about women. He said in a speech at the Audubon Ballroom that he found Muhammad immoral not because he had seduced "nine teenage women," but because he would not publicly admit his doing. During the heat of the paternity suit, Brother Allen (Hakim A. Jamal) remembered Minister Malcolm telling him that he "just want[ed] him [Muhammad] to be a man."[71] In other words, Minister Malcolm did not analyze his leader's behavior in terms of sin; apparently, in a patriarchal system, Muhammad had the right to do what he did. Rather, the lack of responsibility for the protection of (and provision for) his family was the issue.

If the Messenger, or any man who engaged in seemingly promiscuous behavior, willingly admitted to his actions, Minister Malcolm would "shake [their] hand and call" him "a man. A good one too [laughter]."[72]

The Question of Polygamy

Whatever he may have done in private, the Honorable Elijah Muhammad never publicly sanctioned multiple wives. In fact, in January 1974 he published a notice in *Muhammad Speaks* to all members who had written him "asking for freedom to take other women and other men." He responded, "You stand today as much to be charged with committing fornication and adultery as you were before you ever heard Islam!"[73] Obviously, he perceived his own domestic affairs differently, and no follower had the authority to place judgment on Allah's last Messenger. Reports claim that by 1975, he had nineteen children, eight by Sister Clara and the others by the secretaries.

Yet the paternity-suit scandal had a long-lasting hold on the imagination of some Nation members, who continued to feel that Elijah Muhammad's example justified polygamous households. This had a profound effect on women in the NOI, both those in the background and those in the national (and international) spotlight.

After her divorce from her first husband, Brother John 24X, Sister Doris 9X quickly became a target to be "someone's second wife."[74] As she recalled, by this time, in 1974, "rumors were flying right and left about the Honorable Elijah Muhammad having more than one wife. Everybody wanted to jump on the band wagon."[75]

She was first approached by a couple who said they wanted to give her and her daughter a better life. Sister Doris 9X was taken aback and reported them to Minister Jael. Soon thereafter the minister's own wife, Sister Ariel, invited her for tea and inquired if she was interested in becoming a wife. Sister Ariel was fifty years old, childless, and wanted "a baby in the worst way," remembered Sister Doris 9X.[76] Sister Doris 9X replied, "How can a woman ask another woman to have a baby for her husband?" On leaving she said to Sister Ariel, "Allah doesn't want me to share another woman's husband."[77]

For a single mother in the NOI, the pressure to remarry could be either extraordinary or lax, depending on the number of registered mosque brothers. Elijah Muhammad's statements against polygamy did not protect Sister Doris 9X from repeated requests that she become a second wife. Reasoning that the only way to keep second-wife offers at bay was to choose another husband, she married Brother Mahad, even though his income was not enough to create the stable household she craved. Sister Doris 9X paid a high price for that decision when she lost her legal freedom on the charge of welfare fraud, as I discussed earlier.

Around the same time, Sister Belinda Ali's life was complicated by her husband's desire for a second wife. Sister Belinda was the mother of four children (Maryum, born in 1968; the twin girls Rasheda and Jamillah, born in 1970; and Muhammad Jr., born in 1972). Her husband already had two additional daughters outside of their marriage, by two different mistresses: Miya (1972) and Khalilah (1974). Sister Belinda admitted that "for a long time, his seeing other women confused me."[78] He initially kept the other women in secret and then "use[d] the religion as an excuse."[79] Clear about the Qur'an limiting sex to marriage, Sister Belinda believed it gave all fair warning that "it is best to have only one, if you knew." Moreover, she said, "You don't do it the way Ali did."[80]

Sister Belinda, now known as Sister Khalilah (she legally changed her name in 1975), had received a call from Wanda Bolton (Aaisha Ali) when she was pregnant. Both Wanda's mother and Sister Belinda disagreed with Wanda's desire to become a second wife, but in the end, "this is what Ali want[ed]."[81] Recalling the moment of humiliation, Sister Belinda said, "I went along with it because I was trying to get [Ali] to understand, I am going to do this because this is what you think you want, so since you want to roll your oats, you see what happens. And then a baby comes and she [Wanda] names the baby after me. It was the wrong thing to do."[82]

Muhammad Ali moved Wanda and baby Khalilah to his Pennsylvania training camp. Much later, in her 1985 palimony suit, Wanda described how in 1975, when their daughter was eleven months old, Elijah Muhammad, just prior to his death in February, married her and Ali in an Islamic ceremony over the phone.[83] From the eyes of a child, Khalilah recalled, "when I was a toddler we lived for a while in Deer Lake in a cabin right next door to the one occupied by Belinda and her children. My mother and Belinda actually became quite close and cared for each other's children."[84] Whatever the truth of that relationship, there was more to come.

Ali met Veronica Porche in September 1974, shortly after Khalilah was born, and a year later, their relationship was public knowledge. Sister Belinda is reported to have tried to "sort of acquiesce."[85] Porche was explained as "a traveling companion of Belinda's; a cousin of Ali's; a babysitter, and a close friend of the family."[86] As Sister Belinda recalled, "And as much as he tried to stretch Islamic law, it didn't make what he was doing right."[87] In hindsight, Ali would agree: he said, "I had two children by women I wasn't married to. I love them; they're my children. I feel just as good and proud about them as my other children, but that wasn't a right thing to do. And running around, living that kind of life, wasn't good for me. It hurt my wife; it offended God. It never really made me happy."[88] But hindsight came too late: Sister Belinda filed for divorce on September 2, 1976, one month after Ali's daughter with Porche, Hana, was born.

Sister Clara

Though we will never fully know how Sister Clara felt about the paternity suits against her husband, up until her death in 1972 she remained his only public wife. It had never been easy being the first lady of the Nation of Islam, and only Sister Clara fully knew the challenges of the honored status. Over the years she had weathered many storms with her husband. Through Elijah Muhammad's incarceration to his numerous paramours, Sister Clara was sutured to a man whom the NOI converts reverenced as the last Messenger of Allah and a holy apostle. Although Sister Clara herself was never considered divine, she was acknowledged as a living witness to the Nation's history. In Detroit, she had listened to Master Fard's legendary 1930s lectures, and during the World War II persecution of the movement and its members as un-American, she helped keep the NOI afloat. With time, as the pioneering members of the Nation became fewer in number, Sister Clara's importance as a symbol of origin increased. Noted for coming to the aid of her husband in recalling the dates of NOI history, Sister Clara had survived gut-wrenching poverty to reap the material blessings of her husband's Islamic teachings. Her rags-to-riches story speaks to the desire for prosperity of many black American women. Indeed, throughout the NOI's history, a significant number of female converts wanted the financial security and tangible possessions of a first lady. One has to wonder, however, if Sister Clara's status felt akin to wearing golden handcuffs by 1970.

Sister Clara lived within the complicated web of kinfolk as best she could. The FBI electronic intercepts indicate that in the early 1960s her mounting frustration and anger with her husband's extramarital affairs "resulted in domestic strife."[89] By the time Muhammad contemplated bringing all his additional children under one roof in California, because it "would be good to have them all reared by one person," Sister Clara was "sick of being treated like a dog."[90] The birth of Sister June's son Abdullah in December 1960 sealed Sister Clara's public humiliation: he was an identical image of Elijah Muhammad, confirming his father's infidelity to all who dared to look.[91] It was then, determined to keep her sanity, that Sister Clara created physical distance from her husband by choosing to live at their Chicago home while he resided at their Phoenix residence, purchased in 1961. As rumors about disharmony in the Muhammads' marriage swirled, Elijah denied it.

The hot climate of Phoenix was also the drawing card for Sister Ruby Williams, who suffered from rheumatoid arthritis. In January 1962, she relocated there to avoid "becoming a cripple" and found employment in the Royal Family home as a maid and cook in February.[92] Sister Ruby had joined the NOI at Temple No. 1, Detroit, under the teaching of Assistant Minister Malcolm X in 1953. She was appreciative and honored to work in the Muhammads' home a decade later, where she would have unprecedented access to the fountain of knowledge that was the Messenger. Her duties allowed her to become close to Sister Clara, who would occasionally visit. Sister Ruby's insights about Sister Clara are among the very few we have from individuals not connected to her nuclear family or the FBI. Working and living in the residence, Sister Ruby observed family interactions that brought her both happiness and disappointment. In her opinion, Sister Clara was "the one person in Islam I have had contact with that tries so very hard to live up to all the laws of Islam, as taught by the Honorable Elijah Muhammad."[93] Often referred to behind her back as "Madame," or "The Boss Lady," Sister Clara, Sister Ruby wrote, "is often misunderstood because of her direct sincerity and frankness, regardless to whom she is speaking. Usually this makes intimates few."[94] In addition to being forthright, Sister Clara was also shy and had "the ability to sit through an entire evening never uttering a sound — yet, you are aware that she is there."[95] Perhaps this is why her circle of female friends was so small. Sister Clara's confidants were primarily her children, who had witnessed their mother's marital pains and emotional suffering. Sister Lottie said, "I could never walk in my mother's shoes, never, no way. I don't even want to."[96] Even Sister Ruby recalled how Sister Clara's beautiful bright eyes showed "much hurt and sadness."[97]

In the midst of this heartache, Sister Clara did not exercise her NOI right to a divorce. Today we reason that in a court of law, Sister Clara would have been able to prove that the financial success of the Nation occurred during the duration of their marriage and that she was thus entitled to appropriate spousal support. Sister Clara, however, had witnessed how her husband had cut off their children and grandchildren when they critiqued him and his Islamic teachings.[98] If anyone knew the absolute power of her husband, it was Sister Clara, and no doubt she feared an uncertain future. Noted for "just do[ing] everything" her husband said, Sister Clara slowly began to change around 1962.[99] Sister Lottie believed that the reversal hinged on "all this stuff she saw" and the humiliation she was forced to endure.[100] In addition to seeing her husband's six extramarital children, Sister Clara had to share the coveted podium with Sister Tynnetta Deanar at the 1961 Saviour's Day Convention. Sister Tynnetta had received her "X" in 1958, at seventeen years of age, and became a columnist on behalf of the NOI for the *Pittsburgh Courier*. With the publication of *Mr. Muhammad Speaks* in 1960, Sister Tynnetta became a featured writer representing NOI womanhood. Young, smart, attractive, and noted for being "just like a little girl," who was "very humorous and kept you laughing," by 1961, Sister Tynnetta had become one of Elijah Muhammad's favorites.[101]

Determined to maintain her dignity, by 1962, Sister Clara had begun to embrace what brought her pleasure, traveling. In May 1962, she went to Egypt with her son Herbert to visit another son, Akbar, in Cairo. On her return home, she received an anonymous letter highlighting her husband's illicit behavior; on July 25, 1962, the FBI accelerated its campaign to capitalize on what appeared to be the immoral personal affairs of Elijah Muhammad by authorizing the Chicago office to prepare and mail such a letter to Clara Muhammad "upon her return from Egypt."[102] That letter must have felt like salt in an open wound to her. By this point, however, it appears that Mr. and Mrs. Muhammad had come to some sort of agreement, and their daughter, Sister Lottie, recalled that he just "didn't bother her too much."[103] He was also more careful to maintain distance between the children he had fathered with various Nation women. Ishmael, Sister Tynnetta's son with Muhammad, said he "had very little interaction with him," and in fact, met him for the first time when he was seven years old, in 1972.[104]

As Sister Clara attempted to snatch some joy from her life, she was unable to fully keep at bay the weight of her dishonor.[105] By the 1963 Saviour's Day Convention, news of their troubling domestic life had circulated among the membership. In public, Sister Clara tried to remain stoic and as regal as any proud first lady. Sister Ruby recalled that "she has suffered anguish that only one in her position could know, and she has overcome only because of her superiority."[106]

Yet even so, a photo of Sister Clara at the convention captured her looking dejected, with a slightly bowed head and eyes focused on the floor, as she once again sat next to the upright and youthful Sister Tynnetta, who would birth the first of her four children fathered by Muhammad in 1963.[107] After encounters such as this, one can only imagine Sister Clara's crumbled spirit showing behind closed doors. As cancer slowly inched its way through her tiny body, which hardly ever deviated from the 120-pound standard for NOI women, she became even more committed to self-gratification. "I guess when she was finally dying," said Sister Lottie, "she would do all the things she wanted to do," such

Sister Clara Muhammad and Tynnetta Deanar, Saviour's Day
Convention, February 26, 1963. (Sun-Times Media)

as more traveling.[108] When Sister Clara passed away at home, surrounded by her loved ones after her "long illness," on August 12, 1972, she was enshrined as the epitome of perfect NOI virtue.[109]

As more children were born into the NOI by the late 1960s, a new cohort of adults found their way into its Islamic fold as well. Many of them were activists who had watched Minister Malcolm from afar. They became drawn to the NOI as it had slowly mushroomed into a political option when the call for Black Power circulated throughout the country. The boundaries between conservative politics and black nationalist rhetoric were heavily blurred, sparking a movement toward the NOI by black folks who had grown impatient and irritated with desegregation efforts.

CHAPTER NINE

THE APPEAL OF BLACK NATIONALISM
AND THE PROMISE OF PROSPERITY

W hy would the revolutionary poet Sonia Sanchez convert to the NOI after the assassination of Minister Malcolm X? Prior to his brutal murder on February 21, 1965, Minister Malcolm wrote, in his 1965 autobiography as told to Alex Haley, that he knew, "[as] any official in the Nation of Islam would instantly have known, any death-talk [about me] could have been approved of — if not actually initiated — by only one man," the Honorable Elijah Muhammad.[1] Minister Louis Farrakhan stated years later, "There was not a Muslim who loved the Honorable Elijah Muhammad that did not want to kill Malcolm."[2] Even the legendary boxer Muhammad Ali announced to a British audience in 1974, "Malcolm X had to be punished. . . . When you talk against a man who is so loved, the man himself don't have to put the word out to get you, the people themselves are going to get you. The love for that man will get you killed."[3] Farrakhan's and Ali's deflection away from Muhammad's responsibility for the assassination of Minister Malcolm not only served to insulate their leader but also strategically placed the rank-and-file as coconspirators. Through this sleight of hand, no single individual could be held accountable, and all were equally implicated by their love for Elijah Muhammad.

Sonia Sanchez, on the other hand, loved Minister Malcolm X. In a political climate that hosted racist government repression in the form of the state police, his fiercely smart rhetoric had helped to shift the dominant political struggle from a strategy of civil rights liberalism to eclectic expressions of black nationalism. His message combined an encouragement to armed self-defense, "by any means necessary," with a lethal critique of white folks as devils. He appealed to the most socially isolated, politically disposed, and economically desperate black urbanites. For Sanchez, Minister Malcolm X had "said it in a very strong fashion, a very manly fashion, 'I am not afraid to say what you've been thinking all these years.' That's why we loved him so very much. He said it out loud. Not behind closed doors. He took on America for us."[4] This is why Mosque No. 7-A, New York, was burned down after his murder. Amiri Baraka had heard that "people were vowing to go to Chicago and kill Elijah," even after NOI members who had been implicated in the killing were quickly dismissed by the leadership as FBI infiltrators and hypocrites.[5] Sanchez paid tribute to Minister Malcolm X in moving, loving, poetic verse:

> yet this man
> this dreamer,
> thick-lipped with words
> will never speak again
> and in each winter
> when the cold air cracks
> with frost, ill breathe
> his breath and mourn
> my gun-filled nights.[6]

The power of love is difficult to analyze. But love poems, the language, symbols, dialect, and idioms of poetic verse, can speak multiple truths to ailing hearts. Or, as Audre Lorde points out, love poems "insist that you can't separate loving from fighting, from dying, from hurting, but love is triumphant."[7] Sonia Sanchez's 1973 *Love Poems* is a deeply affecting collection of her most memorable work:

> when i felt your warm
> touch, i swelled up until the
> streets were filled with you.[8]

Published during the period of her active membership in the NOI, *Love Poems* frames a historical moment that defies a certain kind of political logic, in the same way that a yearning for romantic love can truncate rational reasoning. Sanchez was an artistic warrior who laced her poems with a sincere love for black people. Love for Ethridge Knight, another amazing poet of the period, whom she had married in 1968, was certainly the motivation for some of her work. Yet being married to a person who suffered from drug addiction proved quite difficult. Sanchez explained that when Knight "tore up the finished manuscript" for *We a BaddDDD People* in 1970, "because he was not writing," she found herself "on the floor, trying to piece together the book." At that instant, she "knew it was time to leave."[9]

The challenge of raising children without her husband was compounded by her growing dissatisfaction with some of her peers in the Black Arts Circle.

Sanchez explained that there were things she had "stopped doing and people who were talking about blackness had not stopped those things at all." Soon she found herself an "alien among them"; even though they were "saying the same kind of things," their "lifestyles were completely different." Specifically, she wanted to distance herself from the drug culture of her peers. Baraka confessed that one time while shooting cocaine he almost overdosed, and "it scared the shit out of me. But it didn't stop me or our drug activities."[10] No longer the "wide-eyed young woman, quiet and self-deprecating" that Baraka had first encountered at a writers' workshop, Sanchez had matured, triggering a search for a new cultural home that would also welcome her children.[11]

Recalling her 1972 NOI conversion, Sanchez explained that she was essentially searching for something positive.[12] Much later, in a 2010 interview, she would say, "I know it sounds odd to say that the reason I ended up in the Nation was really because of Malcolm," who had taught that its "basic doctrine" was "engaging the community, doing work in the community."[13] Sanchez, trying to secure a cultural home and to maintain a vision of herself, "tended to think that it was not the Nation that killed him [Malcolm X] but agent[s] outside that would make use of the people that were in there. And, as a consequence, it still did not deny that there were wonderful decent human beings functioning in the Nation, in a great sense, in a wonderful way."[14]

Life is filled with paradoxes, and seemingly odd choices are usually rooted in desires and needs. By January 1972 Sanchez wrote that the person who had really "brought the idea of 'blackness' among" them was the Honorable Elijah Muhammad. It was Muhammad's "words and His ideas that people had taken and dispersed. They took from him what they wanted and discarded the other things."[15] She was not alone in her thinking. The conversion narrative of Gwendolyn Zoharah Simmons—Sister Gwendolyn 2X—provides another engagement with this pivotal historical moment.

Gwendolyn Simmons had been a member of the Student Non-Violent Coordinating Committee (SNCC), and it was in Laurel, Mississippi, in 1965, that she had first heard "the teachings of Muhammad via his number one spokesperson Malcolm X" on a record album.[16] She listened to the recording alone in a "three-room shotgun-style clapboard house with a tin roof," and the message "both terrified and thrilled" her sensibilities.[17] Minister Malcolm X was preaching the "unvarnished truth" about the white man, and she "loved it," but, similar to most black people, she was not convinced enough to become a Nation follower.[18]

As a native of Memphis, Tennessee, Simmons had firsthand experience of living with Jim Crow violence. Her dark brown skin had "often caused [her]

pain," because she had "internalized the racists' history and ideology and secretly longed to be other than [her]self."[19] She was recruited into the SNCC
while a student in Atlanta and became the project director in Laurel. In Mississippi Simmons began to identify herself as a feminist.[20] From 1964 until the
time she joined the NOI in 1972, Simmons had been active in civil rights,
peace, and women's liberation movement activities.[21] Over the course of eight
years, she had also unlearned the "internalized oppressions," and as a "fully
formed" female had no "desire to re-oppress [her]self as a woman in the name
of religion."[22] Yet the many trials that had engulfed Simmons pushed her to
search beyond her familiar political terrain. The NOI's "messianic nationalism,"
which she understood "as a fairly explicit protest movement against racism and
social stratification in American society," resonated differently for her in 1972
Philadelphia than it had in 1965 Mississippi.[23] Its black nationalist core and its
economic "do for self" mantra now reflected her "own political motivations"
and proved the key for her membership.[24]

It is important to note that Sister Gwendolyn 2X "didn't buy into" all of the
Nation's teachings, especially the idea that her husband had to be the sole breadwinner. Brother Michael had witnessed her leadership in the SNCC and was
aware of her reputation as a "hell raiser." He also knew she had been to jail and
had been beaten as an activist. "There wasn't any expectation that I was going
to change. That was totally out of the question," she said.[25] They "never lived
[their] lives in the way that the Nation said," because Brother Michael knew that
she was his "equal."[26] Admitting that her experience in the Nation was atypical
because of her prior activist life and her well-placed brother-in-law, she was
also celebrated because of it. After they relocated from Chicago to New York,
they joined Mosque No. 7, where Minister Farrakhan would speak from the
podium about how Sister Gwendolyn 2X and Brother Michael had been "freedom fighters and that [they] had been in SNCC and that he wanted all of the
young people to get to know" them. She recalled that he gave them "rock star
status" and on several occasions took them out to dinner, with the FOI in tow.
He shared "his ideas for getting young people involved in community service
and all of that was really amazing"; Sister Gwendolyn 2X "liked him a lot" and
had "tremendous admiration for him."[27] Mosque No. 7 differed from the more
"conservative" Mosque No. 2; it was at No. 7 that Sister Gwendolyn 2X thought,
"Ah-ha, maybe my joining this group was the right thing."[28] Minister Farrakhan
was "a leader who really [had] some of the same vision [I had] for our people so
that was a very bright spot in my time with the Nation."[29]

John R. Howard interviewed nineteen NOI neophytes (including one woman)
on the West Coast in 1965 and concluded that the group attracted individuals

who through their own experiences had already developed a black nationalist perspective. The "recruit comes to the door of the temple with the essence of his ideas already formed. The Black Muslims only give this disaffection a voice," stated Howard.[30] Sanchez and Simmons would definitely fall into this category. But something else was also at work. By the late 1960s, the realignment of white supremacy generated the idea of a color-blind society.[31] A race-neutral future was a worthy goal, but as the SNCC's Chairman, Stokely Carmichael, wrote in 1967, "we must recognize that race is an overwhelming fact of life in this historical period. There is no black man in this country who can live 'simply as a man.'"[32] Rejecting the rhetoric of color-blindness, however, could not check its power, so useful to a racist agenda, to erode a positive black identity. Thus, the sociologists Sidney Willhelm and Edwin Powell argued, the climate of the late 1960s and early 1970s enhanced the value of organizations most committed to elevating individuals as "an identifiable entity," largely based on race and culture. In the long run, extreme communities would attract converts.[33] The NOI persisted "because — untried — they still offer[ed] a hope, a dream, and identity."[34] Simmons herself declared, "Even I, as a skeptic in the midst, could let myself escape into the NOI's utopian vision and pray that it was true."[35]

As the Black Power movement began to fracture and wind down, *Muhammad Speaks*, the NOI's popular organ, offered numerous examples of why revolutionary black women would join a conservative Islamic movement. Naturally, these testimonies must be read as self-justifying tracts, not as reliable history. But this web of self-preservation speaks to the complexity of the Black Power movement and the desperation of former women adherents to belong to what appeared to be a more tangible expression of putting black people first.

Another young revolutionary in the SNCC, Anna Karriem, was also swayed to become a believer in the NOI. Under the direction of Carmichael, who had been heavily influenced by Minister Malcolm X, the SNCC's nonviolent direct-action political strategy shifted to embrace Black Power. Karriem states that many SNCC activists were "willing to arm themselves for revolution in the streets." But teaching that "freedom comes from the barrel of a gun," Karriem learned, ultimately romanticized "the outcome of armed revolution."[36] She soon became critical of Carmichael for not teaching black people in Los Angeles after the 1965 Watts Rebellion how to rebuild their homes. Nor was Carmichael around, argued Karriem, to support the black people in Detroit and Newark in 1967, who had revolted against slum life and dire poverty. Despite Ella Baker's charge that SNCC activists should not rely on a central movement leader, Karriem was disappointed by what she perceived as Carmichael's negligent directorship.

For Karriem, the straw that broke the proverbial camel's back came in 1967. She was working with people living in Alabama and Mississippi counties to secure their right to vote. On election day, however, she observed that local registrars held loaded guns to drive away SNCC members who were supervising the process and that black sharecroppers were pushed off their land and forbidden to take their belongings because they had voted for a black candidate. Karriem found herself, "along with other SNCC workers and members of the homeless families, driving stakes into the ground and building a wooden floor, so that we could set up tents to get them out of the cold."[37] By the end of the year, Karriem concluded that Black Power in the SNCC too often led to "Black Deaths."[38]

The level of violence against black people that Karriem witnessed was heart-wrenching, and she began to question the SNCC's liberation strategies and, ultimately, its leadership. Black people were hurting disproportionately in the United States and Karriem, like many of her comrades, began to take refuge in nationalist thinking, looking for a place where their dreams of peace, progress, and well-being could flourish. Karriem ultimately found herself rooted in the NOI.

Of course, Karriem's critique of the SNCC — that damage was "caused by so called Black leaders who expound on ideas that [had] no foundation in reality"— could certainly have been leveled by others at the NOI's utopian ideals.[39] So what did Karriem latch onto that made her believe in the leadership of Elijah Muhammad, and in the NOI as an organization that avoided the pitfalls of other Black Power offerings? The political lives of Linday Bryant and Joan 4X, both published in *Muhammad Speaks*, provide insight into these questions.

Linday Bryant was initially involved in the Black Student Union (BSU) at the University of California, Santa Barbara, because she sought an organization that would give her "identity as a black woman."[40] Working diligently to "obtain a better education system and a better world in which to live," Bryant soon realized that the slogan "by any means necessary," when applied to achieving the BSU's goals, ironically meant "sleeping with whites and allowing them to integrate into our ranks."[41] Bryant began attending the local mosque and felt inspired each time. Soon, she was completely disillusioned with the BSU, finding it lacked the answers to black suffering. In the end, Bryant decided to unite behind the only man she considered qualified to lead, the Honorable Elijah Muhammad.

Sister Joan 4X also went into the NOI after the BSU, because she "was constantly in search of the qualities embodied in the Nation."[42] Growing up in the South had made her keenly aware of white violence. Joan 4X readily admitted that she was "not quite ready for the Caucasians on the west coast for they have placed a mental fog over the minds of our people that is much worse than any physical danger."[43] This crisis pushed Joan 4X to become a part of the new breed of student activists trying desperately to free themselves from oppression. She put herself on the line and shouted that she was "Black and Proud" to white administrators, because she had the courage to fight for better conditions in the United States. But soon Joan 4X also became disillusioned with the BSU. As a newly formed political movement, BSUs had spread in the late 1960s and were the least structurally organized Black Power group. For both Joan 4X and Linday Bryant, the need for an exclusively black environment made the NOI a viable alternative; that it promised hierarchal infrastructure and protection from harm increased its appeal.

After becoming a member of the NOI, Joan 4X argued in *Muhammad Speaks* that the white press served as a smoke screen to keep black folks from the only true leader in America, the Honorable Elijah Muhammad. Her analysis turned on how and when the white man used the media to convince black folks that a black leader did or did not deserve backing. Joan 4X considered *The Autobiography of Malcolm X* (1964) as the most "obvious sign" that the "devil knows Islam is the only salvation for black people and the only vehicle that really unites us." Pointing out that when Minister Malcolm X taught Islam, "the devils couldn't do enough to blaspheme him and the whole program of the Messenger," she noted that when Malcolm X "turned from the light of Islam, and especially now that he is dead, the white press can't put enough copies of his autobiography in the hands of our people."[44]

This backhanded slap against Minister Malcolm X was typical in *Muhammad Speaks*, which printed countless diatribes against him. Sonia Sanchez raised the question in 2010 of why she and others stayed in the Nation "when they love[d] Malcolm so much and they knew what the people were printing was incorrect?"[45] Her heartfelt reply, that "they had no place else," resonated with political refugees from a variety of organizations.[46] The singer and activist Nina Simone encapsulates the historical moment: The "SNCC was dead in the water, with its most talented members exiled or imprisoned and the rest arguing among themselves. CORE [Congress of Racial Equality] was going the same way. The SCLC was still trying to recover after losing Martin. The antiwar movement had distracted most of the white liberal support we had left. Every black political organization of importance had been infiltrated by the FBI. Police terrorized our communities. Many people refused to admit it, but the plain truth was we were in retreat."[47] The days of real choices were gone for black activists, and many withdrew from political life out of frustration and fear.

It is more than ironic that the NOI filled the vacuum as a Black Power alternative, given that Elijah Muhammad never wavered from his conservative position that his followers eschew mainstream politics. Further, Black Power activists' attachment to Africa as the homeland ran counter to Muhammad's teachings. The pan-African icon Queen Mother Moore of Harlem recalled that Minister Malcolm X had told her that "before he could say the word [Africa] it would have to come from Elijah."[48] Muhammad "was as anti-African as he was anti-white." In fact, he "never had one statement that was pro-African," said Malcolm X.[49] Moore revealed that when she spent three days at Muhammad's home, they argued because "he didn't want to hear nothing about Africa."[50] Muhammad explained his position in 1965 with the following analysis:

> Many of my people, the so-called Negroes, say we should help the nations of Africa which are awakening. This has been said as if we owned America. We are so foolish! What part of America do you have that you can offer to- ward helping Africa? Who is independent, the nations of Africa or we? The best act would be to request the independent governments of Africa and Asia to help us. We are the ones who need help. We have little or nothing to offer as help to others. We should begin to help at home first.[51]

Yet skimming the pages of *Muhammad Speaks*, readers would receive mixed messages about the NOI's view about Africa. Many editions included a huge image of the continent placed next to a map of United States, as if they were reaching out, almost touching, one another. So while Muhammad carped about Africa, he agreed to a newspaper visual that represented the mind-set of many activists, longing for a connection with the motherland. (Perhaps this is why the MGT-GCC in Los Angeles believed that it was appropriate to advertise an "Africa Extravaganza" fund-raiser in a newspaper.[52]) The image went a long way toward allowing activist members to think, or at least hope, that "things were gonna get better" in terms of the NOI's pan-African politics.[53]

In the meantime, at the very least, the NOI offered a wellspring of unity, strength, and cultural identity along with concrete examples of successful nation-building in the midst of purportedly color-blind and neoliberal politics. By 1965, the NOI had moved beyond rhetoric, buying farmland in three states as well as an abundance of properties and small businesses near each of its mosques (grocery stores, restaurants, dry-cleaning shops, bakeries). Its holdings were valued in the millions.[54] Just as important, believers assertively critiqued the United States using language familiar to activists. For example, Sister Chris- tine Delois X of Birmingham, Alabama, explained that "the white man's (devil's) civilization can offer us nothing in the way of security, education, and spiritu- ality. In other words, this capitalist fascist-racist neocolonized society as a whole is falling (or has fallen) as our Beloved Leader and Teacher has taught for more

than 40 years."[55] The writer James Baldwin never joined the NOI, but he also felt
the draw of the Messenger's "peculiar authority." Slender and small in stature,
Elijah Muhammad had a smile, Baldwin remembered, that "promised to take
the burden of my life off my shoulders."[56] Essentially, promising power, peace
of mind, and black wealth, the NOI took on revolutionary meaning within a
context of effete political resistance and racist violence.

The Many Promises Made to Believers

But not all of the NOI's post-1965 female converts were former activists. As
had always been the case, some were women simply seeking to reap Muhammad's promises of stability and wealth: "If you want money, good homes, and
friendships in all walks of life, come and follow me," he declared. His bountiful
membership call yielded a favorable response among black people who had fled
traumatic experiences in the South, but were still catching hell in the northern
Promised Land. They lived in dilapidated housing projects infested with drugs
and hopelessness, the remaining toeholds of generations of economically depressed people. In other words, the NOI's platform offered a lifeline for black
people whose lives remained untouched by civil rights victories.

Many converts explained that when their lives were plagued by drugs, alcohol, and lack of discipline and morals, Muhammad had extended kindness to
them, whereas others had only condemned their behavior. Inside the prisons,
Muhammad would make sure that the jailed believers received encouraging
letters, and Minister Malcolm X recalled how he "sends money all over the
country to prison inmates who write to him."[57] Muhammad cultivated an at-
mosphere of support and caring for his followers, and numerous testimonies
published in *Muhammad Speaks* suggest that he made good on his promise to
improve the conditions of those who believed.[58] Sister Doris 9X's name never
appeared in the newspaper, but her initial conversion story resembles those of
others who sought answers to problems of poverty and racial discrimination.

In 1966, at the young age of fourteen, Doris Jean gave birth to her daughter
Monisha in Columbus, Georgia. She was forced to marry the twenty-year-old
father of her baby, but that union did not last. She migrated to the Bay Area in
1972 to live with her brother. It was at his home that Doris answered a knock
on the door that would change her life. A young man dressed in a nice blue
suit and Elijah Muhammad's signature black bow tie was selling *Muhammad
Speaks* newspapers. He said, "Hello, Sister. I am Tim X, and I am with the Nation of Islam."[59] Doris had never heard of the NOI, but Brother Tim X patiently
explained how the group "cleaned the souls and hearts" of black people.[60] His

words about respecting black women made Doris pay close attention. The following week, Brother Tim X brought her a *Muhammad Speaks* and also sold her a scrumptious bean pie. It did not take long for him to offer a ride to the mosque, and by this time, Doris "was ready to investigate these special powers of the Honorable Elijah Muhammad."[61]

Doris borrowed a long dress, bought a headscarf, and dressed her daughter in comparable attire. Brother Tim X arrived promptly at 9:00 A.M. in a van. In addition to picking up Doris, he went to other homes, and one by one men and women boarded. When they reached Mosque #26, San Francisco, Doris recalled that the brothers, epitomizing gentlemanly behavior, escorted the women to the entrance. Inside the mosque, seats were directed toward a stage with a blackboard; women sat on the left side of the hall. Doris was drawn to the "glow" on the faces of NOI women as they sat proudly dressed in white. She wrote, "They seemed to radiate peace and harmony."[62] She listened eagerly to Minister Jael, who taught about whites being devils, the original black man, and the black woman as the mother of all civilization, but she clung especially to his words about joy and peace of mind. "Who in their right mind," she later wrote, "wanted to pass up peace in their lives? Money! Why not listen to the minister on these matters?"[63] As she left the mosque that day, she thought, "Oh yes, give me a good job and a wonderful home."[64] Her "entire body" felt like it "was flying on cloud nine."[65]

Doris continually thought about the NOI for close to three months. She recalled that Minister Jael "had the power to pound on a racial memory," conjuring the pain of black foreparents.[66] Fretting about providing for her daughter, Doris admitted that she "had a mental image of the wall-to-wall Muslim brothers. Just maybe one of them had [her] name on him."[67] During the summer of 1972, she answered Minister Jael's invitation and joined the NOI with her new friend, Jeanisse. She wrote to receive her "X," and made sure the letter was a direct replica of what she was given to copy, which included duplicating the curves of the alphabet. Thereafter, she began to attend the MGT-GCC. At the classes she recalled being taught how to cook, sew, and parent, but "most of all, their [the women's] responsibility to their black men, and how to carry themselves in order to gain respect."[68]

The classes were intense, and after three months Sister Jeanisse began to question whether she really wanted to be in the Nation. She complained to Sister Doris that "all [she] could hear was how to take care of a man, have babies, cook, sew, and be humble."[69] Sister Doris had heard the same instruction, and replied to Sister Jeanisse, "Oh! I see, you want to be free to attend school, and you're not ready to set a table for a man."[70] Elated that Sister Doris understood,

Sister Jeanisse added that she wanted to be a nurse and that if she married, her education would be cut short. Sister Jeanisse reasoned that she could not "serve two masters at the same time," and that it was important for her to obtain an education before she was an old woman.[71] As Sister Doris listened to Sister Jeanisse explain why she was opting out of the NOI, she quickly factored into the equation that she had no children. As a single mother on welfare, Sister Doris "wanted to stay in the religion and see the many promises made to the believers come true."[72]

Essentially, Elijah Muhammad assured people who had been discarded from the American populace and disinherited from the American dream that they, too, could have the symbols of power and wealth. By offering black people a middle-class lifestyle, Muhammad bypassed the political struggle to extend rights of citizenship. Instead, as T. H. Marshal would argue, he provided a vision couched in an ideal expression of modern citizenship, "against which achievements can be measured and toward which aspirations can be directed."[73] Thus, nationhood success was predicated on establishing a separate existence and presenting Islam as a materially empowering religion. One simply had to become a believer to receive the benefits.

Coming of Age in the Nation

One place where black nationalism and the promise of prosperity seemed to converge was in the education of the Nation's daughters. As a child, Sonsyrea Tate recalled hearing many voices instructing her on how to be a good Muslim girl. The most prominent declarations came from her paternal grandmother, Grand Willie, who had joined the NOI in the early 1950s. As a third-generation member of the Nation, Sonsyrea had vivid memories of her schooling at the University of Islam.

Born in 1966, Sonsyrea began attending the University of Islam at Mosque # 4, Washington, D.C., at the tender age of three. Wearing the school uniform, green pantaloons and a matching long top with a white headscarf, she rode the bus arriving to school by 7:45 A.M. to ensure that her body search was complete before the 8:00 A.M. class. The sister captain, Dean of Girls, and the inspector, from the MGT-GCC, examined each child for cleanliness and appropriate attire. Dirty garments, wrinkled clothing, unclean fingernails, or an overall unkempt appearance constituted reasons to send a child back home. They also looked into book bags for candy and gum, poked under headpieces to ensure neat hair, and slid their hands across each pupil's body. Although the pat-down "felt a little awkward" for Sonsyrea, the enemy was not above using a child to "destroy God's people," she was taught. This is why she also had to lift her small shoes to confirm that no one "had planted a tiny bomb in one of them."[74] Sonsyrea "was glad we had protection," especially after the mosque minister had taught that the devil, in 1963, had bombed a church in Birmingham, Alabama, killing four girls inside.[75] Body searches guaranteed Nation members that they would "never be sitting ducks like the Christians."[76] And, with the FOI outside of the mosque, another layer of protection was added for Sonsyrea and her peers. This inspection was the first stage of her daily school routine.

About two hundred students attended # 4's University of Islam with Sonsyrea in 1969.[77] The miseducation of black children happened in public schools, and the University of Islam sought to correct this wrong. Fifty-one mosques aimed to establish a University of Islam in the tradition of Master Fard's 1930s school, but in 1965, eight schools operated in Detroit, Chicago, Atlanta, Los Angeles, Boston, New York, Philadelphia, and Washington, D.C.[78] Of the eight, only three (Detroit, Chicago, Atlanta) held regular school sessions, while the other five functioned as Saturday schools.[79] Number 4's University of Islam had recently expanded from a Saturday school to a full school when Sonsyrea began attending in 1969. This is probably why she was accepted, since traditionally University of Islam students were aged four and older.[80] If a mosque had a school, the NOI required its members to enroll their children.

As with any parochial school, Nation parents were charged to send their children to the University of Islam. Beginning in 1959, they paid $2 per month for the first child and $1 each for the second, third, and fourth child.[81] There was no charge for a fifth child or more from the same family. Catholics and the NOI accommodated large families because both opposed the use of birth control. Additionally, both religious bodies expected the local mosque or parish to support its school. The NOI followers were resourceful and purchased school supplies for the mosques in the late 1960s and early 1970s with the popular S&H Green and Blue Chip trading stamps.[82]

Uneven mosque membership caused some University of Islam schools to be more elaborate than others. Sister Lottie, Muhammad's daughter, recalled her schooling in a "storefront" temple during the late 1930s and early 1940s, and it was not pleasant. She "begged" her father for permission to go a public school, but he "said, no. What would his followers think if he allowed his own daughter to attend a public school?"[83] By the 1960s only Chicago Mosque No. 2 and Detroit Mosque No. 1 had a separate facility with five classrooms, a library, and a large auditorium.[84] The University of Islam in Washington, D.C., was typical—it was located at the mosque and had makeshift classrooms walled by moving blackboards and plastic curtains. Despite the inadequate edifices, Muhammad's believers took pride in their schools and viewed them as a high priority for the NOI's future.

At the University of Islam, gender separation, beginning in the second grade (usually when the children were aged seven), required the girls to go to school during the first half of the day and the boys during the second half. The school day began at a morning assembly with the students washing (ablution) for prayers. Facing east, they stood with bowed heads and hands raised upward with open palms. Following the lead of the minister, they said together:

> O Allah I seek thy refuge from anxiety and grief and I seek thy refuge from lack of strength and laziness and I seek they refuge from cowardice and niggardliness and I seek thy refuge from being overpowered by debt and oppression of men.
>
> O Allah suffice thou me with what is lawful to keep me away from what is prohibited and with thy grace make me free from want of what is besides thee.
>
> Amen.[85]

Muhammad wrote in the 1966 University of Islam *Yearbook* that "this prayer should be repeated seven times a day as it sums up our greatest hindrances."[86] The students then pledged allegiance to the Muslim flag and sang a song, such as *Our School*, which included the refrain:

> Our school we love so faithfully
> Our school we love so dear
> Our school we love for faith and pride
> All praises to Allah.[87]

The morning gathering framed how Allah would bless the students if they worked hard, were thrifty, and obeyed authority.

The classes numbered twenty-five to thirty-five pupils and grade levels were combined, so the younger students, like Sonsyrea, would benefit from the advanced teachings directed at the older girls.[88] As a kindergartener, she would have received the Nation's *ABC Coloring Book*. Each letter was linked to a NOI principle. For example, under the letter "H," the students' read "'H' is for home. *All* of our people should have good homes, money, clothing, and friendship in all walks of life. Messenger Muhammad teaches us how to get things."[89] The children were taught reverence for Elijah Muhammad, who made material wealth and success possible because his doctrine came directly from Allah, in the person of Master Fard Muhammad. Sonsyrea was also introduced to the Arabic alphabet, safety rules, and the NOI's food practices.

Once Sonsyrea learned to read she was not exposed to silly fairy tales "like white kids," such as Cinderella.[90] Children learned to read from the only text-book published by the NOI, *Muhammad's Children First Grade Reader*. In 1963, Christine X Johnson wrote the textbook with the goal of developing an NOI identity. In the foreword she stated, "Through brief biographical sketches, in-tended for the very young child, I hope to plant the seed of self love and self-respect, that our Messenger and Leader The Honorable Elijah Muhammad has taught us and to strive for higher spheres in life and know why he is striving. To enable them to emulate the lives of great men and women of color and shake off the apathy and shame of being BLACK."[91] In 1963 educators praised the University of Islam as the only school in the country that had published its own elementary textbook and used innovative instruction materials; Sister Christine was often invited to speak outside of Chicago.[92]

The 130-page textbook opens with a photo of two girls. Their young eyes are in-tensely focused on a book page as they sit at a child's desk, wearing knitted white sweaters and head scarves tied under their small chins. Loosely curled bangs, probably rolled tightly the night before on sponge curlers, are hints that little Muslim girls' mothers take pride in their young daughters' grooming. The cap-tion under the photo reads: "I am Roche Muhammad. I am Linda Denise IX. We are Muslims of America. This is the story of our Nation."[93] Roche's and Linda's voices drive the multiple stories in the book. They tell the reader, for example, "This is our Flag," "This is our Messenger," "This is our Mosque of Islam," "This is our Grocery Store," "This is our Bakery," and "This is our Library."

One section of *Muhammad's Children First Grade Reader* that would surely draw the attention of girls was the story, "Barbara's Surprise." As a proud Muslim girl, Roche Muhammad is presented as neat, clean, polite, and full of joy. Her hardworking family has achieved social and economic success, evidenced by their move from a low-income housing project to a spacious suburban home. Barbara is Roche's friend, and the surprise for her, and for Sister Dolly, Barbara's mother, is the purchase of the home. "What!" gasped Sister Dolly in a loud voice when "Roche said with shining eyes" that they had moved. Her family had purchased a house "we could afford to buy, but we didn't tell anyone about it, until we were sure we could get it."[94] "Barbara's Surprise" taught the pros of thrift and self-motivation, NOI values that produced opportunity and up-ward mobility. Here the NOI's mission, as James H. Laue remarks, "becomes a thinly-veiled acceptance and rephrasing of American ideals," as opposed to an un-American doctrine.[95]

Just as crucial, Roche and Linda are also extremely proud of their skin color. Teaching black children to love their hue was no easy feat in a society that deemed everything dark as inferior. The success of the Nation in this area was remarkable and demonstrated on many fronts. Parents gave girls beautiful black dolls and other toys that would affirm self-love. One child wrote, "I am not worried if someone calls me a Nigger. I am not a Negro. I am Black. Black is the original color."[96] When a fifth-grade girl at the University of Islam in Detroit wrote about her future aspirations, she included, "I would like to be a nurse. I would like to have clothes. I would like to work. I would like to be black."[97] The University of Islam, instructors were mandated to inculcate racial pride and they were given tips on how to do so during their teacher orientation. Educating children to take pride in blackness, and being a Muslim, collided with the internalization of self-hatred and was fundamental to their remaking as NOI subjects.

As she grew older, Sonsyrea faced substantially increased academic expectations for herself and her peers. The religion class differed most substantially from traditional schooling. For example, a lesson taught at No. 4's University of Islam included:

1. A Muslim believes in . . . (one God).
2. It is forbidden for us to believe or serve any one other than . . . (Allah).
3. Allah is not a . . . (Spirit).
4. We must have a thorough . . . of ourselves (knowledge).
5. Allah came to North America in the year of . . . (1930).
6. The Uncle of Mr. W. D. Fard lived in the wilderness of . . . (North America).
7. Messenger Muhammad was sent by Almighty . . . (God).[98]

Usually taught over a forty-five-minute period, the religion class provided students the core of the NOI's teachings. The *Teachers' Handbook* that "each teacher MUST be familiar with the program of the MESSENGER. ALIEN or FOREIGN DOCTRINES WILL NOT BE ALLOWED or TOLERATED. ANYONE teaching against the concepts of ISLAM as taught by MESSENGER MUHAMMAD will be DISMISSED WITHOUT NOTICE."[99] All teachers had to observe prayer, and their classes were to support religious instruction and NOI culture. At the same time, the students studied black history from canonical texts. J. A. Rogers's *One Hundred Amazing Facts about the Negro*, John Hope Franklin's *From Slavery to Freedom*, and excerpts from the *Bulletin of African History* were just a few examples.

The pupils were exposed to personalities, events, and contributions that they could be proud of as black people. Even Sister Christine Johnson's *First Grade Reader* included a section, "Stories about Ourselves," wherein she introduced students to her travel to the city of Accra in Ghana, West Africa. She wrote about the importance of drumming and dancers; Shirley and W. E. B. Du Bois, who lived there; and the president of Ghana, Kwame Nkrumah. These words and images showed the power of black people and the possibilities of nation-building. Nonetheless, as the Nation held steadfast onto segregation principles, Martin Luther King Jr. was described as a "coward" in Sonyrea's class.[100] As early as 1959, Sister Thelma X wrote that King was "overloaded with devil's educa-tion" and that "if it were not for the color of his skin you could not tell him from Senator [Kenneth] Keating, both just as evil."[101] Everything about the United States was wicked and doomed, she claimed.

The students were drilled, like adults, on the Actual Facts and the Student Enrollment Rules of Islam. The girls were Elijah Muhammad's little goddesses and there was considerable pressure to perform well. Sonsyrea remembered that she "practiced reciting to [my]self every chance [I] got."[102] Being able to col-lectively articulate NOI teachings meant that they were in unity, special black girls, who would serve as an example of solidarity. But this same instruction disadvantaged Nation youth on standardized tests, where they reportedly scored below average on the multiple-choice aptitude, achievement, and "intelligence" Otis Beta and Gamma exams.[103] Nevertheless, as one educational scholar noted, their scores "are not better or worse than Negro students found in most North-ern inner cities," and at least the University of Islam students were graduating from high school.[104]

Finally, at the University of Islam, they were not allowed any music classes, fine art, or recess time for sport, because Muhammad thought that black people had done enough playing and now needed to get serious. But one could look at pictures painted by the students on the walls at the University of Islam in Chicago for signs of enjoyment. The sun, moon, animals, and rocket drawings produced at home were brought to school and posted.[105] Nation girls took plea-sure in their spare time at home and largely enjoyed their childhood. Whether painting pictures for school, playing board games, or having fun with siblings, their daily lives were filled with positive attention, particularly from their moth-ers. The NOI culture of course also shaped their extracurricular activities. For instance, Sonsyrea remembered having fun at a picnic until she looked up in the sky and thought she saw the Mother Plane.[106]

The University of Islam celebrated student achievement but placed a clear priority on young people becoming productive citizens for the development of the nation. Although about 50 percent of the teachers were not followers of Elijah Muhammad, they wore no makeup, only modest jewelry, and appropri-ate attire.[107] The girls both respected and feared their classroom role models, who had high expectations. As in Catholic schools, the teachers were strict and would use physical punishment to keep the students in line. Out-of-control girls were whacked with rulers on their hands and forced to stand in corners on one foot. One principal explained the use of corporal punishment as follows: "We believe in discipline and if it is necessary to use a stick, we believe in that, especially under the age of nine. We believe that, if, from the time they begin school, from the age of five to nine, we use that stick properly, it will make them recognize authority, and from then on it should not [be] necessary for the teacher to do anything but speak, and they will respond. . . . By the time we have carried them entirely through our system, we do not have any problems."[108] The teachers' discipline was backed up by Nation parents. Sonsyrea remembered that if one got into trouble at school, she was "to get whipped at home, too."[109] Muhammad required all his believers to be disciplined and accept authority. One principal commented on Muhammad's classroom power by saying, "If you want to quiet children, just mention to the children that the Messenger wants them to be quiet. Children knew this with the milk they were fed on."[110] Everyone respected Elijah Muhammad, the last Messenger of Allah, and all his followers had to know their place. For the girls, it was ultimately in the home as a wife and a mother.

Home economics, which largely taught how to cook from scratch, create a household budget, and sew, was a mandatory girls' course reinforced at the Junior (ages fifteen to nineteen) MGT-GCC. But the University of Islam curriculum also added typing and shorthand, secretarial skills used in the professional world, after some high school teens left the University of Islam in Chicago because these subjects were not offered in 1966. These teens had been able to convince their parents that this training was appropriate, and that their professional ambitions did not go against a modest womanhood. To stop the exodus, Muhammad first introduced typing by having six typewriters brought into the Chicago classroom, and he followed this course with shorthand.[111] Dean of Girls Sister Lottie, whose daily presence at the University of Islam in Chicago was felt by teachers and students alike, may have convinced her father to meet the teens' needs, or possibly lose future female NOI enrollment.[112]

Other girls expressed career ambitions beyond the secretarial pool. Ibrahim Mahmond Shalaby conducted a more extensive survey in 1967 of students at the University of Islam in both Chicago and Detroit. His comprehensive work reported that in Chicago, of the seventy-two girls in the fifth through eleventh grades, thirty-two wanted to work as teachers and nurses, eleven as doctors, seven wanted to travel, and six envisioned working as secretaries."[113] Detroiters mirrored the aspirations of the Chicago girls. Of the twenty-nine girls in grades 5 through 9, sixteen wanted to be a nurse, teacher or doctor, and nine wanted to travel.[114] These girls imagined living an adult life beyond domesticity by earning their own money and becoming self-sufficient.

Graduation, University of Islam, Chicago, February 20, 1962.
(Eve Arnold, Magnum Photos)

Elijah Muhammad's granddaughters, Clara Marie Sharrieff and her sister, Sharon Sharrieff, graduated from the University of Islam in 1963 and went directly to Central YMCA Community College in Chicago. Central YMCA, which opened in the fall of 1961, was a popular choice for the University of Islam graduates in Chicago.[115] Clara Marie, who wished to become a physician, planned to study mathematics and science, while Sharon majored in fashion design.[116]

Many Nation girls caught the fashion designing bug largely because they were introduced to sewing at a young age and had instruction at the University of Islam on advanced dressmaking.[117] Helen Joyner was twelve when her mother joined Mosque No. 7, New York, in 1972. She recalled how she learned to sew doll clothing with Sister Lois, who had a doll factory in her East Harlem apartment. Sister Helen's talent was cultivated in the NOI, and as an adult she became a celebrated fashion designer and elementary sewing teacher.[118]

Professional goals did not necessarily mean that a girl had rejected her Islamic roles of marriage and mothering. The fact that Shalaby's 1967 survey included thirty-two females who desired to have "family, home and money" in Chicago, with fifteen in Detroit indicating the same, speaks to this longing.[119] Yet they also wished for more and dreamed of aspirations outside the realm of children and husbands.

Teenage Years

During the teenage years, when self-doubt and self-consciousness creep in and linger on youth, the NOI females generally had a healthy sense of self-worth. They had grown up playing with black dolls and hearing that they were beautiful, princesses of the universe, who were most worthy of respect. And as long as they were at the University of Islam, the mosque, or at home, they knew this to be true. Outside of these safe places, however, they could face taunts and harassment. There are stories of girls having their headpieces snatched off, by "the lost and found children."[120] Sister Doris 9X recalled that when her daughter, Monisha, came home crying because neighborhood children were teasing her about her Muslim clothes, she forced her daughter "to face her attackers," and Sister Doris 9X approached their parents.[121] Sister Doris 9X and Monisha had been taught that civilized people exercised self-control and kept their emotions in check. Unbeknownst to Sister Doris 9X, however, her brother, who was not a member of the NOI, intervened on behalf of his niece. Whenever Monisha visited him, she had access to another set of clothes, which he had purchased, so that she could take comfort in looking like her peers.[122] He had also witnessed Monisha's crying, a natural reaction that she had been taught was inappropriate.

Unlike Christians who hollered at church and raised their voices in public, Nation girls were told to always think five times before speaking and to never act uncivilized by talking loud or showing emotions. A University of Islam motto written on a wall at Chicago was, "There is no substitute for intelligence; the nearest thing to it is silence."[123] Being quiet was a virtue that ran counter to the stereotypically boisterous black woman. Nation of Islam females were refined young ladies who under no circumstances should act like "fools."

Teen gossip was unfiltered foolishness that teachers and parents struggled to keep at bay. In the evenings, the girls would talk on the telephone, replaying school activities and repeating tidbits that they had heard from adults. Some of the sassier, highly opinionated teenagers would openly critique the Nation. Sonsyrea recalled Debra Mitchell, who "could see straight through the grown-ups," pointing out that the FBI infiltrators were not needed to start chaos, because "these people got enough confusion all their own."[124]

At a young age, Sonsyrea recalled the larger-than-life portrait of Elijah Muhammad that hung at the mosque. Like her peers, she saluted it and clicked her shoe heels in Gestapo military precision before passing by it.[125] The Messenger deserved all the respect and honor of a nation leader, and his power was burned into the students' subconsciousness on multiple levels. In school, they read his writings published in *Muhammad Speaks,* and at the mosque they listened to his radio message broadcast once a month on Sunday. When Sonsyrea remembered the radio lectures, she zeroed in on Muhammad's speech, which "was broken and his grammar was bad compared to the grammar" she had learned at the University of Islam.[126] Yet her grandmother and other adults were "spellbound" by "God's man" when they listened. Sonsyrea knew better than to say that Muhammad "didn't sound so smart," so she convinced herself "that he was so supersmart in his mind and that his mouth just couldn't keep up."[127] Over time she and other youth became somewhat "suspicious" of Muhammad's "spiritual food," but they knew enough about his power to keep their thoughts to themselves.[128]

Taking a cue from their elders, many of the teens learned to turn a blind eye on mixed messages from the NOI leadership. For example, at the Adult and Junior MGT-GCC, discussions continued to include diet and weight. Calisthenics and military-type drills were conducted at the classes to keep females in shape. All students were encouraged to eat two meals a day compared to their parents' one daily meal.[129] Sister Supreme Captain Ethel's March 1964 mandate, that all Nation sisters "must lose weight and must not weigh over 120 or 125 pounds, regardless of whether they are tall or short," magnified the focus on weight.[130] Sonsyrea remembered being told about Muhammad's theory that overweight people "breathed too much air and put too much burden on the earth's surface due to their gluttony."[131] But Sister Supreme Captain Ethel, unlike her mother Sister Clara, who always had a slim body, bordered on obese. She was 5'2" or 5'3" and weighed about 175 or 180 pounds at this time.[132] The weight impacted her health to the extent that she was diabetic and on insulin.[133] One can only imagine the whispered commentary among the girls.

University of Islam teens may have questioned contradictions more urgently as they struggled to hold onto girlhood freedoms, because puberty changed everything. As a young woman's body responded to hormonal changes, the mother's charge to monitor her daughter's moral conduct increased as well. Expectations of a modest womanhood intensified with menses. Young women were taught menstrual hygiene at the Junior MGT-GCC. Even men received instruction about the douche. Minister Malcolm X wrote a letter to Muhammad in early 1955, explaining that the FOI wanted to know if their wives should douche immediately after menstruation. If not, "what other means should they [tell their wives to] use to clean themselves out[?]."[134] Meanwhile at their own MGT-GCC meetings, mothers were instructed to make sure their daughters were dressed properly, so that they would maintain their virginity until marriage.[135]

Small gesturers mattered. Girls were instructed to cross their legs at the ankle and not the knee.[136] They were directed to lengthen their dresses to eight inches from the floor (their mothers were told to wear theirs at the ankle). Whether it was body weight or attire, it was crucial for sisters, young and old, to be unified on all things pertaining to the success of the NOI. The unity call, based on self-love, stifled anything that resembled a critique.[137] Girls were told not to question the wisdom of their elders. This applied even when young women simply wanted to experience privileges given to young NOI men. For instance, the protection of girls dictated that they had to ride the school bus until the twelfth grade, whereas boys could stop at grade 6.[138] And beginning in the third grade, boys could sell *Muhammad Speaks*, earning four cents off each paper, whereas girls had no equivalent option.[139] The restrictions made many yearn for the world outside of the NOI. Discontented youth raised in the Nation left when they moved away from home or became legal adults at the age of eighteen.

If a young woman did stay in the NOI, she would inherit the lifestyle of her mother. Similar to Christians who believed that it was better to marry than to burn for having premarital sex, young Muslim women felt pressured to enter legal unions quickly. The culture of the 1960s and 1970s would also certainly influence their possibilities of Nation womanhood.

Scapegoating and Controlling the Black Woman

The making of an NOI woman involved a complicated set of social relationships and obligations. Although rules for belonging always exist, Roger Smith's concept of "civic myths" explains how guidelines, eligibility, and exclusion are used to create political communities and thereby reflect their contested inner workings. In the case of the NOI, membership had always been anchored in gendered prescriptions. That is, men's and women's roles had to be reconfigured based on gendered hierarchies, and regulated differently to achieve black redemption — political emancipation, economic self-sufficiency, and social isolation from whites.

During the late 1960s and early 1970s, the ideal of a Nation woman was in direct conversation with the widespread myth of the matriarchal legacy of slavery. This myth, codified in the famous 1965 report by then Secretary of Labor Daniel Patrick Moynihan, insisted that black women had damned themselves by rendering black men "impotent" by shouldering the responsibilities of their families and working away from home.[140] Male black nationalists, within and outside of the NOI, agreed with the Moynihan Report and advocated the control of black women, stating that they had to assume a passive role, so that real men could rise up. Maulana Ron Karenga led the cultural nationalists with perceptions such as "what makes a woman appealing is femininity and she can't be feminine without being submissive."[141] Moreover, as Akiba ya Emilu stated, the man should be "the leader of the house/nation because his knowledge of the world is broader, his awareness is greater, his understanding is fuller and his application of this information is wiser."[142] That list certainly justified why he should be in charge!

Nation of Islam male leaders added white women to this garbled patriarchal potpourri. They accused black women during this period of mimicking the immoral habits of white women. Utilizing racial pride rhetoric as a form of control, Muhammad told black men to "stop our women from trying to look like them [white women]. By bleaching, powdering, ironing, and coloring their hair, painting their lips, cheeks, and eyebrows; wearing shorts, going half-nude in public places. Stop women form using unclean language in public (and at home), from smoking and drug addiction habits."[143] In sum, slavery as well as the behavior of the aggressive Western women had brought destruction to Allah's social order, generating a renegade black woman.

Imagine the pain felt by a black woman, wrote Abbey Lincoln, "accused as emasculator of the only thing she has ever cared for, her black man."[144] Barbara Smith noted, "Underlying this myth is the assumption that black women are towers of strength who neither feel nor need what other human beings do, either emotionally or materially."[145] This loaded assumption weighed heavily on black women, and wrestling with it could yield odd choices and "irrational extremes" in their effort to secure love, affirmation, protection, and support.[146] The "voguish creed" that many black women adopted in response to the "dangerous fiction" of them as emasculators was to "abandon their 'matriarchal' behavior, learn to speak only when they are spoken to, and take up positions three paces (or is it ten) behind their men," argued Jean Carey Bond and Patricia Peery.[147]

In this pervasively negative context, Elijah Muhammad helped camouflage the gender inequalities in the NOI with the affectionate rhetoric of love, protection, and respect for black womanhood. This proved deeply significant given the scathing, sexualized criticism offered by other black men during this period. The hateful views uttered by Eldridge Cleaver doubtlessly stand as the most misogynistic. He wrote while in prison, prior to his Black Panther Party membership, that he knew that "the white man made the black woman the symbol of slavery." In his mind, this explained his lack of attraction and respect for black women. He gloated, "The only way that I can bust my nuts with a black bitch [is] to close my eyes and pretend that she is Jezebel. If I was to look down and see a black bitch underneath me or if my hand happened to feel her nappy hair, that would be the end, it would be all over."[148]

Within this hostile climate, the Nation could feel like a safe space wherein black women and their children were respected, adored, and protected. Sister Vera X Lewis wrote that the Messenger revered black women. She testified that he was "not afraid to point out how the black woman has been abused for some 400 years." She was thankful that her leader "instills in black men a rebirth to their natural urge to protect black women." White men "or even misguided black men can no longer use black women for ill purposes. We cease being their slaves, both mentally and physically," she remarked.[149] Sister Gertrude Bogans concurred that "all so-called American Negro women should love and cherish our leader for teaching our men how to treat them. We know that we were not used to this kind of [respectful] treatment before. The Messenger is teaching our men how to act and think."[150] He was also teaching them that their manhood was located in what Farah Griffin describes as the "promise of protection."[151]

Appealing to women, particularly poor single mothers, undervalued workers, and dark-skinned black women who, as Griffin aptly points out, "have been excluded from the discourse of the precious, pure, and protected," Muhammad affirmed their womanhood, which continued to be denied.[152] Minister Malcolm X reiterated Muhammad's chastisement of black men and stated: "We treated our own women as if they were mere animals, with no love, respect, or protection, beating and abusing them even in public places, selling them from man to man, letting all other races (even the Slavemaster) mix freely with them, having no regard whatsoever for their feelings, in public or private."[153] Until black men learned to love and respect their women, Muhammad wrote, "we will never be a fit and recognized people on earth. The white people here among you will never recognize you until you protect your woman."[154] Considering societal violence, protection was sometimes warranted, but as Griffin argued, it "need not be equated with possession."[155] Additionally, Muhammad's assertion that "there is no nation on earth that has less respect for and as little control of their woman as we so-called Negroes here in America," indicted the domineering proclivities of black nationalism.[156]

But behind the rhetoric of love and protection, Muhammad believed his own version of an emasculation theory: that women's liberation and the desire for equality left black men unemployed and unable to provide for their families. Sister Dorothy Wedad wrote in *Muhammad Speaks* that "if the black woman would stay in her place, men could find work, and support them like they should." Further, Muhammad bemoaned black women's public lives: "[Our women] are allowed to walk or ride the streets all night long, with any stranger they desire. They are allowed to frequent any tavern or dance hall that they like, whenever they like. They are allowed to fill our homes with children other than our own. Children that are fathered by the very devil [white] himself."[157] Believing that black women were out of control justified tightening restrictions on the NOI's female members, and he instructed the leadership to heavily enforce strict rules regarding women moving about outside alone, especially in the evening.

Nation women who worked or went to school at night faced real dilemmas. At the time of Sister Sonia 5X Sanchez's membership, she served as the chairperson of the Black Studies Department of Amherst College in Massachusetts. To avoid "deep trouble," she initially dealt with the restriction by getting another woman, one outside of the Nation, to travel with her. On other occasions, a Nation brother would serve as security, "as a traveling man," and she would have to pay for his lodging. But these arrangements were not enough, even after she explained to the mosque minister and sister captain that she had no control over the time frames of work-related events. Finally, she "just stopped explaining, cause [she] knew they knew and that they did not want to understand."[158] Other women wrote letters directly to Elijah Muhammad asking for approval to stay out after dark because of school or work. After offering alternatives to their requests (such as asking a professor for a day class as a substitute) and raising issues of safety (such as exposing oneself to the "mercy of rapers and insulting people"), Muhammad concluded that he "did not approve of any Sisters being out at night."[159]

Sister Sonia 5X's fame opened a position of privilege in the Nation, but this did not safeguard her from the challenges of being a woman in a male-dominated organization. "It was not easy being in the Nation," she said in 1983. "I was/am a writer. I was speaking on campuses. In the Nation at that time women were supposed to be in the background. My contribution to the Nation has been that I refused to let them tell me where my place was. I would be reading my poetry some place, and men would get up and leave, and I'd say, 'Look, my words are equally important.' So I got into trouble."[160] Suspension, isolation, intimidation, beatings, and even death ranked among the NOI punishments.[161] The poet's behavior was evidence for some that she did not want to be a Muslim, that she was still a "Pan-Africanist." As a consequence, she began to "treat the Nation the way you would treat a Church. Go on and do your business and if you're in town show up for the sermon. And the rest of the week go to work, take care of your children, and do what you need to do."[162]

The MGT and the Remaking into Muslim Women

Living in Amherst gave Sonia 5X enough distance from the closest Mosque, #11 in Dorchester, near Boston, to excuse her absence from weekly Nation activities. She did make the effort to attend the MGT-GCC classes at Mosque #7 when she was in New York, and the "big joke in the Nation was I traveled so much that they gave [me more] materials to memorize."[163] On her arrival at the MGT-GCC, the sister captain always opened the conversation with, "you know you haven't been here for class," and Sister Sonia 5X would reply, "I've been traveling, I know my lessons, I can recite them." Always, "of course, there was resistance" from the sister captain, who would tell her, "no you cannot recite all of them."[164] When the sister captain refused to let her participate, Sister Sonia 5X would sit in a chair and pull a book out of her purse to read. At one class, Minister Louis Farrakhan came into the room and was surprised to find her reading a book in the corner. He asked, "What are you doing here, Professor Sanchez?" She replied, "Well, I'm actually trying to eventually recite all the things." He asked, "Do you know it?"[165] After Sister Sonia 5X had correctly responded to a question the minister had offered, he then went over to the sister captain to have a private talk with her.

As in the 1950s, the sister captains continued to set the tone for the MGT-GCC classes in the late 1960s and 1970s, and their enforcement of rules controlling women could prove even harsher than the ministers.' Sister Hafeeza Kasif in Washington, D.C., believed that the sister captains were "much harder on the women when giving out restrictions than her husband [who was a mosque minister] ever was."[166] At the MGT-GCC class women were taught to go out only if they had no other choice, and that they should be speedy. Instructions included, "Don't just drag through the street. . . . If you're going somewhere, go. Don't put yourself in the position where someone [can say] 'Oh baby, how you doin' sugar?'"[167] On one occasion Sister Hafeeza wanted to go to Baltimore, but the sister captain denied her request. Sister Hafeeza was clear on the appropriate way to articulate her wants. Out of respect for her husband, if she desired to go anywhere, she never said, "'I'm going'; I just said, 'I'd like to go' or 'I want to go.'"[168] In this instance, she refused to allow the sister captain to control her and went to Baltimore anyway. On her return, the sister captain tried to suspend her for several days. Yet Sister Hafeeza stood up to the sister captain, because she believed that her husband never confined her and therefore would not allow the dictates of the sister captain to control her either.

Sister Baheejah (Bertha) Shakur in Detroit remembered how in 1966 Sister Captain Nettie Mae X "ruled the MGT class with an iron hand." She even put Sister Baheejah out of the Nation one time. At a meeting, when someone said something that Sister Baheejah agreed with, she voiced, "That's right." Immediately, Sister Captain Nettie asked, "who was that that said that's right?" When Sister Baheejah raised her hand, she said, "Well, you could just be dismissed." Sister Baheejah was suspended from the Nation community for thirty days. She could have no contact with NOI members. After the month, Sister Baheejah presented herself, dressed in MGT-GCC garb, and provided her name and number (861) at the mosque. She went to the MGT-GCC class, where it was assumed that she had learned her lesson, so she "melt[ed] right into doing whatever the group was doing."[169]

Despite this experience, Sister Baheejah recalled positively that it was because of Sister Captain Nettie's teachings that they learned the "skill[s] that we would need to become a lady."[170] She taught them how to talk and walk and not to slouch. One's clothes could never be wrinkled, never too tight, too short, nor mismatched. They were also supposed to keep their hair covered, though the example of Sister Baheejah suggests women were flexible in following this rule: she only covered hers at the mosque. When she went to work or even the store, she rarely covered her hair. As she later asserted, the "hijab is internal, it is how you carry yourself." But Sister Baheejah acknowledged that mosque members would have a problem seeing her outside with uncovered hair. Her mother, who was also in the NOI, would tell her all the time, "Baheejah, you know you are supposed to have a scarf on your head." She would reply, "Yeah, you're right," but "if not wearing a scarf is the worst sin that I commit in my lifetime, and I ask Allah for his forgiveness, I think I'm still going to be okay."[171]

The majority of the mosque activities resembled those of earlier decades. The women still got pleasure from their communal gatherings. Sister Sonia 5X recalled how the sisters were "kind and gentle."[172] Sister Doris 9X's favorite night was Tuesday, Unity Night, when the men and women would come together in harmony and enjoy activities. Popular entertainers who were also in the NOI would sometimes be featured, such as Kool and the Gang and Joe Tex.

At the Thursday MGT-GCC class, the women encouraged one another to be their best selves and they shared talents. The women were still taught to eat only one meal daily and were weighed twice monthly. The ideal weight of 120 pounds harkened back to Master Fard's original 1930s mandate and was still enforced: all overweight sisters continued to pay a toll of a penny for each overweight pound. Given the proliferation of the fast-food industry, Nation women found themselves even more challenged than in earlier decades: African American women born after 1955 had a 62 percent chance of obesity.[173] Also in the MGT-GCC, women continued to learn to cook proper meals, sew together, and study the Actual Facts.

The changing times also introduced new discussions. For example, Sister Ruth Mitchner, from Durham, North Carolina, remembered that a mosque search produced a tampon from her purse and she was reported. Playtex introduced the first mass-marketed tampon in 1971, and many religious groups opposed its use. An MGT-GCC class was taught thereafter on the importance of not "stick[ing] anything foreign in your body."[174]

As important as the MGT-GCC was, however, Elijah Muhammad was clear about his role as regulator of the picture the NOI women (and men) presented to the world. Remaking meant not only treating one's female body as a personal temple but also wearing clothing and styles that signaled one's identity to others. Islam is a visible religion, and Muhammad "made" NOI women "respectable" and "civilized" through the adoption of a modest dress code. The tailored uniforms not only combated the myth of the sexually deviant black woman but also gave the appearance of a civilized community with outward forms of religiosity. Sister Shirley X Morton testified that she wore clothes of a civilized people, with dresses far below her knees. This "makes me respect myself better but it also makes other people respect me."[175] Sister Baheejah remembered that the uniform brought "lots and lots of respect back then."[176] If there was an "old drunk on the corner cursing," he would "straighten right up and speak, good afternoon sisters."[177] Everyone respected the Nation women in uniform, "the way they used to do with nuns," said Sister Baheejah.[178] The MGT-GCC uniform was often a protective shield that earned women respect wherever they went.

Women were pressured to purchase their mosque uniforms, priced between $25.75 and $39.95, from the NOI Chicago Clothing Factory.[179] Under the direction of Sister Supreme Captain Ethel, who was in charge of garments fitting properly, the Clothing Factory would become a cash cow for the NOI because women were threatened with six-month suspensions for not purchasing their uniforms directly from the factory.[180] Stipulations around clothing ignited tensions between sister captains and sisters, mothers and daughters, as well as husbands and wives.

Certainly, the uniform clashed with the styles of the vast majority of first-time mosque visitors in the late 1960s and early 1970s, many of whom wore African-inspired apparel and Afro hairstyles. Sister Marguerite X testified that she was "one of those Afro-wearers and was of the opinion that Africans or so-called Negroes imitating Africans was the only beautiful way of life." But her opinion changed after joining the NOI."[181] Sister Evelyn wrote, "If you see a woman dressed as a Muslim sister, you will think that she is a Muslim and treat her with respect due a Muslim woman. By the same token, if you see a woman dressed in hot pants, halter top, afro puff wigs on her head, and mud packed on her face, you will think she must be a loose woman and treat her as one."[182] Nation women were also quick to point out how ridiculous black women looked who preached about Africa being beautiful wearing filthy miniskirts and shorts that exposed their bodies.

Muhammad saw long hair as a "woman's" style.[183] Sister Kathleen X attested to "the fact that [the] wearing of bushy hair is uncivilized."[184] Muhammad charged women to use "only a warm comb" in their hair and to "keep their hair neat."[185] Historian E. Frances White remembered that women in the Nation "resurrected their straighten combs," while revolutionary sisters "experimented with braids and afros."[186] Muhammad did not approve of the Afro-centric styles and exercised his last-resort measure to regain authority through dismissal. He announced in 1968 that if the women were not satisfied "with the styles I give them then I am not satisfied with you being my follower."[187]

Even as sisters worked to remake themselves into proper Muslim women, tensions ran through the Nation. The 1970s brought a greater emphasis on financial tithing and materialism than ever before in the history of the NOI. Many of the sister captains wore furs and expensive jewelry and drove luxury cars, while rank-and-file women were not financially positioned to do so. The paradoxes of membership became more glaring in terms of personal fulfillment and a cultural home. The women were working hard for the Nation, making their homes comfortable, ensuring that their husbands and children were supported, fundraising for the NOI; nonetheless, many remained poor and stressed because of poverty. The vision of power, wealth, and peace of mind that had attracted so many was slipping away from the most sincere and dedicated believers.

Finally, though being a follower of the Honorable Elijah Muhammad might bring both pleasure and pride, it also meant an inability to voice criticism. Women were instructed even at MGT-GCC meetings to write down their questions and submit them to the sister in charge, because a question asked out loud could "discourage a new or a weak Sister in the Temple."[188] If anyone disagreed, they had to leave the mosque immediately. Whatever her attraction to its nationalist core, after five years in the NOI, Sister Gwendolyn Simmons became disenchanted. Her words capture the objections that must have eaten away at many women, whether they remained the laments of believers or became the grievances that spurred a decision to leave:

> The emphasis on money and the "forced" payment of dues, tithes, newspaper sales money, bake sales money, the receipts from the endless fundraisers, which burdened the poor people in the organizations mercilessly, the extravagant lifestyles of the "Royal" Muhammad Family, the structural

and militaristic hierarchy, to which the Believers were forced to submit, the authoritarian and sometimes brutal nature of some of the leadership, the hinted-at and actual violent punishments meted out to the disobedient; and last, but certainly not least for me, the horrible secondary status of women in the movement.[189]

CHAPTER TEN

MODESTY, MARRIAGE,

AND MOTHERHOOD

For women such as Sister Gwendolyn 2X Simmons, the "horrible second-ary status" of women in the Nation of Islam led ultimately to the need to break away. That break was a declaration of resistance to male domination that others such as Sister Clara, or any typical Nation woman who fully accepted the rules, did not make; to suggest otherwise would be false. The NOI was a socio-religious movement framed within masculinist Islamic traditions. But the desire to locate and unpack discrete moments of resistance by NOI women gestures toward an understanding of "agency-as-resistance."[1] Or, said another way, can self-determination itself be read as resistance to power?

There is an assumption, Saba Mahmood brilliantly argues, "that all human beings have an innate desire for freedom, that we all somehow seek to assert our autonomy when allowed to do so, that human agency primarily consists of acts that challenge social norms and not those that uphold them."[2] Exploring how Sister Clara and other NOI women chose to live within the grips of patriarchal power has been a driving focus of this book. In this concluding chapter, I aim to think through their collective choices, which run against feminist sensibilities, to arrive at another way to understand empowerment for black women during the period from 1930 to 1975.

The realities of race, class, gender, sexuality, and religion in black women's lives creates for them an intersectional existence. Legal scholar Kimberlé Cren-shaw argues that the recognition of intersectionality shifts our understanding of patriarchy as the main root of black women's oppression.[3] Because of the "cross-currents of racism and sexism," Crenshaw writes, black people live in an environment that "creates sex-based norms and expectations which racism operates simultaneously to deny; Black men are not viewed as powerful, nor are Black women seen as passive."[4] The result of these "cross-cutting forces," have pushed some in the black liberation struggle "to create institutions and to build traditions that are intentionally patriarchal."[5] The NOI represents one such movement, bent on reversing patterns that seemed to collude with racist gender expectations.

Modesty

Throughout the history of the NOI, the female membership labored to debunk every stereotype that haunted black womanhood. They remade themselves into Islamic women by prioritizing modesty, marriage, and motherhood. All three of these goals are in line with traditional thinking that places women on the periphery of masculine power. Nation women traded any desire for fuller self-determination for their Islamic faith, which gave them a blueprint on how best to disrupt and dismantle harmful racial stereotypes in order to secure honor and protection.

According to Muhammad, exhibiting modesty and restraint would reveal Nation womanhood as the antithesis of the bodacious, hypersexualized black woman. Nation women accepted this direction through a rigorous self-cultivation based on feminine principles scripted and taught at the MGT-GCC weekly meetings.[6] By following specific requirements for proper attire and public conduct, Nation women made a bold outward expression of their religious devotion to Elijah Muhammad's Nation. And many of them were pleased with the results. Standing erect and looking regal brought pride and self-esteem. "When you dress in your Muslim attire, one automatically feels seven feet taller," wrote Sister Ruby.[7] Respect was accorded to them in return. Sister Baheejah recalled how black people gave them ample room to walk on the street when they wore the official uniform.

It is vital to recognize that as NOI women moved throughout their communities, they were exhibiting their "truth." That is, their remaking was not about adopting an alien posture solely for public consumption. Their markers of piety evidenced an interior virtuousness. Modesty and humility were central to their inner sense of themselves, as well as their outer self-presentation.

Many of the feminine virtues NOI women adopted can be read as disempowering behavior. Avoiding the gaze of men, and lowering one's eyes in their company, can be seen as self-deprecating. Additionally, the development of feminine shyness as a means to secure a husband gestures toward problematic cunning.[8] Yet we cannot dismiss the NOI women's own interpretation of their deportment. They saw their behavior as respectful of the men in their lives — men who were not respected by the culture at large.

Moreover, Nation women celebrated their Islamic modesty as "natural beauty," in contrast to other black women whose attire and disposition revealed what they saw as the depravity of the secular world. Of course, the naturalness of their "natural beauty" had its limits. Afro hair styles were not only prohibited but castigated as uncivilized by Muhammad. Nation women's hair needed to be smooth, and if that required a pressing comb, so be it. Still, some black women outside of the NOI acknowledged Nation women's conduct as a courageous attack against hegemonic aesthetics. Wanting to be seen as lovely too often translated into wearing unflattering wigs, ill-fitting clothing, and uncomfortable shoes. On numerous occasions, Nation women reported how their sisters were living on the "dead level" and feared a disinvestment in beauty culture norms.

Not that playing by the rules of the oppressive beautification industry was never rewarded. Years later, Muhammad Ali could still recall the attire worn by his first wife, Sonji Roi, at their first meeting. He told her, "You had on a pair of tight blue jeans with a red-striped, long-sleeved sweater jacket. And when you got up I noticed that you had a beautiful little shape and a slight twist in your hips when you walked past me. I was more convinced that I was going to marry you."[9] As a woman who had won beauty contests, modeled, and worked in "bunny clubs," Roi had grown accustomed to having roaming eyes on her.[10] The same physicality and sensuality that had opened doors of opportunity for her captured Ali's attention. Soon thereafter, Ali also washed Roi's hair because he had noticed her scratching her scalp. "Let me wash out the dandruff," he said.[11] He wanted to see the "beautiful black hair under [her] wig that hadn't been combed for a while."[12]

After marriage to Ali, Roi confronted the mandate that an Islamic woman's beauty must be reserved exclusively for her husband. Unlike other attractive women who joined the NOI, Roi refused to let go of her beauty regimen, which relied on lipstick, wigs, false eye lashes, miniskirts, and form-fitting knit dresses. Her investment in American beauty culture kept her at odds with the NOI standards for women. In the end, Roi left the NOI.[13] But if wearing what she liked gave Roi back an identity she found pleasing, one must still question how much more freedom she, or any other heterosexual American woman, has in submitting to one set of standards for femininity—i.e., the beauty industry—rather than another—i.e., the NOI's rules. One can argue that in both cases, the "epitome of feminization is to be a submissive follower" to someone or something.[14]

Marriage

Given that NOI women were unveiled, wore unique uniforms, and covered their head in creative ways to show a fashionable hairstyle, their outward religiosity differed from that of other Muslims. Nonetheless, their overall deportment positioned them squarely in Islamic traditions; submission was required of all women, not only to a higher being, Allah, but to males, such as fathers, husbands, ministers, and Elijah Muhammad. In particular, the MGT-GCC teachings prioritized marital harmony and the obligation of women to fulfill the needs of their husbands. "One cannot deny that she is humble, considerate, and respectful to all that she encounters," and that "her pleasure is to please her husband," wrote Sister Ruby.[15]

Submission, as a theological concept, makes it difficult to isolate a woman's personal desire and aspirations from her spiritual beliefs. Nevertheless, peeling away the individual from others to locate a detached core provides one way to discover inner passions and yearnings. What were NOI women after when they agreed to submit to their husbands? Can we find agency in that submission?

As we have seen throughout this book, NOI women repeatedly noted their attraction to a family model where the husband (and father, if there were children) provided economic security. Sister Eula and Brother Herbert had a clear understanding that it was the duty of the husband to provide for his wife; thus, Sister Eula envisioned a marriage with the choice of not working outside of the home. This choice was desirable for NOI women, and they were not alone is this regard.

For a good portion of black women, mental health is linked to wealth, and balance is an outgrowth of financial security. Not worrying about the payment of monthly bills brings peace of mind, which opens avenues for self-expression. Yet financial freedom has always proven difficult to achieve as a single black woman in the United States, and it is human nature to want companionship. Seeking relief from their own vulnerability, heterosexual black women have leaned toward marriage for both emotional and financial well-being. In fact, contemporary black women are more likely than white women to report a preference for males' having primary economic responsibility, "despite the remoteness of such a prospect" in the twenty-first century.[16]

At the inception of the Allah Temple of Islam in 1930, there were no national census statistics on households and family characteristics. The 1940 census is the starting point for numbers and a national conversation about the black family.[17] In 1947, one year after Elijah Muhammad was released from prison because of his refusal to be drafted into the Armed Forces, 67.2 percent of black women between the ages of twenty-five and forty-four were married.[18] During the 1950s, the rise of "companionate marriage," based on the "gratification of playing marital roles well: being good providers, good homemakers, and responsible parents," flourished in the United States.[19] Prior to this period, marriages were largely seen institutionally around gendered divisions of labor and responsibility. Love and friendship were now amplified as more meaningful, but the divide between the single-earner male breadwinner and the housewife remained firmly intact. The expansion of the NOI coincided with this larger cultural shift marked by the baby boomer generation. When NOI membership was at its maximum during the early 1960s, marriage was still fundamental to African American life. In 1960, 64.9 percent of black women between the ages of twenty-five and forty-four were living with a husband. Only 10 percent of black women from this same age group in 1960 had never been married.[20] By 1970, this number had decreased slightly to 62 percent, before dropping precipitously to only 44.7 percent in 1980.[21] Though marriage rates among African Americans declined drastically beginning in the 1980s (by 1990, 35 percent of black women age twenty-five to forty-four had never been married), during the years of Muhammad's leadership, Nation women were no different from their black sisters in their desire to be married.

The wish for a husband cannot be reduced to the single variable of a longing for a breadwinner. Nonetheless, William Julius Wilson documents that the black "male marriageable pool" has to a great degree relied on the assumption of employment.[22] And statistical evidence that prior to the 1980s most black men had jobs "supports the hypothesis that the rise of female-headed families is directly related to increasing black male joblessness."[23] When the NOI was established in 1930, 80 percent of black men were employed; this number had dropped to 56 percent by 1983, largely due to global economic shifts.[24] This massive decline has transformed the possibilities of a financially stable male household head. Add to this number the high rate of black male incarceration and premature death, and the ability of black men "to provide economic support is even lower than official employment statistics convey," writes Wilson.[25] This explains a "remoteness" or a "shrinking pool" of marriageable black male household heads by the 1980s. Thus recent lower rates of black marriage do not reflect a simple change in the interest on the part of black women.

Instead, the preference for a male breadwinner has remained consistent among many black heterosexual women. Even the possibility that relinquishing financial power to one's husband might be a direct slide into domination has not diminished black women's fondness for male family heads. Moreover, all the possible harmful elements of an institution so "deeply embedded in its reinforcing of inequality, gender roles, gender hierarchy, and male power" have not dismantled patriarchal marriage as a coveted choice for many women.[26]

So, NOI women were hardly alone in choosing a conventional gender power structure. True, one can argue that there is a difference between desiring economic support and consciously agreeing to be submissive. But there is another factor in women's decision to join and follow the teachings of the NOI. Family structure in African American life has a complicated history, and many scholars have discussed the impact of slavery on that structure.[27] The NOI's teachings were in conversation with this literature in that they also emphasized how slavery allegedly emasculated black men and empowered black women as female heads of household. In the case of NOI women, they agreed with the need to cement masculine power for a strong black nation. An acceptance of a gendered order of creation and authority, wherein "men are inherently and naturally superior to women," is not why African American women largely desire black men as heads of households.[28] Nor is it about "formenism," a concept that seeks to establish romantic patriarchy and the belief that "submission will actually lead to women's liberation and to lifelong happy marriages."[29] Black women ultimately want to make men greatly responsible to them and their families, giving them a sense of security in a violently racist environment. For NOI women, a masculine and feminine arrangement of the world mattered because it dictated that Nation men become responsible to their families.

This is an important distinction. NOI women agreed to submit to their husbands in the context of the NOI teaching that a man should not marry if he was unable to support a family. The logic on this point mirrors contemporary studies that indicate "when men don't work or don't earn adequate wages they do not perceive themselves, nor are they perceived by Black women, to be marriage material."[30] Unlike Christian evangelicals who advance that it is within "a benignly patriarchal family" that "males become men" because they are motivated to be responsible, the NOI teachings advanced that only responsible men should be married.[31] In fact, an irresponsible male proved unworthy of a NOI female.

To study marriage is challenging, because marriage is "often seen as a coveted realm of privacy in a world where little is private."[32] Marriages in the Nation of Islam were conducted by officials of the state, and not by its unlicensed ministers, which supports the idea that "state-sanctioned marriage is a public institution, and the state, not the parties who enter into it, determine the terms of the marriage contract."[33] Scholars document that the marital contract among black people "has always differed in significant ways from that embraced by the dominant white society," because "marriage has not been protective for black women and has rarely provided the substantial economic benefits that white wives could expect."[34] The NOI pledged to give black women what white women took as a given — protection and financial support. At the same time, in line with views from other traditional religions, the NOI saw marriage as the only respectable "form for intimacy and family life."[35] This is why Sister Gwendolyn 2X and Brother Michael Simmons, who had lived together as an unwed couple prior to their NOI membership, had to legally marry, and show proof by bringing the certificate to the mosque, when they joined the Nation. The document represented how "civilized" adults should live together. The NOI cherry-picked aspects of hegemonic society to incorporate into its black nation.

After marriage, as in most pietistic traditions, Nation men faced even more pressure to provide and protect, with the ultimate goal of a "healthy masculinity," which Stu Weber described for Christian men as "initiation—the provision of direction, security, stability and connection," with a wife.[36] "Healthy masculinity"—and the NOI's mandate that "patriarchal authority" be balanced with love, respect, and protection—are interchangeable principles, yet often hard to calculate. It is much easier for scholars to dig in pessimism—to showcase the unloved woman or the disrespected wife as the way to analyze gender domination. But the lived experiences of African American women in general, and of NOI women in particular, demand us to do more. Just as, at the beginning of Sister Clara's Islamic journey, she was pulled toward Master Fard's teachings because of its power to remake her husband into a dependable family man, the establishment of healthy families has been the endmost concern for most black women and the reason why some engage in bargaining within patriarchal relationships.

Within the NOI Islamic paradigm, clear gendered boundaries and roles constituted the only way to make a righteous home for a prosperous black nation. The MGT-GCC teachings required wives to master the disposition of their husbands to successfully uplift and honor manhood for this purpose. Sister Belinda, for example, had to work with a husband, Muhammad Ali, who was temperamental and moody. She carefully trumped patriarchy for her own ends so as not to chip away at her husband's manhood. But Sister Belinda's arsenal also included respectful disagreement with Ali. She was opposed to additional wives and told him so. If, in the end, she yielded to her husband's authority on this matter, it was because she believed that the shortcomings of his decision would become self-evident.

The idea of yielding can be seen as a sleight of hand, a concept meant only to conceal or mystify simple obedience. Because yielding as a strategy fails to resemble a sledgehammer attack against patriarchy, it is missed as a possible form of agency or power. But Sally Gallagher aptly points out that substituting words can create a space for freedom to act. Christian evangelical wives also yield as a strategy and report that "losing is winning." For example, "When women give in, against their better judgment, they see husbands change. Submission becomes a way to encourage husbands to reciprocate both in monitoring what they say and in adopting their wives' perspectives."[37] Sister Belinda banked on this outcome, that Ali would see that additional women would be harmful to their marriage, and that this insight would push him to relinquish the idea. She was not wrong; tragically, however, for Sister Belinda and their four children, Ali's realization came too late. Years later, as we have seen, Ali did admit that his behavior had been shameful: "It hurt my wife; it offended God."[38] In the meantime, nonetheless, Sister Belinda was not bound to wait for Ali to come to grips with his immorality. When her strategy of yielding did not work as she had hoped, she did not obey; she ended her marriage by filing for divorce in 1976, charging Ali with "desertion, adultery, and mental cruelty."[39]

Sister Belinda's story demonstrates both the freedom that could come with financial security and the cost that very freedom might entail. Like other NOI believers, Sister Belinda wanted a breadwinning husband, so that she could be a stay-at-home wife and mother and live according to her religion. Once Muhammad Ali's boxing privileges were restored in 1970, he earned millions, providing Sister Belinda, and their family, a lavish lifestyle. Sister Belinda was able to use her financial freedom to tap into, and expand, her creative interests; she was noted for having many hobbies, and her repertoire for self-expression was vast. Although Ali's superstar stature certainly impacted his moral commitment to his marriage, as a patriarchal head, his income engendered real and tangible freedoms to his wife. On the other hand, Sister Belinda shared that Ali's "psychological games" devastated her spirit and whittled away her self-esteem over time.

Unbalanced power relations can function in both blatant and subtle ways, oppressing women and injuring their identities.[40] Certainly, there is a fine line between service to one's spouse and abuse, and many Nation women walked this tightrope daily. Sister Doris 9X recounted that women within her Northern California circle experienced a range of dominating NOI men; she observed, "Now I see why some of the Muslim marriages didn't make it out of the seventies."[41] Sister Zante, for example, said that "men didn't only want control [;] they got it[—]by force if necessary."[42] Tragically, Sister Zante knew brothers who beat their wives, and others who locked their wives in the home by means of a "padlock on the outside of the door," keeping the sisters confined like prisoners until their husbands returned for the evening.[43] When Sister Zante's husband began to replicate dominating behavior and "started tapping on" her, she refused "to go for that."[44] Although she seems to have stopped the physical abuse, Sister Zante shares that her husband remained "mean and cruel" throughout their marriage.[45] Wounded in homes where love and peace should have resided, Sister Zante and other Nation women experienced harm and humiliation due to their subordinated status.[46]

Nation women who suffered abuse because they took the risk of accepting patriarchal headship and the possibility of yielding and bargaining in their marriages because of their faith in the higher power of Allah, should not, however, be blamed for their own oppression. Instead, we need to understand the choices they made in the context of the options available to them. As political scientist Jennifer Einspahr argues, it is more useful for feminists "to treat both domination and freedom as structural concepts" that highlight the position of the individual in the world.[47]

Black women's position in the world has led to multidimensional frustrations. Historically and in the current moment, African American women too often occupy the lowest rung of the capitalist ladder, at great distance from structural power, which directly informs one's freedom to act. Largely confined to the working class, their status as workers "conflicts with norms that women should not [work], often creating personal, emotional and relationship problems" in their lives.[48] The burden of poverty is compounded by the assumption that their survival tactics emasculate black men. This is why some black women — for instance, those in the NOI — might well wish to achieve a place where they were not working and not being blamed for hurting their men; while other black women have uttered that "hav[ing] to make a man feel like a man" makes them uncertain about marriage.[49]

Equally significant is an analysis that reaches for an understanding of intersectionality. When our picture of patriarchy is extended past the seductive landscape of white privilege, we can look beyond a distorted racist analysis to see how some women are in a position to oppress other women, as well as some men. Class gives rise to wealth disparity and "group inferiority," which is produced by "material inequality."[50] For many women who joined the NOI, their most likely alternative for self-support would have been working as a domestic for a white woman, where there was certainly no more guarantee of fair treatment than in a patriarchal marriage. Interestingly, in the NOI, wealth was not the only way to be affiliated with structural power. For example, a sister captain, as the highest-ranking woman in the mosque, was powerful among the female membership. Nevertheless, all sister captains were also under the leadership of the mosque minister, who ultimately had the last word. And a married sister captain was also under the headship of her husband. Thus the circularity of patriarchal structural power embedded in the NOI regulated the actions of the sister captains, as well as that of rank-and-file Nation women. As a structure for building a black nation, patriarchy reproduced gendered hierarchies and interfered, at times, with what Nation women wanted.

Even within the Nation, a woman's financial position impacted how she might be able to navigate patriarchal structures. For example, some women wanted to attend college but were told that they could not go to night school.

Numerous letters addressed to Elijah Muhammad pleaded their cases. One sister requested an exception, stating that she needed only one last class and that it was at night. Muhammad refused to grant it.[51] Yet Sister Sonia 5X Sanchez, who had the funds to pay for a male escort in order to work in the evening, separated herself from other working-class NOI women. Clearly, NOI women experienced patriarchy unevenly and in unpredictable ways. It was a structure deemed crucial for building a black nation, a goal the women believed in. But where they could negotiate or manipulate, they did. For instance, Sister Gwendolyn 2X Simmons used her brother-in-law's position as a highly placed official in Chicago to cushion her from the dictates of the sister captain and the mosque minister. Time and time again, Sister Gwendolyn 2X usurped power and lived according to her own rules. Prior to her NOI membership, she had never yielded to, nor engaged in, patriarchal bargaining. As a Nation woman, she was excited about building a black community and continued to work for the National Council of Black Women as a field representative. Unwilling to separate her work outside the home from building a black nation, Sister Gwendolyn 2X found ways to evade the direct supervision of her husband, mosque minister, and sister captain. What set her apart from other Nation women was her access to different kinds of structural power.

Sister Gwendolyn 2X's story reveals that the structures of class, race, gender, and sexuality that impacted black folks' lives were interactive and could not be isolated as influences; one could not fight exclusively in one direction. Moreover, her willingness to battle in multiple movements echoes that of other black women, such as Sojourner Truth, who have been essential to feminist critiques of patriarchy. The deep structural inequality in the United States is political and anchored in discrimination; black women's subordination exists along multiple registers, and is therefore, as Crenshaw argues, "greater than the sum of racism and sexism."[52]

Motherhood

Marriage has "remained the only socially acceptable way to have a sexual relationship and raise children in the United States," and Elijah Muhammad's teachings reflect this judgment.[53] And in the NOI, parenthood was a particular duty: believers were also charged with producing children for its black nation. By teaching that birth control went against Allah's law, the Nation asked women to be fruitful and multiply. In what ways can we understand NOI women's choices to comply with these dictates?

Per Muhammad's teachings, motherhood was Allah's blessing to women, and NOI mothers embraced this gift with love, compassion, devotion, and as a serious obligation. Many Nation mothers ran their homes like ship captains; assuming a certain power through their roles, they maintained strict timetables and utilized MGT-GCC instruction to chart everything on a weekly planner. Praying five times a day, under the leadership of the oldest household male, and eating one large meal daily around dinnertime were nonnegotiable in most households. Mothers instilled the importance of punctuality in their children early on, because the NOI considered wasting time unacceptable. We can assume this kind of organization also made work easier on the mother. Sister Eula, a mother of six, kept her children's clothes in drawers that exclusively held specific items, and they learned to keep them neat, so that everyone could dress for school quickly. In fact, her children had the reputation of being early for almost everything. Mothers also supervised homework, chores, and leisure activities. Keeping NOI children on task and disciplined was necessary to build a human foundation that instilled self-control and direction.

Nation mothers were adamant about their children's education. The larger mosques had Universities of Islam — primary and secondary schools — that NOI children were required to attend. By sending their children to these schools, Nation mothers were defiantly rejecting the racism of the larger society. In 1934, parents withdrew their children from the Detroit public school system because of Jim Crow practices. Even when they were harassed by relief works and the Attendance Division, parents stayed committed to the University of Islam. The close supervision of children can be overwhelming and emotionally taxing; no doubt mothers continually prayed to Allah for strength and guidance in the raising of their children. But when their children were in need, they did not rely on Allah alone. Elijah Muhammad's believers represented the hardworking masses of black folk who struggled to make ends meet. Despite their efforts, some mothers had to accept welfare to survive.

Discussions of welfare policy in the United States are riddled with stereotypes regarding black families and their perceived failure to meet traditional family norms.[54] The Moynihan Report, when published in 1965, changed policy and established a view of black family life as pathological and deviant. Scholars, activists, and black religious leaders used it as a means to argue for, or against, patriarchal headship. Essentially, this heated discussion gave the NOI more ammunition for its Islamic masculinist teachings and its mantra "to do for self."

The Honorable Elijah Muhammad taught the members of his black nation that they should not be a financial burden on anyone. If there were no jobs, he asked members to create their own. By doing so, "one gains respect from all mankind," because as Sister Ruby recalled, "No one likes a beggar."[55]

Yet despite the NOI's extreme criticism of those who accepted charity, Muhammad's most destitute mothers bought groceries with food stamps, used Medicaid at doctor's offices, and sometimes kept a roof over their family with a housing voucher issued by the state. Sister Doris 9X was a prime example of a believer who lived with her husband, a brother in the NOI, yet had to accept welfare. Her decision to do what she had to comes through in a statement she wrote after she was convicted of welfare fraud: "All I could think about was the deep, piercing pains of the Muslim brothers proclaiming they would protect their black women and then not doing it. I was paying the price for being my own protector and guide."[56]

Sister Maria X, a mother of twelve, shared Sister Doris 9X's desperation to keep her children "clothed and fed."[57] Also accepting welfare because her "so-called Muslim" husband left the house each time she got pregnant, Sister Maria X said angrily, "These children don't belong to the Mosque or the welfare department. My husband should be found and thrown into jail for the rest of his life."[58]

Sister Maria X had tried to follow the Nation's rules. When asked why she did not use protection, she said, "The Honorable Elijah Muhammad taught against birth control" and that women were charged to "bear a private army."[59] But other Nation women factored in variables such as their health and finances into the decision whether or not to comply. For example, Sister Doris 9X admitted that "I went against the non–birth control idea. For once in my life I used my foresight about letting Mahad use my body as a baby making factory."[60] After giving birth, Sister Doris 9X told her doctor to insert an intrauterine contraceptive device (IUD). Her husband never knew about it, but wondered why she did not become pregnant again. Clear about her family circumstances, Sister Doris 9X added, she "didn't need to add any more children onto the welfare grant."[61]

As NOI mothers loved and cared for their children, a special obligation to daughters increased at puberty. Because of the call to maintain chastity, Nation mothers poured supposedly feminine virtues — modesty and humility — into teenagers wholeheartedly. Given that daughters were seen as a reflection of their mothers, they had to get it right or suffer embarrassment and humiliation. Pregnant and unwed, young and older women were shamed before the entire mosque community. The details of impropriety were confessed at public trials (as was true when one failed to submit to any of Muhammad's Islamic law). Punishments ranged from timeout suspensions to expulsion. To return to the NOI fold, one had to admit a wrongdoing and resubmit to authority, usually in the form of the sister captains or the mosque ministers. (The final authority was of course the person seen as the fountainhead of knowledge and wisdom, Elijah Muhammad.) Faithful mothers transmitted their values, and the rules, in hopes of producing faithful daughters; but no doubt they also passed on their best strategies for how to make the system work for them.

Conclusion

When the women's movement hit full force in the 1970s, the NOI used its Islamic identity to defend modesty, marriage, and motherhood as a natural state for women. The movement's ideals stood in direct contrast to the image of the happy housewife of the 1950s and presented an ongoing challenge to the NOI teachings. In fact, it was in the home, feminist activists argued, that women were reduced to a subservient Other and tragically oppressed. To avoid the feeling of entrapment, the liberal women's movement gave the suburban housewife a language with which to articulate her frustration and anger connected to gendered assumptions. Even mainstream advertisers chimed in and developed a campaign by the mid-1970s that "added new appeals to their repertoire; in addition to the old standbys about women as sex objects and the glories of housework, they sought to capitalize upon the frustrations of the housewife who feels harried and unappreciated. "You deserve a break today" became the well-loved jingle for McDonald's restaurant.[62]

As the movement flourished, small cadres of radical feminists offered provocative insights that critiqued class and race, as well as "the family, marriage, love, normative heterosexuality, and rape."[63] Yet Elijah Muhammad made no distinctions within the women's liberation movement and lumped feminists (liberal, radical, lesbian, socialist, cultural, and conservative) together as white women who would guide black women to "commit evil and indecency."[64] Highly offended by the popular fashions, Muhammad told black women who experimented with new hairstyles and clothing that they "look like wild game in the jungle" and scorned their response when confronted about their "half-nude condition" : 'That is the style.'"[65] The only thing these black women were strutting was their "ignorance," wrote Muhammad, because they were "lost to the knowledge of self" and "think everything white people do, [they] should follow them."[66]

As the liberation movement galvanized young women to protest, NOI leaders used *Muhammad Speaks* to strike blows against what it perceived as indecency. Every week during the 1970s, women's liberation was critiqued through cartoons, and black women outside of the NOI were pictured as carbon copies of white women gone wrong. Skimpily clad women were lascivious and enticed black men into sexual liaisons. These same women also taught their daughters the art of tempting men with "the death-wink."[67] The depiction of a black and a white woman wearing hip-hugging minidresses with plunging necklines, each holding the hand of a girl dressed similarly, was framed by the headline, "The Filth That Produces Filth."[68]

Desperate to keep women in line, the NOI combined three religious authorities against temptation, and by extension, lambasted women's liberation as a movement largely concerned with the flesh.[69] It cited scriptures from Matthew 26:41, "The Devil's last attempt to tempt the righteous [Black] man away from his righteousness to evil and filth," and the Qur'an 7:27, "O, children of Adam let not the devil seduce you as he expelled your parents from the garden, pulling off from them their clothing that he might show their shame." It added a lesson that explained, "This happened to the Black People who followed Yakub from Arabia. He pulled off, from their original Self, the clothes of Righteousness and the clothes to cover their shame."

Black women were also warned to avoid what the NOI leadership described as the abandonment of families by women's libbers. Sister Dorothy Wedad authored a four-part series in *Muhammad Speaks*, "The Black Woman," in which she taught that a black woman who followed "behind the devil woman [i.e., the "liberated woman"] frowns on the idea of woman as homemaker, mother, and wife."[70] These were the most noble, rightful, and beautiful roles for women who were "created for different purposes" than men.[71] As "Mothers of Civilization and the Queens of the Universe," black women were blessed to reproduce human life. But it was the "white man's tricknology" to steer black women's "minds from motherhood" that had created the crisis.[72] She proclaimed, "How better to destroy a Nation, than to destroy the very means by which it reproduces itself?"[73] Women's liberation was nothing short of the devils pushing genocide on African American families.

The NOI took up the theme of genocide in response to the Supreme Court's 1973 *Roe v. Wade* abortion ruling. The Court affirmed a woman's private right to terminate a pregnancy in the safety of a hospital with a physician, freeing women from the risks associated with an illegal procedure. Outraged, the NOI initiated a full-fledged attack against "mass abortions" performed on black women by a "wicked government."[74] Moreover, Sister Dorothy charged, while under the knife, many black women were sterilized without "even know[ing] it."[75] Unwanted sterilization was a real issue for poor black women, giving the NOI factual ammunition for its critique. Yet this harmful truth was not enough to stop black women from exercising their right to an abortion. Unable to stop the execution of choice, the NOI played its "knowledge of self" card, claiming that only a black woman who had internalized self-hatred would abort a fetus.

Clearly, the NOI's most basic assumptions were directly threatened by the women's movement. Nation leaders were outraged by the idea that women should be "liberated from having children when by the very laws of creation, this was [their] purpose."[76] Nation wives, leaders continued to hold out, submitted to Allah's last Messenger, Elijah Muhammad, and their husbands to make life better for themselves and their children. So what does it mean when NOI women, as well as ordinary heterosexual black women, feel that a sense of empowerment resides in a patriarchal structure?

The NOI gave its believers a concrete vision for a prosperous future. The importance of its absoluteness in light of how "uncertainty frames perceptions, attitudes, assessments, decision making, and behaviors about marriage and intimate unions for African Americans" cannot be overestimated.[77] Nation women were promised they would be uncertain only about exactly when heaven on earth (in the form of a financially secure family) would manifest for each of them. Self-confidence, self-love, and an identity that included entitlement to earthly riches gave believers what America had failed to offer. Outside the Nation, African American women had been entitled only to the worst jobs, the poorest schooling, absolutely no protection from violence, and an assault on their beauty. How black women lived under and handled this siege is one theme of this book.

Certainly, we have seen that Nation women's choices were riddled with contradictions. My contention, however, is that the intersection of incongruous impulses and dissemblance reveals women's deepest disappointment, desperation, and desire. In fact, it is here that the heartbeat of black women working to do more than keep body and soul together in America is exposed.

NOI women remade themselves to belong to a religion that billed itself as the antithesis of the racist United States. Their religious practices were framed by Elijah Muhammad's determination to build a black nation. Love of self was intrinsic to its formation, along with living a virtuous life, one filled with a determined spirit to be responsible for the well-being of kinfolk. For more than forty years, Muhammad's believers fought against the "cold calculations of a beast" to ensure stable black families.[78] For that greater goal, Nation women chose to work within a patriarchal structure, yielding where they could, resisting where they had to. Their primary challenge was to the racist norms that determined their lives.

Sadly, the supposed beast was not the only force keeping believers from the lives they desired. "Once upon a time we were puzzled as to why so many seemingly good Muslims became defected or fell by the wayside," remarked Sister Ruby. "It is now obvious that the pressure is too great for those who are trying to be Muslims in its true sense."[79] Referring to the level of self-sacrifice on behalf of rank-and-file believers compared to the indulgences of the NOI leadership, Sister Ruby's comments open a crack to peer on the difficulties faced by some converts. A multiplicity of problems followed many believers who gave all of their time, energy, and financial efforts to the development of the NOI. Sister Doris 9X's first husband quit his job to carry out Muhammad's mandates, leading the family home to go into foreclosure and thereby destroying the family unit. Her experience mirrors that of many others who go unnamed in this book.[80]

The stakes were indeed high for the NOI's most loyal believers. Minister Malcolm X's assassination occurred at the point in his life when he was rethinking engrained beliefs about women. His travels to Africa and the Middle East had accelerated an evolution in his views because "in every country that's progressive, the women are progressive, and in every country that was underdeveloped and backward, it was to the same degree that the women were undeveloped, underdeveloped and backward."[81]

Nation women fought against being labeled backward and uncivilized by promoting a religious lifestyle that was central to their identity. They loved the Nation of Islam, despite its shortcomings. It offered them hope, stability, protection, and freedoms on their own terms. It is my most sincere hope that women who have fallen out of its recorded history, women who gave so much with the purest intention to build a black nation filled with love and possibility, see a glimmer of themselves here.

EPILOGUE

When the Honorable Elijah Muhammad died from heart disease on February 25, 1975, so did his Nation of Islam. He had never publicly named a successor, but the Royal Family proclaimed Wallace D. Muhammad, the seventh son of Mr. Muhammad and Sister Clara, as its new leader. Within six months, Wallace Muhammad had revised many of his father's Islamic teachings, including that depicting whites as devils. It was the mind-set, not the physical pigmentation, that produced devilish behavior, he announced.[1] Releasing white folk from biological culpability in the making of black suffering opened the door for their participation in the movement. Dorothy Dorsey had waited six years for the opportunity, and in 1976 her membership proved sensational news.[2] Acclaimed as the first white woman in the NOI, she had learned at home from her husband, Donald 12X Dorsey, but now "they both could worship together at the Chicago mosque," Sister Dorothy explained.[3]

Sister Dorothy, who held a PhD in sociology and anthropology, received a new name, Dorothy 13X Fardan, from Wallace Muhammad to recognize the "influence of Fard."[4] She was featured in the Nation's newspaper, which Wallace Muhammad had renamed *The Bilalian News* on November 1, 1975, to acknowledge the Prophet Muhammad's African companion Bilal ibn Rabah. The reoccurring media declaration of Sister Dorothy 13X's admission into the Nation was a striking reminder that Mr. Muhammad's divinely inspired racial instruction no longer reigned supreme.

Not all of Elijah Muhammad's original followers welcomed this earth-shattering reversal regarding white people. Although Sister Dorothy 13X insisted that the "hostility toward her" came from "nonbelievers" who saw her as an "intruder" with "ulterior motive," in fact more than a handful of members were disturbed by her inclusion.[5] Additionally, when Wallace Muhammad renamed the organization World Community of Al-Islam in the West (WCIW) in October 1976, he placed further distance between his father's vision and his own religious trajectory. Clearly moving the NOI in the direction of Sunni Islam,

Sister Dorothy Fardan.
(Reprinted courtesy of the *Chicago Tribune*)

Wallace Muhammad sealed the demise of the Nation when he dismantled the main structure of membership accountability, the Fruit of Islam (FOI) and the Muslim Girls Training and General Civilization Class (MGT-GCC). Ayesha Mustafa recalled that "the first thing he [Wallace Muhammad] said was, 'You're not girls anymore.'"[6] Wallace Muhammad reconfigured the MGT-GCC as the Muslim Women Developing Class (MWDC) and relaxed many of the rules and regulations. Sister captains and inspectors were removed from the WCIW hierarchy. While some original believers described these changes as liberating, dissenting voices bewailed them as stimulating undisciplined behavior and confusion among the membership. For example, reports claim that Sister Burnsteen Muhammad (Sharrieff) was in support of Wallace Muhammad, while her husband, Brother John Muhammad (Elijah Muhammad's biological brother), was concerned about the shifts away from Mr. Muhammad's teachings.[7]

A number of splinter groups emerged with the goal of resurrecting the teachings and legacy of the Honorable Elijah Muhammad to contest the leadership of his son. It is difficult to ascertain the real number of splinter groups. Beginning

Sister Burnsteen Muhammad and
Brother John Muhammad, 1988.
(Reprinted courtesy of the *Detroit News*)

in 1978, Louis Farrakhan eventually gathered the largest number of dissenters; Silis Muhammad of Atlanta and Yusuf Bey of Oakland emerged as prominent leaders in their respective cities. As opponents of Wallace Muhammad coalesced under the banner of keeping alive the original teachings of the Nation of Islam, each group cherry-picked from a plethora of Mr. Muhammad's lessons to establish a unique cell. How women figured into these new but familiar black nation-building efforts is as diverse as the experiences of their predecessors in the original Nation of Islam.

Louis Farrakhan distinguished his group by moving Sister Ava Muhammad, a lawyer who had joined his Nation in 1981, into the role of the first female minister for the Atlanta Mosque No. 15 and the Southern region in 1998, signifying a major shift away from Elijah Muhammad's teaching that women should instruct only women.[8] Farrakhan's eldest daughter, Sister Student Minister Donna Muhammad, followed in Sister Ava's footsteps. Still, as female ministers they continue to lecture on appropriate gender roles for women, the importance of femininity and modesty, and the significance of supporting black manhood for the restoration of a nation. At Mosque Maryum in Chicago, Minister Donna's 2013 Father's Day lecture, "Breaking of the Black Woman," demonstrated her commitment to her father's leadership and Elijah Muhammad's teachings by emphasizing that contemporary African Americans are still reeling from the slave masters, upsetting the "natural" order of women and men. She said, "Look at us today, brothers and sisters. Reversed roles. Who is working today, brothers and sisters? The black woman. Who is making more money? The black woman. Who is more educated? The black woman. Who's world are we in? The white man's world. He allows in his world to put the woman in front. If the woman is in front, she is taking the role of who? The male."[9] Moreover, using crisp diction, oratorical flights, and animated hand gestures, Minister Donna described how the black woman has become "bamboozled" because of her income: "With a little money in her pocket, she starts getting a little heavy voice. With a little money in her pocket, her mouth is uncontrollable. What is she saying to you, Father? She is saying I make the money in this house, I pay the cost to be the boss, if you don't like what I say you know what to do." Sadly, she proclaimed, the black woman is "not seeing the bigger picture, the hidden hand, the hidden hand of the white man, the slave master; he is still in all of our affairs."[10]

Louis Farrakhan's daughters are important to his leadership in another way as well. On Valentine's Day 1975, *Muhammad Speaks* published a four-page spread celebrating the double wedding ceremony of two of his daughters to Mr. Muhammad's relatives.[11] Donna married Wali Muhammad, a nephew; Maria married Alif Muhammad, a grandson.[12] Mosque #7, New York, was transformed into a "flower garden" for the event, and Louis Farrakhan concluded the reception by saying that the "Messenger of Allah had once told each of his daughters that he had "'sons for them to marry.'"[13] In 1990, yet another of Farrakhan's daughters, Hanan, married Kamal Muhammad, Elijah Muhammad's son with his former secretary, Sister Ola Muhammad.[14] Louis Farrakhan described Kamal as "the first son of the second generation."[15] Similarly, one of Louis and Khadijah Farrakhan's sons is married to Eva Marie, the daughter of Mr. Muhammad and his former secretary Sister Evelyn (Williams) Muhammad.[16] When introducing these unions at a 1993 Saviour's Day lecture, Louis Farrakhan announced a revised history by stating that the former secretaries were in fact "some of the wives of the Honorable Elijah Muhammad," and that the children showed "vindication and [that] God backed him [Mr. Muhammad] in what he did."[17] Sealing kinship connections elevated Louis Farrakhan to the Royal Family, something he made clear by proudly announcing, "the blood have joined, Farrakhan and Muhammad have become one, that's what he wanted, that's what he has."[18]

Further rooting his movement firmly in Elijah Muhammad's history, Louis Farrakhan elevated Sister Tynnetta Muhammad (formerly Deanar) to the position of Supreme Mother of his Nation. As early as 1961, Sister Tynnetta had used her intellectual gifts to master the Nation of Islam's theology, penning the column, "The Woman in Islam" regularly in *Muhammad Speaks*. Angel Needham-Giles has described her shift from "Mistress to Madonna" by detailing how new members "have no recollection of [Tynnetta] Muhammad as a figure of scandal or disgrace but rather as a champion for protecting and preserving the moral and sexual virtues of Black women."[19] Reciting prayers in Arabic before large audiences, thanking Allah and the Honorable Elijah Muhammad for raising up Louis Farrakhan, Mother Tynnetta had a powerful public presence. She passed away on February 16, 2015, but her legacy continues to be represented in Louis Farrakahan's Nation via her two sons by Elijah Muhammad, Ishmael and Rasul, who form an intricate part of his ministry and public entourage.[20]

Most recently, Louis Farrakhan has also distinguished his Nation from other groups by adding elements of the Church of Scientology into his theology.[21] An extensive introduction of Scientology happened in August 2010 in Rosemont, Illinois,[22] when a Dianetics seminar was offered to hundreds of Louis Farrakhan's followers. *Dianetics: The Modern Science of Mental Health*, Ron L. Hubbard's "Bible" for Scientology, is assigned reading, and Nation members are encouraged to receive training to become auditors. While it is impossible to assess the impact on women in particular of the Scientology goals of "(1) helping individuals rid themselves of any spiritual disabilities; (2) increasing spiritual abilities,"[23] we do have some testimony by Sister Renee Muhammad of Mosque #45, Houston. Sister Renee described how after days of auditing by Sister Captain Valerie Muhammad, the "emotional pull of her husband's death was gone."[24] "I know this will be able to help our people just because of what it's done for me," said Sister Renee.[25] She explained that one is "not put under a trance. It's very calm. No one is being judgmental. It's self-help." Sister Renee also believed it beneficial for "our people," who "don't seek out therapy as a way to solve problems."[26]

Silis Muhammad offers another trajectory for returning African Americans to his version of Elijah Muhammad's Nation. His Lost-Found Nation of Islam (LFNOI), begun in 1977, includes several prominent women leaders and a fascinating twist on gender in the original Nation of Islam.

Departing several months before Louis Farrakhan from Wallace Muhammad's WCIW, Silis Muhammad, a former top *Muhammad Speaks* salesman, initially feared for his life.[27] With his "knees shaking," he boarded an airplane from Phoenix to Chicago to meet with Wallace Muhammad, determined to "sacrifice [him]self for the information or the knowledge that the Honorable Elijah Muhammad was the last Messenger of Allah, willing to sacrifice [his] life to prove that Master Fard Muhammad was Almighty God Allah, that Man is God."[28] Silis Muhammad waited thirty days for a meeting that never happened.

His wife, Sister Harriet Abubakr, was also fully entrenched in the original NOI. She was introduced to the NOI by the youngest son of Sister Clara and Elijah Muhammad, Akbar, and they married in 1961.[29] Together they traveled to Cairo, Egypt, where they both studied at Al-Azhar University.[30] When they returned to the United States, she wrote a popular advice column in *Muhammad Speaks*, "Ask Harriet." In January 1965, when Akbar Muhammad was publicly expelled from the NOI because he disagreed with his father's teachings, Sister Harriet stayed because of her devotion to Mr. Muhammad, eventually marrying Silis Muhammad later that year in Los Angles.[31] While working as the West Coast correspondent for *Muhammad Speaks*, Sister Harriet also completed a bachelor's degree at the University of California, Los Angeles (UCLA).[32] With the encouragement of her husband, in 1977 she began attending the UCLA School of Law, graduating with her Juris Doctor in 1980. Also known as Misshaki Muhammad, or the First Lady of the LFNOI, Sister Harriet's skill set has proven immensely important to the LFNOI: She maintains the LFNOI financial books, ensures that believers meet the financial requirements for mortgage applications, and oversees the legal incorporation of LFNOI mosques.[33]

Now relocated to Atlanta, the LFNOI overall teachings are closer to those of Elijah Muhammad than those of Louis Farrakhan. Yet they, too, diverge strikingly from the original lessons. For example, in its newspaper, also called *Muhammad Speaks*, Minister Malik Al-Akram stated, "Our real Spiritual Father is Master Farad Muhammad who spiritually impregnated our Spiritual Mother, the Honorable Elijah Muhammad, who gave birth to the Body Christ in the person of the Muslim believers and in particular to a special Son, Silis Muhammad."[34] The LFNOI also celebrates the Honorable Elijah Muhammad's birthday, October 7, as "Mother's Day for the African American community."[35] Even the LFNOI letterhead correspondence identifies Mr. Muhammad as "our Spiritual Mother Mary."[36] The apparent feminization of Mr. Muhammad as "the Woman with the Child" is an unlikely twist—but so too is the presence of Ida Hakim, a white woman married to a "God" of the LFNOI.[37]

Ida Hakim's appreciation for the LFNOI was noted in its newspaper and at a 1991 Saviour's Day event. Standing before a large crowd, Hakim knew that she could never qualify as a member of the LFNOI, saying, "I know I am the devil by examining myself."[38] Nevertheless, she appreciated that "Silis Muhammad in his mercy ha[d] accepted me as a Muslim by faith and to be accepted by God is certainly a great blessing."[39] She wanted everyone to know that she was not a "foolish woman, falling in love with a black man and saying anything [she] can to please him."[40] On the contrary, "the God and Goddesses of the Lost Found Nation of Islam [were] the answer to her prayer."[41] Her husband, Khalid Hakim, also provided her with knowledge, thus allowing her to "testify that the Black Man is God, Allah, the Victorious, the Beneficent, the Merciful."[42]

After he relocated from California to Georgia, Silis Muhammad's influence spread, and in 1992 Mattias Gardell documented that the LFNOI had twenty-one Mosques, largely located in the South and Midwest, as well as on the East Coast.[43] Twenty acres of land in College Park, Georgia, was purchased by Silis Muhammad's group for a separate Black Muslim community affectionately embraced as the "Exodus Subdivision" or the "New Mecca."[44] As a premier leader bent on restoring Mr. Muhammad's black nation, Silis Muhammad in 1994 asked Professor C. Eric Lincoln to "serve as impartial facilitator in the merger conversations" between him and Louis Farrakhan.[45] Lincoln had visited Silis Muhammad's home during a research trip to Atlanta. After their exchange, Silis Muhammad believed Lincoln to be in the best position to make the merger happen. Lincoln agreed to assist and sent Louis Farrakhan a letter in which he specifically "offered to impartially mediate a merger if I were requested by both sides to do so."[46] Louis Farrakhan did not reply.

Nevertheless, Silis Muhammad and his wife Harriet Abubakr pushed forward. They believe that their efforts are most deserving of federal support in the form of reparations for African Americans.[47] Focusing on examples of the U.S. government paying reparations to Native and Japanese Americans, the LFNOI has sponsored numerous petitions, including one most recently to then President Barack Obama. Silis Muhammad has argued that separation and reparations lay at the heart of Elijah Muhammad's mission. Moreover, Silis Muhammad is also working toward the legal recognition of African Americans as an oppressed diaspora and has sent representatives to the United Nations.

Although Silis Muhammad and Louis Farrakhan lead separate movements, at one point in 1978 a collective meeting in Oakland attempted to bring the anti–Wallace Muhammad forces together. The gathering was spearheaded by Tynnetta Muhammad and Yusuf Bey, the founder of Your Black Muslim Bakery. With Louis Farrakhan in the audience, Silis Muhammad opened the caucus by crediting Yusuf Bey for "trying to bring some unity and harmony within our black life." He continued, "I suppose that we really should be following you, you seem to be more successful than any the rest of us, at least you are doing what Moses, in the person of the Honorable Elijah Muhammad, told us to do, to teach our people through our action and conduct."[48] Silis Muhammad's declaration only confirmed what Yusuf Bey's followers already believed, namely, that he was the patriarch of a capitalist movement to save black people from the "slave mentality."[49]

Unfortunately, Yusuf Bey would go even beyond Elijah Muhammad in his penchant for additional "wives," and he would become infamous for his treatment of underage females.

Bey's NOI history goes back to 1964. Joseph Stephen, a former cosmetologist, would become Joseph X in the coastal city of Santa Barbara, California. He and his biological brother, Billy X, relocated to their childhood home of Oakland after receiving permission from Mr. Muhammad to start a mosque there. In 1968, Billy X became the minister of Mosque No. 26B (Mosque No. 26 was San Francisco), and Joseph X became the captain of the FOI. The brothers, "fearless businessmen from the start,"[50] answered Elijah Muhammad's black capitalist call by opening Your Black Muslim Bakery. It became the centerpiece of an NOI empire, which also included "an archipelago of bakeries, dry cleaners, security services, and apartment-management gigs," as well as nonprofits throughout the city of Oakland.[51]

Sister Joan X had been a former member of the Black Panther Party for Self-Defense before joining the NOI in Oakland. She recalled that the sisters worked hard at Mosque No. 26B and "fished" for abandoned women, many of whom were drug addicts. Cleaning them up for a righteous life usually began in rented motel rooms, where the sisters cared for them as they "kicked" the drug. The sisters at Mosque No. 26B dressed modestly but with a stylish flair. The latter can be largely attributed to Sister Captain Felicia (Nisa Islam, Nisa Bey, Nisayah Yahudah), a former fashion model connected with the San Francisco mosque. When Sister Captain Felicia "defected" from the San Francisco mosque to the Oakland mosque in 1969, she was brought up on charges, and reports state that at her "trial," she spoke into the tape recorder, addressing Mr. Muhammad directly by saying, "Dear Holy Apostle, I will speak to you in Chicago."[52] She defiantly left her trial with at least twelve other women in tow. Sister Captain Felicia recalled that "when he [Mr. Muhammad] called me there and put me in charge of the females, my assignment was to come back to the Bay Area and clean it up"; "and that's what I did."[53] The talented Sister Captain Felicia "told [the women] that they needed to get out of the beige and white everyday, and put some color on."[54] In addition to color, they proudly wore large Afros visible under their transparent scarves.

By 1971, Captain Joseph X had parted ways with his brother Minister Billy X.[55] He left Mosque No. 26B but took with him the bakery and Sister Captain Felicia. It was at Your Black Muslim Bakery in North Oakland that a separate movement emerged. Delivering weekly sermons at the bakery on Sunday afternoon, Captain Joseph X became Yusuf Bey, surrounding himself with photographs of Elijah Muhammad and Fard Muhammad. As his influence spread, tension increased between him and his brother and members of the San Francisco mosque. Sister Captain Felicia described the period as "a disaster" and claimed "she was almost killed for her leadership during that era."[56] They eventually married, and Sister Captain Felicia became Yusuf Bey's second wife.[57]

Yusuf Bey's sermons, "True Solutions," ultimately reached beyond the four walls of the bakery through the African American–owned public cable television station Soul Beat. In the tradition of Elijah Muhammad, Bey preached that black people were "divine," while whites were "devils." Similar to others determined to honor the legacy of Mr. Muhammad, Yusuf Bey also hammered home the legacy of slavery and Jim Crow, asserting that black people could be saved from the "slave mentality" at Your Black Muslim Bakery.

As his business holdings and political influence increased in Oakland, so did Yusuf Bey's appetite for additional wives. Not all his relationships were consensual, however. In fact, court documents indicate that he molested and raped girls as young as eight years old.[58] In 2002, Kowana Banks, who is known in the public records as Jane Doe 1, went to the Oakland Police Department and shared her horrific story of abuse and rape while growing up at Yusuf Bey's bakery compound.[59] "The first time it [molestation] happened to me, I was eight," she said.[60] It all began when her biological parents were unable to care for her and her siblings. The youngsters were placed with Yusuf Bey and his first wife, Sister Nora, as foster children. At the bakery, Banks learned that "men were the ceiling and women were the floor — that you're better to follow a wrong man than a right woman."[61] Fearful of being alone in Yusuf Bey's presence, Banks went to Sister Nora, telling her that "he's trying to do things to me. And I need you to help me." Yet Banks found no ally in Sister Nora, who told her, "Girl, he's not doing anything to you that he hasn't done to anyone else."[62] Molested at eight and raped at eleven by Yusuf Bey, Banks gave birth to the first of their three children at the age of thirteen.[63]

Tragically, Banks was one of four underage girls at the bakery to have multiple children by Yusuf Bey. All of the young mothers were told not to place his name on the birth certificates, so that they could receive welfare payments. In the end, Yusuf Bey received welfare payments for the bakery's foster children and the children he fathered with them. In 1988, at the age of twenty, Banks escaped the bakery during the night, but her two sons eventually returned. Fourteen years later, when Banks's daughter told Banks that Yusuf Bey had molested her, she went to the authorities.[64] She confessed, "I knew he raped children and I knew he molested children, but never in a million years did I think he was doing that to his own children."[65] Paternity tests provided DNA evidence that Yusuf Bey had fathered Banks's three children.[66] Additional women came forward with similar stories. He was charged with twenty-seven felony accounts of sexual assault and lewd conduct with minors between the years of 1976 and 1995.[67] Court records show that Yusuf Bey fathered more than forty children and called up to seventeen women his "wives."[68] Before the trial on the first case could begin, Yusuf Bey on September 30, 2003, died from colon cancer at the age of sixty-seven.

The tragic nightmare of Kowana Banks serves as a reminder of how innocent people too often get caught in the cross fire of power and violence. This certainly was not the remnant of the NOI that I had hoped to find when I began the current book project. Nor could I have predicted the current state of black America. All the factors that spurred membership into the original Nation of Islam — white supremacy, racial violence, police brutality, poverty, poor schooling, and incarceration — remain ever present. Seeking refuge by building an alternative movement, or nation, is how some black people in the past and present address disrespect, abuse, exploitation, and ultimately being discarded from the American populace. I understand.

NOTES

ABBREVIATIONS

NACP   National Archives, College Park, Md.
RG   Record Group

INTRODUCTION

1. Taylor, "As-Salaam Alaikum, My Sister, Peace Be unto You."
2. Taylor, "Elijah Muhammad's Nation of Islam."
3. Turner, *Islam in the African-American Experience.*
4. Williams, "A Fallen Star," introduction, 2.
5. Ibid., chapter 1, 1.
6. Interview with Doris Shahrokhimanesh, Martinez, Calif., September 16, 2014.
7. Siegel, *The Trials of Muhammad Ali.*

CHAPTER ONE

1. Amatullah-Rahman, "She Stood by His Side and at Times in His Stead," 41. Amatullah-Rhaman interviewed Imam Warith Deen Mohammad who reported that his parents eloped because of Clara's parents' objections.
2. Hatim, "The Nation of Islam," 89; Clegg, *An Original Man*, 8–9; Amatullah-Rahman, "She Stood by His Side and at Times in His Stead," 40.
3. Toomer, *Cane*, 115. *Cane* was originally published in 1923.
4. Ibid., 115.
5. McNicol, *Rural Radicals*, 122.
6. Boyle, *Arc of Justice*, 106. The United States census for 1920 showed 40,838 Negroes in Detroit, compared to the 5,741 reported in 1910.
7. See Bates, *The Making of Black Detroit in the Age of Henry Ford*; Williams, *Detroit: The Black Bottom Community.*
8. Hatim, *The Nation of Islam*, 90.
9. Boyle, *Arc of Justice*, 24.
10. Dancy, *Sand against the Wind*, 177.
11. Clegg, *An Original Man*, 16; Chicago FBI Report on Allah Temple of Islam (9/11/42), Sept. 11, 1942, 11, RG 65, NACP. The 1930 United States census reports that Elijah Poole was an unemployed auto factory worker.
12. Dancy, *Sand against the Wind*, 143.

13. Elijah Poole was arrested by officer John Carlson at a hospital and formally charged with the misdemeanor of "Drunk" by the Detroit Police Department on March 19, 1926. The next day he was convicted of the charge. Best Efforts Inc., Archives, Department of Police, Detroit, Michigan, Bureau of Identification, document number 21177.

14. Meier and Rudwick, *Black Detroit and the Rise of the UAW*, 5; Sanchez de Lozado, Amoush, and Alston, *Henry Ford and the Negro People*, 13–14.

15. Barboza, *American Jihad*, 272.

16. Ibid., 272–73.

17. Tingle, "Interview with Rayya Muhammad," March 10, 1993, 10.

18. Barboza, *American Jihad*, 272.

19. Ibid., 269–70. Ayman Muhammad's birth name was Emmanuel Poole.

20. Ernestine E. Wright, interview in Moon, *Untold Tales, Unsung Heroes*, 115.

21. Wolcott, *Remaking Respectability*, 76.

22. Barboza, *American Jihad*, 269.

23. Ibid., 273.

24. Hatim, *The Nation of Islam*, 90.

25. Mary O. Brookins Ross, interview in Moon, *Untold Tales, Unsung Heroes*, 123.

26. Muhammad-Ali, *The Evolution of the Nation of Islam*, 31.

27. *Fifteenth Census of the United States*: 1930; Census Place: Detroit, Wayne, Michigan; Roll 1040; Page: 1A; Enumeration District: 241; Image: 1036.0.

28. Ibid.

29. Rashid and Muhammad, "The Sister Clara Muhammad Schools."

30. Census takers counted readers usually by asking the question if one could read or write. At times, however, they gave a reading test. The question, "Whether able to read or write," was left blank for the Poole children, but both Elijah and Clara provide a "yes" answer. Marie Thomas answered "yes" for herself and her sons to the literacy question. See *Fifteenth Census of the United States*: 1930; Census Place: Detroit, Wayne, Michigan; Roll 1040; Page: 1A; Enumeration District: 241; Image: 1036.0.

31. *Fifteenth Census of the United States*: 1930; Census Place: Detroit, Wayne, Michigan, Roll 1041; Page 12B; Enumeration District 243; Image 26.0.

32. Hatim, *The Nation of Islam*, 91.

33. Ibid.

34. Ibid.

35. Brown and Hartfield, "Black Churches and the Formation of Political Action Committees in Detroit," 154.

36. The career of Clarence Cobb in Chicago provides a wonderful example. He "never hid is flamboyant style" and was known to "smoke the finest cigars, drive a flashy car and wear cloths of the largest cut." See Best, *Passionately Human, No Less Divine*, 41.

37. Hatim, *The Nation of Islam*, 92.

38. Ibid., 97.

39. Glazier and Helweg, *Ethnicity in Michigan*.

40. Elijah Muhammad Jr., telephone interview broadcast on *The Lance Shabazz Show*, 188, Part 3, YouTube, viewed April 3, 2010.

41. Ibid. Employment of Willie and Addie Poole is listed in the Year: 1930; Census Place:

Hamtramck, Wayne, Michigan; Roll 1072; Page: 1A; Enumeration District: 938; Image: 623.0. Also, Elijah Muhammad's daughter, Lottie [Rayya] Muhammad recalls how her Uncle Willie was her fathers "best brother," "who stood with him during those hard days." See Tingle, "Interview with Rayya Muhammad," 15.

42. *Fifteenth Census of the United States*: 1930, Negro Population, 120,000.

43. Beynon, "The Voodoo Cult among Negro Migrants in Detroit," 895.

44. Hassoun, *Arab Americans in Michigan*, 23, 42.

45. Wolcott, *Remaking Respectability*, 185.

46. Ibid.

47. Naff, *Becoming American*, 2, 157. The first major wave of Arabs into Michigan occurred before the 1924 Immigration and Nationalization Act.

48. Beynon, "The Voodoo Cult among Negro Migrants in Detroit," 896. Also see Bontemps and Conroy, *Any Place But Here*, 216.

49. Beynon, "The Voodoo Cult among Negro Migrants in Detroit," 900.

50. Turner, *Islam in the African-American Experience*, 165.

51. Ibid., 170.

52. "The Journey of the Honorable Elijah Muhammad-Malcolm X (1962)," YouTube, uploaded by Brother Darnell X on June 19, 2011. The sermon was given on November 25, 1962, at Mosque #27, Los Angeles.

53. DeNapoli, "'By the Sweetness of the Tongue.'"

54. The 1930 United States census reports that Hamtramck City's total black population numbered 4,068, compared to the white population of 52,111. See *Fifteenth Census of the United States: 1930; Population Volume III, Part 1; Alabama-Missouri*, 1183.

55. Eggleton, "Belonging to a Cult or a New Religious Movement," 266.

56. For example, Jordan, *White over Black*.

57. Clegg, *An Original Man*, 46–47.

58. Ibid., 42. The origins of the Asiatic Blackman concept have been attributed to Nobel Drew Ali and his Moorish Science Temple. See Deutsch, "The Asiatic Black Man."

59. Reid-Parr, "Speaking through Anti-Semitism," 140.

60. Clegg, *An Original Man*, 47.

61. Deutsch, "The Asiatic Black Man," 197.

62. Hatim, *The Nation of Islam*, 92.

63. The vast majority of the photos taken of Sister Clara Muhammad picture her with gloved hands and a handbag.

64. Hatim, *The Nation of Islam*, 92.

65. Ibid.

66. Ibid.

67. Ibid., 91.

68. Ibid., 93, 126.

69. Essien-Udom, *Black Nationalism*, 84.

70. Hatim, *The Nation of Islam*, 90. In Detroit, the Free and Accepted Masons' Hiram Lodge No. 1 was populated by the black middle class. Using pro-black brotherhood organizations as a way to climb the Talented Tenth ladder, black professionals held offices but seldom attended the monthly meetings.

71. Summers, *Manliness and Its Discontents*, 25–65.
72. Barboza, *American Jihad*, 276.

CHAPTER TWO

1. Nation of Islam Lessons, 3, Box 201, Folder 5, C. Eric Lincoln Collection.
2. Ibid., 1.
3. Ibid., 4.
4. Fard, *This Book Teaches the Lost-Found Nation of Islam*. This document, a ten-page paper, lists thirty-two problems for registered members to memorize and was the property of Robert Pasha.
5. Beynon, "The Voodoo Cult among Negro Migrants in Detroit," 900.
6. Essien-Udom, *Black Nationalism*, 87. Essien-Udom states that "she [Clara Muhammad] often comes to her husband's aid in dating events of the past thirty years."
7. See *Fifteenth Census of the United States: 1930; Population Volume III, Part 1; Alabama-Missouri*, 1183; *Fifteenth Census of the United States:1930; Population Volume II, General Report Statistics by Subjects*, 1276.
8. Karriem, "'Prophet' of Detroit Says Black Man Is Cream of World, Not Foot-Mat," 6. I am indebted to Best Efforts Inc., for locating all six of the previously unknown letters by Elijah Muhammad (Karriem) written to the editor of the *Baltimore Afro-American*.
9. Bontemps and Conroy, *Any Place But Here*, 219.
10. Morris, "Islam as the Black Man's Religion"; Beynon, "The Voodoo Cult among Negro Migrants in Detroit," 900, 902.
11. "A Unity Gathering," *Muhammad Speaks*, 29.
12, Bontemps and Conroy, *Any Place But Here*, 218. Fard, *Secret Ritual of the Nation of Islam, Part 2, Section II*.
13. "The Journey of the Honorable Elijah Muhammad-Malcolm X (1962)."
14. The Holy Bible, Luke: 4:8
15. Ibid., Ephesians 6:11.
16. Ibid., Ephesians 6:16.
17. Beynon, "The Voodoo Cult among Negro Migrants in Detroit," 898.
18. Muhammad, *As the Light Shineth from the East*, 25.
19. Muhammad, "An Invitation to 22 Million Black Americans," 19.
20. Ibid.
21. Ibid.
22. Viswanathan, *Outside the Fold*, 159.
23. Beynon, "The Voodoo Cult among Negro Migrants in Detroit," 902.
24. Dillon, *Problem of School Attendance and the Colored Moslem Families in Detroit*, 16.
25. Barboza, *American Jihad*, 268.
26. Ibid.
27. Tingle, "Interview with Rayya Muhammad," 2.
28. Rashid and Muhamad, "The Sister Clara Muhammad Schools: Pioneers in the Development of Islamic Education in America," 178–85. Muhammad wrongly asserts in her Ed.D. dissertation that the school was founded by Elijah Muhammad. See Ramona

Zakiyyah Muhammad, *Perceptions of the Role of Teachers and the Principal in an Islamic School*, 6.

29. "Voodoo Slayer Admits Plotting Death of Judges."

30. Ibid.

31. Ibid., 2, col. 5.

32. "Negro Leaders Open Fight to Break Voodooism Grip."

33. Ibid.

34. Dancy, *Sand against the Wind*, 183.

35. Cameron, "Detroit as a Cult Capital: Only London and Los Angeles Lead This City as Centers of Novel Beliefs, Sun and Devil Worshippers Have Had Missions Here."

36. Dancy, *Sand against the Wind*, 101.

37. Cameron, "Why Detroit Is Not All 'Cultist.'"

38. "Pastors Decry Growth of Cult Practices Here: Negro Leaders Pledge Support to Wipe Out of Voodooism."

39. Ibid.

40. Ibid.

41. Ibid.

42. Ibid.

43. "Intended Voodoo Victims' Number Still Mounting."

44. Ibid.

45. Ibid.

46. "Suburbs Also in Voodoo Net."

47. "Intended Voodoo Victims' Number Still Mounting."

48. Ibid., 4, col. 8.

49. "Suburbs Also in Voodoo Net," 9. See Martin, *Race First*, appendices, for a discussion of the MSTA and the UNIA connection.

50. *Detroit Free Press*, Department of Police, Detroit, Michigan Record for Wallace D. Farad, charged him with "Viol: Immigration" on November 23, 1932, listed residence, Fraymore Hotel in Detroit. Best Efforts Inc., Archive secured via the Michigan Freedom of Information Act.

51. "Intended Voodoo Victims' Number Still Mounting," 4, col. 3.

52. "Voodoo's Reign Here Is Broken."

53. Ibid.

54. There is no evidence indicating the date when Fard returned to Detroit but the fact that he "disappears" from Detroit in 1934 evidence that he had returned after 1932.

55. I am indebted to Best Efforts Inc., for providing all six of the previously unknown letters by Elijah Muhammad (Karriem) written to the editor of the *Baltimore Afro-American*.

56. Sister Betty Muhammad, *Dear Holy Apostle*, 25. Zain Abdullah brought this text to my attention.

57. In an interview conducted by the FBI on 2/6/1943 its reported that Helen Poole, niece of Elijah Muhammad, stated that "Clara, does the corresponding for Elijah. She said that she did not believe that Elijah could read or write." See Chicago FBI Report on Allah Temple of Islam (2/6/43), 2, RG 65, NACP.

58. Karriem, "'Prophet' of Detroit Says Black Man Is Cream of World, Not Foot-Mat."

59. Ibid.

60. Carter, *Scottsboro*.

61. Karriem, "Moslems are Misrepresented by Caucasians."

62. Karriem, "Preachers Don't Know the Bible and Must Hear the Prophet in Detroit."

63. Elijah Karriem, 3059 Yemans Street, Detroit, Mich., "Whose Christianity?"

64. Elijah Mohammed, Minister of Islam, in North America, 3408 Hasting Street, Detroit, Michigan, "We Teach Ourselves Some Dumb Things, Too, Brother."

65. "DuBois's Church Views Shock Open Forum"; "Colored People Came to U.S. From Europe: Dr. Woodson Tells Local Club of Southalls and Cardozos."

66. "Colored People Came to U.S. from Europe."

67. "DuBois's Church Views Shock Open Forum."

68. Ibid.

69. Karriem, "To the Editor of the Afro."

70. Ibid.

71. Ibid. It is important to point out that the editor added a "note" at the bottom of the letter providing figures from the *World Almanac* disproving Elijah's statement regarding the number of Mohammedans vs. Christians.

72. Elijah Mohammed, "We Teach Ourselves Some Dumb Things, Too, Brother."

73. "Asks State Close 'Islam University': Board of Education to Appeal to Supt. Voelker."

74. "Voodoo University Raided by Police; 13 Cultists Seized: Squad Finds 400 Enrolled at School"; "'Islam' Cult Faces Court: 14 Negro Instructors to Be Arraigned Today, Raid Made on Vodoo Building."

75. "Voodoo University Raided by Police; 13 Cultists Seized."

76. Ibid.

77. "'Islam' Cult Faces Court: 14 Negro Instructors to Be Arraigned Today, Raid Made on Vodoo Building."

78. "Voodoo University Raided by Police; 13 Cultists Seized: Squad Finds 400 Enrolled at School." The reported arrested gave the following names: John Muhammad, head of cult, Tadar Ali, secretary of the school, Abbass Rassouln, assistant secretary, James Mohammed, Mrs. Mary Rozier, Allar Cushmeer, Ravell Shah, Azzad Mohammed, Willie Mapjied, Mrs. Mary Almanza, Jan Sharrief, Miss Alberta Sharrieff, Miss Burnisteen Sharrieff.

79. "'Islam' Cult Faces Court: 14 Negro Instructors to Be Arraigned Today, Raid Made on Vodoo Building."

80. "Editorial: The Islam Issue in Detroit."

81. "University of Islam."

82. "Islam Cult Stages Riot at Police Sta.: Many Hurt as Cult Members Protest Arrest."

83. Ibid.

84. "University of Islam."

85. "Voodoo University Raided by Police 13 Cultist Seized. Squad Finds 400 Enrolled at School"; "Negroes Object to Cult Schools: Leaders Ask Cleanup by Prosecutor."

86. "'Islam' Staff Freed; 'Minister' Convicted."

87. Ibid.

88. Lincoln, *The Black Muslims in America*, 182.

89. Ibid.

90. Attorney Gregrory J. Reed obtained a large private collection of the 1930s NOI but has yet to grant scholars access.

91. "Voodoo University Raided by Police; 13 Cultist Seized"; "'Islam' Cult Faces Court."

92. Ibid.

CHAPTER THREE

1. www.thesoulpit.com/spiritual/?p=246, accessed June 9 (2011).

2. Drury, "The Vocation of "Pastor's Wife: A Tribute to Beatrice Druru, May 16, 1913– April 7, 2002."

3. "Asks State Close 'Islam University': Board of Education to Appeal to Supt. Voelker."

4. Elijah Mohammed, "The Meeting Is Held at Masonic Temple," *The Final Call to Islam*, September 1, 1934, 4.

5. Dillon, *Problem of School Attendance and the Colored Moslem Families of Detroit*, 34. A condensed version of the report was published—Miram S. Dillon, "The Islam Cult in Detroit."

6. Elijah Muhammad Jr., telephone interview broadcast on *The Lance Shabazz Show* 188, Part 3, copyright 2009, YouTube, viewed May 31, 2011.

7. "Graduates of Muhammad's University of Islam Gird for Great Careers," *Muhammad Speaks*, February 25, 1966, 16; *Muhammad Speaks*, September 4, 1970, 15.

8. "The First Honorary," *Muhammad Speaks*, March 13, 1964, 17.

9. "Sister Clara Muhammad Lauds New York University of Islam Educational Plan," *Muhammad Speaks*, May 12, 1967, 20.

10. Rashid and Muhammad, "The Sister Clara Muhammad Schools: Pioneers in the Development of Islamic Education in America," 182.

11. Elijah Muhammad Jr., telephone interview broadcast on *The Lance Shabazz Show* 188, Part 3, Copyright 2009, You Tube, viewed May 31, 2011; "Sister Clara Muhammad Lauds New York University of Islam Educational Plan," *Muhammad Speaks*, May 12, 1967, 20.

12. Upon the disappearance of Master Fard in 1934, there was dissension within the ranks of his leadership. Elijah Mohammad's group was one main offshoot, others were led by his brother Kallot.

13. Dillon, *Problem of School Attendance and the Colored Moslem Families of Detroit*, 3 and 34.

14. Ibid., 4.

15. Frazier, *The Negro Family in Chicago*, 10.

16. Dillon, *Problem of School Attendance and the Colored Moslem Families of Detroit*, 4.

17. Dillon, "The Islam Cult in Detroit," see Editor's Note, 1. An exhaustive search failed to reveal any work by Dillon on Caribbean "cults." Only one published essay is credited to her: Dillon, "Attitudes of Children toward Their Own Bodies and Those of Other Children."

18. Dillon, *Problem of School Attendance and the Colored Moslem Families of Detroit*. A condensed version of the report was published—Miram S. Dillon, "The Islam Cult in

Detroit." The Merrill-Palmer School (later, Institute) was named after Lizzie Pitts Merrill-Palmer. During the 1920, the Institute's efforts were aimed at serving Detroit's children through academic programs in child development. The Institute produced research in the area of child development and trained scientists in the field. The Institute served as a child development laboratory, playing a role in the development of national standards for the federal Head Start program. It is currently linked to Wayne State University. See www.mpsi.wayne.edu, accessed June 20, 2011.

19. Wolcott, *Remaking Respectability: African American Women in Interwar Detroit*, 219. Wolcott discusses how the Alfred District was considered successful because of local activists' efforts to secure resources.

20. Ross, *The Origins of American Social Science*, 388.

21. Dillon, *Problem of School Attendance and the Colored Moslem Families of Detroit*, call no. R326.8, D58, Detroit Public Library. A condensed version of the report was published—Dillon, "The Islam Cult in Detroit."

22. Scott, *Contempt and Pity*, 19.

23. Stein-Roggenbuck, *Negotiating Relief*, 46.

24. Tingle, "Interview with Rayya Muhammad," 10. Interview located in the George Mark Elliott Special Collection Library, Cincinnati Christian University, Cincinnati, OH.

25. Ibid.

26. Ibid.

27. Ibid.

28. Stein-Roggenbuck, *Negotiating Relief*, 59.

29. Dillon, *Problem of School Attendance and the Colored Moslem Families of Detroit*, 4.

30. Wilson, *The Segregated Scholars*, 59.

31. Beulah Whitby, Oral Interview Transcript, 18.

32. Stein-Roggenbuck, *Negotiating Relief*, 129.

33. Ibid., 117. For an introduction to the professional work life of Beulah Whitby, see Shaw, *What a Woman Ought to Be and to Do*, 189–91, 228–29.

34. Beulah Whitby, Oral Interview Transcript, 18–19.

35. Ibid., 18.

36. Ibid.

37. Ibid.

38. Ibid.

39. Dillon, *Problem of School Attendance and the Colored Moslem Families of Detroit*, 6.

40. Ibid.

41. Ibid., 25.

42. Ibid., 29.

43. Ibid., 29.

44. Douglas, *Jim Crow Moves North*, 114.

45. Ibid., 176.

46. Ibid., 177.

47. Fairclough, *Teaching Equality*, 54.

48. Shaw, *What a Woman Ought to Be and to Do*, 190–91.

49. Du Bois, "Does the Negro Need Separate Schools?," 328–29.

50. Scott, *Contempt and Pity*, 38–39.

51. Moehlman, *Public Education in Detroit*, 15, 208; *The Detroit Educational Bulletin: Published Monthly for the Teachers of Detroit by the Board of Education, Detroit, Mich.* (January 1922), 16.

52. Ibid., 12.

53. Ibid., 16.

54. Moehlman, *Public Education in Detroit*, 183–84.

55. Dillon, *Problem of School Attendance and the Colored Moslem Families of Detroit*, 28.

56. Ibid., 30.

57. Ibid.

58. Ibid., 31.

59. Beynon, "The Voodoo Cult among Negro Migrants in Detroit," 896.

60. Dillon, *Problem of School Attendance and the Colored Moslem Families of Detroit*, 28.

61. Ibid.

62. Ibid., 29.

63. Ibid., 26.

64. Ibid.

65. *The Detroit Educational Bulletin: Published Monthly for the Teachers of Detroit by the Board of Education, Detroit*. In Michigan $2.00 per child per week was the legal minimum, though State Welfare Department records indicate that in 1934 many families received only 40 cents per child weekly. Caseworkers could also discontinue payment of the pension because "the law makes it possible for individual counties to pay pensions to some mothers and to refuse them to others who were equally eligible in terms of the state act." These facts regarding the pension probably shaped this Moslem mother's willingness to refuse it; nevertheless, her statement reveals a significant commitment to Master Fard's teachings.

66. Dillon, *Problem of School Attendance and the Colored Moslem Families of Detroit*.

67. Ibid.

68. Ibid., 28.

69. Ibid., 31.

70. Ibid., 27.

71. Ibid., 30.

72. Ibid., 29.

73. Ibid., 28.

74. Ibid.

75. Ibid., 27.

76. Ibid., 28.

77. Ibid., 27.

78. Ibid.

79. Ibid.

80. Ibid., 25.

81. Ibid.

82. Ibid., 15.

83. Ibid., 21.

84. Ibid., 24.
85. Ibid., 28.
86. Ibid., 29.
87. Ibid., 24.
88. Ibid., 26.
89. Ibid., 28.
90. Ibid., 29.
91. Ibid., 28.
92. Ibid., 30.
93. Ibid.
94. Ibid.
95. Ibid., 28.
96. Ibid., 30.
97. Ibid., 28.
98. Ibid., 23.
99. Ibid.
100. Ibid., 32.
101. Ibid., 29.
102. Ibid., 30.
103. Ibid., 28.
104. Ibid., 30.
105. Ibid., 23.
106. Ibid., 28.
107. Ibid., 29–30.
108. Stein-Roggenbuck, *Negotiating Relief*, 180–81.
109. Mink and Solinger, eds., *Welfare*, 44.
110. Stein-Roggenbuck, *Negotiating Relief*, 3.
111. Dillon, *Problem of School Attendance and the Colored Moslem Families of Detroit*, 35.
112. Scott, *Contempt and Pity*, xi.
113. Khalil Gibran Muhammad, *Condemnation of Blackness*, 90, 103.
114. Dillon, *Problem of School Attendance and the Colored Moslem Families of Detroit*, 35.
115. Ibid.
116. Ibid., 34.
117. Frazier, *The Negro Family in Chicago*, 9–10.
118. Dillon, *Problem of School Attendance and the Colored Moslem Families of Detroit*, 34.
119. Lincoln and Mamiya, "Daddy Jones and Father Divine," 32.
120. Ibid., 33–34.

CHAPTER FOUR

1. Hurston, *Their Eyes Were Watching God*, 5.
2. "Voodoo University Raided by Police; 13 Cultists Seized." Another newspaper article states Burnsteen Sharrieff is age seventeen. See "'Islam' Cult Faces Court."
3. Jesus Muhammad-Ali, *The Evolution of the Nation of Islam*, 34.

4. Wolcott, *Remaking Respectability*, 175–76.

5. Burnsteen Sharrieff Mohammed, *I Am Burnsteen Sharrieff Mohammad Reformer and Secretary to Master W. D. F. Mohammad . . . and These Are Some of My Experiences*, 2. Author possession purchased via Pay Pal, Nation of Islam History, www.poolemohammed michigan1.com.

6. Shabazz, *Blood, Sweat & Tears*, 290.

7. Burnsteen Sharrieff Mohammed, *I Am Burnsteen Sharrieff Mohammad Reformer and Secretary to Master W. D. F. Mohammad . . . and These Are Some of My Experiences*, 2.

8. Ibid., 3.

9. Ibid., 5.

10. Ibid., 5.

11. Dorothy Lewis, "WAKE UP!," 5.

12. *I Am Burnsteen Sharrieff Mohammad Reformer and Secretary to Master W. D. F. Mohammad . . . and These Are Some of My Experiences*, 1.

13. Ibid.

14. Ibid.

15. Sharrieff, "The Dangerousness of Overweight," 3.

16. Ibid.

17. Sharrieff, "Reduce and Be Cured of Your Aliments," 3.

18. Ibid.

19. Ibid.

20. Ibid.

21. Farrell, *Fat Shame*, 118.

22. Sister Lt. Gertrude X Mosque No. 24, "Visiting Sister Writes of 'a Few' Blessings She Has Gained from Islam," 17.

23. Burcar, "Re-Mapping Nation, Body and Gender in Michael Ondaatje's *The English Patient*," 99.

24. Detsi-Diamanti, Kitsi-Mitakou, and Yiannopoulou, *The Flesh Made Text Made Flesh*, 2.

25. Farrell, *Fat Shame*, 59.

26. Ibid., 60.

27. Ibid., 59.

28. Ibid., 59.

29. Ibid., 75.

30. Michaels, "From Rejection to Affirmation of Their Bodies," 88.

31. McDannell, *Picturing Faith*, 2.

32. Wright and Rosskam, *12 Million Black Voices*. The photos were taken between the years of 1934 and 1939 in the following locations: Chicago, Illinois; Washington, D.C.; Georgia; Arkansas; Mississippi; North Carolina; South Carolina; Virginia; Alabama; Oklahoma; Missouri; Florida; Pittsburgh, Pennsylvania; Louisiana; New York City; and Dearborn, Michigan.

33. Shaw, "Using the WPA Ex-Slave Narratives to Study the Impact of the Great Depression," 631.

34. Ibid., 634.

35. Dickins, *A Study of Food Habits of People in Two Contrasting Areas of Mississippi Bulletin No. 245*, 33.

36. Mathews, *Food Habits of Georgia Rural People Bulletin No. 159*, 12.

37. Ibid., 9, 22.

38. Moser, *Food Consumption and Use of Time for Food Work among Farm Families in the South Carolina Piedmont, Bulletin 300*, 15.

39. Ibid., 41.

40. Morey, *A Study of the Food Habits and Health of Farm Families in Tompkins County, New York Bulletin 563*, 47, 58.

41. Komlos and Brabec, "The Trend of BMI Values of U.S. Adults by Deciles, Birth Cohorts, 1882–1986, Stratified by Gender and Ethnicity," 243.

42. John Komlos to Ula Taylor, e-mail correspondence, October 10 (2011). In my effort to ensure that I was interpreting the data correctly I emailed the author Komlos.

43. John Komlos and Marek Brabec, "The Trend of BMI values of US Adults by Deciles, Birth Cohorts 1882–1986 Stratified by Gender and Ethnicity," 244.

44. Sharrieff, "Reduce And Be Cured Of Your Aliments," 3.

45. Farrell, *Fat Shame*, 118–19.

46. "Moors Battle in Court; 40 Hurt," 2, col. 2.

47. Ibid.

48. Ibid. Also see "Cultists Riot in Court; One Death, 41 Hurt," 10.

49. "Moors Battle in Court; 40 Hurt," *Chicago Defender* (March 9, 1935), 2, col. 2. "Cultists Riot in Court; One Death, 41 Hurt"; "Forty Cultish Put in Jail for Courtroom Riot," 13.

50. "Cultists Riot in Court; One Death, 41 Hurt," 32.

51. "Moors Battle in Court; 40 Hurt," 1.

52. "Cultists Riot in Court; One Death, 41 Hurt," 1.

53. "Convict 40 'Moors,'" 24.

54. "Forty Cultish Put in Jail for Courtroom Riot," 13.

55. Ibid. Numerous scholars write about the leadership tensions, especially between Elijah Mohammed and his brother Kallot immediately after the disappearance of Prophet Master Fard. See Clegg, *An Original Man*, 38–40.

56. "Moors Battle in Court; 40 Hurt."

57. Ibid.

58. Ibid.

59. "Forty Cultish Put in Jail for Courtroom Riot," 13.

60. Ibid. "Convict 40 'Moors.'"

61. Contemporary documentation on the Bridewell is not available but it is likely that conditions were worse than nearby Cook County Jail because it was older.

62. Loomis, *The Cook County Jail Survey Summarized*, 7.

63. Ibid., 11.

64. Butler, "Prisoners and Prisons"; *U.S. Bureau of Efficiency for the Special Committee on Federal Penal and Reformatory Institutions, House of Representatives*, 70th Cong., 2nd sess. (1929), 228. It's important to note that I am relying on surveys from the decade of the 1920s.

65. Ibid. Also see Harrington, "Progress of Criminal Justice in Chicago," 793.

66. Butler, "Prisoners and Prisons," 183; Kirchwey, *The Survey of the Cook County Jail*, 112.

67. Butler, "Prisoners and Prisons," 224.

68. Loomis, *The Cook County Jail Survey Summarized*, 11.

69. Ibid., 13.

70. Ibid., 11.

71. Ibid., 11.

72. Ibid., 12.

73. Elijah Muhammad, *How to Eat to Live Book 1*, 1.

74. Loomis, *The Cook County Jail Survey Summarized*, 11.

75. Kirchwey, *The Survey of the Cook County Jail*, 132–33.

76. Ibid.

77. Butler, "Prisoners and Prisons," 227.

78. "Moors Battle in Court; 40 Hurt," 2, col. 2.

79. Butler, "Prisoners and Prisons," 222 ; Kirchwey, *The Survey of the Cook County Jail*, 140.

80. Kirchwey, *The Survey of the Cook County Jail*, 127.

81. Butler, "Prisoners and Prisons," 215.

82. Kirchwey, *The Survey of the Cook County Jail*, 114.

83. Hicks, *Talk with You Like a Woman*, 133.

84. "Convict 40 'Moors,'" *Chicago Defender*, 24. The convicted ATOI members names and addressed are listed and neither Zack or Rosetta Hassan are included as defendants jailed.

85. Butler, "Prisoners and Prisons," 212.

CHAPTER FIVE

1. Hill, *The FBI's RACON*, 551, xvii.

2. The Monday and Wednesday meetings began at 8:00pm.

3. Chicago FBI Report on Allah Temple of Islam (9/18/42), 7, RG 65, NACP.

4. Ibid., 2.

5. William J. Conner to J. Albert Woll, "Subversive and Seditious Activities of Negro Groups in Chicago, Washington Park Forum; The Peace Movement to Ethiopia, and the Moslems," August 28, 1942, RG 60, NACP.

6. Chicago FBI Report on Allah Temple of Islam (8/15/42), 15, RG 65, NACP.

7. Chicago FBI Report on Allah Temple of Islam (9/18/42), 13, RG 65, NACP.

8. Ibid.

9. Ronald H. Spector, *Eagle against the Sun*, 547.

10. Chicago FBI Report on Allah Temple of Islam (9/18/42), 13, RG 65, NACP.

11. Ibid., 21

12. Ibid., 21.

13. Ibid., 6.

14. Chicago FBI Report on Allah Temple of Islam (9/11/42), 6, RG 65, NACP.

15. Chicago FBI Report on Allah Temple of Islam (9/18/42), 5, RG 65, NACP.

16. Ibid., 11.

17. This lesson is repeated throughout the files with slight variation, see Chicago FBI

Report on Allah Temple of Islam (9/30/42), 3; Chicago FBI Report on Allah Temple of Islam (9/18/42), 5, RG 65, NACP; Chicago FBI Report on Allah Temple of Islam (8/15/42), 13, RG 65, NACP.

18. Chicago FBI Report on Allah Temple of Islam (9/18/42), 13, RG 65, NACP.

19. Ibid., 12.

20. Ibid., 18.

21. Chicago FBI Report on Allah Temple of Islam (9/30/42), RG 65, NACP, 4; Chicago FBI Report on Allah Temple of Islam (9/11/42), 7, RG 65, NACP.

22. Chicago FBI Report on Allah Temple of Islam (9/30/42), 3, RG 65, NACP.

23. Chicago FBI Report on Allah Temple of Islam (9/18/42), 3, RG 65, NACP. It is unclear why Sister Pauline did not take the last name Karriem.

24. Chicago FBI Report on Allah Temple of Islam (9/11/42), 3, RG 65, NACP.

25. Chicago FBI Report on Allah Temple of Islam (9/18/42), 17, RG 65, NACP.

26. Ibid., 19.

27. Chicago FBI Report on Allah Temple of Islam (9/30/42), 5, RG 65, NACP

28. Chicago FBI Report on Allah Temple of Islam (9/18/42), 3, RG 65, NACP.

29. Chicago FBI Report on Allah Temple of Islam (8/15/42), 16, RG 65, NACP.

30. Chicago FBI Report on Allah Temple of Islam (9/18/42), 2, RG 65, NACP.

31. Chicago FBI Report on Allah Temple of Islam (9/30/42), 7, RG 65, NACP.

32. Ibid.

33. Chicago FBI Report on Allah Temple of Islam (9/18/42), 3, RG 65, NACP.

34. Ibid.

35. Chicago FBI Report on Allah Temple of Islam (9/11/42), 12, RG 65, NACP.

36. Chicago FBI Report on Allah Temple of Islam (9/18/42), 6, RG 65, NACP.

37. Ibid., 12.

38. Ibid., 6.

39. Ibid., 6.

40. Ibid., 8.

41. Chicago FBI Report on Allah Temple of Islam (9/30/42), 5, RG 65, NACP.

42. Chicago FBI Report on Allah Temple of Islam (9/18/42), 9, RG 65, NACP.

43. Ibid., 22.

44. Ibid., 14.

45. William J. Conner to J. Albert Woll, "Subversive and Seditious Activities of Negro Groups in Chicago, Washington Park Forum; The Peace Movement to Ethiopia, and the Moslems," August 28, 1942, RG 60, NACP.

46. Chicago FBI Report on Allah Temple of Islam (9/18/42), 8, RG 65, NACP.

47. Ibid.

48. "12 Negro Chiefs Seized by FBI in Sedition Raids"; Elijah Muhammad, *The Mother Plane*; Clegg, *An Original Man*, 89, 65.

49. Clegg, *An Original Man*, 82. Muhammad, *The Mother Plane*; "Moslem leader nabbed: FBI Holds Moslem Chief on Draft Evasion Charge," 26.

50. Chicago FBI Report on Allah Temple of Islam (9/30/42), 20, RG 65, NACP.

51. Ibid.

52. Ibid.

53. Chicago FBI Report on Allah Temple of Islam (9/18/42), 6, RG 65, NACP.

54. Ibid.

55. Chicago FBI Report on Allah Temple of Islam (9/18/42), 20, RG 65, NACP.

56. Chicago FBI Report on Allah Temple of Islam (9/11/42), 3, RG 65, NACP.

57. Ibid., 10.

58. "12 Negro Chiefs Seized by FBI in Sedition Raids," RG 60, NACP. John Edgar Hoover to Wendell Berge, Allah Temple of Islam, Oct 10, 1942; Muhammad, *The Mother Plane*; Clegg, *An Original Man*, 89, 65.

59. FBI Vault, Wallace Fard Muhammad, , Part 1 of 7, frames 19 and 60. Chicago FBI to Director, "ATOI,"10/14/1943, serial 139, Walker F. Muhammad Consolidated File.

60. Essien-Udom, *Black Nationalism*, 67.

61. "12 Negro Chiefs Seized by FBI in Sedition Raids"; Chicago FBI Report on Allah Temple of Islam (9/30/42), 18.

62. "U.S. Scrutinizes Books Seized in Cult Temple"; Wallace Fard Muhammad, FBI on-line Reading Room, Part 1 of 7, frame 60 (April 2, 1942, Washington, D.C.). Accessed January 11 2011.

63. "Sedition Charges Dropped"; "Drop Sedition Charges against 5 in Chicago"; "Drop Sedition Charges against Islam Leaders"; "$5000 Bond Cult Leader out on Bond in Draft Case," 4.

64. Orro, "Seek Indictments of Sedition Suspects: Cultists Defy Commissioner in U.S. Court."

65. "Moslem Says He 'Registered with Islam.'"

66. Orro, "Seek Indictments of Sedition Suspects: Cultists Defy Commissioner in U.S. Court."

67. Ibid.

68. "Allah Temple of Islam," September 30, 1942, 21, RG 65, NACP.

69. J. Edgar Hoover, director FBI, "Memorandum for Assistant Attorney General Wendell Berge, Re: Allah Temple of Islam; Sedition; Internal Security—J Selective Service," October 9, 1942, RG 60, NACP; J. Albert Woll, to Wendell Berge, Esq., Washington, D.C., October 9, 1942, 1–2, RG 60, NACP.

70. J. Albert Woll to Wendell Berge, October 9, 1942, Re: Allah Temple of Islam; Sedition, 1, RG 60 NACP.

71. "Cultist 'Guilty'; 32 Given Jail Sentences: 3 Others Face Federal Court for Sedition."

72. "6 Cultists Get 3-Year Sentences."

73. Chicago FBI Report on Allah Temple of Islam (9/30/42), 22, RG 65, NACP.

74. The accuracy of FBI documents has generated numerous commentary. One of the best assessments of this intelligence material is the text by Buitrago, with Leon Zimmerman, *Are You Now or Have You Ever Been In the FBI Files? How to Secure and Interpret Your FBI Files*.

75. The ATOI was becoming the NOI by a gradual process.

76. Marable, *Malcolm X*, 78.

77. Chicago FBI Report on Allah Temple of Islam (9/30/42), 19, RG 60, NACP.

78. Criminal Division, "In The District Court of the United States of America for the Northern District of Illinois, Eastern Division" (November 1942) Document No. 33713, RG 60, NACP.

79. Chicago FBI Report on Allah Temple of Islam (9/30/42), 21, RG 60, NACP.

80. Ibid.

81. Ibid.

82. Ibid.

83. Ibid., 19.

84. Ibid., 19.

85. Ibid., 19.

86. Ibid., 19–20.

87. Criminal Division, "In the District Court of the United States of America for the Northern District of Illinois, Eastern Division," October, 1942, RG 60, NACP.

88. "In the District Court of the United States of America for the Northern District of Illinois, Eastern Division," Bench Warrant (October 1942) Document No. 33649, RG 60, NACP. "Seized 84 Negroes in Sedition Raids."

89. "In the District Court of the United States of America for the Northern District of Illinois, Eastern Division," Bench Warrant (October 1942) Document No. 33649, RG 60, NACP.

90. "Cultists 'Guilty'; 32 Given Jail Sentences: 3 Others Face Federal Court for Sedition," 2.

91. Ibid.

92. J. Albert Woll, Office of United States Attorney to Wendell Berge, Assistant Attorney General, Criminal Division, Washington, D.C. (May 15, 1943), 1, RG 60, NACP; J. Albert Woll, Office of United States Attorney, to Wendell Berge, Esq., Assistant Attorney General, Criminal Division, Washington, D.C. (October 9, 1942), 6–7, RG 60, NACP. J. Albert Woll to Wendell Berge, October 9, 1942, Re: Allah Temple of Islam; Sedition, 7, RG 60, NACP.

93. J. Albert Woll, Office of United States Attorney, Criminal Division, Washington, D.C. (May 6, 1943), 2, RG 60, NACP.

94. In the District Court of the United States of America for the Northern District of Illinois, Eastern Division, Bench Warrant (November 1942) Document No. 33713, RG 60, NACP.

95. Chicago FBI Report on Allah Temple of Islam (9/30/42), 4, RG 65, NACP.

96. Ibid.

97. Ibid., 6.

98. Chicago FBI Report on Allah Temple of Islam (9/18/42), 9, RG 65, NACP.

99. Chicago FBI Report on Allah Temple of Islam (9/11/42), 13; Chicago FBI Report on Allah Temple of Islam (8/15/4), 13, RG 65, NACP.

100. "Cultists 'Guilty'; 32 Given Jail Sentences: 3 Others Face Federal Court for Sedition," 1.

101. Curtis, "Islamizing the Black Body: Ritual and Power in Elijah Muhammad's Nation of Islam," 167–68.

102. Chicago FBI Report on Allah Temple of Islam (9/18/42), 10, RG 65, NACP; At Mr. Mohammed's November 1942 draft charge trial in the District of Columbia its reported that a "dozen women followers attired in flowing red ad green satin robes," watched the proceedings. See "Moslem, Tried as Draft Evader, Says Allah Didn't Declare War," 22.

103. "Cultists 'Guilty'; 32 Given Jail Sentences: 3 Others Face Federal Court for Sedition."

104. Bell, *Ritual Theory, Ritual Practice*, 98.

105. "'Mohammed' Is Released' as Wife Posts $5,000 Bond"; "$5,000 in Cash Donated to Free 'Mohammed.'"

106. "$5,000 in Cash Donated to Free 'Mohammed.'"

107. "'Mohammed of U Steel' Pleads Draft Immunity."

108. Warith Deen Muhammad, *As the Light Shineth from the East*, 237.

109. Ibid., 238.

110. Ibid.; Amatullah-Rahman, "She Stood by His Side and at Times in His Stead"; Clegg, *An Original Man*, 96; Marable, *Malcolm X*, 88.

111. Chicago FBI Report on Allah Temple of Islam (9/30/42), 12, RG 65, NACP; Mr. Mohammed states how his brother Kallot betrayed him, see Chicago FBI Report on Allah Temple of Islam (8/15/42), 10.

112. Chicago FBI Report on Allah Temple of Islam (9/18/42), 23, RG 65, NACP.

113. Chicago FBI Report on Allah Temple of Islam (9/30/42), 9, RG 65, NACP.

114. This informant is identified as CGO-71 in the FBI records, see Chicago FBI Report on Allah Temple of Islam (6/7/44), RG 65, NACP; Chicago FBI Report on Allah Temple of Islam (1/19/43), 1, RG 65, NACP.

115. Chicago FBI Report on Allah Temple of Islam (9/11/42), 14.

116. Ibid., 7.

117. The addresses for the meetings were reported as follows: 2963 S. Federal Street, 633 E. 33rd Street, 423 E. 45th Place, and 3735 Wentworth Avenue. See Chicago FBI Report on Allah Temple of Islam (6/7/44), 1, RG 65, NACP. For Pauline Bahar leadership see Chicago FBI Report on Allah Temple of Islam (10/19/43), 1.

118. Chicago FBI Report on Allah Temple of Islam (10/19/43), 1, RG 65, NACP.

119. Ibid., 3.

120. Ibid.

121. Ibid.

122. Ibid.

123. Chicago FBI Report on Allah Temple of Islam (6/7/44), 2, RG 65, NACP.

124. Ibid.

125. Ibid.

126. Chicago FBI Report on Allah Temple of Islam (8/15/42), 18–19, RG 65, NACP.

127. Malcolm X Little to Sister Henrietta (10/16/50), Malcolm X Collection: Papers, 1948–1965, Reel 3, Folder 1.

128. Malcolm X with assistance of Alex Haley, *The Autobiography of Malcolm X*, 169.

129. Ibid., 171.

130. Essien-Udom, *Black Nationalism*, 83.

CHAPTER SIX

1. I have been unable to document exactly when Elijah Muhammad changed the spelling of his name. My estimation is that during World War II, we see the spelling shift from Mohammed to Muhammad.

2. Essien-Udom, *Black Nationalism*, 83.

3. Scholars point out how the Church of Scientology represents the essence of Cold War religion. See Urban, *The Church of Scientology*, chapter 3, "A Cold War Religion." See Horne, *Communist Front?*, for persecution of progressive thinkers.

4. Randle, *The UFO Dossier*.

5. Curtis IV, *Islam in Black America*, 77.

6. Malcolm X, *Autobiography*, 225.

7. Naeem, "Lauds Role and Training of the Muslim Women in the Nation of Islam," 10.

8. Ibid.

9. "Muslim Girls Set Observance, May 27 at Detroit," 35.

10. Jamal, *From the Dead Level*, 109.

11. Ibid., 110.

12. Ibid., 109.

13. Ibid., 118.

14. Clegg, *An Original Man*, 113.

15. Ibid.

16. Elijah Muhammad, "THE MUSLIM GIRLS TRAINING AND GENERAL CIVILIZATION CLASS INSTRUCTION ON THE LAW OF WOMEN IN ISLAM," 1, in *Warnings and Instructions to the M.G.T. and G.C.C.*

17. Ibid., 2.

18. Ibid., 2–5.

19. Ibid., 2.

20. Tate, *Little X*, 90.

21. Ibid., 91.

22. "A SUMMARY OF THE FLAG DEMONSTRATION GIVEN TO THE M.G.T. & G.C.C. BY CAPTAIN BURNSTEEN SHARRIEFF THURSDAY MAY 20TH, 1948," in *Warnings and Instructions to the M.G.T. and G.C.C.*

23. Ibid.

24. "INSTRUCTIONS TO THE M.G.T. & G.C.C. #1, MICHIGAN," 2, in *Warnings and Instructions to the M.G.T. and G.C.C.*

25. Elijah Muhammad, "THE MUSLIM GIRLS TRAINING AND GENERAL CIVILIZATION CLASS INSTRUCTION ON THE LAW OF WOMEN IN ISLAM," 5. Elijah Mohammed to Sister Burnsteen Sharrieff (July 13, 1949) in *Warnings & Instructions to the M.G.T. & C.C.C. From The Honorable Elijah Mohammed: Mothers of the Faithful, Solders for Muhammad, 1930's–1940's,* 1.

26. Ibid., 2.

27. Ibid.

28. Author interview with Sara Sharif (NOI), S. Alimah Sharif, Detroit, Mich., October 4, 2009.

29. Ibid.

30. Ibid.

31. Ibid.

32. Ibid.

33. Ibid.

34. Ibid.

35. Tingle, "Interview with Rayya Muhammad," 7. Also see Malcolm X, *Autobiography*, 224.

36. Ibid., 7.

37. C. Eric Lincoln Collection, Box 278, Folder 27, letter dated April 3, 1959. For Sister Thelma X's last name, Muhammad, see Thelma X Muhammad, "The People Speak," 10.

38. C. Eric Lincoln Collection, Box 278, Folder 27, *Truth Magazine*. The magazine is incomplete. I am thankful to Garrett Felber for bringing this source to my attention.

39. Federal Bureau of Investigation, Criminal Internal Security Sedition, Selection Service Division, Milwaukee, Wisconsin, file no. 14–4 (11/4/42–12/8/42), 2. Report made by: Fred A. Harvey.

40. Ibid.

41. Ibid.

42. C. Eric Lincoln Collection, Box 278, Folder 27, *Truth Magazine*, 3; emphasis original.

43. Ibid.

44. Ibid.

45. Ibid.

46. Ibid.

47. Ibid.

48. Ibid.

49. Ibid.

50. C. Eric Lincoln Collection, Box 278, Folder 27, letter dated April 3, 1959, 2.

51. Ibid.

52. Satter, *Family Properties*, 31.

53. Ibid., 12.

54. Ibid., 57.

55. Ibid., 38.

56. Ibid., 31.

57. C. Eric Lincoln Collection, Box 278, Folder 27, letter dated April 3, 1959, 1, Archives Research Center, Atlanta University Center, Robert W. Woodruff Library. The only hint that Sister Thelma X lived in Chicago is that she gives details on the "Field Museum," which is located there. See 21 of *Truth Magazine*.

58. Ibid., 2.

59. C. Eric Lincoln Collection, Box 278, Folder 27, handwritten notes.

60. C. Eric Lincoln Collection, Box 278, Folder 27, *Truth Magazine*, 21.

61. C. Eric Lincoln Collection, Box 278, Folder 27, handwritten notes.

62. C. Eric Lincoln Collection, Box 278, Folder 27, letter dated April 3, 1959, 3.

63. Ibid., 1

64. Ibid., 3.

65. C. Eric Lincoln Collection, Box 278, Folder 27, *Truth Magazine*, 3.

66. C. Eric Lincoln Collection, Box 278, Folder 27, letter dated April 3, 1959, 1.

67. C. Eric Lincoln Collection, Box 278, Folder 27, *Truth Magazine*, 3.

68. C. Eric Lincoln Collection, Box 278, Folder 27, handwritten notes.

69. Ibid.

70. James A. Emanuel, "Racial Fire in the Poetry of Paul Laurence Dunbar."

71. C. Eric Lincoln Collection, Box 278, Folder 27, handwritten notes.

72. Ibid.

73. Ibid.

74. Ibid.

75. C. Eric Lincoln Collection, Box 278, Folder 27, *Truth Magazine*, 1.

76. Ibid., 21.

77. Ibid., 21.

78. Ibid., 3.

79. Marable, *Malcolm X*, 133.

80. Flomaton Centennial Scrapbook, 21, 29, accessed November 21, 2013, www.escohis
.org/flomaton/flomatonrailroad.pdf

81. Ibid.

82. Wilkerson, *The Warmth of Other Suns*, 10.

83. Ibid., 41; Mormino, *Land of Sunshine, State of Dreams*, 7.

84. Quoted in Wilkerson, *The Warmth of Other Suns*, 62.

85. Hall, "Dramatizing the African American Experience of Travel in the Jim Crow South," 80–94.

86. Green, *The Negro Motorist Green Book*, 4.

87. Ibid., 1.

88. Burns, "Flomaton Works toward Glorious Future," 31.

89. LeFlore, "Negroes Still Segregated on Trains, Buses in Dixie," 8; Equal Justice Initiative, "Federal Agency Bans Racial Segregation in Interstate Transport."

90. Burns, "Flomaton Works toward Glorious Future," 31.

91. Ibid.

92. "Arrest Pair Who Beat White Cop," 5.

93. "Police Chief Beaten for Trying to Enforce Bias"; "Two Negroes Maul Officers."

94. Cox, *The Claude Neal Lynching*.

95. "Two Negroes Maul Officers."

96. Two prominent examples of Minister Malcolm X providing defense for NOI members are in 1958 Queens, New York, and 1962 Los Angeles. See New York FBI Report, "Malcolm K. Little; IS-NOI," (Nov. 19, 1958), cover, 28–229, Sec. 4, serial 27; New York FBI Report, "Malcolm K. Little; IS-NOI," (Nov. 16, 1962), Sec. 8, cover, 16–23.

97. LeFlore, "Negroes Still Segregated on Trains, Buses in Dixie."

98. Supplemental Correlation Summary, "Malcolm K. Little" (September 25, 1963), 9, Sec. 9, serial 71.

99. "Waiting Room JC Gets Two Arrested"; "Arrest Pair Who Beat White Cop."

100. Malcolm X, FBI File Reading Room, Part 3 of 38, frame 10 of 72 (NY 105–8999, 6). Part 3 of 24, BUFile: 100–399321.

101. In the two books that mention the event, neither provide the names of the women. See Marable, *Malcolm X*, 136; and Decaro, *On the Side of My People*. My effort to locate more about the women via Elgin Air Force Base resulted in nothing. *Mr. Muhammad Speaks* newspaper started in May 1960, published in New York, and *Muhammad Speaks* newspaper started in October 1961, published in Chicago. No other news outlet carried the story with interviews of the women.

102. Malcolm Little (Malcolm X), FBI File Reading Room, HQ File Part 2 of 27, frame 62 of 123 (NY 105–8999, 20). Malcolm X Little, file no. 100–399321, Sec. 2, serial 18–20.

103. Ibid., frame 63 of 123 (NY 105–8999, 20).

104. Ibid.

105. Malcolm X, *Autobiography*, 221.

106. Malcolm X Little (Malcolm X), FBI File Reading Room, HQ File Part 2 of 27, frame 74 of 123 (NY 105–8999, 37).

107. Malcolm X, *Autobiography*, 221.

108. Malcolm X Little (Malcolm X), FBI File Reading Room, HQ File Part 2 of 27, frame 79 of 123 (NY 105–8999, 37).

109. Malcolm X Little (Malcolm X), FBI File Reading Room, HQ File Part 2 of 27, frame 79–80 of 123 (NY 105–8999, 37–38).

110. Malcolm X, *Autobiography*, 221.

111. Malcolm X Little (Malcolm X), FBI File Reading Room, HQ File Part 2 of 27, frame 85 of 123 (NY 105–8999, 43).

112. Ibid.

113. Ibid.

114. Ibid.

115. Ibid.

116. Malcolm X Little (Malcolm X), FBI File Reading Room, HQ File Part 2 of 27, frame 86–87 of 123 (NY 105- 8999, 44–45).

117. Ibid.

118. Malcolm X, *Autobiography*, 225.

119. Malcolm X Little (Malcolm X), FBI File Reading Room, HQ File Part 2 of 27, frame 85 of 123 (NY 105–8999, 43).

120. For example, *The Beulah Show*.

121. Malcolm X Little (Malcolm X), FBI File Reading Room, HQ File Part 2 of 27, frame 81 of 123 (NY 105–8999).

122. Malcolm X Little (Malcolm X), FBI File Reading Room, HQ File Part 2 of 27, frame 12–12 of 123 (NY 105–8999, 10).

123. Malcolm X Little (Malcolm X), FBI File Reading Room, HQ File Part 2 of 38, frame 13–14 of 123 (NY 105–8999).

124. Malcolm X Little (Malcolm X), FBI File Reading Room, HQ File Part 2 of 27, frame 14 of 123 (NY 105–8999, 11).

125. Malcolm X Little (Malcolm X), FBI File Reading Room, HQ File Part 2 of 27, frame 12 of 123 (NY 105–8999, 10).

126. Collins with Bailey, *Seventh Child*, 65.

127. Ibid., 66; Marable, *Malcolm X*, 105, 140.

128. Karim with Skutches and Gallen, *Remembering Malcolm*, 74.

129. Collins with Bailey, *Seventh Child*, 130.

130. Malcolm X, *Autobiography*, 226.

131. Marable, *Malcolm X*, 141.

132. Collins with Bailey, *Seventh Child*, 96. Malcolm X, *Autobiography*, 226.

133. Malcolm X Little (Malcolm X), FBI File Reading Room, Part 2 of 27, frame 13 of 123 (NY 105–8999, 10).

134. Lanker, *I Dream a World*, 100; Shabazz and Taylor, "Loving and Losing Malcolm," 50; Rickford, *Betty Shabazz*, 36.

135. Marable, *Malcolm X*, 139.

136. Shabazz, "Loving and Losing Malcolm," 2.

137. Rickford, *Betty Shabazz*, 36.

138. Shabazz, "Loving and Losing Malcolm," 2.

139. Ibid.

140. Ibid.

141. Ibid.

142. Malcolm X, *Autobiography*, 225.

143. Shabazz, "Loving and Losing Malcolm," 2. The physical layout of NOI Temples continued to resemble the 1930s and 40s. Larger spaces included a woman's waiting room, and the chairs were arranged in the direction toward a stage which featured a blackboard. A portrait of a lynched black man next to a Christian cross with the letters "Slavery, Suffering, [and]Death," were featured next to the Islamic symbol, a crescent moon and five-pointed star with the words, "Freedom, Justice, Equality and Islam. See Jamal, *From the Dead Level*, 147.

144. Shabazz, "Loving and Losing Malcolm," 2.

145. Ibid.

146. Ibid., 3.

147. Ibid.

148. Ibid.

149. Ibid.

150. Ibid.

151. Lanker, *I Dream a World*, 100; Shabazz, "Loving and Losing Malcolm," 3.

152. Shabazz, "Loving and Losing Malcolm," 3.

153. Ibid.; Lanker, *I Dream a World*, 100.

154. Shabazz, "Loving and Losing Malcolm," 3.

155. Ibid.

156. Lanker, *I Dream a World*, 100.

157. Shabazz, "Loving and Losing Malcolm," 3.

158. Jamal, *From the Dead Level*, 175.

159. Ibid., 122.

160. Ibid., 121.

161. Ibid., 159–60.

162. Ibid., 160.

163. Ibid.

164. Ibid., 161.

165. Ibid., 160.

166. Ibid., 164–65.

167. Ibid., 165.

168. Rickford, *Betty Shabazz*, 51.

169. Marable, *Malcolm X*, 139.

170. Ibid., 125.

171. Ibid., 126; For a discussion of Minister Malcolm giving time-out to other men for domestic abuse see Shabazz, *Blood, Sweat & Tears*, 231.

172. Lanker, *I Dream a World*, 100.

173. Shabazz, "Loving and Losing Malcolm," 4.

174. Malcolm X, *Autobiography*, 229.

175. Ibid.

176. Ibid., 230.

177. Ibid., 228–229.

178. Shabazz, "Loving and Losing Malcolm," 4.

179. Malcolm X, *Autobiography*, 230. Shabazz, "Loving and Losing Malcolm," 5.

180. Shabazz, "Loving and Losing Malcolm," 5.

181. Malcolm X to Mr. Muhammad (January 13, 1958). Letter archived in Leland's Auction House, Lot 312. Malcolm XTLS- American Autographs, Americana, December 4, 2003. Accessed on-line November 1, 2016.

182. Malcolm X, *Autobiography*, 231.

183. Lee with Wiley, *By Any Means Necessary*, 61.

184. Ibid.

185. Malcolm X, *Autobiography*, 222.

186. Ibid., 232.

187. Collins, *Seventh Child*, 100.

188. *The Messenger Magazine*, vol. 1, no. 1 (1959), Box 175, Folder 16.

189. Gibson and Karim, *Women of the Nation*, 49.

190. Betty Shabazz, FBI Reading Room, Part 1 of 3, frame 93 of 143 (NY 105–29845, 16).

191. Ibid.

192. Malcolm X Little (Malcolm X) FBI Reading Room, HQ File 1 of 41, frame 18–20 of 159. Section 50, 105–8999.

193. Geracimos, "Introducing Mrs. Malcolm X," 6.

194. Rickford, *Betty Shabazz*, 59.

195. Geracimos, "Introducing Mrs. Malcolm X," 6.

196. Ibid.

197. *New York Times Book Review*, April 23, 1961, C. Eric Lincoln Collection, Box 175, Folder 1.

198. "10,000 Hear Muhammad Speak on 'So-Called Negro,'" 3.

199. Thelma X Muhammad, "The People Speak," 10.

200. Ibid., 15.

201. Ibid.

202. Ibid.

203. Ibid.

204. Ibid.
205. Ibid.
206. Ibid.
207. Allen, "The People Speak," 10.
208. Ibid.
209. Thelma X Muhammad, "The People Speak," 10.
210. Ibid.
211. Ibid.
212. Ibid.
213. Ibid.
214. Allen, "The People Speak," 10.
215. Ibid.
216. Ibid.
217. Thelma X Muhammad, "The People Speak," 10.

CHAPTER SEVEN

1. James and Ritz, *Rage to Survive*, 37.
2. Ibid., 37.
3. Ibid., 111.
4. Ibid., 107.
5. Ibid., 107.
6. Ibid., 112.
7. Ibid., 112.
8. Ibid., 84.
9. Ibid., 112, 113.
10. Ibid., 112.
11. Ibid., 62.
12. Ibid., 112.
13. Ibid., 112.
14. Ibid., 113. In a July 14, 2015, telephone interview with Rahman Ali, Muhammad Ali's brother, he said that he remembered meeting Etta James at the Apollo with his brother but did not remember her talking about being a Muslim. I am thankful to H. Ron Brashear for connecting me with Rahman Ali.
15. Ibid., 112.
16. Ibid.
17. Ibid.
18. Ibid. James adds that "My religious practices might have been erratic, and my wildness surely overwhelmed my piety, but for ten years I called myself a Muslim."
19. Lomax, *When the Word Is Given . . .*, 29; Goldman, *The Death and Life of Malcolm X*, 56.
20. Brown, "Black Muslims and the Police," 119.
21. Ibid.

22. *Biennial Report to the Alabama Legislature by the Alabama Legislative Commission to Preserve the Peace* in the Social Protest Collection, Reel 13, ctn. 4.6, Anti-War National Folder, Bancroft Library, University of California, Berkeley. The Alabama Legislative Committee to Preserve the Peace was created in 1963. This report was brought to my attention by Robyn Spencer.

23. Author interview with Waheedah Muhammad, November 4, 2014.

24. Hauser, *Muhammad Ali*, 182.

25. Author Skype interview with Khalilah Ali, daughter of Inez (Aminah) Ali, March 5 (2015).

26. Author Skype interview with Khalilah Ali, March 5, 2015.

27. Ibid.

28. Alvardo, "Khailah Camacho-Ali Stood by Muhammad Ali through Exile and Trump."

29. Hauser, *Muhammad Ali*, 364.

30. Alvardo, "Khailah Camacho-Ali Stood by Muhammad Ali through Exile and Trump."

31. Author Skype interview with Khalilah Ali, March 5 (2015).

32. "Secret Honeymoon of the Champ," 149; Witt, "After Their Chilla in Manila, Belinda Ali Launches a New Career—Alone."

33. Author Skype interview with Khalilah Ali, March 5 (2015).

34. See photos of Muhammad Ali and Belinda Boyd at a Chicago NOI bakery.

35. Alvardo, "Khailah Camacho-Ali Stood by Muhammad Ali through Exile and Trump."

36. "Secret Honeymoon of the Champ," 144.

37. Alvardo, "Khailah Camacho-Ali Stood by Muhammad Ali through Exile and Trump."

38. Hauser, *Muhammad Ali*, 183–84.

39. Ibid., 184.

40. Author Skype interview with Khalilah Ali (March 5, 2015).

41. Hauser, *Muhammad Ali*, 184.

42. Ibid., 184.

43. Ibid., 182.

44. Ibid., 182–83.

45. "Secret Honeymoon of the Champ," 161.

46. Author interview with Waheedah Muhammad (November 1, 2014).

47. Ibid.

48. Ibid.

49. Ibid.

50. Ibid.

51. Ibid.

52. Author interview with Doris Sharokhimanesha, Martinez, Calif. (September 16, 2014).

53. Ibid.

54. Author interview with S. Alimah Sharif (Sara Sharif), Detroit, Mich. (October 4, 2009).

55. Author telephone interview with Zoharah Simmons (Gwendloyn Robinson) (August 27, 2014).

56. Author telephone interview with Zoharah Simmons (Gwendloyn Robinson) (September 9, 2014).

57. Author telephone interview with Zoharah Simmons (Gwendloyn Robinson) (August 27, 2014).

58. Author telephone interview with Zoharah Simmons (Gwendloyn Robinson) (September 9, 2014).

59. Ibid.

60. Author interview with Baheejah Shakur (Bertha), Southfield, Michigan (October 5, 2009).

61. See photo of Sister Christine in Johnson, *Muhammad's Children*, 8.

62. Zoharah Simmons to Ula Taylor, email correspondence (October 29, 2014).

63. Wedad, "The Black Woman: Must Have Islam," 15.

64. Elijah Muhammad, *Message to the Blackman in America*, 64.

65. Weisbord, "Birth Control and the Black American," 581.

66. Lepore, "Birth Control in the Cabinet." Lepore attached the Malcolm X document as a jpeg, accessed December 8, 2011.

67. Ibid.

68. Baylor, "Ameenah Rasul, Leader of Women in the Nation of Islam, Dies at 90," 35. I am thankful to Gerald Horne for sharing this citation.

69. Ibid.

70. Ibid.

71. Ibid.

72. Currin, "Portrait of a Woman," 19.

73. Ibid., 20.

74. Ibid., 18.

75. Ibid., 20.

76. Ibid., 16.

77. Ibid., 17.

78. Ibid., 20.

79. Ibid., 17.

80. Ibid., 17.

81. Author interview with Waheedah Muhammad, November 4, 2014.

82. Ibid.

83. Author interview with Waheedah Muhammad, November 1, 2014.

84. Ibid.

85. Ibid.

86. Ibid.

87. Ibid.

88. Clegg, *An Original Man*, 159.

89. Magida, *Prophet of Rage*, 93.

90. Karim, Skutches, and Gallen, *Remembering Malcolm*, 149.

91. Author interview with Doris Sharokhimanesh, Martinez, Calif. (September 16, 2014).

92. Shabazz, *Blood, Sweat & Tears*, 22, 268–69.

93. Author interview with Doris Sharokhimanesh, Martinez, Calif. (September 16, 2014).

94. Shahrokhimanesh, *Under the Veil*, 22.

95. Ibid., 22.

96. Ibid., 22.

97. Ibid., 23.

98. Ibid., 16.

99. Ibid., 20.

100. Ibid., 22.

101. Ibid.

102. Author interview with Doris Shahrokhimanesh, Martinez, Calif. (September 16, 2014). Also see Kuruvila, "Bakery Leader Defiant in Sermons after Arrest"; Mary Fricker, "Officer's Diligence Paid Off in Bust"; Askia Muhammad, "Your Muslim Bakery's Recipe for Mayhem"; Thompson, "The Sinister Side of Yusuf Bey's Empire."

103. Shahrokhimanesh, *Under the Veil*, 47.

104. Sister Betty Muhammad, *Dear Holy Apostle*, 60.

105. Many of the prominent officials and members in the Nation married two and three times. For example, Ethel Muhammad married Harry W. Hudgens at the age of nineteen in 1942, divorced, and subsequently married Raymond Sharrieff in 1948. See Ethel Sharrieff, FBI file, FOIPA No: 1139512, Field Office file no.: 100–31804 (December 6, 1961), 8–9 of 48 pages. See Sister Betty Muhammad, *Dear Holy Apostle*, 60. Also, Lance Shabazz writes that, "Islam has not stopped many Muslims from marrying four or five times." See Shabazz, *Blood, Sweat & Tears*, 31.

106. Shahrokhimanesh, *Under the Veil*, 25.

107. Author interview with Waheedah Muhammad November 1, 2014.

108. Ibid.

109. Ibid.

110. Ibid.

111. Shahrokhimanesh, *Under the Veil*, 61.

112. Ibid., 62.

113. "Secret Honeymoon of the Champ."

114. "Early 1967 Wedding Photo," 9; "Happy Birthday for Wife of the Champ," 25.

115. "First Photos of the Champ and His Baby," 9; "Reappearance by Request," 29; "Maryam Ali"; "At Home with the Champion and His Daughter."

116. Hauser, *Muhammad Ali*, 184.

117. Eurpublisher02, "Ali's Second Wife Khalilah on Their Marriage."

118. "Joe Tex the Real Story (Khalilah Ali on Polygamy and James Brown)."

119. Alvardo, "Khailah Camacho-Ali Stood by Muhammad Ali through Exile and Trump."

120. Ibid.

121. Hauser, *Muhammad Ali*, 184.

122. Ibid., 185.

123. Eurpublisher02, "Ali's Second Wife Khalilah on Their Marriage."

124. Siegel, *The Trials of Muhammad Ali.*

125. Hauser, *Muhammad Ali*, 190.

126. Ibid., 190.

127. Eurpublisher02, "Ali's Second Wife Khalilah on Their Marriage." Camacho-Ali spoke onstage during the Independent Lens/Trails of Muhammad Ali panel discussion at the PBS portion of the 2014 Winter Television Critics Association tour at Langham Hotel on January 21, 2014, in Pasadena, California. "Eur" stands for Electronic Urban Report.

128. Alvardo, "Khailah Camacho-Ali Stood by Muhammad Ali through Exile and Trump."

129. Ibid.

130. *The John Lewis Show* with cohost Ron Jefferson and featured guest Khalilah Ali. Milesaheadinc.com. Uploaded December 25, 2009, accessed October 15, 2014, YOUTUBE.

131. Hauser, *Muhammad Ali*, 187.

132. Shabazz, *Blood, Sweat & Tears*, 311.

133. Eurpublisher02, "Ali's Second Wife Khalilah on Their Marriage."

134. Elijah Muhammad, "We Tell the World We're NOT with Muhammad Ali," 2.

135. Author Skype interview with Khalilah Ali, March 5 (2015).

136. Siegel, *The Trails of Muhammad Ali.*

137. Author Skype interview with Khalilah Ali, March 5 (2015).

138. Bill Siegel, *The Trails of Muhammad Ali* video

139. I am thankful to Sunni Khalid for pointing out this difference.

CHAPTER EIGHT

1. Bush, "Ethel Muhammad Sharrieff, 80: Nation of Islam leader's daughter."

2. Hakim and Muhammad, "Ethel Sharieff, daughter of Hon. Elijah Muhammad."

3. Ibid.

4. Ibid.

5. Bush, "Ethel Muhammad Sharrieff, 80: Nation of Islam leader's daughter."

6. Ibid.

7. Ethel Sharrieff, FBI file, FOIPA No: 1139512, Field Office file no.: 100–31804 (January 3, 1967), 7 of 15. Date within document 5/12/66.

8. Ibid., 12 of 23.

9. Shabazz, *Blood, Sweat & Tears: The Nation of Islam and Me*, 89.

10. Cha-Jua, "A Life of Revolutionary Transformation," 168; Malcolm X, *Malcolm X Speaks*, 207. Malcolm X estimates the NOI's 1965 membership at 15,000.

11. Williams, "A Fallen Star," chapter 3, 35.

12. "Nab Suspects in 23G Black Muslim Theft," 1; "Gunmen Take Black Muslim for $23,000," 1.

13. Ibid.

14. Clegg, *An Original Man*, 254.

15. Williams, "A Fallen Star," chapter 3, 52.

16. Clegg, *An Original Man*, 158.

17. Williams, "A Fallen Star," chapter 3, 35, 52.

18. Ibid., 53.

19. Clegg, *An Original Man*, 254.

20. Ibid., 252.

21. Ibid.

22. Ibid., 254.

23. On several occasions Mr. Muhammad refused to give financial support to his sons W. D. Mohammad and Akbar Muhammad as well as his grandson Hasan Sharrieff because of their critique of his leadership.

24. Williams, "A Fallen Star," chapter 3, 36.

25. http://www.finalcall.com/artman/publish/National_News_2/article_102165.shtml. Accessed June 1, 2015

26. Ethel Sharrieff, FBI file, FOIPA No: 1139512, Field Office file no.: 100–436766 (November 6, 1968), 6 of 10 pages. Contract dated 10/15/1963.

27. Sister Betty Muhammad, *Dear Holy Apostle:*, 25. I am thankful to Zain Abdulah for identifying this source.

28. Muhammad, *Dear Holy Apostle*, 25.

29. Ibid., 24.

30. Shabazz, *Blood, Sweat & Tears*, 13.

31. Muhammad, *Dear Holy Apostle*, 25.

32. Sister Margary Hassain was a secretary in charge of proofreading and approving the Orientation letters. Sister Betty 2X West's article, "The Love Our Leader Has For His People" was published June 1968.

33. Muhammad, *Dear Holy Apostle*, 34.

34. Ibid.

35. Ibid., 45.

36. Ibid., 16.

37. Ibid., 28.

38. Shabazz, *Blood, Sweat & Tears*, 148.

39. Malcolm X, *The Final Speeches, February 1965*, 207.

40. The Honorable Louis Farrakhan, "The Honorable Elijah Muhammad & Malcolm X —28 Years Later—What Really Happened," Saviour's Day 1993, the U.I.C. Pavilion, Chicago, Ill, February 21, 1993. Sister Ola Muhammad states that she is "forty something years old" and her son is thirty-two. It should be noted that Farrakhan's daughter is married to Kamal Muhammad.

41. Malcolm X, *Autobiography*, 98.

42. Ethel Sharrieff, FBI file, FOIPA No: 1139512, Field Office file no.: 100–31804 (December 14, 1962), 10 of 18; Malcolm X, *Autobiography*, 298.

43. Clegg, *An Original Man*, 186–187.

44. Shabazz, *Blood, Sweat & Tears*, 187.

45. Kimmel, *Manhood in America*, 7.

46. Evanzz, *The Judas Factor*, 170.

47. Tingle, "Interview with Rayya Muhammad," 11.

48. Ethel Sharrieff, FBI file, FOIPA No: 1139512, Field Office file no.: 100–31804 (January 3, 1967), cover page of 23.

49. Clegg, *An Original Man*, 171.

50. Goldman, *The Death and Life of Malcolm X*, 112.

51. The Honorable Louis Farrakhan, "The Honorable Elijah Muhammad & Malcolm X — 28 Years Later — What Really Happened."

52. "Muslim Leader Named in Two Paternity Suits."

53. Rosary, *Superior Court of the State of California for the County of Los Angeles*, 2.

54. "Elijah's Two Paternity Suits — The Will of Allah: He Claims."

55. Rosary, *Superior Court of the State of California for the County of Los Angeles, Case Number*, 2.

56. Williams, *Superior Court of the State of California for the County of Los Angeles Case Number* D652475 (July 2, 1964).

57. Jamal, *From the Dead Level*, 266.

58. Ibid., 262.

59. Ibid., 263.

60. Ibid., 253.

61. Ibid., 253.

62. Tingle, "Interview with Rayya Muhammad," 12.

63. Ibid.

64. "Elijah's Two Paternity Suits — The Will of Allah: He Claims."

65. Tingle, "Interview with Rayya Muhammad," 11.

66. Ibid.

67. Ibid.

68. Kondo, *Conspiracys*, 260–61.

69. Perry, *The Life of a Man Who Changed Black America*, 305.

70. I think this is why Minister Malcolm's brothers and others who disagreed with the leadership stayed in the NOI during this horrific moment.

71. Jamal, *From the Dead Level*, 266.

72. Malcolm X, *The Final Speeches, February 1965*, 116.

73. Elijah Muhammad, "Messenger of Allah Special: Read," 13.

74. Shahrokhimanesh, *Under the Veil*, 29.

75. Ibid.

76. Ibid.

77. Ibid.

78. Hauser, *Muhammad Ali*, 308.

79. Ibid., 308.

80. Ibid., 308.

81. Author Skype Interview with Khalilah Ali, March 5 (2015).

82. Ibid.

83. *Jet*, January 14, 1985.

84. Rush, Molly, Ogunnaike, and Anderson, "Ali Daughter Tosses Book in Ring."

85. Hauser, *Muhammad Ali*, 312.

86. Ibid., 308.

87. Ibid.

88. Ibid., 310.

89. Elijah Muhammad FBI Reading Room, Part 07 of 20, frame 30 of 124 (April 26, 1962, 100–35635), 105–24822, Sec. 7.

90. Elijah Muhammad FBI Reading Room, Part 08 of 20, frame 106 of 234. 105–24822, Sec. 8. Elijah Muhammad, 07 of 20, frame 5–6 of 124 (100–6989, Cover Page B-C); Clegg, *An Original Man*, 188.

91. See video, "Elijah Muhammad and Malcolm X, 28 Years Later, What Really Happened." Sister June states that Malcolm X said to her, "if I have you I will also have Muhammad" in relation to her joining the paternity law suit. For birthdate of Abdullah see http://www.finalcall.com/artman/publish/National_News_2/article_102165.shtml. Accessed June 1, 2015

92. Williams, "A Fallen Star," chapter 2, 10.

93. Ibid., 13.

94. Ibid. chapter 3, 56.

95. Ibid., chapter 2, 13.

96. Tingle, "Interview with Rayya Muhammad," 10 and 14.

97. Williams, "A Fallen Star," chapter 3, 26.

98. Wallace, Akbar and Ethel's son, grandson Shariff were the most isolated at different times in their lives. Wallace accused his father of "immorality, religious deception and political sterility." Akbar disassociated himself from his father because of "immorality." See FBI Reading Room, Elijah Muhammad, 08 of 20, frame 181–182 of 234 (8/17/1964).

99. Tingle, "Interview with Rayya Muhammad," 14.

100. Ibid.

101. Starla Muhammad, "Mother Tynnetta Muhammad—A Heartfelt and Fitting Tribute to a Perfect Example," 3, http://www.finalcallcall.com/artman/publish/National _News_2/article_102165.shtml, accessed June 3, 2015.

102. FBI Records: The Vault, "Elijah Muhammad," 07 of 20, frame 45 of 124 (July 31, 1962, 100–35635). File 105–24822, Sec. 7.

103. Tingle, "Interview with Rayya Muhammad," 14.

104. "Donna Farrakhan: Breaking of the Black Woman 1/3" (November 14, 2013). YouTube upload by Richard Ekiye.

105. FBI Records: The Vault, "Elijah Muhammad," 08 of 20, frame 103 of 234 (PX 105–93, 2).

106. Williams, "A Fallen Star," chapter 3, 26.

107. "Empty Chair," *Muhammad Speaks*, March 18, 1963, 4. For birth years and names of Mr. Muhammad's extra marital children see http://www.finalcall.com/artman/publish /National_News_2/article_102165.shtml. Accessed June 1, 2015

108. Tingle, "Interview with Rayya Muhammad," 14.

109. "Mrs. Elijah Muhammad, 72, Black Muslim Leader's Wife," *New York Times*, August 14, 1972, 30.

CHAPTER NINE

1. Malcom X, *Autobiography*, 303.

2. Clegg, *An Original Man*, 228.

3. Ibid., 332, note 84.

4. William Strickland, oral histories selected and edited by Cheryll Y. Greene, *Malcolm X: Make It Plain*, 231.

5. Baraka, *The Autobiography of Leroi Jones*, 296.

6. Sanchez, *Shake Loose My Skin*, 6.

7. Evans, ed., *Black Women Writers (1950–1980)*, 264.

8. Sonia Sanchez, *Love Poems*, 69.

9. Johnson-Bailey, "Poet Sonia Sanchez Telling What We Must Hear," 217.

10. Baraka, *The Autobiography of Leroi Jones*, 262–63.

11. Ibid., 311.

12. Melhem, "Sonia Sanchez: Will and Spirit," 73–98, 94.

13. Author interview with Professor Sonia Sanchez, October 3, 2010, Raleigh, North Carolina.

14. Ibid.

15. "Reflections: A Conversation with Sis Sonia 5X Sanchez," S-3.

16. Simmons, "African American Islam as an Expression of Converts' Religious Faith and Nationalist Dreams and Ambitions," 181. The 1965 album *Ballots or Bullets* by Malcolm X represented Malcolm's independent beliefs.

17. Ibid.

18. Ibid.

19. Simmons, "Striving for Muslim Women's Human Rights," 199.

20. Ibid., 200.

21. Simmons, "Are We Up to the Challenge?," 244, note 3.

22. Ibid., 236. Simmons, "Striving for Muslim Women's Human Rights," 201.

23. Ibid., 179.

24. Simmons, "African American Islam as an Expression of Converts' Religious Faith and Nationalist Dreams and Ambitions," 180.

25. Author telephone interview with Zoharah Simmons (Gwendolyn Robinson), September 9, 2014.

26. Ibid.

27. Ibid.

28. Ibid.

29. Ibid.

30. Howard, "The Making of a Black Muslim," 255.

31. For a great discussion on the power of color-blind rhetoric, see Gomer, "Colorblindness, A Life."

32. Carmichael, *Black Power*, 53–54.

33. Willhelm and Powell, "Who Needs the Negro?," 347.

34. Ibid.

35. Simmons, "African American Islam as an Expression of Converts' Religious Faith and Nationalist Dreams and Ambitions," 182.

36. Karriem, "The Preacher of Pan-Africanism," 15.

37. Ibid.

38. Ibid.

39. Karriem, "The Preacher of Pan-Africanism," 15.

40. Bryant, "What Islam Has Done for Me," 13.

41. Ibid.

42. Joan 4X, "What Islam Has Done for Me," 17.

43. Ibid.

44. Ibid.

45. Author interview with Professor Sonia Sanchez, October 3, 2010, Raleigh, North Carolina.

46. Ibid.

47. Simone with Cleary, *I Put a Spell on You*, 118.

48. Audley (Queen Mother) Moore interview, June 6 and 8, 1978, in Ruth Edmonds Hill, 151.

49. Malcolm X in Steve Clark, ed., *February 1965: The Final Speeches*, 205.

50. Audley Moore interview, 151.

51. Elijah Muhammad, *Message to the Blackman in America*, 35.

52. "MGT & GCC Present Africa Extravaganza."

53. Author interview with Professor Sonia Sanchez, October 3, 2010, Raleigh, North Carolina.

54. Jackson and Gaines, "Nation of Islam: Power and Money," 16.

55. Sister Christine Delois X, "Dope, Alcohol and Devil's Tricks Strip Blacks of Human Dignity," 18.

56. Baldwin, *The Price of the Ticket*, 360.

57. Malcolm X, *Autobiography*, 169.

58. See *Muhammad Speaks* regular column "What Islam Has Done for Me."

59. Shahrokhimanesh, *Under the Veil*, 6.

60. Ibid.

61. Ibid.

62. Ibid., 8.

63. Ibid., 9.

64. Ibid., 9.

65. Ibid., 9.

66. Ibid., preface, 2

67. Ibid., 9.

68. Ibid., 10.

69. Ibid., 12.

70. Ibid., 12.

71. Ibid., 12.

72. Ibid., 13.

73. Marshall, *Citizenship and Social Class*, 29.

74. Tate, *Little X*, 28.

75. Ibid. The minister was making reference to the 1963 bombing of the 16th Street Baptist Church in Birmingham, Alabama.

76. Ibid.

77. The enrollment of students at the University of Islam is difficult to ascertain. Ibrahim Mahmond Shalaby's dissertation provides stats for 1965. The University of Islam in Detroit enrollment numbered 196, Chicago numbered 488, and Atlanta numbered 72. See Shalaby, "The Role of the School in Cultural Renewal and Identity Development

in the Nation of Islam in America," 317–18. I rely heavily upon this dissertation because the author visited each school and interviewed Mr. Muhammad, principals, students and teachers. It's the most comprehensive work on the University of Islam schools that I was able to locate.

78. Vontress, "Threat, Blessing, or Both?," 86.

79. Shalaby, "The Role of the School in Cultural Renewal and Identity Development in the Nation of Islam in America," 47.

80. Ibid., 256.

81. Essien-Udom, *Black Nationalism*, 263. This cost was slightly higher than Catholic schools which had a three tier range in 1960: lowest annual rate was $24 per child; medium annual rate was $30 per child and sixty per family; maximum annual rate was $60 per child and $100 per family.

82. Shalaby, "The Role of the School in Cultural Renewal and Identity Development in the Nation of Islam in America," 284. Blue Chip Stamps and S&H Green Stamps were the most popular trading stamp and were issued at grocery stores and gas stations. The stamps could be redeemed at stores for merchandise.

83. Vontress, "Threat, Blessing, or Both?," 87.

84. Ibid., 89.

85. Shalaby, "The Role of the School in Cultural Renewal and Identity Development in the Nation of Islam in America," 120.

86. Ibid., 121.

87. Ibid., 103.

88. Ibid., 251, 260.

89. Ibid., 78.

90. Tate, *Little X*, 11.

91. Johnson, *Muhammad's Children*.

92. Brazziel and Gordon, "Replications of Some Aspects of the Higher Horizons Program in a Southern Junior High School," 142. See *New York Amsterdam News*, September 16, 1961, 12.

93. Johnson, *Muhammad's Children*, 12.

94. Ibid., 26.

95. Laue, "A Contemporary Revitalization Movement in American Race Relations," 321.

96. Shalaby, "The Role of the School in Cultural Renewal and Identity Development in the Nation of Islam in America," 113.

97. Ibid.

98. Ibid., 117–18.

99. Ibid., 249.

100. Tate, *Little X*, 30.

101. Dunnigan, "Washington Inside Out," 6.

102. Tate, *Little X*, 30.

103. Vontress, "Threat, Blessing, or Both?," 89.

104. Ibid.

105. Shalaby, "The Role of the School in Cultural Renewal and Identity Development in the Nation of Islam in America," 151.

106. Tate, *Do Me Twice*, 265.

107. Shalaby, "The Role of the School in Cultural Renewal and Identity Development in the Nation of Islam in America," 71. There were some teachers who were not in the Nation of Islam but members were preferred. See Essien-Udom, *Black Nationalism*, 261.

108. Shalaby, "The Role of the School in Cultural Renewal and Identity Development in the Nation of Islam in America," 263.

109. Tate, *Little X*, 34.

110. Shalaby, "The Role of the School in Cultural Renewal and Identity Development in the Nation of Islam in America," 264.

111. Essien-Udom, *Black Nationalism*, 267. Shalaby, "The Role of the School in Cultural Renewal and Identity Development in the Nation of Islam in America," 276.

112. Vontress, "Threat, Blessing, or Both?," 87.

113. Shalaby, "The Role of the School in Cultural Renewal and Identity Development in the Nation of Islam in America," 312.

114. Ibid., 315.

115. Ibid., 267, footnote 39. Vontress, "Threat, Blessing, or Both?," 89.

116. "Islam Grads Move into Top Colleges," 18

117. "Expanding Curriculum," 20.

118. Baylor, "Ameenah Rasul, Leader of Women in the Nation of Islam, Dies at 90," 35.

119. Shalaby, "The Role of the School in Cultural Renewal and Identity Development in the Nation of Islam in America," 312 and 315.

120. Tate, *Little X*, 25.

121. Shahrokhimanesh, *Under the Veil*, 41–42.

122. Author interview with Doris Jean Sharokhimanesh.

123. Shalaby, "The Role of the School in Cultural Renewal and Identity Development in the Nation of Islam in America," 264.

124. Tate, *Little X*, 101.

125. Ibid., 59. Vontress, "Threat, Blessing, or Both?," 90.

126. Tate, *Little X*, 51.

127. Ibid.

128. Ibid., 52. Sister Betty Muhammad, *Dear Holy Apostle*, 13.

129. Shalaby, "The Role of the School in Cultural Renewal and Identity Development in the Nation of Islam in America," 76.

130. Ethel Sharrieff, FBI file, FOIPA No: 1139512, Field Office file no.: 100–31804 (March 17, 1964), 19 of 32 pages.

131. Tate, *Do Me Twice*, 265.

132. Ethel Sharrieff, FBI file, FOIPA No: 1139512, Field Office file no.: 100–31804 (December 6, 1961), 44 of 48 pages.

133. Ethel Sharrieff, FBI file, FOIPA No: 1139512, Field Office file no.: 100–31804 (December 14, 1962), 5 of 18.

134. Malcolm X to Dear Holy Apostle (April 19, 1955), FBI Reports (Individuals) Malcolm K. Little, AKA BUfile 105–24822.

135. Sister Ethel Sharrieff MGT Captain's instruction to MGT class No. 6, Baltimore,

Maryland, February 20, 1964. See Ethel Sharrieff, FBI file, FOIPA No: 1139512, Field Office file no.: 100–31804 (11/5–12/11/64) 18 of 32.

136. Author interview with Sara Sharif, Detroit, Michigan (October 4, 2009).

137. Ethel Sharrieff, FBI file, FOIPA No: 1139512, Field Office file no.: 100–31804 (January 3, 1968), 6 of 12.

138. Shalaby, "The Role of the School in Cultural Renewal and Identity Development in the Nation of Islam in America," 100.

139. Ibid., 79.

140. Moynihan, *The Negro Family*.

141. Baraka, *African Congress*, 177.

142. Ibid., 177, 179.

143. Elijah Muhammad, *Message to the Black Man*, 60.

144. Lincoln, "Who Will Revere the Black Woman?," 82.

145. Smith, "Some Home Truths on the Contemporary Black Feminist Movement," 255.

146. Bond and Peery, "Is the Black Male Castrated?," 113–14.

147. Ibid., 113.

148. Cleaver, *Soul on Ice*, 160–61.

149. Sister Vera X Lewis (Teaneck, New Jersey), *Muhammad Speaks*, November 4, 1966, 25.

150. Sister Gertrude Bogans (Detroit, Michigan), *Muhammad Speaks*, January 1, 1965, 7.

151. Griffin, "'Ironies of the Saint'"; Griffin, "Black Feminists and Du Bois."

152. Griffin, "'Ironies of the Saint,' 216.

153. Elijah Muhammad, *The Supreme Wisdom*, 9.

154. Naeem, "Lauds Role and Training of the Muslim Women in the Nation of Islam," 58.

155. Griffin, "'Ironies of the Saint,' 218.

156. Muhammad, *Message to the Blackman*, 59.

157. Ibid., 59.

158. Author interview with Professor Sonia Sanchez, October 3, 2010, Raleigh. North Carolina.

159. Sister Betty Muhammad, *Dear Holy Apostle*, 42.

160. Tate, *Black Women Writers at Work*, 139.

161. Goldman, *The Death and Life of Malcolm X*.

162. Author interview with Professor Sonia Sanchez, October 3, 2010, Raleigh. North Carolina.

163. Ibid.

164. Ibid.

165. Ibid.

166. Currin, "Portrait of a Woman," 22–23.

167. Ibid., 23.

168. Ibid., 22.

169. Author interview with Baaheejah Shakur, Southfield, Mich., October 5, 2009.

170. Ibid.

171. Ibid.

172. Author interview with Professor Sonia Sanchez, October 3, 2010, Raleigh, N.C.

173. Komlos and Brabec, "The Trend of BMI values of US Adults by Deciles, Birth Cohorts 1882–1986 Stratified by Gender and Ethnicity."

174. Currin, "Portrait of a Woman," 23.

175. Sister Shirley X Morton (San Francisco), *Muhammad Speaks*, June 3, 1966, 25.

176. Author interview with Baaheejah Shakur, Southfield, Mich., October 5, 2009.

177. Ibid.

178. Ibid.

179. Sister Ethel Sharrieff, March 2, 1961. See Ethel Sharrieff, FBI file, FOIPA No: 1139512, Field Office file no: 100–31804 (December 6, 1961), 41 of 48.

180. Ethel Sharrieff, FBI file, FOIPA No: 1138512, Field Office file no.: 100–31804 (December 14, 1962), 9 of 18.

181. Marguerite X, "What Islam Has Done for Me," 17.

182. Sister Evelyn X, "Modest Muslim Dress Dignifies Blackwoman," 18.

183. Elijah Muhammad. "Beards," 5.

184. Sister Kathleen X (Newark, New Jersey), *Muhammad Speaks*, September 12, 1969, 21.

185. Ibid.

186. E. Frances White, "Listening to the Voices of Black Feminism," *Radical America*, Vol. 18, no. 2–3, 9.

187. Elijah Muhammad, "Warning to the MGT and GC Class," *Muhammad Speaks*, June 28, 1968, 4.

188. Ethel Sharrieff, FBI file, FOIPA No: 1139512, Field Office file no.: 100–31804 (December 19, 1963), 8 of 20.

189. Simmons, "African American Islam as an Expression of Converts' Religious Faith and Nationalist Dreams and Ambitions," 184–85.

CHAPTER TEN

1. Mahmood, *Politics of Piety*, 32.

2. Ibid., 5.

3. Crenshaw, "Demarginalizing the Intersection of Race and Sex," 314–43.

4. Ibid., 327.

5. Ibid., 327.

6. Mahmood, *Politics of Piety*, 158.

7. Williams, "A Fallen Star," chapter 3, 20.

8. Einspahr, "Structural Domination and Structural Freedom," 7.

9. Muhammad Ali with Richard Durham, *The Greatest*, 185.

10. Ibid., 200.

11. Ibid., 187.

12. Ibid., 187.

13. Ibid., 189.

14. Nadar and Potgieter, "Liberated through Submission?," 148.

15. Williams, "A Fallen Star," chapter 3, 20–21.

16. Burton and Tucker, "Romantic Unions in an Era of Uncertainty," 142.

17. Yet even here, it is difficult to get at real numbers because census reports on populations separate races into two categories, white and nonwhite or colored, which grouped Negroes, Japanese, Chinese, Indians, and Mexicans as a collective.

18. Wilson, *The Truly Disadvantaged*, 69.

19. Cherlin, "The Deinstitutionalization of American Marriage," 851.

20. Dickson, "The Future of Marriage and Family in Black America," 474.

21. Wilson, *The Truly Disadvantaged*, 69.

22. Ibid., 95.

23. Ibid., 96

24. Ibid., 82.

25. Ibid., 95.

26. Josephson, "Citizenship, Same-Sex Marriage, and Feminist Critiques of Marriage," 270.

27. See Moynihan, *The Negro Family*, and Frazier, *The Negro Family in Chicago*.

28. Nadar and Potgieter, "Liberated through Submission?," 143.

29. Ibid., 144.

30. Dickson, "The Future of Marriage and Family in Black America," 477.

31. Gallagher, *Evangelical Identity & Gendered Family Life*, 156.

32. Josephson, "Citizenship, Same-Sex Marriage, and Feminist Critiques of Marriage," 270.

33. Ibid., 271.

34. Burton and Tucker, "Romantic Unions in an Era of Uncertainty," 143.

35. Josephson, "Citizenship, Same-Sex Marriage, and Feminist Critiques of Marriage," 271.

36. Gallagher, *Evangelical Identity & Gendered Family Life*, 156.

37. Ibid., 161.

38. Hauser, *Muhammad Ali*, 310.

39. Ibid., 342.

40. Brown, *States of Injury*.

41. Shahrokhimanesh, *Under the Veil*, 87.

42. Ibid., 83 and 86.

43. Ibid., 87.

44. Ibid., 86.

45. Ibid., 85.

46. There is a lot of scholarship that links violence against women and patriarchal religions. See Horton and Williams, *Abuse and Religion*; and Johnson, *Religion and Men's Violence against Women*.

47. Einspahr, "Structural Domination and Structural Freedom," 4.

48. Crenshaw, "Demarginalizing the Intersection of Race and Sex," 328.

49. Burton and Tucker, "Romantic Unions in an Era of Uncertainty," 132.

50. Einspahr, "Structural Domination and Structural Freedom: A Feminist Perspective," 7.

51. Sister Betty Muhammad, *Dear Holy Apostle*, 42.

52. Crenshaw, "Demarginalizing the Intersection of Race and Sex," 315.

53. Cherlin, "The Deinstitutionalization of American Marriage," 851.

54. Josephson, "Citizenship, Same-Sex Marriage, and Feminist Critiques of Marriage," 275.

55. Williams, "A Fallen Star," chapter 3, 22.

56. Shahrokhimanesh, *Under the Veil*, 67.

57. Ibid., 82.

58. Ibid., 82–83.

59. Ibid., 82.

60. Ibid., 89.

61. Ibid., 89.

62. Evans, *Personal Politics*, 216.

63. Echols, *Daring to Be Bad*, 3–4.

64. Elijah Muhammad, Messenger of Allah, "To the Black Woman in America," 16.

65. Ibid.

66. Ibid.

67. "Temptations of Christianity," 4.

68. "The Filth That Produces Filth." This cartoon is printed weekly during the 1970s.

69. "The Filth of Filth," 2; "The Filth That Produces Filth."

70. Wedad, "The Black Woman Part I," 15.

71. Ibid.

72. Wedad, "The Black Woman Part II," 15.

73. Wedad, "The Black Woman Part I," 15.

74. Ibid.

75. Ibid.

76. Wedad, "The Black Woman Part II," 15.

77. Burton and Tucker, "Romantic Unions in an Era of Uncertainty: A Post-Moynihan Perspective on African American Women and Marriage," 144.

78. Wedad, "The Black Woman Part I," 15

79. Williams, "A Fallen Star," chapter 3, 73.

80. Lance Shabazz, *Blood, Sweat & Tears: The Nation of Islam and Me*, 179.

81. I am thankful to Paul Lee for sharing his memo to Spike Lee, which details this transition of Minister Malcolm X.

EPILOGUE

1. Clegg, *An Original Man*, 280.

2. Reynolds, "First White Woman Becomes a Muslim."

3. Ibid.

4. Shabazz, *Blood, Sweat & Tears*, 85.

5. Reynolds, "First White Woman Becomes Muslim."

6. Gibson and Karim, *Women of the Nation*, 104.

7. Shabazz, *Blood, Sweat & Tears*, 289–90.

8. It is important to point out that there were occasions when women, Sister Captains

specifically, lectured before men and women but they were careful to state that their talk was directed toward the women in the audience. See "Sister Captain Bayyinah Shareef-Hamzal-The Woman in Islam," YouTube, uploaded by Sha'Allah Shabazz (March 26, 2013).

9. "Donna Farrakhan: Breaking of the Black Woman 1/3," YouTube, November 14, 2013, uploaded by Richmond Ekiye.

10. Ibid.

11. Mary Eloise X, "Two Great Families Unite!"

12. Gardell, *In the Name of Elijah Muhammad*, 125.

13. Mary Eloise X, "Two Great Families Unite!," S-4.

14. Gardell, *In the Name of Elijah Muhammad*, 125.

15. The Honorable Louis Farrakhan, "The Honorable Elijah Muhammad and Malcolm X—28 years later—What Really Happened" (Saviour's Day 1993, The U.I.C. Pavilion-Chicago, ILL—February 21, 1993).

16. Ibid.

17. Ibid.

18. Ibid.

19. Needham-Giles, "Message from the Black Woman."

20. Gardell, *In the Name of Elijah Muhammad*, 125.

21. Ortega, "Scientology and the Nation of Islam."

22. Gray, "The Mothership of All Alliances."

23. Official Church of Scientology website, "Video: Auditing in Scientology, Spiritual Counseling, Frequently Asked Questions—What Is Auditing?," accessed August 5, 2015.

24. Charlene Muhammad, "Nation Adopts New Technology to Serve Black Nation," FinalCall.com News (April 4, 2011), accessed August 5, 2015.

25. Ibid.

26. Ibid.

27. Ancient Order of Free Asiatics and Son of Man God, publication, "The Science of Everything in Life," chapter 4, "The Leaders of the Nation of Islam," www.ancientorderof freeasiatics.com/SupremeMathematics.html, accessed August 10, 2015. For top newspaper seller, see Shabazz, *Blood, Sweat & Tears*, 192.

28. "Silis Muhammad Tells What Happened, 21 August 1977 to Mattias Gardell." Uploaded by Hasan (October 24, 2000).

29. Gibson and Karim, *Women of the Nation*, 53.

30. "A Phenomenal Woman."

31. Gardell; *In the Name of Elijah Muhammad*, 397, note 184.

32. "A Phenomenal Woman."

33. Ibid.

34. Gardell, *In the Name of Elijah Muhammad*, 217.

35. Ibid.

36. Silis Muhammad to Professor C. Eric Lincoln (May 6, 1994); Silis Muhammad to Dr. C. Eric Lincoln (April 26, 1994), Box 358, Folder 39, C. Eric Lincoln Collection, Archives Research Center, Atlanta University Center, Robert W. Woodruff Library.

37. Gardell, *In the Name of Elijah Muhammad*, 221.

38. Ibid., 217.

39. Ibid., 217.

40. Ibid., 397, note 180.

41. Ibid.,

42. Ibid., 217.

43. Ibid., 221, 396, note 169.

44. Ibid.; "A Phenomenal Woman," the Farrakhan Factor, August 29, 2010.

45. C. Eric Lincoln to the Honorable Louis Farrakhan (March 23, 1994), C. Eric Lincoln Collection, Box 358, Folder 39.

46. C. Eric Lincoln to Silis Muhammad (April 2, 1994), C. Eric Lincoln Collection, Box 358, Folder 39.

47. Gardell, *In the Name of Elijah Muhammad*, 397, note 184.

48. "Muhammad, Farrakhan, 1978, Your Muslim Bakery, Oakland, Calif.," YouTube.

49. Kuruvila, "Bakery Leader Defiant in Sermons after Arrest."

50. Askia Muhammad, "Your Muslim Bakery's Recipe for Mayhem."

51. Thompson, "The Sinister Side of Yusuf Bey's Empire."

52. Askia Muhammad, "Your Muslim Bakery's Recipe for Mayhem." The year of Sister Captain Felicia's "defection" is an estimate based on the fact that it occurred soon after Mosque #26B had been established.

53. Kuruvila, "Bey's Second Wife Was a Confidant of Chauncey Bailey."

54. Ibid.

55. Ibid.

56. Ibid.

57. Ibid.

58. Fricker, "Officer's Diligence Paid Off in Bust," 11.

59. "Jane Doe 1."

60. Ibid.

61. Ibid.

62. Ibid.; Kuruvila, "Bakery Leader Defiant in Sermons after Arrest."

63. "Jane Doe 1."

64. Fricker, "Officer's Diligence Paid Off in Bust," 11.

65. "Jane Doe 1."

66. Fricker, "Officer's Diligence Paid Off in Bust," 11.

67. Ibid.

68. "Jane Doe 1"; Kuruvila, "Bakery Leader Defiant in Sermons after Arrest."

BIBLIOGRAPHY

MANUSCRIPT COLLECTIONS

Dunham, Katherine. "The Occurrence of Cults among Deprived People." Federal Writers Projects, Works Progress Administration, Chicago, Illinois, 1937. VeVe Amasa Clark Collection, Bancroft Library, University of California, Berkeley.

Hassen, Aliya, Papers, 1910–1991. Bentley Historical Library, University of Michigan.

The Malcolm X Collection: Papers, 1948–1965, Box 3, Folders 1–4, Reel 3. Schomburg Center for Research in Black Culture, New York Public Library, New York, N.Y.

Military Intelligence Division Relation to "Negro Subversion," 1917–1941. National Archives, Northeastern Region, College Park, Md.

Nation of Islam Lessons. Box 201, Folder 5. C. Eric Lincoln Collection, Archives Research Center, Atlanta University Center, Robert W. Woodruff Library.

Shabazz, Betty. The Malcolm X Collection: Papers, 1948–1965, Box 2, Reel 2. Schomburg Center for Research in Black Culture, New York Public Library, New York, N.Y.

PAMPHLETS

Dillon, M. S. *Problem of School Attendance and the Colored Moslem Families in Detroit.* Detroit: Department of Public Welfare, 1934/1935. Burton Historical Collection, Detroit Public Library Main Branch.

Fard, Prophet W. D. *Secret Ritual of the Nation of Islam.* Bentley Historical Library, University of Michigan, Ann Arbor.

———. *This Book Teaches the Lost-Found Nation of Islam: A Thorough Knowledge of Our Miserable State of Condition in a Mathematical Way, When We Were Found by Our Savior W. D. Fard. Registered Moslems Only in North America.* Bentley Historical Library, University of Michigan, Ann Arbor.

REPORTS AND RECORDS

Anti-War National Folder. *Biennial Report to the Alabama Legislature by the Alabama Legislative Commission to Preserve the Peace.* Social Protest Collection, Reel 13, Bancroft Library, University of California, Berkeley.

Archives of Michigan. Government Records, Executive Department: Negro Matters, Reel 49, 1939–1940. Lansing, Mich.

Department of Corrections, State Archives of Michigan Records of the Bureau of Prisons.

Department of Police, Detroit, Michigan. Record for Wallace D. Farad, charged him with "Viol: Immigration" on 11/23/1932, listed residence, Fraymore Hotel in Detroit. Best Efforts Inc., Archives, Detroit, Mich.

———. Bureau of Identification, document number 21177. Best Efforts Inc., Archives, Detroit, Mich.

Detroit Commission on Community Relations/Human Rights Department Collection Records, 1940–1984. Archives of Labor and Urban Affairs, Reuther Library, Wayne State University.

Detroit Urban League Records, 1916–1992. Bentley Historical Library, University of Michigan.

Muslims, Racial Report and Segregated Housing Units, 1973. Records of the Bureau of Prisons.

Rosary, Lucille. *Superior Court of the State of California for the County of Los Angeles,* Case Number D652479, July 2, 1964.

U.S. Penitentiary, Leavenworth, KS, 1895–1920. Records of the Bureau of Prisons.

Williams, Evelyn. *Superior Court of the State of California for the County of Los Angeles,* Case Number D652475, July 2, 1964.

GOVERNMENT PUBLICATIONS

Fifteenth Census of the United States: 1930; Census Place: Detroit, Wayne, Michigan; Roll 1040; Page: 1A; Enumeration District: 241; Image: 1036.0. Washington, D.C.: Government Printing Office, 1931.

Fifteenth Census of the United States: 1930; Census Place: Hamtramck, Wayne, Michigan; Roll 1072; Page: 1A; Enumeration District: 938; Image: 623.0. Washington, D.C.: Government Printing Office, 1931.

Fifteenth Census of the United States: 1930; *Population Volume III, Part 1; Alabama-Missouri.* Washington, D.C.: Government Printing Office, 1932, 1183.

Fifteenth Census of the United States: 1930; *Population Volume II, General Report Statistics by Subjects.* Washington, D.C.: Government Printing Office, 1933, 1276.

INTELLIGENCE

Federal Bureau of Investigation Files

Allah Temple of Islam. Headquarters file, no. 146-28-344. National Archives at College Park, Md., Record Group 65, Classification 44 (Civil Rights) Case Files.

Little, Malcolm X [Malcolm X]. Headquarters file, no. 100-388321. Available on the FBI's The Vault website, https://vault.fbi.gov/Malcolm%20X.

———. New York File, no. 105-8999. Available on the FBI's The Vault website, https://vault.fbi.gov/malcolm-little-malcolm-x.

Muhammad, Elijah. Headquarters file, no. 105-24822. Available on the FBI's The Vault website, https://vault.fbi.gov/elijah-muhammad.

Muhammad, Wallace Fard. Consolidated file (headquarters and field offices). Available on the FBI's The Vault website, https://vault.fbi.gov?Wallace%20Fard%20 Muhammad.

Sharrieff, Ethel. FBI headquarters file, no.100-436766. Released to author September 10 and December 7, 2010.

Shabazz, Betty. Headquarters file, no. 100-71186. Available on the FBI's The Vault website, https://vault.fbi.gov/betty-shabazz.

Department of Justice

Allah Temple of Islam. Record Group 60, Class 25 (Selective Service Act), Litigation Case Files, 1920–1974, National Archives at College Park, Md.

NEWSPAPERS AND POPULAR JOURNALS

Afro American (Baltimore)

Afro American (Washington, D.C.)

The Afro-American

Chicago Daily Defender

Chicago Daily Tribune

Chicago Defender

Chicago Tribune

Detroit Educational Bulletin: Published Monthly for the Teachers of Detroit by the Board of Education (Detroit, Mich. [January 1922])

Detroit Free Press

Detroit News Burton

Detroit Saturday Night

Detroit Tribune Weekly

Ebony

Essence

Evening Star (Washington, D.C.)

The Final Call to Islam. Elijah Mohammed, Minister of Islam in North America, vol. 1, no. 1 (August 11, 1934), and vol. 1, no. 4 (September 1, 1934). Bentley Historical Library, University of Michigan.

Los Angeles Sentinel

The Messenger Magazine. Vol. 1, no. 1 (1959), box 175, folder 16. C. Eric Lincoln Collection, Archives Research Center, Atlanta University Center, Robert W. Woodruff Library.

Muhammad Speaks

New Times Broward-Palm Beach

New York Amsterdam News

New York Herald-Tribune

Oakland Tribune
People
Philadelphia Tribune
San Francisco Chronicle
San Francisco Gate
Time
The Tribune Independent
Truth Magazine. Box 278, folder 2,. C. Eric Lincoln Collection, Archives Research
     Center, Atlanta University Center, Robert W. Woodruff Library.

CITED INTERVIEWS

Interviews are by author unless noted otherwise.
Ali, Khalilah. March 5, 2015. Skype.
Muhammad, Waheedah. November 1, 2014. Telephone.
———. November 4, 2014. Telephone.
Shakur, Baheejah (Bertha). Southfield, Mich. October 5, 2009.
Shahrokhimanesh, Doris Jean. Martinez, Calif. September 16, 2014.
Sharif, Sara. (NOI), S. Alimah Sharif. Detroit, Mich. October 4, 2009.
Sanchez, Sonia. Raleigh, N.C. October 3, 2010.
Simmons, Zoharah (Gwendolyn Robinson). August 27, 2014. Telephone.
———. September 9, 2014. Telephone.
Tingle, Donald S. "Interview with Rayya Muhammad (Formerly Called Lottie; Sister
     of Imam W. Deen Mohammad and Daughter of Elijah and Clara Muhammad)."
     March 10, 1993. Cincinnati, Ohio. George Mark Elliott Special Collection Library,
     Cincinnati Christian University.
Whitby, Beulah. Oral History Collection. Archives of Labor and Urban Affairs, Reuther
     Library, Wayne State University.

SECONDARY SOURCES

Books
Abdullah, Zain. *Black Mecca: The African Muslims of Harlem*. New York: Oxford Uni-
     versity Press, 2010.
Ali, Muhammad, with Richard Durham. *The Greatest: My Own Story*. New York:
     Random House, 1975.
Baldwin, James. *The Price of the Ticket: Collected Nonfiction, 1948–1985*. New York:
     St. Martin's Press, 1985.
Baraka, Amiri. *The Autobiography of Leroi Jones*. Chicago: Lawrence Hill Books, 1997.
Baraka, Imamu Amiri, editor. *African Congress: A Documentary of the First Modern
     Pan-African Congress*. New York: William and Morrow, 1972.
Barboza, Steven. *American Jihad: Islam after Malcolm X*. New York: Doubleday, 1993.

Bates, Beth Tompkins. *The Making of Black Detroit in the Age of Henry Ford*. Chapel Hill: University of North Carolina Press, 2012.

Bell, Catherine. *Ritual Theory, Ritual Practice*. New York: Oxford University Press, 1992.

Best ,Wallace. *Passionately Human, No Less Divine: Religion and Culture in Black Chicago, 1915–1952*. Princeton, N.J.: Princeton University Press, 2005.

Beynon, E. D. *Master Fard Muhammad: Detroit History*. Newport News, Va.: United Brothers & Sisters Communications Systems, 1990.

Bontemps, Arna, and Jack Conroy. *Any Place But Here*. New York: Hill and Wang, 1966.

Boyle, Kevin. *Arc of Justice: A Saga of Race, Civil Rights, and Murder in the Jazz Age*. New York: Henry Holt, 2004.

Boyd, Stephen, W. Merle Longwood, and Mark W. Muesse, eds. *Redeeming Men: Religion and Masculinity*. Louisville, Ky.: Westminster John Know Press, 1996.

Braden, Charles Samuel. *These Also Believe: A Study of Modern American Cults and Minority Religious Movements*. New York: Macmillan, 1956.

Brown, Wendy. *States of Injury*. Princeton, N.J.: Princeton University Press, 1995.

Brumberg, Joan Jacobs. *The Body Project: An Intimate History of American Girls*. New York: Vintage Books, 1997.

Buitrago, Ann Mari, with Leon Andrew Zimmerman. *Are You Now or Have You Ever Been in the FBI Files? How to Secure and Interpret Your FBI Files*. New York: Grove, 1981.

Carmichael, Stokely. *Black Power: The Politics of Liberation*. New York: Vintage Books, 1967.

Carter, Dan T. *Scottsboro: A Tragedy of the American South*. Baton Rouge: Louisiana State University Press, 1979.

Chireau, Yvonne, and Nathaniel Deutsch, eds. *Black Zion: African American Religious Encounters with Judaism*. New York: Oxford University Press, 2000.

Clarke, John Henrik, ed. *Malcolm X: The Man and His Times*. New York: Collier Books, 1969.

Cleaver, Eldridge. *Soul on Ice*. New York: Delta, 1968.

Clegg, Claude. *An Original Man: The Life and Times of Elijah Muhammad*. New York: St. Martin's Press, 1997.

Collins, Rodnell P., with A. Peter Bailey. *Seventh Child: A Family Memoir of Malcolm X*. Secausus, N.J.: Carol Publishing Group, 1998.

Cox, Dale. *The Claude Neal Lynching: The 1934 Murders of Claude Neal and Lola Cannady*. Basom, Fla.: Old Kitchen Books, 2012.

Curtis, Edward. *Islam in Black America: Identity, Liberation, and Difference in African-American Islamic Thought*. Albany: State University of New York Press, 2002.

Dancy, John C. *Sand against the Wind: The Memoirs of John C. Dancy*. Detroit: Wayne State University Press, 1966.

Decaro, Louis. *On the Side of My People: A Religious Life of Malcolm X*. New York: New York University Press, 1997.

Detsi-Diamanti, Zoe, Katherina Kitsi-Mitakou, and Effie Yiannopoulou. *The Flesh*

Made Text Made Flesh: Cultural and Theoretical Returns to the Body. New York: Peter Lang, 2007.

Dickins, Dorothy. *A Study of Food Habits of People in Two Contrasting Areas of Mississippi Bulletin No. 245.* Mississippi State, Miss.: Mississippi Agricultural Experiment Station Agricultural College, 1927.

Dorman, Jacob S. *Chosen People: The Rise of American Black Israelite Religions.* New York: Oxford University Press, 2013.

Douglas, Davison M. *Jim Crow Moves North: The Battle over Northern School Segregation, 1865–1954.* New York: Cambridge University Press, 2005.

Deutsch, Sarah. *Women and the City: Gender, Space, and Power in Boston, 1870–1949.* New York: Oxford University Press, 2000.

Evans Mari, ed. *Black Women Writers (1950–1980): A Critical Evaluation.* New York: Anchor Books, 1984.

Evanzz, Karl. *The Judas Factor: The Plot to Kill Malcolm X.* New York: Thunder's Mouth Press, 1992.

Echols, Alice. *Daring to Be Bad: Radical Feminism in America, 1967–1975.* Minneapolis: University of Minnesota Press, 1989.

Essien-Udom, E. U. *Black Nationalism: A Search for an Identity in America.* Chicago: University of Chicago Press, 1962.

Evans, Sara. *Personal Politics: The Roots of Women's Liberation in the Civil Rights Movement and the New Left.* New York: Vintage Books, 1980.

Fairclough, Adam. *Teaching Equality: Black Schools in the Age of Jim Crow.* Athens: University of Georgia Press, 2001.

Farrell, Amy Ardman. *Fat Shame: Stigma and the Fat Body in American Culture.* New York: New York University Press, 2011.

Frazier, E. Franklin. *The Negro Family in Chicago.* Chicago: University of Chicago Press, 1932.

Gallagher, Sally K. *Evangelical Identity and Gendered Family Life.* New Brunswick, N.J.: Rutgers University Press, 2003.

Gardell, Mattias. *In the Name of Elijah Muhammad: Louis Farrakhan and the Nation of Islam.* Durham, N.C.: Duke University Press, 1996.

Gibson, Dawn-Marie, and Jamillah Karim. *Women of the Nation: Between Black Protest and Sunni Islam.* New York: New York University Press, 2014.

Glazier, Jack, and Arthur W. Helweg. *Ethnicity in Michigan: Issues and People.* East Lansing: Michigan State University Press, 2001.

Goldman, Peter. *The Death and Life of Malcolm X.* Urbana: University of Illinois Press, 1979.

Green, Victor H. *The Negro Motorist Green Book, an International Travel Guide, U.S.A., Alaska, Bermuda, Mexico, Canada 1949 Edition.* New York: Victor H. Green, 1949.

Hassoun, Rosina J. *Arab Americans in Michigan.* East Lansing: Michigan State University Press, 2005.

Haber, William, and Paul L. Stanchfield. *The Problem of Economic Insecurity in Michigan: A Preliminary Study of the Place of Unemployment Insurance and Other*

Systematic Measures for Economic Security in a State Plan for Michigan. Lansing, Mich.: State Welfare Relief Commission, August 1936.

Hauser, Thomas. *Muhammad Ali: His Life and Times.* New York: Touchstone Book, 1991.

Hicks, Cheryl D. *Talk with You Like a Woman: African American Women, Justice, and Reform in New York, 1890–1935.* Chapel Hill: University of North Carolina Press, 2010.

Hill, Robert, ed. *The Marcus Garvey and Universal Negro Improvement Association Papers Vol. V: September 1922–August 1924.* Berkeley: University of California Press, 1987.

———. *The Marcus Garvey and Universal Negro Improvement Association Papers Vol. VII: November 1927–August 1940.* Berkeley: University of California Press, 1991.

Hill, Robert A., ed. *The FBI's RACON: Racial Conditions in the United States during World War II.* Boston: Northeastern University Press, 1995.Holy Bible. King James Version. Nashville, Tenn.: Thomas Nelson, 1977.

Horne, Gerald. *Communist Front? Civil Rights Congress, 1945–1956.* Rutherford, N.J.: Fairleigh Dickinson University Press, 1988.

Horton, Anne L., and Judith A. Williams, eds. *Abuse and Religion: When Praying Isn't Enough.* Lexington, Mass.: Lexington Books, 1988.

Howard, Clark, *Zebra: The True Account of the 179 Days of Terror in San Francisco.* New York: Richard Marek Publishers, 1979.

Hurston, Zora Neale. *Their Eyes Were Watching God.* New York: Harper & Row, 1990.

Jamal, Hakim A. *From the Dead Level: Malcolm X and Me.* New York: Random House, 1972.

James, Etta, and David Ritz. *Rage to Survive: The Etta James Story.* New York: Da Capo Press, 1995.

Johnson, Andy J., ed. *Religion and Men's Violence against Women.* New York: Springer, 2015.

Johnson, Christine. *Muhammad's Children: A First Grade Reader.* Chicago: University of Islam, 1963.

Jordan, Winthrop. *White over Black: American Attitudes toward the Negro, 1550–1812.* Baltimore: Penguin Books, 1969.

Karim, Benjamin, with Peter Skutches and David Gallen. *Remembering Malcolm: The Story of Malcolm X from inside the Muslim Mosque by His Assistant Minister Benjamin Karim.* New York: Carroll and Graf, 1992.

Kimmel, Michael. *Manhood in America: A Cultural History.* New York: The Free Press, 1996.

Kirchwey, George W. *The Survey of the Cook County Jail.* Chicago: The Chicago Community Trust, 1922.

Kondo, Zak A. *Conspiracys: Unraveling the Assassination of Malcolm X.* Washington, D.C.: Nubia Press, 1993.

Lanker, Brian. *I Dream a World: Portraits of Black Women Who Changed America.* New York: Stewart, Tabori & Chang, 1989.

Lee, Martha F. *The Nation of Islam: An American Millenarian Movement*. Lewiston, N.Y.: The Edwin Mellen Press, 1988.

Lee, Spike, with Ralph Wiley. *By Any Means Necessary: The Trials and Tribulations of the Making of Malcolm X*. New York: Hyperion, 1992.

Lincoln, C. Eric. *The Black Muslims in America*. Boston: Beacon Press, 1961.

Loomis, Frank D. *The Cook County Jail Survey Summarized*. Chicago: The Chicago Community Trust, 1922.

Lomax, Louis. *When the Word Is Given . . .* New York: Signet Books, 1963.

Magida, Arthur J. *Prophet of Rage: A Life of Louis Farrakhan and His Nation*. New York: Basic Books, 1997.

Mahmood, Saba. *Politics of Piety: The Islamic Revival and the Feminist Subject*. Princeton, N.J.: Princeton University Press, 2005.

Marable, Manning. *Malcolm X: A Life of Reinvention*. New York: Penguin Books, 2011.

Marsh, Charles. *God's Long Summer: Stories of Faith and Civil Rights*. Princeton, N.J.: Princeton University Press, 1997.

Marshall, T. H. *Citizenship and Social Class*. Cambridge: Cambridge University Press, 1950.

Martin, Tony. *Race First: The Ideological and Organizational Struggles of Marcus Garvey and the Universal Negro Improvement Association*. Dover, Mass.: Majority Press, 1976.

Mathews, Susan J. *Food Habits of Georgia Rural People Bulletin No. 159*. Athens: Georgia State College of Agriculture, Georgia Experiment Station, 1929.

McNicol, Catherine. *Rural Radicals: Righteous Rage in the American Grain*. New York: Cornell University Press, 1996.

Meier, August, and Elliott Rudwick. *Black Detroit and the Rise of the UAW*. New York: Oxford University Press, 1979.

Mink, Gwendolyn, and Rickie Solinger, eds. *Welfare: A Documentary History of U.S. Policy and Politics*. New York: New York University Press, 2003.

Moon, Elaine Latzman. *Untold Tales, Unsung Heroes: An Oral History of Detroit's African American Community, 1918–1967*. Detroit: Wayne State University Press, 1994.

Moehlman, Arthur B. *Public Education in Detroit*. Bloomington, Ill.: Public School Publishing Company, 1925.

Morey, Nancy Booker. *A Study of the Food Habits and Health of Farm Families in Tompkins County, New York Bulletin 563*. Ithaca, N.Y.: Contributions from Studies in Home Economics Cornell University Agricultural Experiment Station, 1933.

Mormino, Gary R. *Land of Sunshine, State of Dreams: A Social History of Modern Florida*. Gainesville: University Press of Florida, 2005.

Moser, Ada M. *Food Consumption and Use of Time for Food Work among Farm Families in the South Carolina Piedmont, Bulletin 300*. Clemson, S. C.: Agricultural Experiment Station of Clemson Agriculture College, 1935.

Muhammad, Betty. *Dear Holy Apostle: Experiences and Letters of Guidance with the Honorable Elijah Muhammad*. Gilbert, Ariz.: Ashanti Enterprises, 2004.

Muhammad, Elijah. *How to Eat to Live, Book 1*. Chicago: Muhammad's Temple of Islam No. 2, 1967.

———. *Message to the Blackman in America*. Philadelphia: Hakim Publishing, 1965.

———. *The Mother Plane*. Atlanta: Secretarius Memps Publications, 1995.

———. *The Supreme Wisdom: Solution to the So-Called Negroes*. Newport News, Va.: National Newport News and Commentator, 1957.

Muhammad, Khalil Gibran. *The Condemnation of Blackness: Race, Crime, and the Making of Modern Urban America*. Cambridge, Mass.: Harvard University Press, 2010.

Muhammad, Warith Deen. *As the Light Shineth from the East*. Chicago: WDM Publishing, 1980.

Muhammad-Ali, Jesus. *The Evolution of the Nation of Islam: The Story of the Honorable Elijah Muhammad*. Birmingham, Ala.: JMA Publishing, 2002.

Naff, Alixa. *Becoming American: The Early Arab Immigrant Experience*. Carbondale: Southern Illinois University Press, 1985.

Moynihan, Daniel P. *The Negro Family: The Case for National Action*. Washington, D.C.: U.S. Government Printing Office, 1965.

McDannell, Colleen. *Picturing Faith: Photography and the Great Depression*. New Haven, Conn.: Yale University Press, 2004.

Peele, Thomas. *Killing the Messenger: A Story of Radical Faith, Racism's Backlash, and the Assassination of a Journalist*. New York: Crown Publishers, 2012.

Perry, Bruce. *Malcolm: The Life of a Man Who Changed Black America*. New York: Station Hill, 1992.

Randle, Kevin D. *The UFO Dossier: One Hundred Years of Government Secrets, Conspiracies and Cover-Ups*. Canton, Mich.: Visible Ink Press, 2015.

Ross, Dorothy. *The Origins of American Social Science*. Cambridge: Cambridge University Press, 1991.

Rouse, Carolyn Moxley. *Engaged Surrender: African American Women and Islam*. Berkeley: University of California Press, 2004.

Rickford, Russell J. *Betty Shabazz: Surviving Malcolm X*. Naperville, Ill.: Sourcebooks, 2003.

Sanchez, Sonia. *Love Poems*. New York: The Third Press, 1973.

———. *Shake Loose My Skin: New and Selected Poems*. Boston: Beacon Press, 1999.

Sanchez de Lozado, Boris, Robert Amoush, and Christopher C. Alston. *Henry Ford and the Negro People*. Ann Arbor, Mich. : Nation Negro Congress and Michigan Negro Congress, 1940.

Satter, Beryl. *Family Properties: Race, Real Estate, and the Exploitation of Black Urban America*. New York: Metropolitan Books, 2009.

Scott, Daryl Michael. *Contempt and Pity: Social Policy and the Image of the Damaged Black Psyche, 1880–1996*. Chapel Hill: University of North Carolina Press, 1997.

Shabazz, Candace. *Muslim Girl's Training: M.G.T & G.C.C. Notebook*. San Bernardino, Calif.: Createspace Publisher, 2015.

Shabazz, Lance. *Blood, Sweat, and Tears: The Nation of Islam and Me*. Raleigh, N.C.: Lulu Publishing Services, 2015.

Shahrokhimanesh, Doris Jean. *Under the Veil: A True Life Story*. San Francisco: Giant Horse Printing, 1996.

Shaw, Stephanie J. *What a Woman Ought to Be and to Do: Black Professional Women Workers during the Jim Crow Era*. Chicago: University of Chicago Press, 1996.

Simone, Nina, with Stephen Cleary. *I Put A Spell on You: The Autobiography of Nina Simone*. New York: Da Capo Press, 1991.

Spector, Ronald H. *Eagle against the Sun: The American War with Japan*. New York: The Free Press, 1985.

Stein-Roggenbuck, Susan. *Negotiating Relief: The Development of Social Welfare Programs in Depression-Era Michigan, 1930–1940*. Columbus: Ohio State University Press, 2008.

Strickland, William, with Cheryll Y. Greene. *Malcolm X: Make It Plain*. New York: Viking-Penguin, 1994.

Summers, Martin. *Manliness and Its Discontents: The Black Middle Class and the Transformation of Masculinity, 1900–1930*. Chapel Hill: University of North Carolina Press, 2004.

Tate, Claudia. *Black Women Writers at Work*. New York: Continuum, 1983.

Tate, Sonsyrea. *Do Me Twice: My Life after Islam*. New York: Strebor Books, 2007.

———. *Little X: Growing Up in the Nation of Islam*. New York: HarperSanFrancisco, 1997.

Toomer, Jean. *Cane*. 1923. New York: W. W. Norton, 2011.

Turner, Richard Brent. *Islam in the African-American Experience*. Bloomington: Indiana University Press, 1997.

Urban, Hugh B. *The Church of Scientology: A History of a New Religion*. Princeton, N.J.: Princeton University Press, 2011.

Viswanathan, Gauri. *Outside the Fold: Conversion, Modernity, and Belief*. Princeton, N.J.: Princeton University Press, 1998.

Wilkerson, Isabel. *The Warmth of Other Suns: The Epic Story of America's Great Migrations*. New York: Random House, 2010.

Williams, Jeremy. *Detroit: The Black Bottom Community (Images of America)*. Charleston, S.C.: Arcadia Publishers, 2009.

Wilson, Francille Rusan. *The Segregated Scholars: Black Social Scientists and the Creation of Black Labor Studies, 1890–1950*. Charlottesville: University of Virginia Press, 2006.

Wilson. William Julius. *The Truly Disadvantaged: The Inner City, the Underclass, and Public Policy*. Chicago: University of Chicago Press, 1987.

Wolcott, Victoria W. *Remaking Respectability: African American Women in Interwar Detroit*. Chapel Hill: University of North Carolina Press, 2001.

Wright, Richard, and Edwin Rosskam (photo director). *12 Million Black Voices: A Folk History of the Negro in the United States*. New York: Viking Press, 1941.

X, Malcolm, with Alex Haley. *The Autobiography of Malcolm X*. New York: Grove Press, 1966.

———. *The Final Speeches, February 1965*. New York: Pathfinders, 1992.

———. *Malcolm X Speaks: Selected Speeches and Statements*. Edited by George Breitman. New York: Grove Press, 1965.

Journal Articles

Berg, Herbert, "An African American Muslim Mufassir?" *Arabica* 45, no. 3 (1998): 320–46.

Beynon, Erdmann Doane. "The Voodoo Cult among Negro Migrants in Detroit." *American Journal of Sociology* 43, no. 6 (May 1938): 895.

Brazziel, William F., and Margaret Gordon. "Replications of Some Aspects of the Higher Horizons Program in a Southern Junior High School." *National Association of Secondary School Principals (NASSP) Bulletin* 47, no. 281 (March 1963): 135–43.

Brown, Lee P. "Black Muslims and the Police." *Journal of Criminal Law, Criminology, and Police Science* 56, no. 1 (March 1965): 119–26.

Burns, Charles J. "Flomaton Works toward Glorious Future." *Alabama Municipal Journal* 14, no. 7 (January 1957): 31.

Burton, Linda M., and M. Belinda Tucker. "Romantic Unions in an Era of Uncertainty: A Post-Moynihan Perspective on African American Women and Marriage." *Annals of the American Academy of Political and Social Science* 621 (Jan. 2009): 132–48.

Butler, Amos W. "Prisoners and Prisons." *Journal of Criminal Law and Criminology* 20, issue 2 (August 1929): 182–245.

Cherlin, Andrew J. "The Deinstitutionalization of American Marriage." *Journal of Marriage and Family* 66, no. 4 (November 2004): 848–61.

Curtis, Edward E. "Islamizing the Black Body: Ritual and Power in Elijah Muhammad's Nation of Islam." *Religion and American Culture: A Journal of Interpretation* 22, no. 2 (2002): 167–96.

DeNapoli, Antoinette E. "'By the Sweetness of the Tongue': Duty, Destiny, and Devotion in the Oral Life Narratives of Female Sadhus in Rajasthan." *Asian Ethnology* 68, no. 1 (2009): 81–109.

Deutsch, Nathaniel. "'The Asiatic Black Man': An African American Orientalism?" *Journal of Asian American Studies* 4, no. 3 (October 2001): 193–208.

Dickson, Lynda. "The Future of Marriage and Family in Black America." *Journal of Black Studies* 23, no. 4 (June 1993): 472–91.

Dillon, Miriam S. "Attitudes of Children toward Their Own Bodies and Those of Other Children." *Child Development* 5, no. 2 (June 1934): 165–76.

———. "The Islam Cult in Detroit." *The Compass Needle: The Professional Social Worker, the Intelligent Philanthropist, and the Socially Minded Layman* 2, no. 2 (October 1935): 35.

Du Bois, W. E. B. "Does the Negro Need Separate Schools?" *Journal of Negro Education* 4, no. 3 (July 1935): 328–35.

Einspahr, Jennifer. "Structural Domination and Structural Freedom: A Feminist Perspective." *Feminist Review* 94 (2010): 1–19.

Hall, Michael Ra-Shon. "Dramatizing the African American Experience of Travel in the Jim Crow South: The Negro Motorist Green Book in the African American Literary Imagination." *South Carolina Review* 44, no. 2 (2014): 80–94.

Harrington, Cornelius J. "Progress of Criminal Justice in Chicago." *Journal of Criminal Law and Criminology (1931–1951)* 29, no. 6 (March–April 1939): 785–98.

Josephson, Jyl. "Citizenship, Same-Sex Marriage, and Feminist Critiques of Marriage." *Perspectives on Politics* 3, no. 2 (June 2005): 269–84.

Komlos, John, and Marek Brabec. "The Trend of BMI Values of U.S. Adults by Deciles, Birth Cohorts, 1882–1986, Stratified by Gender and Ethnicity." *Economics and Human Biology* 9 (2011): 234–50.

Laue, James H. "A Contemporary Revitalization Movement in American Race Relations: The Black Muslims." *Social Forces* 42, no. 3 (March 1964): 315–23.

Melhem, D. H. "Sonia Sanchez: Will and Spirit." *MELUS* 12, no. 2 (Autumn 1985): 73–98.

Nadar, Sarojini, and Cheryl Potgieter. "Liberated through Submission? The Worthy Woman's Conference as a Case Study of Formenism." *Journal of Feminist Studies in Religion* 26, no. 2 (Fall 2010): 141–51.

Nance, Susan. "Mystery of the Moorish Science Temple: Southern Blacks and American Alternative Spirituality in 1920s Chicago." *Religion and American Culture: A Journal of Interpretation* 12, no. 2 (Summer 2002): 123–66.

———. "Respectability and Representation: The Moorish Science Temple, Morocco, and Black Public Culture in 1920s Chicago." *American Quarterly* 54, no. 4 (December 2002): 623–59.

Rashid, Hakim M., and Zakiyyah Muhammad. "The Sister Clara Muhammad Schools: Pioneers in the Development of Islamic Education in America." *Journal of Negro Education* 61, no. 2 (Spring 1992): 178–85.

Reid-Parr, Robert. "Speaking through Anti-Semitism: The Nation of Islam and the Poetics of Black (Counter) Modernity." *Social Text* 14, no. 4 (Winter 1996): 133–40.

Shaw, Stephanie J. "Using the WPA Ex-Slave Narratives to Study the Impact of the Great Depression." *Journal of Southern History* 69, no. 3 (August 2003): 623–58.

Taylor, Ula. "As-Salaam Alaikum, My Sister: Peace Be unto You: The Honorable Elijah Muhammad and the Women Who Followed Him." *Race & Society* 1, no. 2 (1998): 177–96.

Turner, Richard B. "The Ahmadiyya Mission to Blacks in the United States in the 1920s." *Journal of Religious Thought* 44, no. 2 (Winter/Spring 1988): 50–66.

Vontress, Clemmont E. "Threat, Blessing, or Both? The Black Muslim Schools." *The Phi Delta Kappan* 47, no. 2 (October 1965): 86–90.

Weisbord, Robert G. "Birth Control and the Black American: A Matter of Genocide?" *Demography* 10, no. 4 (November 1973): 571–90.

White, E. Frances. "Listening to the Voices of Black Feminism." *Radical America* 18, nos. 2–3 (1984): 7–25.

Essays and Short Pieces in Edited Collections

Bond, Jean Carey, and Patricia Peery. "Is the Black Male Castrated?" In *The Black Woman: An Anthology*, edited by Toni Cade, 113–18. New York: New American Library, 1970.

Brown, Ronald E. and Carolyn Hartfield. "Black Churches and the Formation of Political Action Committees in Detroit." In *Black Churches and Local Politics: Clergy*

Influence, Organizational Partnership, and Civic Empowerment, edited by R. Drew Smith and Frederick C. Harris, 151–70. New York: Rowan & Littlefield, 2005.

Burcar, Lilijana. "Re-Mapping Nation, Body, and Gender in Michael Ondaatje's *The English Patient*." In *The Flesh Made Text Made Flesh: Cultural and Theoretical Returns to the Body*, edited by Zoe Detsi-Diamanti, Katherina Kitsi-Mitakou, and Effie Yiannopoulou, 99–110. New York: Peter Lang, 2007.

Cha-Jua, Sundiata Keita. "A Life of Revolutionary Transformation: A Critique of Manning Marable's *Malcolm X: A Life of Reinvention*." In *A Lie of Reinvention: Correcting Manning Marable's Malcolm X*, edited by Jared A. Bell and Todd Steven Burroughs, 57–87. Baltimore: Black Classic Press, 2012.

Clark, Steve. *February 1965: The Final Speeches*. New York: Pathfinders, 1992.

Crenshaw, Kimberlé. "Demarginalizing the Intersection of Race and Sex: A Black Feminist Critique of Antidiscrimination Doctrine, Feminist Theory, and Antiracist Politics." In *Feminism and Politics*, edited by A. Philips, 314–43. New York: Oxford University Press, 1998.

Emanuel, James A. "Racial Fire in the Poetry of Paul Laurence Dunbar." In *Singer in the Dawn: Reinterpretations of Paul Laurence Dunbar*, edited by Jay Martin, 75–93. New York: Dodd, Mead, 1975.

Eggleton, Martin. "Belonging to a Cult or a New Religious Movement: Act of Freewill or Form of Mind Control?" In *Religious Conversion*, edited by Christopher Lamb and M. Darrol Bryant, 263–75. London: Cassell, 1999.

Griffin, Farah Jasmine. "Black Feminists and Du Bois: Respectability, Protection and Beyond." *Annals of the American Academy of Political and Social Science* 568 (March 2000): 28–40.

——. "'Ironies of the Saint': Malcolm X, Black Women, and the Price of Protection." In *Sisters in the Struggle: African-American Women in the Civil Rights and Black Power Movements*, edited by Bettye Collier-Thomas and V. P. Franklin, 214–28. New York: New York University Press, 2001.

Howard, John R. "The Making of a Black Muslim." In *Down to Earth Sociology: Introductory Readings*, edited by James M. Henslin, 244–55. New York: The Free Press, 1972.

Johnson-Bailey, Jaunita. "Poet Sonia Sanchez Telling What We Must Hear." In *Flat-Footed Truths: Telling Black Women's Lives*, edited by Patricia Bell-Scott and Jaunita Johnson-Bailey, 209–22. New York: Henry Holt, 1998.

Lincoln, Abbey. "Who Will Revere the Black Woman?" In *The Black Woman: An Anthology*, edited by Toni Cade, 80–84. New York: New American Library, 1970.

Lincoln, C. Eric, and Lawrence II. Mamiya. "Daddy Jones and Father Divine: The Cult as Political Religion." In *Peoples Temple and Black Religion in America*, edited by Rebecca Moore, Anthony B. Pinn, and Mary R. Sawyer, 28–46. Bloomington: Indiana University Press, 2004.

Mohammed, Elijah, to Sister Burnsteen Sharrieff. In *Warnings and Instructions to the M.G.T. and G.C.C. from the Honorable Elijah Mohammed: Mothers of the Faithful, Soldiers for Muhammad, 1930's–1940's*. Detroit: MohammadPoole, 2012.

Audley (Queen Mother) Moore interview, June 6 and 8, 1978. In *The Black Women Oral History Project*, edited by Ruth Edmonds Hill, 1–84. Westport, Conn.: Meckler, 1991.

Michaels, Jennifer E. "From Rejection to Affirmation of Their Bodies: The Case of Afro-German Women Writers." In *The Flesh Made Text Made Flesh: Cultural and Theoretical Returns to the Body*, edited by Zoe Detsi-Diamanti, Katerina Kitsi-Mitakou, and Effie Yiannopoulou, 87–98. New York: Peter Lang, 2007.

Muhammad, Elijah. "The Muslim Girls Training and General Civilization Class Instruction on the Law of Women in Islam." In *Warnings and Instructions to the M.G.T. and G.C.C. from the Honorable Elijah Mohammed: Mothers of the Faithful, Soldiers for Muhammad, 1930's–1940's*. Detroit: MohammadPoole, 2012.

———. "A Summary of the Flag Demonstration Given to the M.G.T. and G.C.C. by Captain Burnsteen Sharieff Thursday May 20th, 1948." In *Warnings and Instructions to the M.G.T. and G.C.C. from the Honorable Elijah Mohammed: Mothers of the Faithful, Soldiers for Muhammad, 1930's–1940's*. Detroit: MohammadPoole, 2012.

Simmons, Gwendolyn Zoharah. "African American Islam as an Expression of Converts' Religious Faith and Nationalist Dreams and Ambitions." In *Women Embracing Islam: Gender and Conversion in the West*, edited by Karin Van Nieuwkerk, 172–91. Austin: University of Texas Press, 2006.

———. "Are We Up to the Challenge? The Need for a Radical Re-Ordering of the Islamic Discourse on Women." In *Progressive Muslims on Justice, Gender, and Pluralism*, edited by Omid Safi, 235–48. Oxford, England: Oneworld, 2003.

———. "Striving for Muslim Women's Human Rights — Before and beyond Beijing: An African American Perspective." In *Windows of Faith: Muslim Women Scholar-Activists in North America*, edited by Gisela Webb, 197–225. Syracuse, N.Y.: Syracuse University Press, 2000.

Smith, Barbara. "Some Home Truths on the Contemporary Black Feminist Movement." In *Words of Fire: An Anthology of African-American Feminist Thought*, edited by Beverly Guy-Sheftall, 254–67. New York: The Free Press, 1995.

Taylor, Ula. "Elijah Muhammad's Nation of Islam: Separatism, Regendering, and a Secular Approach to Black Power after Malcolm X (1965–1975)." In *Freedom North: Black Freedom Struggle outside the South, 1940–1980*, edited by Komozi Woodard and Jeannie Theoharis, 177–98. New York: Palgrave and Macmillan, 2003.

Willhelm, Sidney M., and Edwin H. Powell, "Who Needs the Negro?" In *Down to Earth Sociology: Introductory Readings*, edited by James M. Henslin. New York: The Free Press, 1972.

Articles in Newspapers and Popular Periodicals

Allen, James. "The People Speak, Dear Editor." *Chicago Daily Defender*, March 12, 1962.

———. "The People Speak, Dear Editor." *Chicago Daily Defender*, April 16, 1962.

Alvardo, Francisco. "Khailah Camacho-Ali Stood by Muhammad Ali through Exile and Trump." *New Times Broward-Palm Beach*, April 14, 2011.

"Arrest Pair Who Beat White Cop." *Chicago Defender*, March 9, 1957.

"Asks State Close 'Islam University': Board of Education to Appeal to Supt. Voelker." *Detroit News*, March 28, 1934.

"At Home with the Champion and His Daughter." *Muhammad Speaks*, September 13, 1968, 33.

Baylor, Leroy. "Ameenah Rasul, Leader of Women in the Nation of Islam, Dies at Ninety." *New York Amsterdam News*, July 17–July 23, 2014.

Bogans, Gertrude. *Muhammad Speaks*, January 1, 1965, 7.

Bryant, Lindsay. "What Islam Has Done for Me." *Muhammad Speaks*, October 24, 1969, 13.

Cameron, Charles D. "Detroit as a Cult Capital: Only London and Los Angeles Lead This City as Centers of Novel Beliefs, Sun and Devil Worshippers Have Had Missions Here." *Detroit Saturday Night*, August 21, 1926, sect. 2, 3.

———. "Why Detroit Is Not All 'Cultist': Many New Adherents Are Found Each Year in the Assemblies of the Novel Philosophers, But the Adherents Do Not Remain." *Detroit Saturday Night*, September 4, 1926, Section 1, 10.

"Colored People Came to U.S. from Europe: Dr. Woodson Tells Local Club of Southalls and Cardozos." *The Afro-American*, January 14, 1933.

"Convict 40 'Moors.'" *Chicago Defender*, March 16, 1935.

"Cultists 'Guilty'; Thirty-Two Given Jail Sentences: Three Others Face Federal Court for Sedition." *Chicago Defender*, October 10, 1942. Nation of Islam clipping file, Martin Luther King Jr. Memorial Library, Washington D.C.

"Cultists Riot in Court; One Death, Forty-One Hurt." *Chicago Daily Tribune*, March 6, 1935.

"Drop Sedition Charges against Five in Chicago." *Chicago Defender*, June 19, 1943.

"Drop Sedition Charges against Islam Leaders." *The Afro-American*, June 19, 1943.

"DuBois's Church Views Shock Open Forum." *The Afro-American*, December 24, 1932.

Dunnigan, Alice. "Washington Inside Out." *Pittsburgh Courier*, September 12, 1959.

"Early 1967 Wedding Photo." *Muhammad Speaks*, January 19, 1968.

"Editorial: The Islam Issue in Detroit." *The Tribune Independent*, April 28, 1934.

"Elijah's Two Paternity Suits—The Will of Allah: He Claims." *Los Angeles Herald Examiner*, July 10, 1964.

"Empty Chair." *Muhammad Speaks*, March 18, 1963, 4.

"Expanding Curriculum." *Muhammad Speaks*, July 22, 1965, 20.

"The Filth of Filth." *Muhammad Speaks*, April 5, 1968, 2.

"The Filth That Produces Filth." *Muhammad Speaks*, September 4, 1970, 16–17.

"First Photos of the Champ and His Baby." *Muhammad Speaks*, July 5, 1968, 9.

"The First Honorary." *Muhammad Speaks*, March 13, 1964, 17.

"$5,000 Bond Cult Leader out on Bond in Draft Case." *Washington Post*, July 24, 1942.

"$5,000 in Cash Donated to Free 'Mohammed.'" *Evening Star*, Washington, D.C., July 24, 1942.

"Forty Cultish Put in Jail for Courtroom Riot." *Chicago Daily Tribune*, March 7, 1935.

4X, Joan. "What Islam Has Done for Me." *Muhammad Speaks*, August 29, 1969, 17.

Fricker, Mary. "Officer's Diligence Paid Off in Bust." *Oakland Tribune*, February 10, 2008.

Geracimos, Ann. "Introducing Mrs. Malcolm X." *New York Herald-Tribune*, June 30, 1963.

"Graduates of Muhammad's University of Islam Gird for Great Careers." *Muhammad Speaks*, February 25, 1966, 16.

Gray, Eliza. "The Mothership of All Alliances." *New Republic*, October 5, 2012.

"Gunmen Take Black Muslim for $23,000." *Mt. Vernon Register-News*, February 6, 1969.

"Happy Birthday for Wife of the Champ." *Muhammad Speaks*, March 29, 1968.

"Intended Voodoo Victims' Number Still Mounting: Another Attack Made by Harris before Murder Bared." *Detroit Free Press*, November 27, 1932.

"'Islam' Cult Faces Court." *Detroit News*, April 17, 1934.

"'Islam' Cult Faces Court: Fourteen Negro Instructors to Be Arraigned Today, Raid Made on Vodoo Building." *Detroit News*, April 17, 1934.

"Islam Cult Stages Riot at Police Sta.: Many Hurt as Cult Members Protest Arrest." *The Tribune Independent*, Detroit, Michigan, April 21, 1934.

"Islam Grads Move into Top Colleges." *Muhammad Speaks*, September 27, 1963, 18.

"'Islam' Staff Freed; 'Minister' Convicted." *Detroit Free Press*, April 25, 1934.

Jackson, David, and William Gaines. "Nation of Islam: Power and Money." *Chicago Tribune*, March 12, 1995.

Jet magazine, January 14, 1985, 16.

Karriem, Anna. "The Preacher of Pan-Africanism." *Muhammad Speaks*, April 16, 1971, 15.

Karriem, Elijah (Detroit, Mich.). "Moslems Are Misrepresented by Caucasians." *The Afro-American*, May 6, 1933.

———. "Preachers Don't Know the Bible and Must Hear the Prophet in Detroit." *The Afro-American*, April 1, 1933.

———. "'Prophet' of Detroit Says Black Man Is Cream of World, Not Foot-Mat." *The Afro-American*, April 15, 1933.

———. "To the Editor of the Afro." *The Afro-American*, January 28, 1933.

———. "Whose Christianity?" *The Afro-American*, April 22, 1933.

Kihss, Peter. "In Return for Years of Slavery, Four or Five States." *New York Times Book Review*, April 23, 1961.

Kuruvila, Matthai. "Bakery Leader Defiant in Sermons after Arrest." *San Francisco Chronicle*, December 23, 2007.

LeFlore, J. L. "Negroes Still Segregated on Trains, Buses in Dixie." *Philadelphia Tribune*, January 4, 1958.

Lepore, Jill. "Birth Control in the Cabinet: Planned Parenthood in the Archives." *New Yorker*, November 4, 2011.

Lewis, Dorothy. "Wake Up!" *The Final Call to Islam*, September 1, 1934.

Lewis, Vera X. *Muhammad Speaks*, November 4, 1966, 25.

"Maryam Ali." *Muhammad Speaks*, July 26, 1968, 15.

"MGT and GCC Present Africa Extravaganza." *Los Angeles Sentinel*, February 13, 1964.

"'Mohammed of U Steel' Pleads Draft Immunity." *Evening Star* (Washington, D.C.),

August 26, 1942. Nation of Islam clipping file, Martin Luther King Jr. Memorial Library, Washington, D.C.

Mohammed, Elijah. "We Teach Ourselves Some Dumb Things, Too, Brother." *The Afro-American*, April 21, 1934.

"'Mohammed' Is Released as Wife Posts $5,000 Bond." *Evening Star* (Washington, D.C.), July 23, 1942. Nation of Islam clipping file, Martin Luther King Jr. Memorial Library, Washington, D.C.

"Moors Battle in Court; 40 Hurt." *Chicago Defender*, March 9, 1935.

Morris, J. B. "Islam as the Black Man's Religion." *Tribune Independent*, July 7, 1934.

Morton, Shirley X. "What the Teachings of the Messenger Mean to Women." *Muhammad Speaks*, June 3, 1966, 25.

"Moslem Leader Nabbed: FBI Holds Moslem Chief on Draft Evasion Charge." *Washington Afro American*, May 16, 1942.

"Moslem Says He 'Registered with Islam.'" *Washington Post*, August 2, 1942.

"Moslem, Tried as Draft Evader, Says Allah Didn't Declare War." *Washington Post*, November 22, 1942.

"Mrs. Elijah Muhammad, 72, Black Muslim Leader's Wife." *New York Times*, August 14, 1972.

Muhammad, Clara. "An Invitation to 22 Million Black Americans." *Muhammad Speaks*, January 13, 1967, 19.

Muhammad, Elijah. "Beards." *Muhammad Speaks*, July 4, 1969, 5.

——. "Messenger of Allah Special: Read." *Muhammad Speaks*, January 11, 1974.

——. "To the Black Woman in America." *Muhammad Speaks*, September 4, 1970, 16–17.

——. "Warning to the MGT and GCC Class." *Muhammad Speaks*, June 28, 1968, 4.

——. "We Tell the World We're NOT with Muhammad Ali." *Muhammad Speaks*, April 4, 1969, 3.

——. "Thelma X Speaks." *Chicago Daily Defender*, April 13, 1961.

——. "Tornado Aftermath." *Chicago Daily Defender*, May 2, 1961.

——. Quoted in Alice A. Dunnigan, "Washington Inside Out." *Pittsburgh Courier*, September 2, 1959, national edition.

Muhammad, Thelma X. "The People Speak." *Chicago Daily Defender*, March 20, 1962.

[Muhammad], Thelma X. "Muhammad Savior of Negro Women." *Pittsburgh Courier*, magazine section, April 25, 1959, national edition.

"Muslim Girls Set Observance, May 27 at Detroit." *Pittsburgh Courier*, May 24, 1958.

"Muslim Leader Named in Two Paternity Suits." *Washington Post*, July 4, 1964.

"Nab Suspects in 23G Black Muslim Theft." *Pittsburgh Courier*, March 8, 1969.

Naeem, Abdul Basit. "Lauds Role and Training of the Muslim Women in the Nation of Islam." *Muhammad Speaks*, October 28, 1966, 10.

"Negroes Object to Cult Schools: Leaders Ask Cleanup by Prosecutor." *Detroit Free Press*, March 30, 1934.

"Negro Leaders Open Fight to Break Voodooism's Grip." *Detroit Free Press*, November 24, 1932.

New York Times Book Review, April 23, 1961.

"19 Children of Muslim Leader Battle a Bank for $5.7 Million." New York Times, November 3, 1987.

Orro, David H. "Seek Indictments of Sedition Suspects: Cultists Defy Commissioner in U.S. Court." *Chicago Defender*, October 3, 1942.

Ortega, Tony. "Scientology and the Nation of Islam: A Heartwarming Independence Weekend Parable." *Village Voice*, July 1, 2011.

"Pa. Mom of 10-Year-Old Sues Ali for $2 Million." *Jet*, January 14, 1985.

"Pastors Decry Growth of Cult Practices Here: Negro Leaders Pledge Support to Wipe Out of Voodooism." *Detroit Free Press*, November 28, 1932.

"Police Chief Beaten for Trying to Enforce Bias." *The Plaindealer* (Kansas City), March 3, 1957.

"Reappearance by Request." *Muhammad Speaks*, July 12, 1968, 29.

"Reflections: A Conversation with Sis Sonia 5X Sanchez." *Muhammad Speaks*, June 13, 1975.

Reynolds, Barbara. "First White Woman Becomes a Muslim." *Chicago Tribune*, March 2, 1976.

"Secret Honeymoon of the Champ." *Ebony*, November 1967, 161.

"Sedition Charges Dropped." *Philadelphia Tribune*, June 19, 1943.

"Seized Eighty-Four Negroes in Sedition Raids." *New York Times*, September 22, 1942.

Shabazz, Betty, and Susan Taylor. "Loving and Losing Malcolm." *Essence*, February 1992.

Sharrieff, Reformer Burnsteen. "The Dangerousness of Overweight." *The Final Call to Islam*, September 1, 1934.

———. "Reduce and Be Cured of Your Aliments." *The Final Call to Islam*, August 25, 1934.

"Sister Clara Muhammad Lauds New York University of Islam Educational Plan." *Muhammad Speaks*, May 12, 1967.

"Six Cultists Get Three-Year Sentences." *Chicago Defender*, April 17, 1943.

"Suburbs Also in Voodoo Net: Poll Book List Bring Literature Seizure." *Detroit Free Press*, November 29, 1932.

"Temptations of Christianity." *Muhammad Speaks*, November 5, 1965.

"Ten Thousand Hear Muhammad Speak On 'So-Called Negro.'" *Chicago Daily Defender*, February 26, 1962.

"Twelve Negro Chiefs Seized by FBI in Sedition Raids." *Chicago Daily Tribune*, September 22, 1942.

"Two Negroes Maul Chief in Flomaton." *Pensacola News*, February 23, 1957.

"U.S. Scrutinizes Books Seized in Cult Temple." *Chicago Defender*, October 17, 1942.

"University of Islam." *Time*, April 30, 1934, 37.

"Voodoo Slayer Admits Plotting Death of Judges." *Detroit Free Press*, November 22, 1932.

"Voodoo's Reign Here Is Broken: Slayer Held Insane; Farad Quits City." *Detroit Free Press*, December 7, 1932.

"Voodoo University Raided by Police; Thirteen Cultists Seized: Squad Finds Four Hundred Enrolled at School." *Detroit Free Press*, April 17, 1934.

"Waiting Room JC Gets Two Arrested." *Afro-American*, March 9, 1957.

Wedad, Dorothy. "The Black Woman: Must Have Islam." *Muhammad Speaks*, April 6, 1973.

——. "The Black Woman Part I." *Muhammad Speaks*, March 2, 1973, 15.

——. "The Black Woman Part II." *Muhammad Speaks*, March 23, 1973.

Witt, Linda. "After Their Chilla in Manila, Belinda Ali Launches a New Career— Alone." *People*, March 1, 1976.

X, Christine Delois. "Dope, Alcohol, and Devil's Tricks Strip Blacks of Human Dignity." *Muhammad Speaks*, January 29, 1971, 18.

X, Evelyn. "Modest Muslim Dress Dignifies Blackwoman." *Muhammad Speaks*, April 6, 1973, 18.

X, Sister Lt. Gertrude. "Visiting Sister Writes of 'a Few' Blessings She Has Gained from Islam." *Muhammad Speaks*, September 12, 1969.

X, Kathleen. "What Islam Has Done for Me." *Muhammad Speaks*, September 12, 1969, 21.

X, Marguerite. "What Islam Has Done for Me." *Muhammad Speaks*, August 2, 1969, 17.

X, Mary Eloise. "Two Great Families Unite!" *Muhammad Speaks*, February 14, 1975, 24.

X, Thelma. "The People Speak, Thelma X Speaks." *Chicago Daily Defender*, April 13, 1961.

UNPUBLISHED WORKS

Ali, Randal Omar. "The Foundation: Women in the Nation of Islam." Master's thesis, University of Iowa, 1998.

Amatullah-Rahman, Ajile Aisha. "She Stood by His Side and at Times in His Stead: The Life and Legacy of Sister Clara Muhammad, First Lady of the Nation of Islam." Diss., Clark Atlanta University, 1999.

Currin, Katherine. "Portrait of a Woman: The Inaccurate Portrayal of Women in the Original Nation of Islam." Undergraduate Honors thesis, University of North Carolina–Chapel Hill, 2004.

Edwards, Harry. "The Black Muslim Family: A Comparative Study." Master's thesis, Cornell University, 1966.

Fanusie, Fatimah Abdul-Tawwad. "Fard Muhammad in Historical Context: An Islamic Thread in the American Religious and Cultural Quilt." Diss., Howard University, 2008.

Gomer, Justin Daniel. "Colorblindness, a Life: Race, Film, and the Articulation of an Ideology." Diss., University of California, Berkeley, 2014.

Hatim, Sahib. "The Nation of Islam." Master's thesis, University of Chicago, 1951.

Jeffries, Bayyinah Sharief. "A Nation Can Rise No Higher Than Its Women: The Critical Role of Black Muslim Women in the Development and Purveyance of Black Consciousness, 1945–1975." Diss., Michigan State University, 2009.

Mohammed, Burnsteen Sharrieff. *I Am Burnsteen Sharrieff Mohammed Reformer and Secretary to Master W. D. F. Mohammad . . . and These Are Some of My Experiences.* Detroit, Mich.: Poole Muhammad, pamphlet, 2014. Purchased online via PayPal.

Mohammed, Medina. *Some of the First Women Who Accepted Islam: Beginning in the 1930s.* Detroit, Mich.: Poole Mohammad, pamphlet, 2014. Purchased online via PayPal.

Muhammad, Kathy Makeda Bennett. "Humble Warrioress: Women in the Nation of Islam; A Comparative Study, 1930–1975 and 1978–2000." Diss., Union Institute and University, Cincinnati, Ohio, 2008.

Muhammad, Ramona Zakiyyah. "Perceptions of the Role of Teachers and the Principal in an Islamic School." Diss., Columbia University Teacher College, 1986.

Muhammad, Raquel Ann. "Black Muslim Movement after the Death of Elijah Muhammad." Diss., United States International University, 1980.

Needham-Giles, Angela. "Message from the Black Woman: Gendered Roles of Women in the Nation of Islam from 1995 to 2005." Senior Capstone Project, Paper 329, Vassar College, 2014.

Pope, Jacqueline C. "The Status of Women in the Nation of Islam 1965 and 1975." Master's thesis, Queens College of the City University of New York, 1971.

Shalaby, Ibrahim Mahmond. "The Role of the School in Cultural Renewal and Identity Development in the Nation of Islam in America." Diss., University of Arizona, Education, Theory and Practice, 1967.

Warnings & Instructions to the M.G.T. & C.C.C. from the Honorable Elijah Mohammed: Mothers of the Faithful, Solders for Muhammad, 1930's–1940's. Detroit, Mich.: Mohammad Poole, pamphlet, 2012. Purchased online via PayPal.

Williams, Ruby. "A Fallen Star, 1964." Subject Files, Box 15, Folder 10, Reel 15, manuscript, The Malcolm X Collection: Papers, 1948–1965. Schomburg Center for Research in Black Culture, New York Public Library, New York, N.Y.

AUDIO/VIDEO

The Beulah Show. Directed by Richard L. Bare and Abby Berlin. American Broadcasting Company, 1950–1952.

"Donna Farrakhan: Breaking of the Black Woman 1/3." YouTube video, 46:12. Posted by "Richmond Ekiye." November 14, 2013. https://www.youtube.com/watch?v=gIeN8 darRPY.

"The Hon. Elijah Muhammad & Malcolm X: 28 Years Later, What Really Happened." YouTube video, 3:57:05. Posted by "BRO.IRONMUHAMMAD," July 14, 2016. https://www.youtube.com/watch?v=FxCFg1OmLHQ.

"Jane Doe 1." YouTube video, 10:05. Posted by "Reveal," August 1, 2012. https://www.youtube.com/watch?v=GWyHINcJdHI.

"Joe Tex the Real Story (Khalilah Ali on Polygamy)." YouTube video, 14:59. Posted by "Lance Shabazz," August 16, 2012. https://www.youtube.com/watch?v=yST-yRaHCSo.

"John Lewis Show — Khalilah Ali." YouTube video, 3:24. Posted by "MilesAheadMusic," December 25, 2009. https://www.youtube.com/watch?v=s74_AOZoPxM.

"The Journey of the Hon. Elijah Muhammad — Malcolm X." YouTube video, 2:19:50. Posted by "King_Alamgir," June 19, 2011. https://www.youtube.com/watch?v=P8Y8IU 23dL4.

The Killing Floor. Directed by Bill Duke. Arlington, Va.: Public Broadcasting Service, 1984.

Muhammad, Elijah, Jr. Telephone interview, *The Lance Shabazz Show*, 188, Part 3. YouTube, viewed April 3, 2010.

"Muhammad, Farrakhan, 1978 Your Muslim Bakery, Oakland, CA." YouTube video, 10:54. Posted by "TrueMedia99," August 21, 2014. https://www.youtube.com/watch?v=3eNqG9Haztk. Accessed August 12, 2015.

Shabazz, L. *The Lance Shabazz Show.* YouTube. Last modified February 12, 2017. http://www.lanceshabazz.com/lance-shabazz-show.

"Sister Captain Bayyinah Shareef-Hamzah — The Woman in Islam." YouTube video, 22:22. Posted by "Shah-Allah Shabazz," March 26, 2013. https://www.youtube.com/watch?v=aqLAX3dX6vE.

The Trials of Muhammad Ali. Directed by Bill Siegel. Chicago, Ill.: Kartemquin Films, 2013.

WEBSITES

Bush, Rudolph. "Ethel Muhammad Sharrieff, 80: Nation of Islam Leader's Daughter." *Chicago Tribune*, December 13, 2002. http://articles.chicagotribune.com/2002-12013/news/0212130102_1islam-elijah-muhammad-nation. Accessed November 21, 2014.

Drury, Keith. "The Vocation of 'Pastor's Wife': A Tribute to Beatrice Drury. May 16, 1913–April 7, 2002." *Drury Writing.* http://www.drurywriting.com/keith/2bea.htm. Last modified April 2002. Accessed June 9, 2011.

Equal Justice Initiative. "Federal Agency Bans Racial Segregation in Interstate Transport." http://racialinjustice.eji.org/timeline/1950s/. Accessed November, 23, 2013.

Eurpublisher02. "Ali's Second Wife Khalilah on Their Marriage: 'It Was a Wonderful Struggle.'" http://www.eurweb.com/2014/01/alis-second-wife-khalilah-on-their-marriage-it-was-a-wonderful-struggle/#. Accessed October 12, 2014.

Flomaton Centennial Scrapbook. "The Beginnings." http://www.escohis.org/flomaton/flomatonrailroad.pdf. Accessed November 21, 2013.

Hakim, Hashim, and Sandra Muhammad. "Ethel Sharieff, Daughter of Hon. Elijah Muhammad." *The Final Call*, January 1, 2003. http://www.finalcall.com/artman/publish/National_News_2/Ethel_Sharieff_daughter_of_Hon_Elijah_Muhammad_325.shtml. Accessed November 22, 2014.

Kuruvila, Matthai. "Bey's Second Wife Was a Confidant of Chauncey Bailey." *San Francisco Gate*, December 30, 2007. http://www.sfgate.com/bayarea/article/Bey-s-second-wife-was-a-confidant-of-Chauncey-3299307.php. Accessed August 15, 2015.

Malcolm X to Mr. Muhammad, January 13, 1958. Letter archived in Leland's Auction House, Lot 312. Malcolm XTLS — American Autographs, American, December 4, 2003. Accessed online, November 1, 2016.

Muhammad, Askia. "Your Black Muslim Bakery's Recipe for Mayhem." *East Bay Times*,

August 16, 2007. http://www.eastbaytimes.com/2007/08/16/your-black-muslim-bakerys
-recipe-for-mayhem/. Accessed August 15, 2015.

Muhammad, Starla. "Mother Tynnetta Muhammad—A Heartfelt and Fitting Tribute
to a Perfect Example." *The Final Call*, March 3, 2015. http://www.finalcallcall.com
/artman/publish/National_News_2/article_102165.shtml. Accessed June 3, 2015.

"A Phenomenal Woman." The Farrakhan Factor, 29 August 2010, www.farrakhanfactor
.com/clients/Factor/forums/viewtopic.php?p=230641. Accessed August 10, 2015.

Rush, George, Joanna Molly, Lola Ogunnaike, and Kasia Anderson. "Ali Daughter
Tosses Book in Ring." *New York Daily News*, March 18, 2001. http://www.nydailynews
.com/archives/gossip/ali-daughter-tosses-book-ring-article-1.906525. Accessed November 10, 2014.

The Soul Pitt. "Church Spotlight Sep 08: Lovely Ladies Women's Department of Sanctuary of Love Church of Deliverance." http://www.thesoulpitt.com/spiritual/?p=246.
Accessed June 9, 2011.

Thompson, Chris. "The Sinister Side of Yusuf Bey's Empire: The Troublesome History
of Oakland's Most Prominent Black Muslims—and the Political Establishment That
Protects Them." *East Bay Express*, November 13, 2002. http://www.eastbayexpress.com
/oakland/the-sinister-side-of-yusuf-beys-empire/Content?oid=1068749. Accessed August 14, 2015.

INDEX